Best American Political Writing 2002

Best American Political Writing 2002

Edited by Royce Flippin

Thunder's Mouth Press
New York

The Best American Political Writing 2002

Published by
Thunder's Mouth Press
An Imprint of Avalon Publishing Group Incorporated
161 William St., 16th Floor
New York, NY 10038

Library of Congress Cataloging-in-Publication Data

The best American political writing 2002 / edited by Royce N. Flippin, III.
    p.cm.
    ISBN 1-56025-410-6 (trade paper)
      1. United States – Politics and government – 2001 – 2. Political
    culture – United States. 3. American essays. I. Flippin, Royce.

    E902.B47 2002
    973.931 – dc21

                                                          2002072434

9 8 7 6 5 4 3 2 1

Book design by Sue Canavan
Printed in the United States of America
Distributed by Publishers Group West

CONTENTS

National Conversation: Election Aftermath

Part Two: Politics in the Bush Era

The National Conversation: The Bush Tax Cut

Part Three: (Not) Politics as Usual

The National Conversation: Global Warming

Part Five: September 11, 2001

The National Conversation: The War on Terror

Part Six: America's Future in an Uncertain World

This book is dedicated to my grandmother, Elizabeth Bellah Flippin, who loves talking politics more than anyone I know.

Acknowledgments

I'd like to express my appreciation to all the contributors who allowed their work to appear in this anthology, and to their publishers, permissions reps and agents for helping to facilitate the process. I'm also grateful to my family, friends and colleagues for their ideas and input. In particular, I want to thank publisher Neil Ortenberg for making this anthology happen, Shawneric Hachey for his dedicated and superb work in securing all the reprint rights, and my wife Alexis Lipsitz for her invaluable advice and editing skills. Finally, I'd especially like to thank Dan O'Connor for supporting this project from the beginning, and for his ongoing guidance in putting it together.

Preface: by Royce Flippin

Welcome to the first edition of *Best American Political Writing*. This book represents an idea that's long overdue—a one-volume collection of the year's sharpest and best-written political reporting and analysis from the country's leading authors, magazine writers, newspaper reporters and columnists, scholars, and speech makers. Its debut couldn't be more timely, for the year 2001 was like no other in our nation's history. The American public had only just digested the results of the controversial 2000 presidential election and was starting to settle into the rhythms of a new administration—one with very different views than its predecessor on how to conduct itself domestically and internationally—when September 11 happened. Suddenly we found ourselves plunged into a global struggle against an elusive enemy: U.S. troops were on the ground in Afghanistan, we were busy trying to decipher multi-color "terrorist alerts" here at home, and George W. Bush had morphed from a stumbling neophyte (at least in the eyes of some) into an overwhelmingly popular commander in chief.

As a result, 2001 was also a year in which people relied on the media like never before. On the most basic level, we had a greater hunger than ever to be kept informed, quickly and accurately, about the uncertain world we live in. Just as important, though, we needed to seek out the opinions and interpretations of those reporters and thinkers who were trying to make sense of it all—and, in the process, test our own opinions about what's going on around us. When we share in Paul Krugman's thoughts about the latest federal budget numbers, or Henry Kissinger's views on U.S. foreign policy, or Meg Greenfield's perspective on the hopes and fears lurking inside the well-coiffed heads of Washington's politicians, it elevates our own critical thinking as well—whether or not we agree with their conclusions.

One of the most remarkable aspects of editing this book was to see first-hand how impressively the media rose to the occasion: Between the burgeoning numbers of television pundits and interviewers, the coast-to-coast free-for-alls on talk radio, the columnists and editorialists holding forth on the nation's op-ed pages, the analysts-in-residence at our universities and nonprofit institutions, and the huge host of skilled and insightful journalists writing for both traditional brick-and-mortar publications and upstart webzines, we are currently immersed in what is undeniably a golden age of political commentary. This rich and diverse national dialogue is the voice of democracy making itself heard—and our country is stronger for it.

In the following pages, we've assembled what we believe are some of the brightest and most influential pieces of writing from the past year. While the general focus is on politics, the subject matter itself ranges from the partisan fights in Washington to the working poor on Main Street and their struggle to make rent, taking readers from the American heartland to the diplomatic outposts of Europe and the Middle East. The anthology contains two speeches, President Bush's historic address to Congress on September 20, 2001, and a thought-provoking soliloquy, "On Politics and the Art of Acting," from playwright Arthur Miller. There are also nine book excerpts (including chapters from the latest works by Kissinger and David Halberstam and selections from Barbara Ehrenreich's best-seller *Nickel and Dimed*), 30 magazine and journal articles, 12 newspaper stories and op-ed pieces, and three columns that first appeared online—one of them the post-9/11 essay by Tamim Ansary entitled "An Afghan-American Speaks," which became known as the "e-mail read around the world."

Our goal was not to endorse any particular viewpoint, but instead to present a wide variety of thoughtful political and social perspectives. This year's selections range from a pro-tax-cut opinion piece by Fred Barnes, executive editor of the conservative *Weekly Standard* ("Surprise, Surprise, He Meant It"), to an article by Lani Guinier on the need for a better electoral process ("What We Must Overcome"), written for the liberal journal *The American Prospect*. We also tried to strike a balance between being informative and being entertaining: What red-blooded American could resist Marjorie Williams' *Vanity Fair* behind-the-scenes look at the disintegration of Bill Clinton and Al Gore's relationship ("Scenes From a Marriage"), or Jennifer Senior's *New York* magazine profile of how Hillary Clinton is faring in the Senate ("Hill Climbing")? Other must-reads include Katha Pollitt's notorious column from *The Nation*, "Put Out No Flags"—if only to see what the fuss was all about—and Seymour Hersh's analysis in *The New Yorker* of how our intelligence agencies let us down on September 11 ("What Went Wrong").

Best American Political Writing 2002 is divided into six main parts, plus five shorter connecting sections called "The National Conversation." The six main segments correspond roughly to the year's chronology of events: Part One reports on the 2000 election (including Jeff Greenfield's TV-anchor's-view account of that wacky election night, "Oh, Waiter! One Order of Crow!") and the subsequent court battles over Florida's electoral votes; Part Two covers the political landscape during the first months of the Bush presidency, including Senator Jim Jeffords' startling decision to quit the Republican Party ("How Jeffords Got Away'"); Part Three is made up of think pieces such as "Digital Disjuncture"—two political scientists' prescription for how to make our government less beholden to special interests; Part Four, "The View From Main Street," focuses on the political realities of average Americans; Part Five is dedicated to September 11 and its aftermath; and Part Six, "America's Future in an Uncertain World," explores the United States' role in international politics.

The connecting National Conversation segments contain mostly column-length opinion pieces. Each section offers an assortment of views on a single topic: the fallout from the Supreme Court's decision to halt the Florida recount; the battle over the Bush tax cut; the moral debate on stem cell research and cloning; the increasingly urgent issue of global warming; and the country-wide argument over how (and whether) to conduct the new war on terrorism. Our hope in these sections was to convey some of the political give-and-take that occurs daily on the pages of the nation's periodicals.

Of course we weren't able to address every important issue of 2001, much less include all the thousands of insightful, well-written pieces that enriched our national dialogue last year. This book inevitably leaves out many, many terrific writers and columnists. Fortunately, there's always next year. As I write this, the big stories of 2002 are already unfolding: Legislation banning soft money has finally passed both houses of Congress; the F.B.I. has admitted its intelligence failures and pledged to become a new and better anti-terror outfit, complete with a new license to spy domestically; India and Pakistan (along with their nuclear arsenals) have a million soldiers facing off across their common border; Enron-type accounting scandals continue to pile up here in the U.S.; and the Middle East violence drags on with no end in sight. Oh yeah, and midterm elections are just around the corner.

Meanwhile, the scribblers and sages push onward, doing their best to make sense of it all. We can't wait to see what they have to say.

Best American Political Writing 2002

Part One: Election 2000

"Oh, Waiter! One Order of Crow!"
Jeff Greenfield

from *"Oh, Waiter! One Order of Crow!": Inside the Strangest*
Presidential Election in History

As 2001 dawned, the election of the previous fall still cast a shadow over the polit-
ical landscape. While the outcome of that presidential race was decided in the
courts, it started out as an Election Night comedy of errors, at least as far as the
media was concerned: At 8:00 on the evening of November 7—using shared exit-
poll data supplied by the Voter News Service—the television networks announced
they were calling Florida's 25 electoral votes (and in all likelihood the presidency)
for Al Gore. Two hours later, the networks took the prediction back. At quarter-past
two in the morning, they called Florida again—this time for George W. Bush.
Finally, at 3:30 A.M., after Gore had already phoned Bush to concede, they reversed
themselves one last time and declared the race "too close to call."

No one had a better seat for the madness than CNN's political analyst Jeff Green-
field. Here is his version of the first part of the evening, as witnessed from the CNN
anchor desk. . . .

Maybe it was Ross Perot's fault.

One of the major achievements of the shorthaired, short-fused billionaire's presidential campaigns was the harsh light it shone on the ballot
access laws: a collection of two-party protection rules that strangled new
political parties in their cribs. No state was more hostile to third-party politics than Florida. In 1996, for example, the Green Party tried to put Ralph
Nader's name on the ballot. Under state law, the party needed to collect
more than sixty-five thousand signatures—an impossible task for a party
with no money and no foot solders. Two years later, a broad coalition of
reform groups succeeded in putting Amendment 11 on the Florida ballot.
Its aim: to "grant equal ballot access for independent and minor parties."
It was approved by a nearly two-to-one margin. Now, all a minor party
needed to do was to pay a small filing fee.

The result? In November 2000, ten different tickets qualified for the
Florida ballot: not just Gore, Bush, Nader, and Pat Buchanan, but the Natural Law Party, the Socialist Party, and the Workers' World Party.

All this clutter worried local election officials, such as Theresa LePore in Palm Beach County, who'd been working in the field since the age of sixteen. She'd seen firsthand what could happen with a cluttered ballot. In a very close 1988 Florida race for the U.S. Senate, the candidates for that office were buried on the bottom of the first page of the punch-card ballot booklet. Some one hundred seventy thousand Floridians overlooked that highly competitive race. Moreover, LePore knew her constituents. There were so many old folks in Palm Beach County that even the STOP signs featured supersized letters. There was, LePore concluded, only one way to put all those presidential candidates on the ballot with type big enough for her voters to read easily. She decided to put the names on *both* sides of the page, with the punch holes in the middle. Most other local election officials in Florida rejected that idea; they even talked about it among themselves when they met in September in Tampa for their big annual meeting. LePore did not hear the conversation; she was out of the room at the time (the group that met was the Urban and Large County Election and Registration Supervisors: ULCERS).

In Duval County, which includes Jacksonville, voting officials decided on a different approach—they put the presidential candidates on *two* pages rather than one. No one took much notice of the change—including local officials of the NAACP and the Democratic Party, intent on getting out the African-American vote for president and for U.S. senator. Their mailings and leaflets all urged voters—many of them first-time voters, who had never seen a ballot before—to "punch every page" on their ballots. Those instructions assumed that the ballot this time would be like the Duval County ballots in the past—one office, one page.

On Election Day, the confusion spawned by the "butterfly ballot" in Palm Beach County and the "caterpillar" ballot in Duval County cost Al Gore thousands of votes from his two most loyal constituencies. Gore lost the state of Florida by 537 votes. Because he lost Florida, he lost the White House.

• • •

At two minutes after five o'clock on the evening of November seventh, 2000, Judy Woodruff turned to me on the anchor set at CNN's World Headquarters in Atlanta for my first words of wisdom.

"Jeff Greenfield, our senior analyst, this is the kind of election those of us who love politics have been living for."

"Judy, and folks out there," I said, "if you've ever longed for those nights that you've heard about, when people waited late to find out who their leader was, pull up a chair—this may be it."

Who knew?

Well, to be honest about it, we did—sort of. We just didn't know quite how late it would be.

We knew because, in one sense, every Election Night is a ritual of concealment. Hours before the networks take to the air, the first wave of exit polls starts flowing into the headquarters of Voter News Service, then to the television networks, and then—almost instantly, in flat violation of solemn contractual pledges—into the ears of every decently connected campaign operative, journalist, campaign contributor, and kibbitzer from one end of the country to the other.

("No kidding . . . a wipeout in Illinois? And the whole California rumor was nothing, right? What about Ohio? . . . Yeah, I figured that. . . . ")

For the last twenty years, those early exit polls had pointed to a decisive outcome—sometimes in striking contrast to the last preelection surveys (Reagan romping over Carter in 1980), sometimes reflecting those surveys (Reagan demolishing Mondale in '84, Clinton putting away Bob Dole in '96). So, by the time the TV networks hit the air, every anchor, reporter, and analyst knew what the voters had done—not only nationally, but in most cases state by state. The rules of the game, however, strictly forbade us from reporting to our viewers and listeners the facts that all of us knew, thus turning the whole Election Night into something of a dramatic re-creation— a little like reporting the World Series *after* learning how every key moment of the game would turn out.

"You know, Bernie, I'd keep a close eye on Bill Buckner down at first base in the late innings; he's not the best in the world at picking up a slow ground ball rolling right at him—just the kind of nubber a guy like Mookie Wilson could hit."

For an analyst like myself, this early-warning system had clear advantages; back in 1992, for example, the sure and certain knowledge that Bill Clinton was going to win New Jersey provided plenty of time for remarkably thoughtful instant analysis of Clinton's ability to lure suburban Jerseyites back to the Democratic Party, thus ending the Republicans' string of six consecutive triumphs in that state. Long before sunset in that same year, we had prepared our comments about the Reagan Democrats in Michigan, secure in our understanding that Clinton had reclaimed Michigan as well—because the exit polls had told us so while the sun was still high in the sky.

But this time? This time the exit polls were telling us exactly what we had been reporting all weekend long: This one was up for grabs.

At 4 P.M. on Election Day, a few dozen staffers jammed into a conference room in the Executive Corridor, one floor above the cavernous CNN newsroom in Atlanta—a 16,500-square-foot room jammed with 136 workstations, thirty-five edit bays, fifty-two computer pods in the satellite-feed areas, and close to 200 people, all of which forms the background behind the Atlanta anchor desk. Bill Schneider, the owlish, genial academic-turned-TV-analyst, sat at one end of the conference table, armed with a yellow legal pad.

"Well," he said with a small smile, "remember we told you it would be close? It's going to be very close." How close? Well, the national popular vote was splitting right down the middle—48 percent to 48 percent.

Some parts of the picture were clear: Bush's late sweep through California, which had cost him seven days and more than ten million dollars in television and radio advertising, had been a fool's venture—Gore was going to win California without breaking a sweat. He was winning comfortably in New Jersey as well, another state where Bush had made a late foray, on the heels of reports that he was "closing fast." And Illinois, once considered a key battleground, was also safely in hand for the Democrats. In other states that Gore desperately needed, however, there was potential trouble brewing. These were the "Dukakis" states—half a dozen won by the hapless 1988 Democratic presidential nominee, and assumed during the early stages of the campaign to be solidly in Gore's column.

("If *Dukakis* can win a state," the mantra went, "no Democrat can lose it.")

Now it was clear, that assumption was in doubt. Yes, New York, Massachusetts, Hawaii, the District of Columbia, these were safely in Gore's column. The only way that Gore could lose any of those would be to appear on national TV with horns sprouting out of his head, chanting "All praise to Satan!"—and even then, New York would only shift to "Undecided." But some of those "Dukakis" states were precisely those where Ralph Nader could be costing Gore precious votes—Wisconsin, Iowa, Minnesota, Oregon, Washington. No, Nader would not be getting that 5 percent of the national popular vote, which would entitle his Green Party to millions of dollars in future federal funds—but he could still turn out to be a key player. And then there was West Virginia, a reliably Democratic state, but one where a lot of Democrats mined for coal and hunted with guns. Here, Gore's passion for the environment evoked images not of pastoral hills and valleys, but of shuttered mines and food stamps. West Virginia was in play on this Election Night, and in a race this close, even those five electoral votes could be decisive.

And what about Florida? Too close to call, Schneider said, but Gore does have a three-point lead in the exit polls.

"We may be up late with that one," he said. . . .

• • •

There was something wrong about Florida.

At Bush campaign headquarters in Austin, Texas, the bad news was that African-Americans were turning out in huge numbers. Two years earlier, Jeb Bush had been elected governor on a theme of inclusion; he'd campaigned heavily in black neighborhoods, something Florida Republicans rarely if ever did. But in 1999, an anti-affirmative-action proposal by Bush turned the African-American community solidly against him.

"We will take our case to the polls," warned Representative Corrine Brown. "We will let people understand the message that the Bush family has delivered to Florida." Now that promise seemed more like prophecy. Moreover, the Bush folks knew full well that Bill Clinton had almost carried Florida in 1992. In fact, the president had always kicked himself for not putting more resources into the state. Four years later, Clinton had actually carried Florida against Bob Dole. This time, the presence of Joe Lieberman on the ticket was bound to encourage a heavier Jewish turnout ("A heavier Jewish turnout? Impossible!" longtime political reporter Hal Bruno maintained. "Every Jew who can *move* votes. I think it's the eleventh commandment.") In 1996, blacks made up 10 percent of the total vote; if that percentage increased, so did the chances that Bush would lose the state he had once assumed would be his.

In the Gore camp, the worry was what was going on in Palm Beach—one of the heaviest Democratic areas of the state. "The polls opened at 7 A.M.," one Palm Beach Democrat recalls, "and the first call came in to our headquarters eight minutes later. People were saying it was terribly confusing, that they thought they'd voted for Buchanan by mistake."

• • •

On his first Election Day as chairman of the Palm Beach County Canvassing Board, Judge Charles Burton, the forty-two-year-old chairman of the board, was expecting a highly uneventful day.

"The only reason I was named chairman in the first place was because they had to have a judge who'd been elected without opposition," he recalled a few weeks later in his ninth-floor office in the modern, sandstone-and-glass Palm Beach County Courthouse. "When they said I'd be chairman of the board, the only thing I asked was, 'What's a canvassing board?' " Before Election Day, Burton remembers, the board had met a few times to go over the rules and regulations—"strictly routine, by-the-book stuff."

But shortly after Election Day began, Burton dropped into the Supervisor of Elections office in a nearby building, and found a distraught Theresa LePore with a sample butterfly ballot, which she handed to him.

"Take this, and see if you can vote for Gore," she asked him. He did.

"We're getting calls about the ballot," she said. "People are saying it's confusing." She decided to send out an advisory to clear up the confusion, and let worried Democrats get it to the polls before turnout began to spike up again in the late afternoon.

The advisory read:

"Attention all poll workers. Please remind all voters coming in that they are to vote for one (1) presidential candidate and that they are to punch the hole next to the arrow next to the number next to the candidate they wish to vote for. Thank you."

In Atlanta, we knew little if anything about the Palm Beach troubles. What we did know was unsettling enough: that the Voter News Service was reporting trouble with some of its early numbers from a series of states when its first exit-poll numbers came in at one o'clock in the afternoon.

"We've got a lot of 'bads,' " Bill Schneider had told the group jammed into the CNN conference room in midafternoon. Schneider was not trying to imitate a homeboy; he was talking about precincts where the exit-poll data seemed at odds with past track records, or with preelection polls. (The early numbers, for instance, pointed to a clear Bush win in Pennsylvania, a state Gore would wind up winning by four percentage points.) In each key state, exit polls are taken in about four dozen precincts; if two of those precincts produce "bads," the number crunchers can go about their work with a fair measure of confidence. On this Election Day, roughly 10 percent of the precincts were showing up with shaky numbers. At 4:47 P.M., VNS sent out a reassuring alert to subscribers: "The problems with the state survey weighting are cleared up. We have cleaned out the bad precinct problems." This was not all that reassuring to CNN co-anchor Judy Woodruff, who was openly uneasy about a vote-gathering operation—the *only* vote-gathering operation—deciding in the middle of Election Day that its model might have a bug or two in it. It was, said another colleague, like looking out the window of a jumbo jet ten minutes before departure time, and noticing a group of mechanics huddling around engine number 4 shaking their heads and flipping through the maintenance manual.

So at 7 P.M.., when most of the polls in Florida closed, none of us in front of the cameras was surprised that the numbers were showing the state "too close to call."

But less than a half-hour later, in a room in New York City jammed with computers and people, a group of analysts was looking at numbers that were pointing very clearly to a call: the numbers that Voter News Service were dumping into computers were saying that Al Gore was going to carry Florida.

The men and women were part of a "Decision Desk" assembled by Warren Mitofsky, one of the Founding Fathers of modern political analysis. On this day, he was simultaneously working for CNN and CBS News, communicating with both networks through an open telephone line. Similar teams were at work for the other broadcast news divisions and cable networks. But *every one* of these teams was looking at exactly the same data at exactly the same time: the information popping up on the computer screens programmed by Voter News Service.

• • •

So it was that CNN Political Director Tom Hannon, at 7:50 P.M., opened the microphone to the anchor desk and announced in our ears, "We are calling Florida for *Gore*—Florida for *Gore*."

("I was surprised by the early call for Florida," Hannon said, weeks later. "But it's like a laboratory situation. You look at the numbers, the models, the percentages. There was no reason to assume there was a problem.")

Judy Woodruff announced our call at the instant the commercial break ended.

"A *big* call to make. CNN announces that we call Florida in the Al Gore column. This is a state both campaigns desperately wanted to win."

"This is a roadblock the size of a boulder to George W. Bush's path to the White House," I said. "They had counted these twenty-five electoral votes from the moment George Bush entered the campaign, before he was even nominated. . . . whether it was Social Security, the turnout, Joe Lieberman, now George W. Bush has to look to Michigan, Pennsylvania, Ohio, and those smaller states really become critical."

And for the next two hours, our coverage focused on one question: Could George W. Bush win the White House without Florida? What we did *not* do was assume that Gore had the race won. What we *did* do was assume the accuracy of our call, even as the Bush campaign and its partisans were loudly questioning the call—and question it they did—loudly, urgently, almost desperately. In Austin, Bush political strategist Karl Rove was calling correspondents and news executives alike, with one message: *Your Florida call is wrong! The polls in the Panhandle are still open! You're gonna have egg all over your faces!*

• • •

In Austin, the Florida call for Gore came as a special shock to some twenty close Bush friends and family members who had gathered on the ninth floor of the Four Seasons Hotel. It was an optimistic group; the final polls, the campaign assured them, pointed to a comfortable victory. According to the schedule, Bush would dine at a restaurant next-door to the hotel with his parents and brother, Florida Governor Jeb Bush, and come over to the hotel about 7:45 (Central time) to celebrate. But when the networks called Florida for Gore, everything changed. Jeb Bush was "in tears, very, very emotional," one intimate remembers. Bush called Campaign Chair Don Evans, and said simply, "I have to take my family back to the mansion."

• • •

The Bush campaign did not have to wait for the networks to put Rove or other official campaign representatives on the air. Every network had partisans of the two candidates ready to offer commentary throughout the evening; these partisans, in turn, had telephone access to the campaign headquarters. So at 8:24 P.M., barely twenty minutes after CNN called Florida for Gore, Mary Matalin was armed with her talking points when CNN put her and Mike McCurry on the air. After McCurry credited the selection of Joe Lieberman and the Social Security issue as the decisive factors in Florida, it was Matalin's turn:

"I'm going to go out on a limb here," she began. "We have early data. The spread is two percent. The raw total is four thousand votes at this point. If it continues at this pace, there are a half a million absentee ballots out there. I'm just telling you, this reminds me of Deukmejian in California [referring to a very close 1982 race for governor that was decided by absentee ballots]: lost on Tuesday, won on Thursday."

"What are you suggesting, Mary?' asked Judy Woodruff.

"I'm suggesting," replied Matalin, "that when the real count is in, the absentee ballots are counted, that they're—they are extensive in there, and that state's going to flip. I really feel that way."

• • •

Sometime after 9 P.M., Larry Rosen, one of the people at Warren Mitofsky's Decision Desk in New York, began to notice that the raw, county-by-county vote in Florida was starting to indicate a probable win for Bush. In the VNS system, there are half a dozen statistical models that project a state race's likely outcome. They factor in everything from geographic patterns to past voting history to actual votes from sample precincts. Now, the county vote—the so-called "CORE estimator"—was pointing to Bush. Tom Hannon, CNN's political director, recalls that "the news about the county vote *electrified* us. It's like the green lights on a NASA control panel—when one of them suddenly goes red, you pay attention." And when Rosen saw that the numbers were pointing to Bush, "everybody on the decision team dropped what they were doing, and asked, 'My God, what's going on?' "

For Hannon, the news did *not* suggest an immediate recall.

"My first thought was that, if they're in doubt, we'll wait on a 'recall' until we know that the 'winner' has in fact become the loser. Because otherwise, you're just adding to the confusion."

That restraint seemed prudent at 9:20, when Gore picked up twenty thousand more votes. That increase in Gore's lead made the projection look much more solid—except that these were *phantom* votes, the result of a computer glitch tallying the numbers from Duval County. Once that error was caught and corrected, CNN and every other network knew the truth: The exit polls from Florida had *overestimated* Gore's actual vote total. The absentee vote was *much* larger than the VNS projection had assumed; the current VNS projections were showing a dead heat.

On the anchor set, we knew nothing of the drama building in the control room. In fact, at about 9:50, we were chatting again with Mary Matalin and Mick McCurry. And Matalin was still insisting that Florida—and for that matter, Pennsylvania—was in play.

"I want to reiterate the competition in Florida and Pennsylvania isn't over, but as the Bush campaign looks west to the states you're looking at, there is a way to add thirty-three states up to two hundred seventy plus. . . . It's threading the needle, as we say, but they see their way there and again are not giving up on Pennsylvania and Florida."

A few moments later, Bush himself sought to rally the troops; the campaign permitted cameras into the governor's mansion, where he and Laura were watching the returns.

"This was Governor [Tom] Ridge calling when you came up, and he doesn't believe the projections. He believes there are votes outstanding. . . . We're getting the same report out of Florida as well. The networks called this thing awfully early, and people who are actually counting the votes have a different perspective, so . . . "

Time for a little perspective, I thought.

"I think, in fairness, these projections are not infallible. There are times when the networks have to eat a hearty portion of crow. It happened to Senator Bob Smith in New Hampshire in 1996. The networks called it for his opponent, had to bring it back."

This would have been a perfect time to stop. But no-o-o-o-o-o . . .

"But I think, Bill, and you're the maven on this one, that generally networks do not call unless they have a pretty high degree of assurance, correct?"

"That is correct," Bill Schneider said. "We have a pretty high degree of assurance that Florida and Pennsylvania have gone for Al Gore."

About fifty seconds later, as Schneider and I were discussing likely recriminations among Republicans for the coming presidential loss, Tom Hannon opened his key to Bernie Shaw, and Shaw took over.

"Stand by, stand by," he said. "CNN right now is moving our earlier declaration of Florida back to the too-close-to-call column. Twenty-five very big electoral votes and the home state of Governor Bush's brother are hanging in the balance. This is no longer a victory for Gore."

And I blurted out the only thing I could think of that fit the moment:

"Oh, waiter! One order of crow!"

Follow the Bouncing Polls

Dana Milbank

from *Smashmouth: Two Years in the Gutter with Al Gore and George W. Bush*

The title of Dana Milbank's book Smashmouth, a warts-and-all account of his travels with the 2000 presidential candidates, refers to the modern, attack-dog style of political combat—not that there's necessarily anything wrong with that, in his view. "Our problem," Milbank writes, "is not negative campaigning but an increasingly puritanical press that often makes no distinction between negative comparisons (which are common and useful) and gratuitous personal attacks (which are harmful but rare)."

Fortunately, no one's accusing Milbank of puritanism—after all, he did break the story behind Al Gore's new, uptempo speaking style ("tight underwear," explained an aide). The following excerpt concerns a side trip he made to Utica, New York, where he explores the dark underbelly of the Zogby tracking polls. . . .

As we enter the homestretch of the election, the Bush campaign is rebounding (unless, of course, it still happens to be stumbling). Al Gore's operation, by contrast, is slipping into disarray (or perhaps it is becoming highly disciplined). Candidate Bush (or is it Gore?) is connecting with voters, while Candidate Gore's (or is it Bush's?) morale is falling.

In the real world, presidential campaigns progress slowly and steadily over many months. But this is considered boring in the alternate reality occupied by campaign staffs, party hacks and, particularly, journalists. Instead, they occupy themselves by hunting for subtle (and sometimes overnight) mood swings. They call this stuff "momentum."

"There are natural cycles of puff and collapse," says Paul Begala, the former Clinton hand and a Gore enthusiast. Bush adviser Ed Gillespie concurs: "Everything is just going swimmingly or everything is a misstep."

Recently, Bush has been in misstep mode. In front of a microphone he didn't know was on, he pointed out *New York Times* reporter Adam Clymer at a rally and told Dick Cheney the fellow was a "major league asshole." Replied Cheney: "Big time." Then came the word *RATS* exploding from the word *BUREAUCRATS* in a Bush ad for a fraction of a second. Bush, in front of the cameras, denied that the rodents were meant to be "subliminable" (rhymes with abominable).

Armed with such patterns of speech, Gail Sheehy, writing in *Vanity Fair*, diagnosed Bush with dyslexia. I had ruled out dyslexia when I accused Bush of having speech apraxia in the spring, but no matter: the story had legs. Bush, forced to respond, didn't appear to be joking when he uttered, "The woman who knew that I had dyslexia—I never interviewed her." The Bush malapropisms have since come fast and furious, the latest being about how he wants "wings to take dream."

Not long ago, though, the currently "focused" Gore was the one in the dumps. Remember the stiff and programmed Gore, the earth-toned, faux farm-working, pot-smoking, Fairfax Hotel–living, slumlord Gore? Don't worry—he'll be back, when the cycle turns again. We're due for a Bush recovery any day now.

Asked to forecast the campaign's boom-and-bust cycles over the next two months, Mindy Tucker, Bush's press secretary, drew a chart that "goes all over the place," as she put it, much like the Carter-Reagan race of 1980, when the two often traded leads in polls. Not surprisingly, her chart ends in an upswing for Bush.

The newly smug Gore campaign declined to provide an illustration. Instead, it volunteered Begala, who sees an equally volatile race ahead. Bush survives the first debate without throwing up, and Gore plunges; Cheney "does throw up" in the VP debate, and Gore surges; Bush holds his own in the third debate, and Gore plunges; analysts predict a Bush victory; Gore wins.

The smallest event can set the cycle in motion. It might start when an adviser to one of the candidates starts talking to the media about something that's "off message." The process, as one Bush adviser explains it, goes like this: "You get the stories that you're 'thrown off course.' . . . Then all the people who called a week before to say what a good job you're doing now have new ideas about how to fix things."

And then comes rock bottom: the dreaded panic: "There's nothing stupider than a campaign in panic," says Mark Fabiani, Gore's communications director. "You feel there's no way out of a downward cycle. It piles on. You get criticized. People get dispirited."

Predicting the cycles is rather like predicting the weather. There are underlying climate changes. There are seasonal changes. And then there are the usual cold fronts every few days, punctuated occasionally by a hurricane. "If a thunderstorm is on the way and you don't have an umbrella, you're in trouble," explains Tad Devine, a top Gore strategist.

Gore is hoping that the dominant cycle will be an overall warming pattern—his own political El Niño. Gore spokesman Chris Lehane prefers a different metaphor. He likens the Gore campaign to the Boston Celtics of the late 1960s: They would just barely make the playoffs, then grow steadily stronger and win the championship.

Bush, on the other hand, hopes that the recent troubles are just a passing storm. "There will be another twist," predicts Gillespie. "Maybe two or three before it's over." Each of the three scheduled presidential debates could cause a cycle reversal. So could a yet-unknown scandal or a major mistake by a candidate.

The feast-or-famine swings often have a kernel of reality. A candidate who is having trouble making his case is more likely to get knocked down by petty events (a Naomi Wolf scandal or a major-league expletive). Begala likens it to teaching his four-year-old daughter to ride a bicycle: "If you don't have forward momentum, anything can push you over."

The polls—now being done daily—are partly to blame for the swings. A jump in the polls sends political watchers searching for a sign—something in the candidate's message or demeanor—to explain the change. Usually there's no cause and effect. "It's like the way the old Incas worshiped: when the sun moved and something changed, they thought the sun did it," says Matt Dowd, Bush's polling director. "They want to attribute immediate cause and effect, and there are much longer-term patterns."

Reporters fuel the cycles with their constant desire to make the race competitive—knocking down the front-runner and building up the underdog. More insidiously, reporters also want to ingratiate themselves with the eventual winner. As soon as Gore pulled ahead in the polls, reporters traveling with Bush suddenly deluged Gore advisers with phone calls. When Gore was down, these same reporters wouldn't even return Gore advisers' calls.

For the campaigns, the trick is to be at a peak and have your opponent in a trough on Election Day. This is not easy. When a candidate finds himself in a trough, often the only way out is to "retool" or to have a shakeup, even if nobody feels one is warranted.

"You cannot get out of it until you admit something's wrong—whether or not it is," muses one Bush adviser. "It's like an intervention." The campaign must enroll itself in a 12-step recovery process, come up with the requisite staff change or a new slogan. The latest case is the rash of headlines about Bush's new plan to target the middle class. Who, pray tell, was he targeting before?

Before you know it, your campaign is back "on message," back to talking about Medicare or taxes or Social Security. Then it's time for the other guy to be off message or "on the defensive." Your candidate gets "traction," while the other guy concedes that his campaign is "tentative" and possibly "losing footing."

The game is easy. You don't need to be a political professional or a practicing journalist to play along at home. Simply select the words of your choice in the following sentences to construct your own cycle-turning news report—just as the pros do.

Thank you, (Tom/Peter/Dan/Bernie). Tonight, the campaign of (Al Gore/George W. Bush) is (losing momentum/on a roll). The candidate had a (tentative/self-assured) day of campaigning, proving that he is (connecting with/struggling to connect with) the voters of (Michigan/Florida/Missouri). In fact, Mr. (Bush/Gore) seems to be more (focused/off message) than at any point I've seen him in the last few (weeks/days/hours). At stop after stop, he is (rallying crowds/mangling syntax) to a degree unseen before. Clearly, this is a sign that the candidate is (stumbling/losing footing/cruising). With a few more days of (smooth sailing/fumbling) it is likely that he will encounter a (healthy bounce/bump in the road). On the other hand, we hear that Mr. (Bush's/Gore's) rival is (retooling/panicking/soaring in overnight polls), a development that has the potential to send the race into a period of heightened (tension/tension/tension), which should lead to (higher turnout/higher ratings). Reporting from (Austin/Nashville), I'm (your name here) for (ABC/CBS/NBC/CNN) news. Back to you, (Tom/Peter/ Dan/Bernie).

As if on cue, the Gore plunge has begun—within days of my prediction of a turn in the cycle. It came after Gore's first debate performance in Boston. Though his tough style won the debate, according to the polls, his theatrical sighing and his exaggerations began to sink him. He told the story of a Florida girl forced to stand during class for lack of desks—but the story was subsequently denied by the school's principal—and he falsely claimed that he traveled to Texas with the head of the Federal Emergency Management Agency. The bloopers weren't that much by themselves, but it reminded everybody of I-invented-the-Internet Al. Now Bush is effectively using Gore's trouble with the truth to discredit the v.p.'s entire program. Suddenly, Bush is on top again.

It's getting hard to keep track of the quick shifts in Big Mo. To get a better grip on who's ahead, I have come, of all places, to Utica, New York.

Genesee Street, running south from downtown, becomes Religion Row. There's the steeple of First Presbyterian Church and the yellow-brick Temple Beth El on your left. On the right, you'll pass Saviour Lutheran Church. Then, just before the Church of our Lady of Lourdes and the Church of the Nazarene, right next to the AMF Pin-O-Rama bowling alley, is a Cathedral of our Civic Religion.

This is the headquarters of Zogby International, pollsters.

In this election season, the operation is a frenzied factory of public opinion, tracking every hiccup and sigh in the presidential race. Callers begin at 9 A.M. and end at midnight, when number-crunchers figure out who's winning and release the Reuters/MSNBC/Zogby daily tracking poll to the breathless media.

In politics this year, polling is everything. The results of these surveys drive the candidates' moves and the press coverage, which may in turn influence the election's outcome. For this reason, I have made a pilgrimage here to worship at the altar of public opinion.

The dinner hour is approaching. I put on my headset and push the button that tells the computer to dial a number. I call Washington State— no answer. I call Colorado—answering machine. I call Kansas—no reply. I call Michigan, where a man shouts, "No!" and hangs up. I click "refusal— hostile" on my computer, and forge on.

My success doesn't improve much over the next hour. I get busy tones in Ohio and Kansas, disconnected numbers in Montana and Illinois, no answer in Virginia, Kentucky, Maine, Oklahoma and Massachusetts, a fax machine and a call-waiting "privacy manager" in Ohio, and a tree and shrub service in upstate New York. In New York City, a woman advises me, "Sweetheart, you're in the middle of our dinner," and another hangs up on me. A Virginia man, shouting over a crying baby, exclaims, "Excuse me? Nah!" Click. A California woman asks me, "No habla español?" A New Jersey woman informs me, "I'm one of Jehovah's Witnesses and there are certain things we don't do."

My hour of calling produces only one hit in 25 attempts: a 51-year-old woman in Cincinnati who is for Bush. The result of my piece of the tracking poll:

Bush: 100 percent
Everyone else: 0 percent
Margin of error: +/- 98 percent

Apparently, I'm not cut out for this. "You did a couple of things we would yell at our interviewers for," explains Steven McLaughlin, my tutor. "You've got to read your script word for word," he tells me.

But perhaps I shouldn't feel bad. With all the busy signals and disconnected numbers, it takes Zogby callers nearly 6,000 calls to get 400 complete responses. Only 35 percent of people reached by phone answer pollsters' questions, a number that has declined from 65 percent fifteen years ago. Answering machines, caller ID, and telemarketers poisoning the well have made poll-taking difficult. Even among those reached, it becomes immediately obvious that a large number of our compatriots have only the vaguest notion that there's an election happening.

But such cynicism is not necessarily warranted. Though large numbers of Americans are ill informed, ill mannered and ill prepared to choose a leader, when you add them up something magical happens. Individuals are transformed into a wise and noble creature: the American electorate. The polls, in their aggregate, invariably show a temperate and thoughtful nation. It would make Tocqueville smile.

"There's a collective wisdom that emerges," says John Zogby, who started the firm in the 1980s. "When it all adds up there's a clear message. The community is never stupid."

Still, Zogby is the first to acknowledge polling's shortcomings. The polls, particularly daily ones, are just snapshots. "We're not predicting," Zogby says. "You can't read too much into the day-to-day change or try to read causality into it."

But the press tends to look for some fault in the declining candidate to justify a poll drop. The explosion of cable and Internet news outlets, which commission polls and hype the results, exacerbates the problem. "Having it govern the way a campaign gets covered is dangerous," Zogby says. "It becomes a tremendous disservice."

Another caveat: While polls are good at measuring trends, the numbers tend to reflect the pollsters' hunches as much as the respondents' answers. The raw numbers in a poll are meaningless until "weighted" (certain categories of voters are over- or underemphasized) to mirror the population and to reflect the pollster's guess about who will vote. Most poll-watchers don't realize that a Bush lead in raw numbers can become a Gore lead in weighted numbers.

"Twenty percent of this business is art, 80 percent is science," Zogby says. "Ultimately, you have to make a call about who's going to turn out to vote." Pollsters adjust their responses by gender, race, religion, age, region and income. The time of day a call is made, the response rate, how the questions are phrased and ordered, the suggestiveness of the questioner, and how a pollster defines a "likely voter" and "undecided" can all alter the results. Zogby, controversially, also weighs party identification, which he gauges through a series of questions.

Some other pollsters think Zogby favors Republicans (he says he's a Democrat and works for both sides). But Zogby has a good record among the three major public tracking polls. In 1996, he got Clinton's eight-point victory exactly right. Lately, his tracking poll has had a smoother pattern than the Gallup tracking poll (which recently galloped 18 points in a couple of days) and has been more consistent with larger polls than the Voter.com/Battleground tracking poll.

Zogby's calling center is a collection of 94 cubicles in a decrepit, dank office building abandoned by the phone company. The callers, whose pay starts at $6.25 an hour, are a mixture of students, retirees, immigrants from Eastern Europe and part-timers with day jobs. The place smells of pizza or whatever else is in the break area, which also includes a snack machine that sells Chicken Cordon Bleu. One woman's lapdog naps on the floor of her cubicle as she makes calls.

"Hello, my name is Fanny and I'm doing a poll of U.S. voters for Reuters News Agency and Zogby International," says Fanny George, a retired nurse. She calls numbers that pop up on her screen courtesy of the "computer-aided telephone interview" or CATI system, pronounced "Katie." CATI sends Fanny plenty of duds: no answer, a law office, a couple of refusals. But George, an expert caller with a grandmother's gentle voice, completes interviews at the clip of three an hour. Each one requires her to give voters choices for president that most have never heard of: Harry Browne, John Hagelin, Howard Phillips and David McReynolds.

As night approaches, there are fifty callers in the room, and a round of "Very likely? Somewhat likely? Unlikely?" rises from the din. The callers struggle with a confounded electorate. Mark Carchedi interviews a woman who can't understand what he means when he asks how likely she is to vote. Later comes the man who agrees to offer his phone number in case a reporter wants to ask about the poll. "Your area code?" Carchedi asks. The respondent doesn't respond. "What's your area code?" Nothing. "Sir, do you have an area code? . . . Area code! . . . What's your area code? . . . If somebody's calling you long distance, what do they dial?" Carchedi finally procures the desired digits.

Callers here have heard it all. Many get obscenities and propositions, one polled Rodney Dangerfield, one respondent believed he was Jesus, another put her dog on the phone, and one woman described her status as "married, wanting to get divorced."

By 9 P.M., Frank Calaprice, a night supervisor, has begun to keep careful track of the tracking poll. He has met his quota of 93 responses from Zone 1 (Eastern) and must get 11 more in Zone 2 (Midwest) and 13 more in Zone 3 (South) by 10 P.M., when he turns his attentions to Zone 4 (California). He watches the tally on his computer, shifting callers from other Zogby polls as needed. He completes his last call in Zone 3 at 9:58, with two minutes to spare.

"It's very nerve-racking," Calaprice says. At 10 P.M., he begins to work on getting 26 more responses from the West Coast. By 11 P.M., he has ten to go. He could add callers and finish the whole thing in five minutes, but he's been instructed that this could skew results. "I know there's a logic to everything they do," he says. "I just don't personally know what it is."

"I'm going in," says Joe Mazloom.

It's midnight, and Mazloom, a wild-haired young man wearing blue jeans and a T-shirt, enters the response database and commands his computer to "export off CATI system." After a brief scare before midnight—several West Coast respondents don't respond because of the baseball playoffs—Calaprice has reached his 400-call quota, and it's time to crunch numbers.

In his office, next to the Cordon Bleu snack machine, Mazloom hits a few buttons and pulls up the day's raw numbers: Bush leads Gore by 44.6 percent to 40.1 percent overall, and 49.1 percent to 42.9 percent in a hypothetical two-way matchup. That gives an unweighted three-day average of 44.2 for Bush and 42.8 for Gore, and a three-day average in the two-way race of 47.3 for Bush and 45.1 for Gore.

Now the fun begins. Mazloom begins to balance the day's sample so it conforms with Zogby's hunches (based on exit polls from previous elections) about which type of people will show up on election days. Republicans, men and Jews are overrepresented in the day's sample, while African-Americans and young voters must be doubled. Mazloom whips through spreadsheets, hitting buttons, adjusting regions, typing incomprehensible numbers (1071 0.805, 499 0.483). After several runs, the sample is weighted: slightly more women and Democrats, a quarter Catholic, more than a quarter elderly, and four-fifths white.

The weighted results invert the findings: now Gore leads in the three-day average, 45.0 to 41.0; in the two-way race, Gore leads 47.5 to 44.5. The inversion, Mazloom says, comes mostly from the weighting for party identification.

Mazloom sends the results to a bleary-eyed Alan Crockett, Zogby's press man, who is waiting in his office to write the 2 A.M. press release. "The midnights are killing my social life," Crockett says. He slaps on the 3 percent margin of error and fields a call from Zogby, who dictates the day's headline and a quote. "Race Now Just a 4-Point Lead," the release says. "Make no mistake about it, this is a very tight race."

By daybreak, political reporters everywhere will be using the results to do just what Zogby warned against: to find a reason why one candidate is doing badly and the other is doing well.

Endgame
the Political Staff of *The Washington Post*

from *Deadlock: The Inside Story of America's Closest Election*

The book Deadlock is a blow-by-blow description of the five weeks between Election Day, 2000 and December 12—the day when the U.S. Supreme Court announced its final ruling in Gore v. Bush, effectively handing the election to George W. Bush. In this excerpt, we pick up the action on the morning after the Florida Supreme Court's momentous December 8 ruling, in which they overturned an earlier decision by Judge N. Sanders Saul and ordered a statewide manual recount of all Florida undervotes (ballots that had not registered a vote), to commence immediately. The court also ruled that the ballots already hand-counted in Palm Beach and Miami-Dade counties should be added to the certified total. This gave Al Gore a net gain of 383 votes— and left George W. Bush hanging by his fingernails to a 154-vote lead. . . .

Bright and early Saturday morning, December 9, the phone rang at Karen Hughes's house. George W. Bush was on the line. The Texas governor relied powerfully on Hughes for advice and friendship, and he often began her day with a call at dawn. "Have we won yet?" Bush asked jokingly.

If the disputed election was the first test of Bush's presidential abilities, he felt he was passing admirably. "I remained very steady," Bush said afterward, taking inventory of the things he'd done right. "I was pretty peaceful throughout. . . . I called upon the very best people I could find to solve the problem, and when called upon I was able to make decisions." Field marshal James A. Baker III, running mate Richard B. Cheney and chief of staff-designate Andrew H. Card Jr. crystallized the questions and proposed answers, and once Bush pulled the trigger, the whole team moved on.

Bush considered morale one of his most important jobs. Routinely during the War for Florida, he placed calls to people who were doing a good job pursuing his cause. After Supreme Court arguments he called his constitutional lawyer, Ted Olson, to say thanks. When a Democrat from Tallahassee, Barry Richard, did a good job for him in court, Bush called the man's house and had to convince his wife that yes, this really was George W. Bush. "Somebody had told me he had twin kids," Bush later recalled. "I said, 'It's hard to be away from your wife and the twin babies but tell your wife how much I appreciate it, tell her it's going to end. Wish her all the best. You're looking great.' " On Thanksgiving, Bush phoned a large group of loyalists sharing a holiday dinner far from home.

So here he was, the former prep school cheerleader, trying to start a bad day on an up note for his communications director. In these waning days of the election dispute, Bush became "fully engaged," he said later. "I've got a lot of Lyndon Johnson in me, I guess. I'm on that phone: What does it mean? What are you seeing? What are you hearing?"

Bush also called Josh Bolten, his campaign policy director, who was working with Baker in Florida. Bolten gave him a pessimistic report. "I told him that counting was bad for us from a PR standpoint," Bolten remembered, "because it posed the risk that at some point Bush would fall into deficit and then we'd have serious public relations problems."

In Florida that Saturday morning, officials in nearly every county were preparing to start scrutinizing ballots, looking for uncounted votes that might just tip the election to Al Gore. When he called Hughes—"Have we won yet?"—she wondered if she had missed some big event overnight. "Not that I'm aware of yet, sir," she hedged.

Hughes wasn't in a joking mood. On Friday afternoon, Gore had been on the mat. Now, thanks to the Florida Supreme Court, he was back where he wanted to be—counting ballots.

Ron Klain, the hub of Al Gore's Florida wheel, had read the deeply split decision of the Florida Supreme Court with a mixture of excitement and foreboding. The excitement was simple: Just as he had expected, the Florida justices, by a 4 to 3 vote, had ordered further examination of ballots rejected as unreadable by the state's counting machines. All Gore's hopes rested on those ballots.

Klain's foreboding was more complex. Nowhere in the Florida four's opinion was there any direct mention of the fact that, just a few days earlier, the U.S. Supreme Court had vacated the lower court's previous work on the dispute. Klain wasn't sure the Florida justices intended to provoke the highest court. But as he read their opinion—and the passionate dissent of Chief Justice Wells—Klain realized that he must immediately begin preparing for a new hearing at the U.S. Supreme Court.

Meanwhile, in Washington and in Tallahassee, the Gore team began a mass mobilization, as Klain had recommended the day before. Phone calls went out to union activists and local party loyalists and Democratic attorneys around the country, pleading with them to get to Florida as quickly as possible. Observers would be needed all over the state.

Joe Allbaugh faced the same task on behalf of Bush. When the imposing Oklahoman heard the news of the Florida Supreme Court's decision, he got so angry he stalked into his cubbyhole office and fumed. Eventually, he emerged and started organizing an airlift. Allbaugh and his aides were on the phone all night rousting volunteers to come watch the counts—by Saturday morning, they had pulled in more than 450 people from across the country. "We were moving and mobilizing an army, and getting them not only there, but briefed up the next morning to go into the counties that were starting to recount," Allbaugh explained later, "and what they needed to be prepared for, and what did they need to look for, and what was the law, and what do they do in case this crops up or that crops up."

Watchers were needed in every county, and lawyers to advise the watchers, and another layer of attorneys to coordinate the lawyers, and so on. Allbaugh caught a couple of hours of sleep after 2 A.M. When he got back to the office at 6:30, he was amazed to find the first waves of recruits were already arriving. He walked into a little meeting room and there were perhaps 100 people crammed inside, sweaty and stifling, yet hanging on to each instruction.

The key, the volunteers were told, was to keep track of every interpretation by the counters, because Leon County Circuit Court Judge Terry P. Lewis had declined the night before, when he set up the recount process, to set specific standards for counting votes. Lewis would order only that the examiners seek "the intent of the voter," whatever that might mean from ballot to ballot. For the sake of speed, though, the judge barred party observers from making objections. Instead, they were to keep a list of disputed ballots. He would let them complain later, maybe.

Bush attorney Phil Beck had protested this lack of a uniform standard— not because he thought Lewis would change his mind, but because he hoped a few U.S. Supreme Court clerks—maybe even a few justices—might be watching the proceedings on television. The seemingly hopeless issue raised by the Bush team weeks earlier in federal court—that the recounts violated equal protection standards in the U.S. Constitution—was now ripening by the minute. This hasty statewide recount would involve dozens of counties devising their own standards for discerning votes. By order of the court, roughly 20 percent of the Miami-Dade ballots would be certified according to the county canvassing board's partial count, while the rest of the Miami undervotes were to be counted in Tallahassee by an entirely different group of judges with their own set of standards. In that case, Beck believed, the standard was not even consistent in one county. "My whole point was, you must have a coherent standard that applies uniformly throughout the state of Florida," he said later.

Beck called Mike Carvin to urge that the standards issue be front and center in Bush's appeal to the U.S. Supreme Court. Carvin was already there. He had been watching the equal protection argument getting a little bit stronger—and stronger and stronger, he felt—with each step in the election dispute. Of all the lawyers in the tangled dispute, Beck mused, Carvin got the rawest treatment. Because of the battering he took in the initial oral argument before the Florida Supreme Court, Carvin had become the butt of jokes and whispers throughout the political world. Radio host Don Imus loved to dump on him. Carvin had been pulled unceremoniously from the public eye. Yet he remained, Beck believed, one of the most creative thinkers in the crucial area of federal litigation.

Indeed, people on the Bush team began to feel that their once-doomed argument was turning into a winner. George Terwilliger and Ben Ginsberg barreled out of Lewis's courtroom so quickly that Terwilliger bumped shoulders with David Boies. Instead of apologizing, the tall, bearded Terwilliger said, "You know what, David? We just won this case."

"This is so bad it's good," Ginsberg added.

Boies looked at them as if they were crazy. "I'm sure he thought I was out of my mind," Terwilliger recalled. But as he explained to a crowd of reporters as he strode down the courthouse hallway: "It's exactly the kind of chaotic, confusing, standardless situation that we had warned the U.S. Supreme Court about."

Nearly five weeks after the election had ended in a virtual tie, an elections supervisor in Leon County named Ion Sancho stood up in the community room of the county public library and said simply: "The process may begin."

With scarcely a murmur, eight judges and their assistants hunkered down to tally the roughly 9,000 undervotes left unstudied when the Miami-Dade canvassing board halted its recount on Thanksgiving eve. In Duval County—greater Jacksonville—election officials met a computer programmer from Miami bearing the software to instruct their counting machines to separate nearly 5,000 undervotes from the mountain of 292,000 ballots cast on Election Day. In Sarasota, a county judge corralled an official van and headed to a satellite office at the other end of the county to collect 65 boxes of ballots.

In Collier County, on the Gulf Coast, the canvassing board needed five hours that Saturday just to decide how to count 40 absentee ballots. "We've set up a system that has a built-in margin of error of 3 percent, one way or another," the board's chairman lamented. "To tell us on Friday to count them by Monday is ridiculous."

In Pinellas County, on Tampa Bay, Commissioner Robert Stewart pondered the recount effort and mused: "Damn, we need a better process."

And so it went all over Florida. As it was from the beginning, the reliability of hand counting was in the eye, or party affiliation, of the beholder. Democrats extolled a heroic effort moving along quickly with noble intentions. Republicans saw chaos. In Austin, Hughes felt her stomach sink as she watched on television. "Well," she thought, "once again, we're counting votes."

But no one had much chance to contemplate the matter. At 2:40 P.M., CNN reported that the U.S. Supreme Court had ordered an immediate halt to the effort. Gore was on the phone with Ron Klain when the news broke. It was the vice president's lowest moment.

In Tallahassee, the chief local judge, George S. Reynolds III, confirmed the news and issued his order 12 minutes later. At 3 P.M., court spokesman Terre Cass was once more at the microphones. "We have stayed the recount," she said.

The simmering divisions in the U.S. Supreme Court had boiled over. The stay order—and the related decision to hear oral arguments on Bush's appeal on Monday, December 11—was issued by a bare 5 to 4 majority, perfectly splitting the court's most conservative members from its most liberal ones.

The liberals reacted to the stay with a published dissent—a very rare form of writing at the Supreme Court. It read like the work of people who suspect their colleagues are not dealing with them in good faith. Citing the necessary standard for a stay order—namely, that there must be a risk of "irreparable harm" unless the action is halted—the liberals scoffed at the idea that counting ballots threatened to harm Bush. If anyone was threatened with irreparable harm it was Gore, they said, who could be deprived of his challenge if time ran out. As Justice John Paul Stevens wrote for the four: "Preventing a recount from being completed will inevitably cast a cloud on the legitimacy of the election. . . . The Florida court's ruling reflects the basic principle, inherent in our Constitution and our democracy, that every legal vote should be counted."

At that, Justice Antonin Scalia, the court's leading conservative theorist, felt he had no choice but to issue an even more unusual document—an opinion concurring with the brief, boilerplate stay order. "The counting of votes that are of questionable legality does in my view threaten irreparable harm to petitioner" he wrote, "and to the country, by casting a cloud upon what [Bush] claims to be the legitimacy of his election. Count first, and rule upon legality afterwards, is not a recipe for producing election results that have the public acceptance democratic stability requires."

In this unusually public dispute, Scalia added a so-there that his liberal colleagues could not answer. Under the court's rules, he noted, the stay grant meant that Bush had a "substantial probability" of prevailing in the case. In other words, he had five votes going into the Monday hearing. The case was Bush's to lose.

The Justice Who Picked the President
David Kaplan

from *The Accidental President: How 413 Lawyers, 9 Supreme Court Justices, and 5,963,110 Floridians (Give or Take a Few) Landed George W. Bush in the White House*

Could the Supreme Court's final decision in Election 2000 have gone the other way? Cynics claim that the court's 5-4 ruling to stop all Florida recounts—thus sealing the presidential victory for George W. Bush—was a preordained vote along party lines. But Newsweek's David Kaplan portrays a less clear-cut scenario.

In this excerpt from his book The Accidental President, Kaplan focuses on the Supreme Court justice who represented the swing vote: Justice Anthony Kennedy. Kennedy was the last court member to embrace the Republicans' "equal protection" argument—which asserted that going ahead with the hand recounts in Florida would violate voters' rights to a fair election. We join him and the other eight justices on the bench, as Gore's superstar attorney David Boies prepares to argue his client's case. . . .

Unlike Olson or Klock, Boies did have to swing for the fences—for both his client and, as Boies explained later, for posterity. Whatever else happened, he wanted future generations to hear what was going down in the election of the forty-third president of the United States.

Boies faced the same two lines of questioning the others had: Did the Florida Supreme Court change the law and, even if it didn't, was the statewide recount unfair? On the first, Kennedy led the charge. "Could the Florida Legislature have done what the [state] supreme court did?" he asked with a glower.

"I really haven't thought about that question," Boies replied. "I think they probably could not . . . because it would be a legislative enactment as opposed to a judicial interpretation of an existing law."

"I'm not sure why," said Kennedy, seeing that Boies was begging the question. "If the legislature does it, it's a new law and when the supreme court does it, it isn't?" If it had been the legislature that had effectively "truncated" the contest period by nineteen days, Kennedy said, wouldn't that have occasioned squawks?

O'Connor, still stewing over the fact that the Florida justices had yet to respond to the vacate-and-remand, seconded Kennedy's point. Didn't both the U.S. Constitution and the Electoral Count Act require the state court to give "special deference" to the state legislature? "General elections" were one thing, she lectured, "but in the context of selection of presidential electors, isn't there a big red flag up there [saying] 'Watch out'?"

The challenge of oral argument, particularly before a bench of nine jurists, is to keep so many balls in the air. While Boies wanted to keep all his interrogators happy as his forty-five minutes whizzed by, he knew who was most important and who was a lost cause. As the various justices competed with each other to steer the argument, Boies had to keep weaving to take the direction he wanted. It was impossible. O'Connor wanted to hear more about being dissed by the Florida Supreme Court; Scalia professed not to understand how any further ballots could be added to Harris's initial certification now that its supposed extension had been vacated by the Court. Neither of those inquiries was going to get Boies anywhere, nor were they even close to getting to the much larger issue that Boies wanted to engage: Were any of these specific items really matters for the U.S. Supreme Court or were they best left to Florida's courts to resolve?

Kennedy wanted to go back to the equal-protection problem and prevailed in making it the center of the rest of the argument. What he demanded to know was whether Boies acknowledged that "there must be a uniform standard for counting the ballots" under the Florida Supreme Court order in the contest proceeding.

"I do, Your Honor," Boies said. "The standard is whether or not the intent of the voter is reflected by the ballot. That is the uniform standard throughout the state of Florida."

Kennedy had enough of this dodge-and-weave. "That's very general," he remonstrated Boies. "Even a dog knows the difference in being stumbled over and being kicked. . . . From the standpoint of the Equal Protection Clause, could each county give their own interpretation to what intent means?"

"It can vary from individual to individual."

"This is susceptible of a uniform standard," Kennedy asked with incredulity, "and yet you say it can vary from [recount] table to table within the same county?"

Boies was digging himself in, but not because he was a fool. If he proposed specific rules about, say, dimples or hanging chads, he'd be tacking too near the proscriptions of the Electoral Count Act and out of the December 12 safe harbor he'd long ago conceded as significant. How do you articulate the uniform standards that equal protection seemed to require, while also *not* changing the law that existed on Election Day—especially a law that was so vague about standards ("clear indication of the intent of the voter") that it amounted to no standard at all? Boies wanted it both ways and ended up satisfying nobody. There may very well have been no way out of the bind, though Boies probably should've just tried to solve the equal-protection problem—which had constitutional proportions—and taken his chances that a majority of the Court would find the counting rules hadn't been illegally changed.

Kennedy wouldn't let Boies off. "You're not just reading a person's mind," he said. "You are looking at a piece of paper." Was there not "something objective" about how to evaluate a mark on it?

Boies again proffered nothing, except to note that states like Texas, which had statutorily delineated standards, included a "catch-all provision that says, 'Look at the intent of the voter.'" How was this practically any different from Florida? he said.

Souter tried next. "I think what's bothering Justice Kennedy—and it's bothering a lot of us—is we seem to have a situation here in which there is a subcategory of ballots in which we are assuming for the sake of argument, since we know no better, that there is no genuinely subjective indication beyond what can be viewed as either a dimple or a hanging chad, and there is a general rule being applied in a given county that an objective intent, or an intent on an objective standard, will be inferred, and that objective rule varies, we are told, from county to county."

Huh? What did all *that* mean?

It was just a reflection of how confusing the facts could be to those who hadn't been following them for a month, and another indication for the Court that trying to unravel the mess swiftly wasn't a task for which justices were well suited. But Souter did figure out his point. "Why shouldn't there be one objective rule for all counties?" he asked. "And if there is not, why isn't it an equal-protection violation?" If Souter wanted to make it any clearer to Boies what might be needed to entice Kennedy (or, possibly, O'Connor), the justice would've had to get up from the bench and walk to the lectern and bonk Boies over the head with a law book.

Yet Boies wouldn't go there. "Objective criteria," he said, didn't exist in Recountland, any more than they did in other areas of the law, including how juries and public officials went about making decisions.

Did that mean the same "physical characteristic" constituted a legal vote in one county but not the next? Souter inquired. Wasn't a dimple always a dimple?

"I don't think so," Boies insisted. That was because there wasn't evidence that counties were behaving that way. "Maybe if you had specific objective criteria in one county that said we're going to count indented ballots and another county that said we're only going to count the ballot if it's punched through—if you knew you had those two objective standards and they were different, then you might have an equal-protection problem."

Hallelujah! Boies was admitting the theoretical possibility of the problem, even if he was denying the factual reality that it had to happen with sixty-four counties recounting, almost half of them using punch-card voting systems.

Souter pointed out the obvious: "We can't send this thing back for more fact-finding." So, he said, he was going to assume the counties were acting inconsistently and in violation of equal protection. With that hypothesis, "we would have a responsibility to tell the Florida courts what to do about it.

"On that assumption," Souter asked one last time, "what would you tell them to do about it?"

"Well," Boies said, "that's a very hard question."

It took an awfully long time for him to come around to that unhelpful conclusion. And despite Boies later tepidly offering up the Texas chad standards as a guide, he had largely wasted whatever slender chance there might have been to win Kennedy over. You can't replay the inning—another first baseman might've missed Mookie Wilson's grounder just the same as Bill Buckner did, and the Red Sox still would've lost the game—but Souter and Breyer knew they had given Boies a chance, relentlessly so, and he had muffed it.

• • •

One had to be a careful reader to find the ruling's essence—that the standardless recounts were an unconstitutional violation of equal protection and there was no time left for Florida to do anything about it. Not until the fourth page did the ruling even mention equal protection; not until three pages later was it discussed further. In retrospect, the best way to distill the meaning was to read not the main opinions, but the dissents. Page after page of the ruling was a rote recitation of the case history. (In the old days, even the Kremlin didn't do this good a job of burying its decisions in some long-winded edict.) There was no method to the Court's obtuseness—just proof that good writing takes time. Justices don't handle short deadlines well.

Despite its sixty-five pages, consisting of six different opinions, *Bush v.*

Gore came down to another unsigned statement, just as the first election case before the High Court had. That one, however, was unanimous, as virtually all unsigned "per curiam" ("for the Court") orders were. This one, given the various signed concurrences and dissents that followed, was obviously the view of only Kennedy or O'Connor, or both, but it nonetheless represented the law of the land. Later, it became clear that Kennedy himself had drafted the opinion. The internal dynamics of the Court made sense. The four liberals wrote dissents: Breyer and Souter conceded there was an equal-protection problem (which is why a few commentators mistakenly said it was a 7-to-2 ruling), but one that should be sent back to Florida for repair; Ginsburg and Stevens argued more vociferously that the Court should have stayed out of this political thicket altogether.

• • •

When Kennedy, in the thirteen-page per curiam opinion, got around to discussing equal protection, he noted that an individual's right to vote for presidential electors came not from the Constitution itself, but from the eventual decisions by state legislatures to relinquish that right themselves. This was an implicit dig by Kennedy at both Gore's and the Florida Supreme Court's propensity for invoking the "will of the people." Once individuals had the privilege of picking the electors, Kennedy wrote, their respective votes had to be accorded "equal weight" and "equal dignity." Having "granted the right to vote on equal terms," he said, "the state may not, by later arbitrary and disparate treatment, value one person's vote over that of another." According to Kennedy, citing both Boies's admission at oral argument and the dissent by Florida's chief justice, the recount procedures ordered by the Florida Supreme Court did precisely that. Palm Beach provided the best evidence, where, Kennedy said, "the process began with a 1990 guideline which precluded counting completely attached chads, switched to a rule that considered a vote to be legal if any light could be seen through a chad, changed back to the 1990 rule, and then abandoned any pretense of a *per se* rule."

The process struck Kennedy as farce. "The recount mechanisms implemented in response to the decisions of the Florida Supreme Court do not satisfy the minimum requirement for non-arbitrary treatment of voters necessary to secure the fundamental right" of voting, he wrote. The mere incantation of following the "intent of the voter" was "unobjectionable as an abstract proposition and a starting principle," but not without "specific standards to ensure" equal treatment for voters. "The formulation of uniform rules to determine intent," Kennedy concluded, was "practicable" and "necessary."

But isn't evaluating "intent" inherently subjective? Kennedy argued that assessing a witness's testimony at trial is thoroughly different from interpreting "marks or holes or scratches on an inanimate object." How so? "The fact-finder confronts a thing, not a person." It wasn't much of a distinction—and Kennedy said nothing more about it. Nor, tellingly, did he think through what he really meant by equal protection. Just what was the exact harm of, say, County A counting a dimpled chad as a legal vote and County B not doing so? The worst that could happen is that ballots in County B would remain invalid. Which candidate did that hurt, though? (Remember, it was the candidates who brought the lawsuits.) Was there not the same probability of those ballots going for either Bush or Gore? The fact is, neither would suffer more harm as a result of County B running its recount differently from County A—*unless* the greater risk was to Bush because he was the guy *ahead*. Kennedy's equal-protection logic sounded a lot like Scalia's embarrassing attempt the prior Saturday to justify halting the recounts.

• • •

It was not surprising that the *Bush v. Gore* majority might worry about the logic of its ruling, so wholly unreceptive as the five justices had long been to expanding any voting rights under the Fourteenth Amendment. The five conservatives believed that voting disputes were the province of the elected branches. But *Bush v. Gore* seemed totally disconnected from any prior opinions. And the justices wanted to make sure it remained unmoored from anything that might follow. "The problem of equal protection in election processes generally presents many complexities," Kennedy wrote, purportedly explaining why the ruling was "limited to the present circumstances." But that was mush—generalities wrapped in platitudes inside a haze. Of course the transmogrification of electoral inequalities into constitutional violations is "complex." Carried to its extremes, the *Bush v. Gore* rationale could invalidate most statewide elections in America, run as they are at the county level. Why should recounts be treated any differently from the initial counts known as elections? Standards are standards.

States, counties, and even local communities use different voting machines, tabulation equipment, and ballot designs; lines are short in affluent neighborhoods and around the block in poorer precincts; the polls are open for twelve hours in some places, fifteen in the next; election officials have varying degrees of experience. Lurking behind many of the inequities, intentional or otherwise, is their disparate effect on blacks, which has always been the lodestar of equal-protection jurisprudence; African-Americans tend to live in poorer areas, which tend to have less reliable voting equipment. But the Court had never found that local variations in "election processes," unless specifically animated by bias, were actionable.

So, for Kennedy and the other four justices to declare a bold change in the law that worked to the *detriment* of blacks and minorities in Florida in this presidential election—and, in the next breath, to say that the revolutionary principle could never be used again—was more than ironic. It was brazen. It seemed to prove that *Bush v. Gore* wasn't about "equal protection" at all—only the realpolitik end of putting the Republican in the White House and ensuring that he'd be naming new justices for the next four years. This, in effect, was the conservatives choosing their potential successors.

• • •

Given the inescapable partisanship of the decision, the amazing aspect of *Bush v. Gore* is that it just might have gone the other way. Kennedy wavered, enough that Souter thought until the very end that he'd get him, and that the 5-to-4 ruling for Bush would become a 5-to-4 verdict for Gore. They'd find an equal-protection violation, send the case back to the Florida justices to fix standards and administer the best recount they could under the circumstances and before December 18, and then leave it to the political branches—the Florida legislature and, if need be, the U.S. Congress—to settle it for good.

A month after the decision, Souter met at the Court with a group of prep-school students from Choate. He told them how frustrated he was that he couldn't broker a deal to bring in one more justice—Kennedy being the obvious candidate. Souter explained that he had put together a coalition back in 1992, in *Planned Parenthood v. Casey*, the landmark abortion case in which the Court declined by a 5-to-4 vote to overturn *Roe v. Wade;* Souter, along with O'Connor and Kennedy, made the unusual gesture of writing a joint opinion for the majority.

If he'd had "one more day—*one more day*," Souter now told the Choate students, he believed he would have prevailed. Rehnquist, Thomas, and Scalia had long ago become part of the Dark Side. O'Connor seemed beyond compromise. But Kennedy seemed within reach. *Just give me twenty-four more hours on the clock.* While a political resolution to the election—in the Florida legislature or in the Congress—might not be quick and it might be a brawl, Souter argued that the nation would still accept it. "It should be a political branch that issues political decisions," he said to the students. Kennedy, though, wouldn't flip. He thought the trauma of more recounts, more fighting—more *politics*, as it were—was too much for the country to endure.

In the end, the margin of victory for George W. Bush wasn't 154, 165, 193, or 204 votes (depending on what numbers you believe from the abbreviated recounts). Nor was the operative margin Katherine Harris's initial number, 930. The sands of history will show Bush won by a single vote, cast in a 5-to-4 ruling of the U.S. Supreme Court. The vote was Tony Kennedy's. One justice had picked the president.

None Dare Call It Treason
Vincent Bugliosi

from *The Nation* | February 5, 2001

The Supreme Court has been criticized roundly for its 5-4 decision to stop the recounts in Florida and award the 2000 presidential election to George W. Bush. One of the harshest attacks came from their own colleague, Justice John Paul Stevens, who wrote in his dissenting opinion: "Although we may never know with complete certainty the identity of the winner of this year's election, the identity of the loser is perfectly clear. It is the nation's confidence in the judge as an impartial guardian of the rule of law."

Justice Stevens doesn't begin to approach the ferocity of Vincent Bugliosi, however. Bugliosi, the former federal prosecutor best known for putting Charles Manson behind bars, published a blistering legal critique in The Nation magazine, taking apart the ruling by the five-justice majority of Rehnquist, Scalia, Thomas, O'Connor and Kennedy point by point. His indictment—he bluntly refers to the five justices

*as "criminals"—generated the greatest reader response in the magazine's history.
Following is a condensed version of Bugliosi's article, daggers and all. . . .*

In the December 12 ruling by the U.S. Supreme Court handing the election to George Bush, the Court committed the unpardonable sin of being a knowing surrogate for the Republican Party instead of being an impartial arbiter of the law. If you doubt this, try to imagine Al Gore's and George Bush's roles being reversed and ask yourself if you can conceive of Justice Antonin Scalia and his four conservative brethren issuing an emergency order on December 9 stopping the counting of ballots (at a time when Gore's lead had shrunk to 154 votes) on the grounds that if it continued, Gore could suffer "irreparable harm," and then subsequently, on December 12, bequeathing the election to Gore on equal protection grounds. If you can, then I suppose you can also imagine seeing a man jumping away from his own shadow, Frenchmen no longer drinking wine.

From the beginning, Bush desperately sought, as it were, to prevent the opening of the door, the looking into the box—unmistakable signs that he feared the truth. In a nation that prides itself on openness, instead of the Supreme Court doing everything within its power to find a legal way to open the door and box, they did the precise opposite in grasping, stretching and searching mightily for a way, any way at all, to aid their choice for President, Bush, in the suppression of the truth, finally settling, in their judicial coup d'état, on the untenable argument that there was a violation of the Fourteenth Amendment's equal protection clause— the Court asserting that because of the various standards of determining the voter's intent in the Florida counties, voters were treated unequally, since a vote disqualified in one county (the so-called undervotes, which the voting machines did not pick up) may have been counted in another county, and vice versa. Accordingly, the Court reversed the Florida Supreme Court's order that the undervotes be counted, effectively delivering the presidency to Bush.

Now, in the equal protection cases I've seen, the aggrieved party, the one who is being harmed and discriminated against, almost invariably brings the action. But no Florida voter I'm aware of brought any action under the equal protection clause claiming he was disfranchised because of the different standards being employed. What happened here is that Bush leaped in and tried to profit from a hypothetical wrong inflicted on someone else.

Even assuming Bush had this right, the very core of his petition to the Court was that he himself would be harmed by these different standards. But would he have? If we're to be governed by common sense, the answer is no. The reason is that just as with flipping a coin you end up in rather short order with as many heads as tails, there would be a "wash" here for both sides, i.e., there would be just as many Bush as Gore votes that would be counted in one county yet disqualified in the next. . . . .So what harm to Bush was the Court so passionately trying to prevent by its ruling other than the real one: that he would be harmed by the truth as elicited from a full counting of the undervotes?

And if the Court's five-member majority was concerned not about Bush but the voters themselves, as they fervently claimed to be, then under what conceivable theory would they, *in effect,* tell these voters, "We're so concerned that *some* of you undervoters may lose your vote under the different Florida county standards that we're going to solve the problem by making sure that *none* of you undervoters have your votes counted"? Isn't this exactly what the Court did?

Gore's lawyer, David Boies, never argued either of the above points to the Court. Also, since Boies already knew (from language in the December 9 emergency order of the Court) that Justice Scalia, the Court's right-wing ideologue; his Pavlovian puppet, Clarence Thomas, who doesn't even try to create the impression that he's thinking; and three other conservatives on the Court (William Rehnquist, Sandra Day O'Connor and Anthony Kennedy) intended to deodorize their foul intent by hanging their hat on the anemic equal protection argument, wouldn't you think that he and his people would have come up with at least three or four strong arguments to expose it for what it was—a legal gimmick that the brazen, shameless majority intended to invoke to perpetrate a judicial hijacking in broad daylight? And made sure that he got into the record of his oral argument all of these points? Yet, remarkably, Boies only managed to make one good equal protection argument, and that one near the very end of his presentation, and then only because Justice Rehnquist (not at Boies's request, I might add) granted him an extra two minutes. . . .

This was Boies's belated argument: "Any differences as to how this standard [to determine voter intent] is interpreted have a lot less significance in terms of what votes are counted or not counted than simply the differences in machines that exist throughout the counties of Florida." A more powerful way to make Boies's argument would have been to point out to the Court the *reductio ad absurdum* of the equal protection argument. If none of the undervotes were counted because of the various standards to count them, then to be completely consistent the Court would have had no choice but to invalidate the entire Florida election, since there is no question that votes lost in some counties because of the method of voting would have been recorded in others utilizing a different method.[1] [*Footnotes at end of article*]. . . .

. . . . Varying methods to cast and count votes have been going on in every state of the union for the past two centuries, and the Supreme Court has been as silent as a church mouse on the matter, never even hinting that there might be a right under the equal protection clause that was being violated. Georgetown University law professor David Cole said, "[The Court] created a new right out of whole cloth and made sure it ultimately protected only one person—George Bush." . . . As Yale law professor Akhil Reed Amar noted, the five conservative Justices "failed to cite a single case that, on its facts, comes close to supporting its analysis and result."

If the Court majority had been truly concerned about the equal protection of all voters, the real equal protection violation, of course, took place when they cut off the counting of the undervotes. As indicated, that very act denied the 50 million Americans who voted for Gore the right to have their votes count at all. It misses the point to argue that the five Justices stole the election only if it turns out that Gore overcame Bush's lead in the undervote recount. We're talking about the moral and ethical culpability of these Justices, and when you do that, the bell was rung at the moment they engaged in their conduct. What happened thereafter cannot unring the bell and is therefore irrelevant. To judge these Justices by the final result rather than by their intentions at the time of their conduct would be like exonerating one who shoots to kill if the bullet misses the victim. . . .

Other than the unprecedented and outrageous nature of what the Court did, nothing surprises me more than how it is being viewed by the legal scholars and pundits who have criticized the opinion. As far as I can determine, most *have* correctly assailed the Court for issuing a ruling that was clearly political. As the December 25 *Time* capsulized it, "A sizable number of critics, from law professors to some of the Court's own members, have attacked the ruling as . . . politically motivated." A sampling from a few law professors: Vanderbilt professor Suzanna Sherry said, "There is really very little way to reconcile this opinion other than that they wanted Bush to win." Yale's Amar lamented that "for Supreme Court watchers this case will be like B.C. and A.D. For many of my colleagues, this was like the day President Kennedy was assassinated. Many of us [had] thought that courts do not act in an openly political fashion." Harvard law professor Randall Kennedy called the decision "outrageous."[2]

The only problem I have with these critics is that they have merely lost respect for and confidence in the Court. . . . The "conventional wisdom" emerging immediately after the Court's ruling seemed to be that the Court, by its political ruling, had only lost a lot of credibility and altitude in the minds of many people. But these critics of the ruling, even those who flat-out say the Court "stole" the election, apparently have not stopped to realize the inappropriateness of their tepid position vis-à-vis what the Court did. You mean you can steal a presidential election and your only retribution is that some people don't have as much respect for you, as much confidence in you? That's all?. . .

The stark reality, and I say this with every fiber of my being, is that the institution Americans trust the most to protect its freedoms and principles committed one of the biggest and most serious crimes this nation has ever seen—pure and simple, the theft of the presidency. . . . No technical true crime was committed here by the five conservative Justices only because no Congress ever dreamed of enacting a statute making it a crime to steal a presidential election. . . .

Though the five Justices clearly are criminals, no one is treating them this way. As I say, even those who were outraged by the Court's ruling have only lost respect for them. And for the most part the nation's press seems to have already forgotten and/or forgiven. Within days, the Court's ruling was no longer the subject of Op-Ed pieces. Indeed, just five days after its high crime, the caption of an article by Jean Guccione in the *Los Angeles Times* read, "The Supreme Court Should Weather This Storm." The following day an AP story noted that Justice Sandra Day O'Connor, on vacation in Arizona, had fired a hole-in-one on the golf course.

The lack of any valid legal basis for their decision and, most important, the fact that it is inconceivable they would have ruled the way they did for Gore, proves, *on its face,* that the five conservative Republican Justices were up to no good. . . . But for those who want more, let me point out that there is no surer way to find out what parties meant than to see what they have done. And like typical criminals, the felonious five left their incriminating fingerprints everywhere, showing an unmistakable consciousness of guilt on their part.

1. Under Florida statutory law, when the Florida Supreme Court finds that a challenge to the certified result of an election is justified, it has the power to "provide *any* relief appropriate under the circumstances" (§ 102.168(8) of the Florida Election Code). On Friday, December 8, the Florida court, so finding, ordered a manual recount (authorized under § 102.166(4)(c) of the Florida Election Code) of all disputed ballots (around 60,000) throughout the entire state. As a *New York Times* editorial reported, "The manual recount³ was progressing smoothly and swiftly Saturday . . . with new votes being recorded for both Vice President Al Gore and Governor George W. Bush . . . serving the core democratic principle that every legal vote should be counted" when, in midafternoon, the U.S. Supreme Court "did a disservice to the nation's tradition of fair elections by calling a halt" to the recount. The stay (requested by Bush), the *Times* said, appeared "highly political."⁴

Under Supreme Court rules, a stay is supposed to be granted to an applicant (here, Bush) only if he makes a substantial showing that in the absence of a stay, there is a likelihood of "irreparable harm" to him. With the haste of a criminal, Justice Scalia, in trying to justify the Court's shutting down of the vote counting, wrote, unbelievably, that counting these votes would "threaten irreparable harm to petitioner [Bush] . . . by casting a cloud upon what *he* claims to be the legitimacy of *his* election." [Emphasis added.] In other words, although the election had not yet been decided, the absolutely incredible Scalia was presupposing that Bush had won the election—indeed, had a *right* to win it—and any recount that showed Gore got more votes in Florida than Bush could "cloud" Bush's presidency. . . .

The *New York Times* observed that the Court gave the appearance by the stay of "racing to beat the clock before an unwelcome truth would come out." Terrance Sandalow, former dean of the University of Michigan Law School and a judicial conservative who opposed *Roe v. Wade* and supported the nomination to the Court of right-wing icon Robert Bork, said that "the balance of harms so unmistakably were on the side of Gore" that the granting of the stay was "incomprehensible," going on to call the stay "an unmistakably partisan decision without any foundation in law."

As Justice John Paul Stevens wrote in opposing the stay, Bush "failed to carry the heavy burden" of showing a likelihood of irreparable harm if the recount continued. In other words, the Court never even had the legal right to grant the stay. "Counting every legally cast vote cannot constitute irreparable harm," Stevens said. "On the other hand, there is a danger that a stay may cause irreparable harm to the respondent [Gore] and, more importantly, the public at large because of the risk that the entry of the stay would be tantamount to a decision on the merits in favor of the applicant. Preventing the recount from being completed will inevitably cast a cloud on the legitimacy of the election." Stevens added what even the felonious five knew but decided to ignore: that it is a "basic principle inherent in our Constitution that every legal vote should be counted." From the wrongful granting of the stay alone, the handwriting was on the wall. Gore was about as safe as a cow in a Chicago stockyard. . . .

2. When prosecutors present their circumstantial case against a defendant, they put one speck of evidence upon another until ultimately there is a strong mosaic of guilt. One such small speck is that in its 5-to-4 decision handing the election to Bush, the Court's ruling was set forth in a thirteen-page "per curiam" (Latin for "by the court") opinion (followed by concurring and dissenting opinions). Students of the Supreme Court know that per curiam opinions are almost always issued for unanimous (9-to-0) opinions in relatively unimportant and uncontroversial cases, or where Justices wish to be very brief. But as *USA Today* pointed out, "Neither was the case here." Again, on the run and in a guilty state of mind, none of the five Justices, even the brazenly shameless Scalia, wanted to sign their name to a majority opinion of the Court reversing the Florida Supreme Court's order to recount the undervotes. A per curiam opinion, which is always unsigned, was the answer. It is not even known who wrote the per curiam opinion, though it is believed to be O'Connor and/or Kennedy, neither of whose names is mentioned anywhere in the Court's sixty-two-page document. After they did their dirty work by casting their two votes on the case for their favorite—two votes that overruled and rendered worthless the votes of 50 million Americans in fifty states—O'Connor and Kennedy wanted to stay away from their decision the way the devil stays away from holy water. Indeed, by their per curiam opinion, it was almost as if the felonious five felt that since their names would not be on the legally sacrilegious opinion, maybe, just maybe, the guilt they knew they bore would be mitigated, at least somewhat, in posterity.

3. The proof that the Court itself knew its equal protection argument had no merit whatsoever is that when Bush first asked the Court, on November 22, to consider three objections of his to the earlier, more lim-

ited Florida recount then taking place, the Court only denied review on his third objection—yeah, you guessed it, that the lack of a uniform standard to determine the voter's intent violated the equal protection clause of the Fourteenth Amendment. Since the Court, on November 22, felt that this objection was so devoid of merit that it was unworthy of even being considered by it, what did these learned Justices subsequently learn about the equal protection clause they apparently did not know in November that caused them just three weeks later, on December 12, to embrace and endorse it so enthusiastically? The election was finally on the line on December 12 and they knew they had to come up with something, anything, to save the day for their man. . . .

4. The Court anchored its knowingly fraudulent decision on the equal protection clause of the Fourteenth Amendment. But wait. Since the electors in the fifty states weren't scheduled to meet and vote until December 18, and the Court's ruling was on December 12, if the Court was really serious about its decision that the various standards in the counties to determine the voter's intent violated the equal protection clause, why not, as Justices Stevens, Souter, Ginsburg and Breyer each noted in separate dissents, simply remand the case back to the Florida Supreme Court with instructions to establish a uniform, statewide standard and continue the recount until December 18? The shameless and shameful felonious five had an answer, which, in a sense, went to the heart of their decision even more than the bogus equal protection argument. The unsigned and anonymously written per curiam opinion noted that under Title 3 of the United States Code, Section 5 (3 USC § 5), any controversy or contest to determine the selection of electors should be resolved "six days prior to the meeting of the Electoral College," that is, December 12, and inasmuch as the Court issued its ruling at 10 P.M. on December 12, with just two hours remaining in the day, the Court said, "That date [December 12] is upon us," and hence there obviously was no time left to set uniform standards and continue the recount. But there are a multiplicity of problems with the Court's oh-so-convenient escape hatch. Writing in the *Wall Street Journal*, University of Utah law professor Michael McConnell, a legal conservative, pointed out that the December 12 "deadline" is only a deadline "for receiving 'safe harbor' protection for the state's electors" (i.e., if a state certifies its electors by that date, Congress can't question them), not a federal deadline that must be met. New York University law professor Larry Kramer observed that if a state does not make that deadline, "nothing happens. The counting could continue."

Justice Stevens observed in his dissent that 3 USC § 5 "merely provides rules . . . for Congress to follow when selecting among conflicting slates of electors. They do not prohibit a state from counting . . . legal votes until a bona fide winner is determined. Indeed, in 1960, Hawaii appointed two slates of electors and Congress chose to count the one appointed on January 4, 1961, well after the Title 3 deadlines" of December 12 and 18. Thus, Stevens went on to say, even if an equal protection violation is assumed for the sake of argument, "nothing prevents the majority . . . from ordering relief appropriate to remedy that violation without depriving Florida voters of their right to have their votes counted."

But even if December 12 were some kind of actual deadline, nothing was sillier during this whole election debate than the talking heads on television, many of whom were lawyers who should have known better, treating the date as if it were sacrosanct and set in stone (exactly what the Supreme Court majority, on the run and trying to defend their indefensible position, said). In the real world, mandatory dates always have an elliptical clause attached to them, "unless there is just cause for extending the date.". . . If extending the December 12 (or the December 18 date, for that matter)[5] deadline for a few days for the counting of votes to determine who the rightful winner of a presidential election is does not constitute a sufficient cause for a short extension of time, then what in the world does? No one has said it better than columnist Thomas Friedman: "The five conservative Justices essentially ruled that the sanctity of dates, even meaningless ones, mattered more than the sanctity of votes, even meaningful ones. The Rehnquist Court now has its legacy: In calendars we trust.". . .

What could be more infuriating than Chief Justice Rehnquist, who knew he was setting up a straw man as counterfeit as the decision he supported, writing that the recount "could not possibly be completed" in the two hours remaining on December 12? The Supreme Court improperly stops the recounting of the votes from Saturday afternoon to Tuesday, December 12, at 10 P.M., then has the barefaced audacity to say that Gore ran out of time? This type of maddening sophistry is enough, as the expression goes, to piss off a saint. How dare these five pompous asses do what they did?

It should be noted that the recount that commenced on Saturday morning, December 9, was scheduled to conclude by 2 P.M. that Sunday, and the vote counters were making excellent progress. . . . Justice Breyer wrote that the alleged equal protection "deficiency . . . could easily be remedied." But that's assuming the felonious five wanted a remedy. They did not. All of the above are further indicia of their guilty state of mind.

5. If there are two sacred canons of the right-wing in America and ultra-conservative Justices like Scalia, Thomas and Rehnquist, it's their ardent federalism, i.e., promotion of states' rights (Rehnquist, in fact, wrote in his concurring opinion about wanting, wherever possible, to "defer to the decisions of state courts on issues of state law"), and their antipathy for Warren Court activist judges. So if it weren't for their decision to find a way, any way imaginable, to appoint Bush President, their automatic predilection would have been to stay the hell out of Florida's business. The fact that they completely departed from what they would almost reflexively do in ninety-nine out of a hundred other cases is again persuasive circumstantial evidence of their criminal state of mind.

6. Perhaps nothing Scalia et al. did revealed their consciousness of guilt more than the total lack of legal stature they reposed in their decision. . . . [T]he Court knew that its ruling (that differing standards for counting votes violate the equal protection clause) could not possibly be a constitutional principle cited in the future by themselves, other courts or litigants. Since different methods of counting votes exist throughout the fifty states (e.g., Texas counts dimpled chads, California does not), forty-four out of the fifty states do not have uniform voting methods, and voting equipment and mechanisms in all states necessarily vary in design, upkeep and performance, to apply the equal protection ruling of *Bush v. Gore* would necessarily invalidate virtually all elections throughout the country.

This, obviously, was an extremely serious problem for the felonious five to deal with. What to do? Not to worry. Are you ready for this one? By that I mean, are you sitting down, since if you're standing, this is the type of thing that could affect your physical equilibrium. Unbelievably, the Court wrote that its ruling was *"limited to the present circumstances, for the problem of equal protection in election processes generally presents many complexities."* . . . Of the thousands of potential equal protection voting cases, the Court was only interested in, and eager to grant relief to, one person and one person only, George W. Bush.[6] Is there any limit to the effrontery and shamelessness of these five right-wing Justices? Answer: No. This point number six here, all alone and by itself, clearly and unequivocally shows that the Court knew its decision was not based on the merits or the law, and was solely a decision to appoint George Bush president. . . .

These five Justices, by their conduct, have forfeited the right to be respected, and only by treating them the way they deserve to be treated can we demonstrate our respect for the rule of law they defiled, and insure that their successors will not engage in similarly criminal conduct. . . .

At a minimum, I believe that the Court's inexcusable ruling will severely stain its reputation for years to come, perhaps decades. This is very unfortunate. As Justice Stevens wrote in his dissent: "Although we may never know with complete certainty the identity of the winner of this year's presidential election, the identity of the loser is perfectly clear. It is the nation's confidence in [this Court] as an impartial guardian of the rule of law.". . . .

That an election for an American president can be stolen by the highest court in the land under the deliberate pretext of an inapplicable constitutional provision has got to be one of the most frightening and dangerous events ever to have occurred in this country. Until this act—which is treasonous, though again not technically, in its sweeping implications—is somehow rectified (and I do not know how this can be done), can we be serene about continuing to place the adjective "great" before the name of this country?

1. A total of 3,718,305 votes were cast in the Florida election under the Votomatic punch-card system, and 2,353,811 votes were cast under the optical-scan system. The percentage of votes not picked up using the punch-card system was 3.92 percent, the rate under the more modern optical-scan system being only 1.43 percent. Put in other terms, for every 10,000 votes cast, the punch-card system resulted in 250 more nonvotes than the optical-scan system. *Siegel v. LePore*, No. 00-15981. See also Ford Fessenden, "No-Vote Rates Higher in Punch-Card Counts," *New York Times*, December 1 [2001].

2. The ruling was so bad that it was very difficult to find even conservative legal scholars who supported it, and when the few who attempted to do so stepped up to the plate, their observations were simply pathetic. University of California, Berkeley, law professor John Yoo, a former law clerk for Thomas, wrote that "we should balance the short-term hit to the court's legitimacy with whether . . . it was in the best interest of the country to end the electoral crisis." Translation: If an election is close, it's better for the Supreme Court to pick the President, *whether or not he won the election*, than to have the dispute resolved in the manner prescribed by law. Pepperdine Law School's Douglas Kmiec unbelievably wrote that "the ruling of the U.S. Supreme Court was not along partisan or ideological lines," and that its ruling "protected our cherished

democratic tradition with a soundly reasoned, per curiam voice of restraint." I won't dignify this with a translation.

3. Actually, not a recount since the Votomatic machines, for whatever reason, never did detect the votes on these particular ballots. The manual count would be examining these ballots for the *first* time to see if, as provided for under § 101.5614(5) of the Florida Election Code, there was a "clear indication of the intent of the voter." One example: The stylus punches a clear hole in the paper ballot, but the chad is still attached (hanging) by one or more of its four sides. In that situation the Votomatic machine frequently does not detect the vote, though the intent of the voter could not be any clearer.

4. Earlier in the day, the conservative-leaning U.S. Court of Appeals for the Eleventh Circuit in Atlanta voted 8 to 4 to deny Bush's companion attempt to have that court stop the recount.

5. In fact, L. Kinvin Wroth, dean of the Vermont Law School and an expert on the Electoral College, said that "a recount could have gone on right up to the last day of Congress' joint session" on January 6, when the votes of the College were counted in Congress.

6. And this, mind you, in an election in which Bush was leading in Florida by only a few hundred votes while losing the popular vote nationwide to Gore by, at last count, 539,000 votes.

The Final Word?

Dan Keating and Dan Balz

The Washington Post, November 12, 2001

This Washington Post headline says it all. . . .

Florida Recounts Would Have Favored Bush—But Study Finds Gore Might Have Won Statewide Tally of All Uncounted Ballots

In all likelihood, George W. Bush still would have won Florida and the presidency last year if either of two limited recounts—one requested by Al Gore, the other ordered by the Florida Supreme Court—had been completed, according to a study commissioned by *The Washington Post* and other news organizations.

But if Gore had found a way to trigger a statewide recount of all disputed ballots, or if the courts had required it, the result likely would have been different. An examination of uncounted ballots throughout Florida found enough where voter intent was clear to give Gore the narrowest of margins.

The study showed that if the two limited recounts had not been short-circuited—the first by Florida county and state election officials and the second by the U.S. Supreme Court—Bush would have held his lead over Gore, with margins ranging from 225 to 493 votes, depending on the standard. But the study also found that whether dimples are counted or a more restrictive standard is used, a statewide tally favored Gore by 60 to 171 votes.

Gore's narrow margin in the statewide count was the result of a windfall in overvotes. Those ballots—on which a voter may have marked a candidate's name and also written it in—were rejected by machines as a double vote on Election Day and most also would not have been included in either of the limited recounts.

The study by *The Post* and other media groups, an unprecedented effort that involved examining 175,010 ballots in 67 counties, underscores what began to be apparent as soon as the polls closed in the nation's third most populous state Nov. 7, 2000: that no one can say with certainty who actually won Florida. Under every scenario used in the study, the winning margin remains less than 500 votes out of almost 6 million cast.

For 36 days after the election, the results in Florida remained in doubt, and so did the winner of the presidency. Bush emerged victorious when the U.S. Supreme Court, in a 5 to 4 ruling, agreed with his lawyers' contention that the counting should end. Since then, many Gore partisans have accused the court of unfairly aborting a process that would have put their candidate ahead.

But an examination of the disputed ballots suggests that in hindsight the battalions of lawyers and election experts who descended on Florida pursued strategies that ended up working against the interests of their candidates.

The study indicates, for example, that Bush had less to fear from the recounts underway than he thought. Under any standard used to judge the ballots in the four counties where Gore lawyers had sought a recount—Palm Beach, Broward, Miami-Dade and Volusia—Bush still ended up with more votes than Gore, according to the study. Bush also would have had more votes if the limited statewide recount ordered by the Florida Supreme Court and then stopped by the U.S. Supreme Court had been carried through.

Had Bush not been party to short-circuiting those recounts, he might have escaped criticism that his victory hinged on legal maneuvering rather than on counting the votes.

In Gore's case, the decision to ask for recounts in four counties rather than seek a statewide recount ultimately had far greater impact. But in the chaos of the early days of the recount battle, when Gore needed additional votes as quickly as possible and recounts in the four heavily Democratic counties offered him that possibility, that was not so obvious.

Nor was there any guarantee that Gore could have succeeded in getting a statewide recount. Florida law provided no mechanism to ask for a statewide recount, only county-by-county recounts. And although he did at one point call on Bush to join him in asking for a statewide recount, it was with the condition that Bush renounce all further legal action. Bush dismissed the offer, calling it a public relations gesture by his opponent, and Gore never took any further steps toward that goal.

White House press secretary Ari Fleischer, responding to the study, said, "The voters settled this election last fall, and the nation moved on a long time ago. The White House isn't focused on this; the voters aren't focused on it." Fleischer called the results "superfluous."

Gore, in a written statement, did not respond directly to the study. "As I said on Dec. 13th of last year, we are a nation of laws and the presidential election of 2000 is over," he said. "And of course, right now our country faces a great challenge as we seek to successfully combat terrorism. I fully support President Bush's efforts to achieve that goal."

Gore said he remained appreciative of the support he received last year and "proud of the values and ideals for which we fought."

The National Conversation:
Election Aftermath

Defenders of the Law . . .

Charles Krauthammer

The Washington Post | December 15, 2000

In the weeks following the conclusion of the 2000 presidential contest, every political commentator worth his or her salt was busily dissecting the U.S. Supreme Court's decision and the legal drama that led up to it. In the first installment of our "National Conversation," Charles Krauthammer, a columnist for The Washington Post, *accuses the the Florida Supreme Court of having embarked on a hopeless quest for "cosmic justice".* . . .

Democratic partisans are complaining that the presidential election has been settled not by the people but by judges. This is amusing. Who turned this into a lawyers' contest anyway? Within hours of Election Night, the Gore campaign parachuted dozens, ultimately hundreds of lawyers into Florida with one objective: to find judges to undo their loss.

They went judge shopping, court shopping, venue shopping, loophole shopping. They sued everywhere and anywhere: To overturn the "illegal" butterfly ballot in Palm Beach County; to force selective manual recounts in heavily Democratic counties; to impose on these counties scandalously loose criteria for judging "voter intent" (the notorious dimpled chad). They sent lawyers to every county to disqualify overseas ballots; Democratic activists sued to throw out 25,000 valid absentee ballots in Seminole and Martin counties.

Where did they expect all this lawyering to wind up if not in the U.S. Supreme Court? After five weeks of testing every legal mechanism to overturn the results, they are now shocked—shocked—that the Supreme Court has, by its final verdict, determined the identity of the next president. Live by the courts, die by the courts.

The Democrats, nonetheless, now impute illegitimacy to the final outcome because it was decided by the Supreme Court. But who is the real agent of illegitimacy in this saga? Has everyone forgotten where we were last Friday? After a trial, Circuit Court Judge N. Sanders Sauls had resoundingly, methodically, unmercifully rejected Gore's challenge to the second recount.

That recount had been granted by the Florida Supreme Court in a victory Democrats had cheered lustily. It was said at the time: Let that recount, however questionable, go forward and if Gore fell short, that would produce the most legitimate possible outcome.

Well, it went forward. Gore lost the count. He then lost the case. We were on the threshold of legitimacy and finality. The country was ready to accept Sauls's ruling. So was Gore, who had his concession speech prepared.

Re-enter the Florida Supreme Court, with gusto. In an astonishing burst of willfulness, it reversed the trial court judge and created yet another electoral scheme: a statewide, undervote-only recount to be completed in four days. More than one dissenting Florida justice denounced it for "departing from the essential requirements of the law"—a scheme both "impossible to achieve and which will ultimately lead to chaos."

The Florida court's willfulness had a point. In an election this close, there are two ways to resolve the issue: procedural fairness or cosmic fairness. Procedural fairness simply says: We'll never know who "really" won (because the margin of victory is smaller than the margin of a vote-counting error), so we'll go by the rules as they were on Election Day and let the chips fall where they may. By this accounting, George Bush won twice, weeks ago.

But for good liberals like the Florida Supreme Court, mere procedural justice is inferior to abstract right and cosmic justice. They would therefore invent new and better rules and impose them ex post facto on this election.

They were on a mission. They let nothing stand in their way. They overturned critical lower court rulings not once, but twice. They stripped the executive officer in charge of Florida elections of any discretion to regulate and certify elections. They even thumbed their noses at a unanimous opinion of the U.S. Supreme Court that vacated their original election concoction because it found their justification indiscernible.

Undeterred, the Florida Supremes created yet another concoction, invalidating their first invented deadline (cosmic justice requires such constant refinement) and ordering another recount—selective, standardless, seat-of-the-pants.

That is where they were hoist by their own petard. The U.S. Supreme Court found that this scheme, dreamed up in the name of fairness, was so arbitrary and capricious as to be not only unfair but unconstitutional. Not five but seven justices found it offensive to elementary notions of equal protection.

Justice David Souter, who agreed that there were constitutional problems with the recount, dissented nonetheless from the majority, arguing that the Supreme Court should have stepped aside and let the process continue. "It is entirely possible that . . . political tension could have worked itself out in the Congress"—meaning, Congress selecting the president by choosing between a Gore and a Bush set of electors.

Would that have been better? On the contrary. Political tension would only have grown—this would not have been resolved until January!—and created a train wreck. The majority of the court wisely declined this reckless invitation to a true constitutional crisis—a crisis created by the willfulness of a rogue state supreme court and averted by a U.S. Supreme Court that decided finally to step in and play Daddy to a court playing God.

What if they hijacked an election, and no one cared?

Jake Tapper

salon.com | November 14, 2001

The media's unofficial recount of the Florida undervotes and overvotes in the 2000 presidential race, completed in the fall of 2001 (see p. 44), revealed that Al Gore may well have carried the state of Florida after all. In the wake of this news, salon.com's Jake Tapper asks why Gore supporters—and Gore himself—aren't raising more of a ruckus. . . .

WASHINGTON—Last December, in the throes of the post-election fight, Senate Majority Leader Tom Daschle, D-S.D., flew down to Tallahassee, Fla. There he warned the public that the state's open-government sunshine laws meant that eventually the media would be able to conduct a full recount of all the 175,000 unread ballots in the state—even if the courts and the Legislature blocked it.

"There will be an accurate count," Daschle said, adding that it would be "tragic" if we only learned who really won months later, from the media, when it no longer counted.

Nearly a year and almost $1 million later, the media consortium that reviewed all the Florida ballots finally produced results indicating that, for whatever reason—whether voter screw-ups, vast and sundry conspiracies or just simple fate—the will of a plurality of voters in the Sunshine State was thwarted last year. "The media recount confirms what many of us have believed for a long time," says Ron Klain, who headed the Gore team's legal effort last year. "If you count all the legal ballots in Florida, Al Gore won."

But Klain is one of the few talking about the matter; Daschle has had nothing to say about the media recount now that it's a reality. With President Bush experiencing approval ratings near 90 percent and the nation in crisis, few have had anything to say.

The media consortium even held off a few weeks before releasing the information, so as not to do so in the midst of the tense few weeks post-Sept. 11. Not that it was released on a better day, with more consequential news—the crash of American Airlines Flight 587 that killed at least 260 people, the Taliban fleeing Kabul—making the reexamined ballots seem all the more silly. What's a few thousand unread ballots in the face of thousands of Americans being killed by al-Qaida?

Still, the biggest, most comprehensive and most thoroughly conducted media recount indicates that if there had been a statewide review of all the 175,000 overvotes and undervotes unread on Election Day 2000, Al Gore would have ultimately beaten George W. Bush by anywhere from 42 to 171 votes, depending upon the method of counting.

Gruffed White House spokesman Ari Fleischer: "The election was settled a year ago, President Bush won and the voters have long since moved on."

That's perfectly true. The election is settled, Bush won and the voters have moved on. But in the world of politics, that wouldn't necessarily matter. This was the most controversial election in a century, and whatever one thinks about Al Gore, the consortium's data proposes a fairly shocking notion on its face—that the wrong man may well have taken the oath of office last January. Especially when one contemplates that Gore nationally garnered 537,000 more popular votes than did President Bush.

But for a number of reasons this fairly stunning conclusion has been downplayed significantly. Even by some of the media organizations that paid for the recount, which include the Associated Press, CNN, the *New*

York Times, the *Washington Post,* the *Wall Street Journal,* the *Palm Beach Post,* the *St. Petersburg Times* and Tribune Publishing.

Some of this is because there seems to be little outrage—and few Democratic talking heads willing to take up the cause. "People are either more concerned about terrorism, and/or they prefer Bush and his team handling the terrorist threat," speculated former Sen. Bob Kerrey, D-Neb. "Or maybe the story is too long to read."

Another reason is that, as during the recount fiasco itself, Gore still remains unable to generate much enthusiasm even among those who would be his natural supporters.

Many Democrats are upset that Gore himself hasn't raised more of a stink. One former senior Gore campaign strategist confessed to being so disheartened after reading Gore's benign statement about the consortium recount ("As I said on December 13 of last year, we are a nation of laws, and the presidential election of 2000 is over," Gore said. "And of course, right now, our country faces a great challenge as we seek to successfully combat terrorism. I fully support President Bush's efforts to achieve that goal") that he crumpled the newspaper in a ball and tossed it out angrily.

But of the 20 precincts of significant size that showed the highest rate of spoiled ballots, all were at least 80 percent African-American. Many Democrats don't see the fight as just about Gore, but about the right to vote, and by being quiet, Gore is infuriating many Democrats who feel cheated.

By being silent, Gore is clearly defusing any attention the story would otherwise have received.

"If Gore's saying that 'George W. Bush is my commander in chief,' and Joe Lieberman's saying it, no matter what the results are, who cares?" says Florida Democratic Party spokesman Tony Welch. "I care, by the way. But in the overall analysis, it's a really big nonstory."

But there are other reasons for the lack of buzz, for the failure of the recount and its potentially troublesome conclusions to generate much discussion. One is the ambiguous nature of the recount and the ambiguous way many in the media have portrayed its conclusions. "It doesn't slam-dunk it for anyone," says Welch. "There's a lot to muddle through to come to the conclusion that Gore was the winner and anyone can point to another story that says he wasn't."

Another reason may be a general lack of enthusiasm for Gore among many Democratic officials, who believe Gore was a dud of a candidate who will blow it again if given a chance in 2004. Still other rank-and-file Democrats feel let down by Gore's reticence since last December.

"I don't think Al Gore acts like a man who wants to be president of the United States," Rep. Maxine Waters, D-Calif., said on CNN in August. "He's been away for almost eight months now," said the feisty liberal. "We've had a lot going on in that eight-month period of time." But Gore—who is "supposed to be the titular head of the party"—has been absent, Waters complained. "There's been some terrific battles in the Congress of the United States dealing with this tax cut by the president of the United States, and Social Security, and stem cells. You name it. And where's Al Gore?"

Donna Brazile, Gore's campaign manager, is upset that the Florida fiasco hasn't resulted in serious election reform, and she sees the resounding thud of the recount news in that context. "For an entire year we have not have a spiritual leader on election reform, the same way that John McCain is the spiritual leader of campaign finance reform," Brazile says. "Even before Sept. 11, election reform had died."

One senses that Brazile wishes Gore would try to become that "spiritual leader."

Brazile, who is teaching at the University of Maryland's Academy of Leadership, says that "the only groups and the only constituencies who are talking about Florida are African-Americans, with some progressive elements. But by and large people walked away. They said, 'O.K. So what?' We kept saying a disproportionate number of African-Americans didn't have their votes counted and people said, 'Move on, move on.' And the 'Move on' crowd won."

"Why do you think I'm sitting at home and teaching instead of pounding the pavement for candidates?" Brazile asks. "If people are not going to stand up for you, why should I work hard for them?"

The recount indicated that African-Americans were "three times as likely to have their ballots discarded," she says. But there hasn't been any serious investigation as to whether there was a purposeful spoilage of these ballots. "I don't believe in my heart of hearts that African-Americans would make that big a mistake," she says. "Something happened to some of those ballots. Somebody tampered with the process."

Even if some of the mistakes were innocent—like the Duval County elections supervisor, who put the instructions on the sample ballot to "Vote all pages," though the list for presidential candidates was two pages long, thus possibly resulting in overvotes—there was little actual fallout, Brazile says. "We should have caught that, someone should have caught that, but did that official get fired? No. Was he made an example of? No."

She pauses. Sighs. "I'm trying not to relive 2000," she says. "It's taking a lot of time. I'm trying to put away some of my anger, but it's been a very difficult process."

A final reason for the story's resounding thud may be a certain media relishing of the consortium's ironic conclusions. After all, if either of Gore's recount strategies pursued by his legal team had been acted upon, then Bush would have won, according to the consortium's review.

It's only through a full statewide recount of both the undervotes and the overvotes—an option advocated by Gore recount lawyers such as Jack Young, and blithely dismissed by the Gore kingpins—that Gore would have won. (That Gore's legal eagles did so because they thought that option would result in Gore's being slammed for dragging the process out is certainly understandable, though P.R. considerations are hardly lofty ones.)

For the early "protest" phase of the recount, for instance, Gore hand-picked four Democratic-leaning counties for his hand recounts—Broward, Palm, Miami-Dade and Volusia—thus ignoring the state's other 63 counties and their approximately 110,000 unread ballots, both undervotes and overvotes. The consortium's recount indicated that if Florida's 25 electoral votes had been assigned according to this plan, Bush would have won by 225 votes.

In the "contest" period of the recount, Gore's lawyers managed to get the Florida Supreme Court to implement a statewide recount of just the 65,000 undervotes. Had that not been stopped by the U.S. Supreme Court, then Bush would have won by 490 votes. If the county election supervisors who planned on counting the overvotes had done so, Bush would have won by 493 votes. (Not that the Bush recount team was playing any more honorably, blocking any recount that they could.)

These, however, are questions of strategy. And clearly Gore and his team chose the wrong one. Their strategy was unfair, since it initially focused on four Democratic-leaning counties and ignored the others precisely because they were Republican-leaning; and then because it focused on undervotes and ignored overvotes, where voter intent could clearly be discerned—and had been discerned and counted in places like Gadsden and Volusia counties, where there were clearly votes for both Gore and Bush in the overvotes.

And in the end it ended up not only being unfair, but stupid, too. Some

Democratic strategists who early on in the post-election battle argued for a statewide recount of all 175,000 ballots—but were overruled—confessed to feeling some vindication with news of the consortium's recount.

Others didn't feel anything but anger—at the Bush team, and at the media, and seemingly at the unfairness of life itself.

"Just because he happened to choose the wrong formula to get there doesn't negate the fact that he got more votes and that he should be president," says one Democratic strategist.

Shoulda woulda coulda. The lesson learned: Next time you say "Count every vote," *mean* it.

Part Two: Politics in the Bush Era

Scenes from a Marriage

Marjorie Williams

Vanity Fair | July 2001

There were plenty of rumors that the relationship was in trouble, but no one really knew for sure what went on between the two of them behind closed doors. No, this isn't about Hillary and Bill: we're referring to Bill Clinton and Al Gore. People said it wouldn't last—they seemed so different—and yet they made things work for the better part of eight years. Vanity Fair's ace political writer Marjorie Williams explores why the nation's ultimate power couple finally went bust. . . .

January 6 may have been the worst day of Al Gore's life. He spent the early afternoon in the chamber of the House of Representatives, presiding with fortitude over the joint session of Congress that certified the presidential victory of his opponent, George W. Bush. After almost two hours of that, he patiently signed his autograph on tally sheets and admission tickets for a stream of pages, spectators, and even senators, former colleagues who stood in line to collect evidence that they had been present when, for the first time in 40 years, a vice president had to ratify the election of his opponent.

Then he went back to the White House, to a party in a vast white tent on the South Lawn that gathered staffers from all eight years of the Clinton-Gore administration for one last hurrah. The Clintons arrived at the party on the famous bus that had borne the Clintons and the Gores on their triumphal cross-country campaign trip of 1992; Al and Tipper Gore arrived later.

Gore got a rousing ovation when he came in, but it was hard not to notice something strange about the long, elaborate program the White House staff had organized. It had testimonials from men and women who had served in every part of Clinton's presidency—his personal assistants, his political consultants, even Hillary Clinton's chiefs of staff. The tributes went on and on, interspersed with video clips enumerating Clinton's many trips abroad, his major legislative achievements, his political victories. The only thing the program did not include was much mention of Al Gore. "You had to work at not having Gore included in that," says a former White House aide. "They obviously did."

It was a fitting obituary for what had once been the successful partnership of Bill Clinton and Al Gore. The president and vice president were barely on speaking terms by then, after a campaign that had pitted the two men and their staffs—in many cases, old friends and comrades-in-arms—against each other in a battle of wills.

The pair had faced each other down in a bitter White House meeting, a few days after Gore conceded the election, that matched grievance for grievance. The sit-down, which took place at Gore's request, aired the fury the vice president had been carrying for months, even years. In response, Clinton vented his anger that Gore had refused to run on the record of their administration.

Their fight has been mirrored ever since in acrimonious post-mortems among Democrats all over Washington. The Gore side argues that Clinton's affair with Monica Lewinsky cost Gore the election, and that Clinton compounded his sins with obstructive complaints about the competence of Gore's campaign. The Clinton side argues that Gore bungled a simple campaign he should have won—and, in sidelining Clinton for the duration, showed wretched disloyalty in the bargain.

Clinton has told a confidant that "[Hillary] was able to figure out how to deal with her relationship with me and win by 10 points. *He* should have been able to as well." This source adds, "It was clear [Clinton] was just in total disbelief that Gore had run the kind of campaign he had."

And Gore has complained to associates about Clinton's "trashing his campaign," in the words of one man who has discussed it with Gore. "I think Gore thinks that if it weren't for all the mistakes the president made in the second term he'd be president now."

The break appears complete. As of mid-May, the two men had not spoken since the day of Bush's inauguration. "They're both leading very separate and very busy lives," says Clinton spokeswoman Julia Payne, with the matter-of-fact brightness that Hollywood publicists bring to discussing celebrity divorce.

For eight years we watched the marriage of Bill and Hillary Clinton, marveling at the glue that kept it together, wondering if Bill's misdeeds would finally blow it apart, certain that if the end came it would make for a spectacular explosion.

And all that time, it turns out, we were watching the wrong marriage.

The split between Clinton and Gore presents itself as everything from a personal spat to an ideological divide, from a battle between pollsters and consultants with a huge stake in the question of why Gore lost to a shell-shocked lack of consensus over who will now have the standing to lead the party.

But most accounts of the schism, which assign all of the blame for the break to Gore's repulsion and fury over Clinton's affair with Monica Lewinsky, are somewhat off the mark. "The idea that this relationship just went off the skids when Monica came along, and Gore said, 'Oh, shocking. As a husband and a father, I just can't stomach this,' is wrong," says a former White House official. "It was all there, in a deep and profound way, long before Monica Lewinsky ever showed up."

Months after the campaign's end, the bitterness of the Clinton-Gore split is vividly present in the language of former aides and associates on both sides, who sound like the children of a bad divorce.

"I'm telling you, these are Zantac moments," says Gore's campaign manager, Donna Brazile, summarizing what it was like to run interference between the Gore campaign and the Clinton White House. "It tore me up. It was personally excruciating."

It is hard to say which side is more withering in its view of the other. Former Gore consultant Bob Boorstin says, "Did we make mistakes? Yes. Would I say that Clinton was the only reason we lost? No. Would I say with absolutely zero doubt in my mind that we would have won the election if Clinton hadn't put his penis in her mouth? Yes. I guarantee it. The guy blew it!"

From the Clinton side: "It's about incompetence," says a close former staffer. "It's unbelievable how [Gore] fucked the Clinton relationship up as it related to his own campaign."

The truth, of course, is that all their complaints have some justice. Here on the far side of the separation, interviews about it have the quality of psychotherapy: time and again, I sat down with a witness to the relationship who, once invited to talk, could scarcely seem to stop. Almost no one would agree to speak for the record, but it is appropriate, in a way, that the story should be narrated by a Greek chorus of former aides and officials. For like many bonds that are described in Washington as warm friendships, this was a relationship heavily mediated—glued together, maintained, and eventually undermined—by staff.

On Clinton's side, this is the story of his generosity to a smart, relentless, ungainly successor—a man who, in exchange for his loyal service, got a political opportunity he could never have had if Clinton hadn't chosen him for vice president and then given him unprecedented authority.

On Gore's side, it is the story of his uneasy alliance with a much greater political talent and much more unruly, undisciplined man than himself. Gore's struggle to serve the two masters of Clinton's need and his own career recapitulated some of the most painful themes of his dutiful, self-dimming life, investing the final disillusionment with an explosive power. "If people are shocked now by the way the relationship hit the skids, they shouldn't be," says a former White House official. "There was an almost unnatural suppression and denial in the first six years."

Ultimately, it is this side of the story that is harder—and more important—to understand. Bill Clinton, as the alpha dog, controlled the terms of the relationship at its founding. But it was Al Gore who insisted on its destruction.

A few scenes from the earliest days of the partnership:

In 1992 the Clinton campaign conducted its vice-presidential search under a cloak of darkest secrecy, smuggling potential candidates through a service entrance of Washington's Capitol Hilton.

When campaign staffer Mark Gearan called Gore's scheduler to set up a meeting, he recalls, "I can remember telling [her], 'We'll be by to pick up the senator at 11.' She said, 'A.M.?' I said, 'No, P.M.' She said, 'P.M.?' I said, 'Yeah.' From the start, it was an interesting little window into the respective body clocks and approaches of the two men."

Al Gore, the most ordered, most analytical politician you could hope to meet, was stepping onto the ride of his life.

When Bill and Hillary and Al and Tipper embarked on the famous bus ride across America, the media covered "the boys on the bus" as instant friends and boon companions, the foursome as two fun couples on a marvelous double date.

But the friendship was always oversold. "The whole bus tour, the foursome thing, the press really wanted to believe that," says a former White House official. "The press went with it, and there was no reason for the president or the vice president to shoot it down."

Already, Al Gore was learning the special discipline of a partnership with Clinton. Not far into the trip, he had a knockdown fight with Clinton scheduler Susan Thomases, who drew her clout from a close friendship with Hillary, over extending the bus tour. Gore had talked Clinton (or so he thought) into a longer trip than originally planned; Thomases disagreed, and "Clinton crumbled," says a close Gore associate. This was Gore's first clue that in dealing with Clinton you couldn't always trust what you heard. "Invariably, you're going to come away thinking he said yes," says the Gore associate. "It doesn't mean that at all; it just means Clinton isn't going to look you in the eye and say no. . . . It took a while to kind of refine the language, dealing with Clinton, to get a good understanding that you've got to pin Clinton down, and then you've got to get someone else in the room, to memorialize it."

It's one thing to learn that you're going to need a witness every time the president makes you a promise. But there was something more: Gore's ability to plunge headlong into the role of helper, guide, stalwart sidekick. It took him no time at all to fall into the newlywed's cardinal error of trying to fix his partner—beginning with Clinton's atrocious junk-food diet. "I can remember him getting to an advance person to have only fruit on the buses, for Clinton's weight," says someone who spent time on the bus. "So he was both big brother and little brother, trying to make sure he was eating an apple instead of a Milky Way bar."

Clinton, of course, continued to ask for his Milky Ways. "And, of course, someone would deliver him a Milky Way," continues this source. "But at least it would delay him a stop: at least you'd get to Terre Haute before he had a Milky Way."

Of all the thankless jobs a vice president could be called on to perform, serving as Bill Clinton's superego has to be one of history's most challenging. But that was Gore, loyal son of an outsize southern senator who had methodically raised his namesake to follow in his own footsteps. Gore had spent the first 44 years of his life, with only a few diversions along the way, dutifully fitting himself to the role that had been laid out for him at birth. Al Gore was the reliable boy, the sensible man, the one who steadied the more mercurial souls around him. He brought these lifelong habits to the task of making himself indispensable to Bill Clinton.

"Gore was absolutely determined to make it work. . . . He knew the ability to get anything done depended directly on the president's goodwill," says Roy Neel, who worked for both men in the White House. "In the early days, there were a hundred reasons to keep that relationship working well."

"Work," almost everyone agrees, is the operative word. "Gore worked his way into a relationship with Clinton," says a former Clinton staffer, "but Gore always *worked* to have a relationship."

Still, this achievement can't be underrated. The historic relationships among presidents, vice presidents, and their staffs offer an endless chronicle of mutual suspicion, contempt, alienation, and backbiting. Clinton and Gore did a remarkable job of containing the tensions inherent in the deal, and of wringing the best from their association.

On the president's side, you have to credit his intellectual security: Clinton knew that Gore knew things he didn't, and was happy to delegate specific areas of responsibility—technology, the environment, government reform, and several foreign-policy subjects—and to give great weight to Gore's advice across the board. When you put aside the uncertainties that make it so difficult for Gore to present a coherent political persona, the truest, most reliable parts of the man reside in his grasp of the substance of government. At his best, Gore can be formidably decisive, straightforward, and tough. He offered a desperately needed steadiness to the storm-tossed White House of Clinton's first term, and Clinton was smart enough to accept it.

Additionally, Clinton trusted Gore as a smart, bureaucratically savvy peer. "At the end of the day, a lot of being president is, you're in a meeting, and two smart guys say something, and three smart guys say something else, and it's really hard to decide," says a former Clinton adviser. "Gore was a huge player in this."

The relationship "didn't stretch beyond the kind of day-to-day business that they had to confront," says former Clinton chief of staff Leon Panetta. But even Clinton partisans who are now dumping on Gore's campaign grant him warm praise for his contributions to the administration's successes. When Clinton worked himself into a temper, only Gore could step in with his dry, ironic humor to lance the boil; press secretaries learned never to schedule a press conference when Gore wouldn't be in town for the "pre-brief."

"He had a really light touch with Clinton," recalls former press secretary Dee Dee Myers, describing the scene at a typical press-conference rehearsal. "Clinton would say, 'You sons of bitches don't care about the future of the country.' And Gore would go, 'I think that's exactly the right tone.' "

From the start, however, it was possible to see where the alliance began and ended. There was, for one thing, the past to consider: Clinton had declined to endorse Gore when he ran for president in 1988, and Gore had returned the favor during the early 1992 primaries. Some of those around Clinton were acutely aware that Gore had never been a particular help to them until he was tapped for vice president. And it must have been complicated for Gore to watch Clinton prosecute, successfully, the game plan Gore felt he'd pioneered in the 1988 campaign, running as a southern moderate "New Democrat." But it was a plus that the two men had never run against each other—indeed, while each had long eyed the other as a potential rival, Gore's 1988 endorsement request was the most substantive encounter they ever had before Clinton chose his running mate.

Gore came into the White House determined to hold the Clinton staff to every part of the bargain the two men had struck, which gave Gore unusual bureaucratic power: an inviolable weekly lunch alone with the president, a staff presence in all important West Wing meetings, and a say in all major appointments. Gore aides studied Clinton's schedule intently so that the vice president could be at any important meeting. "He had people there all day long telling him what was going on," says a former Clinton staffer. Under the rule that face time is all, Gore would cancel meetings of his own in order to shadow the president, accommodating himself to Clinton's unpredictable rhythms—even if it meant sprinting down the hall to make it to a meeting he had learned about at the last minute.

Gore especially policed the sanctity of his weekly lunch with the president, the one place he could sit down alone with Clinton to take up his own agenda. And Gore, as one might expect, came to these meetings armed with a multi-item memo and plenty of backup material. One Clinton aide remembers, "Clinton would come in, 'What's for lunch?' Gore would come in with a stack of work under his arm." On one Friday in January of 1996, Clinton aides cleared a room in a Nashville restaurant so that the president and vice president could have a belated meal after a day of joint political appearances. Gore insisted on it despite the fact that Air Force One was standing by to take the president to visit U.S. troops in Bosnia. Aides eyed their watches incredulously as Gore marched through his agenda, not at all daunted by the knowledge that Clinton faced a nine-hour flight into a tense situation.

"He wouldn't let Clinton skip one of those lunches if the fucking missiles were coming in from Russia," says a former White House official. No one on Clinton's side of the house blamed Gore for his insistence on these prerogatives, exactly: he was only doing the smart thing. But they did laugh at him a bit, and constantly pushed back for bureaucratic reasons of their own.

For Gore, there was also the Milky Way problem to contend with—the gargantuan indiscipline of the president's work habits, his ability to talk a thing to death, the experience of thinking you'd talked him around only to discover the next morning that he'd sought five more opinions in the middle of the night. "Clinton drove Gore nuts," says a former Gore aide. "Gore's much more disciplined in terms of how he makes decisions and the way he demands things to happen. There's nothing more irritating as vice president than to be waiting around for a Clinton meeting that starts 45 minutes late."

The two men were, at bottom, as different as could be: Clinton had a thousand friends; Gore, former associates believe, had either few or none. Clinton's famous temper blew hard at anyone in his path, but then passed like a summer storm, whereas Gore did everything with a profound correctness, confiding in almost no one outside of his family, controlled by an inner thermostat that held his manner at a constant room temperature. "He was always very measured and disciplined about what he said around people he didn't trust, which was virtually everybody," says a former White House staffer. Aides learned to read Gore's feelings by small signs. He "was careful about what he said [about Clinton], but didn't hide his feelings that much," says a former Clinton aide who remembers Gore's "winks, nods, facial expressions, sort of the rolling of the eyes. . . . The thing about him always leaching Clinton's anger out—that was true. But underneath that was a very real dismay about Clinton's weaknesses."

One of Gore's roles, from the outset, was to bring the president to closure. A famous episode chronicled in Bob Woodward's *The Agenda*, an account of Clinton's first year in office, had Gore admonishing the president to "get with the goddamn program!" White House staffers learned that this was one of the vice president's great uses. "It would be common to say, 'O.K., it's time to go see Gore,' and get him to tell the president to do something," says a former White House official who has ties to both men. "And it made a lot of sense at the time. 'This works well for everyone' was the feeling. But inside each man's head, it stops being cute after a while."

This source believes that "the abiding bathtub ring it left with Gore was 'Omigod, the guy is undisciplined, and now they're going to send me in there again.' And if you're Clinton, to read in every account that Gore always had to come in at every crucial moment and tell you what to do, that is going to create some real resentment."

Some associates also saw in Gore an occasional wistful awareness that, while Clinton trusted him, they weren't exactly friends. One official from the first term remembers Gore looking at a schedule that included one of the Clintons' movie nights at the White House, and saying, "You know. I've never been invited." This former senior aide continues, "There were so many emblems of uncertainty. . . . He felt Clinton genuinely cared about his success. But I think it was also really important to him that he feel needed, valued, and respected. And sometimes when your older brother doesn't show you need, value, and love, you yearn for it."

And there was, too, the question of Tipper Gore's role in the administration. Given Hillary Clinton's high profile, "Al was always trying to make sure Tipper had standing," says a former aide. "There was always a perception that Al was trying to give her standing that in Clinton's mind she didn't have."

While Tipper and Hillary had done a great job during the campaign of playing up their bond, the truth was that their relationship contained all the tensions that this era can create between women who have chosen radically different paths in life. "Hillary thinks that Tipper is an unintellectual, nice lady who doesn't have a brain in her head," says one source who watched them closely. "And Tipper thinks Hillary's an ambitious, rather uncoordinated, grasping, difficult woman." During the first term, says a former White House official, "there were little reminders that [Tipper] was not an equal, and they rankled. It would come up in discussions with Gore and the First Lady's staff about who was getting what plane to go somewhere."

It all added up to a delicate collaboration. In his every action, Gore reconciled himself to the hard truth that the best way for him to succeed was to help Clinton succeed. But "the fact that they managed to form an effective team professionally never really cured these tensions," says a former White House official with ties to both men. "And in some ways, Gore's approach to the job exacerbated them. The more Gore was rigidly disciplined, and rigidly played his part, the more his resentment grew. . . . This is a guy who, instead of blowing up sometimes and venting at all of the natural tensions in the vice-presidential role, is letting it accumulate and accumulate, and build and build. . . . There was just a lot of shit being built up inside."

Gore's frustrations had their pale mirror image on Clinton's side of the house. Most sources for this story insist that Clinton's grudges were shorter-lived than Gore's; Clinton is a more elastic, more forgiving soul than Gore—"His favorite saying," a Clinton supporter reminds me, "is 'He can't help it, he was born that way' "—and, significantly, he held the upper hand through the first six years in the White House.

But there were limits on his side, too. Sometimes he chafed under the relentlessness of Gore's help. "I never saw resentment on Clinton's part," says a key former staffer. "What I saw more was 'When is this guy just going to leave me alone? Give me a break!' "

In its best hours, the Gore staff was adept at mediating the relationship. "I always viewed my job as 80 percent prosecuting Gore's agenda with the Clinton team," says one former Gore aide. "But the other 20 percent was the hardest part: going into Gore's office and saying, '*Stop*—don't ask for more. Enough, you need to back off.' "

It is also worth remembering that the Clintons never successfully made peace with the Washington establishment—the same elite in which the Gores were utterly at home. And Gore got glowing press throughout Clinton's first term, while Clinton got hammered—for his administration's lack of discipline, for Hillary's health-care debacle, for the dreadful congressional losses of 1994, for Whitewater and Travelgate and Troopergate.

"Clinton felt he gave a lot to Gore, and did a lot for Gore, and tolerated a lot from Gore," recalls a well-placed observer. "And what he's reading in the paper are stories about how Gore did a lot for him."

"I think they had a good relationship early on," says a staffer from the first term. "And I think it was pretty good for quite a while. But I think the more stupid shit Clinton did, the more disapproving Gore got. And Clinton's attitude was 'Yeah, buddy, and when you can do what I do, then you can stand in judgment of me.' "

"They did a pretty good job of holding it together" throughout the first term, says a Clinton supporter. But then came the first serious tear in the fabric—the 1996 campaign-finance scandals.

Reports of Gore's fund-raising phone calls from his office, and of his visit to what turned out to be an illegal fund-raiser at a Buddhist temple in California, made him the emblem for the party's omnivorous attempts to evade campaign-finance laws. Up to that point, Gore had been miraculously free of any taint from the scandals that followed Bill and Hillary Clinton like Pigpen's dirt cloud. Now, suddenly, Establishment Washington was arching its collective brow at the formerly golden vice president. When you lie down with dogs, you get up with fleas, they said—and Gore was receptive to this construction of his problem.

In truth, he had been an enthusiastic participant in both devising and carrying out the campaign's plan to raise huge amounts of "soft" money—large donations made to the party instead of the candidate—and then spend it on ads that would circumvent federal limits on the campaign's spending. But from the moment Gore read a March 2, 1997, Bob Woodward story in *The Washington Post* that termed him the "solicitor-in-chief," he seems to have begun to question whether he could survive his close association with Clinton. "The Woodward story really affected Gore's head a lot," says a former senior official. "It was the first time he'd gotten slapped down by the old guard inside the Beltway."

By September of that year, Gore's favorability rating was more than 20 points lower than Clinton's. And "he was envious that Clinton had gotten off scot-free," says another close associate. Most infuriating was the fact that Gore was in trouble because he had done what he'd said he'd do—dialing at least 45 donors from his desk—while Clinton had ducked the phone calls assigned to him. "It's the whole nature of his being—of Gore's, and Clinton's—writ large," says a former White House staffer. " 'Cause Clinton is out there not doing what he's supposed to be doing, and somehow that protects him? Wait a minute—is that in the rule book? We all know people like that. We went to college with them. They never came to class, then they'd write a brilliant thesis and get an A. . . . You always think, Oh, it's going to catch up with guys like that. And somehow it never does."

The scandal unnerved Gore in a way that he never quite seemed to recover from, and it was amid this crisis of confidence that the Monica Lewinsky affair detonated.

We can't know exactly what Bill Clinton said to Al Gore, in the early days of the Lewinsky scandal, about what he had or hadn't done with the comely intern. The great likelihood, most observers feel, is that Clinton lied to him only indirectly, in the sense of including him in the great, finger-wagging lie he told the entire country. Gore knew his boss well by then, and sophisticated students of the relationship doubt that Gore would have sought a direct yes-or-no answer.

"I know that Gore deliberately never put Clinton in the position of having to lie to him," says a Gore confidant. "It was 'I'm not asking anything you don't want to tell me, but if I were you and I had anything to say, I would say it.' " When Clinton persisted in his cover-up strategy, this source says, Gore was "flabbergasted that Clinton would handle it in a way that was so contrary to logic. I know Gore thinks that if Clinton had just fessed up, apologized, said he'd made a mistake and moved on, it would have been a lot better for everybody."

Even with his closest staffers Gore had enormous discipline: no gossip, no words of anger, above all no speculation about whether Clinton might resign. Staffers, how ever, did see hints of his feelings—above all, incredulity. ("I think he can barely even comprehend why Clinton would behave the way he behaved," says a friend.) But, as always, Gore sucked it up and did what he had to do, which in this case was to express his full support.

And here is the fascinating thing about Gore's support for Clinton over the next difficult year—the tendency that explains almost everything about the bitterness with which Gore eventually turned on his patron: at every step in the Lewinsky saga, Gore went even further than he had to in his statements of support. Faced with any repugnant task that he perceives as his duty, Al Gore will do it to the extreme. As a young man, he had enlisted to go to Vietnam. As a politician, he had prodded himself into being one of the best fund-raisers on Capitol Hill. This gritting of teeth is, in one way, an admirable trait. But it is also what drives him to the opposite extreme after the fact, when emotion has had a chance to catch up to duty and intellect.

The week after the scandal broke, Clinton and Gore traveled together to the Midwest. The trip had originally been planned as a way to shore up Gore politically, to let him share in the lift that Clinton's State of the Union addresses always brought. Instead, it turned out to be yet another chance for Gore to help his boss. At the University of Illinois, he delivered a full-throated defense of Clinton, writing the closing lines of the speech himself: "He is the president of the country," Gore told a roaring crowd in Champaign. "He is also my friend. And I want to ask you now, every single one of you, to join me in supporting him and standing by his side."

That August, when Clinton finally testified before a grand jury and admitted to his affair with Lewinsky, the Gores were on vacation in Hawaii, a trip that had been planned months before. When Gore's office wrote a statement of support, several aides questioned the wisdom of the words "I am proud of him," but Gore insisted on leaving them in.

And on the afternoon of December 19, when the House voted to impeach the president, Gore stood with him on the South Lawn and made his famous assertion that Clinton would be "regarded in the history books as one of our greatest presidents." That line was extemporized, despite the advice of anxious staffers that he not go too far.

But from Clinton's perspective, says another observer, it only made sense that Gore should be giving him cover. "Gore was simply helping him out in a way that seemed natural, given everything he'd done for Gore," says a former White House official. "Clinton just kind of felt like Gore was doing his job."

Al Gore may be slow to act on his feelings, but that makes them all the more forceful when he finally does. From the time he began seriously pressing his own campaign, in late 1998 and early 1999, Gore brooded about how Clinton's behavior might hurt him. The conventional wisdom at the time said it would not: Democrats had done very well in the 1998 midterm elections. The economy was flying high, and Clinton's job-approval ratings along with it. And many of Gore's advisers assumed that the vice president's straight-arrow personal life would insulate him from any association with the one part of Clinton that dismayed voters.

But Gore's poll numbers were stubbornly low. And one easy explanation was that the problem wasn't him. Sources say his family—both Tipper and the couple's oldest daughter, Karenna—felt strongly that Clinton was at fault. Smart observers suggest that there was more at work here than simple personal outrage at Clinton's behavior. Both of the Gores, after all, had gone into their partnership with the Clintons knowing of his "zipper problem," and both had spent decades in politics, where womanizing (if not on the presidential scale) was common—frowned on, to be sure, but common. As much as anything, sources say, Tipper's antipathy to Clinton was a means of loyally seeking a palatable explanation for why her husband left voters so cold. "What the Clinton people underestimated," says a former White House official, "was how much influence Gore's family had, and how much shit he was getting at home."

In any case, Gore had few outlets for his gathering concern: he and Clinton had done too good a job of knitting together their staffs—placing Gore people in the White House and Clinton people in Gore's campaign, and essentially merging their political operations. Gore's pollster, Mark Penn, and media adviser, Bob Squier, both worked for Clinton too; his campaign manager, Craig Smith, was a Clinton loyalist whose ties dated back to Arkansas.

Enter Naomi Wolf, the feminist writer whose role in the campaign would eventually make Gore a laughingstock. In late '99, political reporters discovered that Wolf had been handsomely paid to advise Gore that he needed to shed his "beta male" image and adopt warm earth tones for his wardrobe. But this caricature of her advice greatly understated her true significance, which was her role in persuading Gore that his anguish over Clinton was well founded. Having started a full year earlier, she played "an absolutely critical role in the unraveling of this relationship," says some one who observed Gore closely in this period. "She is the Lady Macbeth of this drama."

It was Karenna who drew Wolf into Gore's orbit, and his early consultations with her took place outside the campaign's staff structure. Aides sensed that she revved him up: "Her biggest danger was that too often she told him what he wanted to hear," says a former Gore associate. "When he was pissed off, she'd tell him he was right to be pissed off."

"She becomes a tremendously powerful force in taking those dynamics and playing them up," says another insider. "It all resonated with Gore's sense that for six years he's been the guy cleaning up after Clinton."

In addition to hardening Gore's growing fury, Wolf had another important effect. Up to that time, success within GoreWorld, as it had come to be known by the White House, was defined by how well you could work with (and work) ClintonWorld. Wolf's example taught people coming into the Gore campaign that the fastest path to the candidate's heart was now anti-Clintonism. And within the White House, presidential staffers watched the shift in sentiment around Gore with growing alarm.

Throughout the summer and early fall of '99, Gore jettisoned advisers who had ties to Clinton, including Penn, Squier, and Smith. Many in the replacement cast had their own difficult history with Clinton, having either worked for candidates who had run against him or been cast out of the Clinton circle at some point. (One pollster, Harrison Hickman, while working for Senator Bob Kerrey's presidential-primary campaign in 1992, had urged reporters to dig into the story of Clinton's draft-dodging; another, Stan Greenberg, had been pushed aside by Clinton after the disastrous midterm elections of 1994.) And the new boss of the campaign, former congressman Tony Coelho, consolidated his own power by pushing out of Gore's circle many of the people—including his vice-presidential chief of staff, Ron Klain—who had the strongest working ties to ClintonWorld.

At the same time, Gore pretty much vanished from the White House.

"People would joke, 'Gore? I haven't seen him around here in decades,'" says a former Clinton staffer. "Gore really made a decision to get out of the White House in 1999—to stop being vice president. And Clinton thought he was kicking away another of his assets."

And so the relationship crumbled.

"You've got to look at it as a series of little, small breaks," says Gore campaign manager Donna Brazile. But the first break that was irreparable came with Gore's announcement speech on June 16, 1999. The same day he opened his campaign on the steps of the courthouse in his hometown of Carthage, Tennessee, ABC aired an interview with Diane Sawyer in which Gore said three times that the president's behavior had been "inexcusable."

"From then on, the antipathy was much more public," says someone with ties to both camps. "It was a match on the huge pool of gasoline that had been accumulated." The White House, which had received no warning, felt blindsided by the attack, and assumed it had been orchestrated. "We couldn't figure it out," says a Clinton partisan. "Why launch your candidacy that way? We were pissed because of how he was treating Clinton, and we were pissed because we thought it was stupid politically."

In truth, according to senior campaign officials, there was no grand strategy to make separation the theme of Gore's announcement. The choice of language, and its vehemence, seems to have come from Gore alone. This episode was the template for all that would follow in the campaign: Gore, by insisting on his independence from Clinton, seemed at every turn to tangle himself more fully in the drama of his difficult relationship with the president, all the while asserting that this was just the routine separation that every vice president goes through when it's his turn to run. It was at this stage that the Clinton factor became a self-fulfilling prophecy.

"It seems that this was something that really paralyzed the campaign internally," says someone who had a ringside seat. "They got further and further behind on that, and it got away from them, fundamentally."

The confusion over Clinton went way beyond the question—heavily picked over in the press—of whether the president should have campaigned for Gore. Even many people on the Clinton side understood the risk of having Clinton out in public, given the importance, in several battleground states, of independent voters who had very negative feelings about the president.

The bigger problem was the campaign's resolve to steer clear of Clinton's record. "I would have done whatever was necessary to elect Al Gore," says pollster Stan Greenberg. "I would have had Bill Clinton carry Al Gore around on his back if I thought it would get Al Gore elected president." But, he insists, "what our research showed . . . was that when Al Gore went out running on that record, he performed more weakly." It made a crude kind of sense, on paper: all the data said that talking about the past—even to brag about the unparalleled prosperity of the '90s—led voters to unwelcome thoughts of Bill Clinton.

The only thing this calculus omits is common sense, for it left Gore without a strong rationale for his run, making him a candidate who seemed less than the sum of his parts. "If Gore were to find in the polling data that having worked with Clinton was a negative, it doesn't mean that pretending *not* to have was a positive," says Bill Curry, a Connecticut politician and former Clinton aide. "He was so connected to Clinton that it was impossible to separate himself from Clinton. . . . And in his anxiousness to separate himself from Clinton, he separated himself from himself."

What Gore presented instead, starting with his convention speech, was a sort of diffuse neopopulism. It even worked for a time, producing spikes in the tracking polls. But it wasn't enough to counteract voters' larger impression that Al Gore wasn't a coherent figure whose real substance was available for examination. "With Gore, [voters] see this lurching back and forth, indecision, uncertainty about his relationship with Clinton," says a longtime Gore ally. "They see a guy who is, bottom line, in some ways unsteady."

Perhaps Gore would have faced this bedrock problem without the drama of the Clinton factor. But his anxiety over Clinton magnified it, making it the very backdrop of his entire campaign. He ended up wrapping himself in the most dangerous parts of the Clinton legacy—voters' doubts about values and trustworthiness—while getting no credit for the parts that had sustained Clinton's approval ratings throughout the impeachment process. Curry says flatly, "[The Gore campaign] skewed all their own data out of pique. . . . Someone had to misread the data horribly to choose that strategy. It was so much about people's grievances and wounds."

"The psychodrama overpowers everything," says someone who knows Gore well. "I think the guy just so much wanted for this to be *his* victory, and not Clinton's. He didn't want to wear the older sibling's jeans."

This, finally, is the other explanation for why Gore seemed so unnerved by his Clinton problem. As the son of a forceful father who had bragged of raising him for the presidency, Gore had struggled all his life with the assumption that he was wearing borrowed clothes. Even under the best of circumstances, it might have been harder for him than for others to manage with grace the eternal vice-presidential conundrum of how to stop looking like a second fiddle when his turn finally came. On some level, in addition to the real difficulties he posed, Bill Clinton was a very persuasive foil for Gore's drama of filial rebellion.

But try telling that to the squire of Chappaqua, who spent the entire campaign yearning—burning—to be part of the action. "Clinton is going nuts," says someone who spoke to him in the late stages of the campaign. "He's going, 'Don't use me, O.K. But, God knows, use my presidency. Use my record!'"

Clinton's frustration, says one observer, "ran infinitely deeper than just 'He isn't running on my record.' He felt he had spent eight years basically knocking obstacles out of Gore's way."

Staffers on both sides learned to manage a volatile, high-test battle of wills between Clinton and Gore, trying to satisfy Clinton's great hunger for information and a role in the campaign while also tiptoeing around Gore's great determination to exclude him.

"This dynamic developed," says a Clinton partisan, "where the Clinton guys thought the Gore guys were stupid, and the Gore guys thought the Clinton guys were assholes, that we weren't giving them enough room."

A constant struggle was being waged in which the White House pressed for a bigger role, and the Gore campaign labored to contain the 800-pound gorilla. Campaign chairman Bill Daley, who had served in the Clinton Cabinet as commerce secretary, fielded phone calls from the president as often as three times a week. Brazile recalls being buttonholed by the president at a White House social event: How were the polls? In Arkansas? In Pennsylvania? What about Michigan?

The Gore campaign sent occasional delegations to brief the president on the campaign's progress. On one occasion, Daley and strategist Tad Devine were primed to tell Clinton, in no uncertain terms, the limited number of appearances they wanted from him. Just before the meeting, Devine said to Daley, "You're the chairman, you're going to do it, right?" And Daley replied, "Oh, no, Tad, you're going to do it. The guy put me in the Cabinet."

Then there were the back channels. Even when the White House appeared to bow to the campaign's wishes, it was trying other angles of attack: Gore aides received constant phone calls saying that Congressman So-and-so was begging the president to come to his district, that Senate candidate Thus-and-such had demanded an appearance. "I believe Clinton used practically everyone he could get his hands on to send messages to Al Gore," says Donna Brazile.

Direct conversations between the president and the vice president had slowed to a trickle by the late summer of 2000, according to aides. And on the few occasions when they did talk—and the even rarer occasions when they met in person—Gore aides tied themselves in knots to conceal the contact from a press corps that had fixated on the story of the tension between the two men. "Sometimes they would just talk, without our scheduling it," says a former Clinton adviser. "Clinton would say, 'I need to talk to him,' and pick up the phone. And then [the Gore side] would get all in a lather about whether to tell anyone about it."

Tensions may have reached their apogee on October 20, when the Clintons and the Gores both attended the funeral of Missouri governor Mel Carnahan, who had died in a plane crash. That very morning, *The New York Times* had published a yeasty, highly detailed story about the disaffection between the two families. "So everyone had to go through the motions of being friendly," recalls a former Clinton aide. "It was a brutal article—it had everyone but the pets in the families at war with each other. It picked over every scab there was." Yet there they all were, sharing a motorcade together. "It was all very awkward and very weird," recalls the aide. "They didn't erupt or anything . . . but it had a feel like, your family gets together over someone who died, and people haven't talked for a while, and they sort of have to go through the motions."

Gore's behavior seemed to those in the White House to ignore the plain fact that, had it not been for Clinton, it is unlikely Gore would have reached the nomination. "Clinton just felt, 'Suck it up, man!' " says a close associate.

But Gore's sense of grievance ran far deeper than Clinton's, for the obvious reason that he had much more at stake. "Look. He kept his end of the bargain," says Marla Romash, a former Gore press secretary. "The deal was: I will do everything I can to make your presidency successful, and you'll try to help me get elected. . . . He stood by every decision, even the ones he didn't agree with, bless him. He carried Clinton's water politically, substantively, every way. And Clinton broke the deal in the one way that could undermine everything Gore had worked for."

In the wake of Gore's loss, recriminations flew almost immediately. On

Gore's side, because he won the popular vote (and, many Democrats argued, the electoral vote too), there was a certain zany insistence that the operation had been a success if you could only overlook the fact that the patient had died. Of course our strategy was sensible, this argument ran; we won the campaign, didn't we? To the extent that we failed to actually get our guy inaugurated—well, that was Clinton's fault.

Gore strategist Carter Eskew published a *Washington Post* op-ed piece suggesting that Clinton had been "the elephant in the living room" during the campaign—the one insuperable obstacle. Eskew says Gore did not read the piece in advance, but he was told about it—and tacitly approved by not protesting Eskew's plans to publish it.

Clinton partisans responded to the piece and to other anti-Clinton analyses with contemptuous statements of their own. "[Gore's] failure in this last campaign is indicative of the fact that he can't carry himself," rails a Clinton supporter. "He didn't have the juice." They pointed out, too, that Gore's loss involved blunders—including his performance in the debates with Bush and his failure to carry his home state, Tennessee—that had little or nothing to do with Clinton.

Clinton himself considered but then dropped the idea of authorizing some response to the Eskew piece. Wrapped up in the drama of his own farewell to the White House, he didn't have nearly the level of rage that Gore did. "His feelings are hurt, he thinks he should have been used, he doesn't really understand why Gore didn't ask him to help, and he doesn't think Gore is a great politician," says a friend. "But under all that, he feels badly about what happened."

Moderate Democrats gathered in earnest confab to debate whether Gore lost because he turned away from the supple centrism of Clinton to a more "old Democratic" populism. And the pollsters who had worked for the party's two principals during the campaign—each of whom had at one time in his career been dumped by the other side—published contending polls supporting the wisdom of their own camp's view.

But this was really just the same Clinton-Gore divorce dressed up in ideological clothing. "It's a big intellectual debate that is being driven by the big personal stakes of the guys around them," says a former Clinton adviser. "As a party, if we want to spend the next decade the way we spent the '80s, we couldn't make a better start than creating a lot of false choices about why we lost the election."

And this, ultimately, is one of the reasons why the sour end to their relationship poses a larger problem for their party. Gore's campaign turned out to be the field on which Democrats in some sense thrashed out their ambivalence over what Clinton had cost them, and the ongoing bitterness of the debate about why Gore lost continues to obscure the party's path out of the Clinton years and into the next stage of its life.

A few days after Gore conceded the election, he and Clinton finally had it out themselves in their tense White House meeting. Clinton aides had the sense that Gore—who instigated the meeting—came in loaded for bear, with years' worth of anger to get off his chest. Both men laid out the nature of their grievances, including, on Gore's side, his fury that Clinton had spent the weeks after the election deriding the competence of Gore's campaign. But it was far too late for the meeting to do anything more than anatomize why the partnership lay in ruins.

Both men had some truth on their side. "It's not fair for Gore's people to say he lost because of Clinton," says one judicious soul. "And it's not fair for Clinton's people to say that Gore's loss had nothing to do with Clinton."

But it is fair to say that, to the extent that candidates' fears and feelings shape their campaigns, Al Gore's history with Bill Clinton cost him the 2000 election.

On the day of Bush's inauguration, Clinton and Gore walked together through the labyrinthine halls of the Capitol to take their places on the stage. Television cameras caught them in a last characteristic tableau of their partnership—Clinton glad-handing every guard along the route, waving and smiling, while at his side Gore gazed stoically ahead.

With that, the two men seem to have walked out of each other's life. In mid-February, guests at a dinner thrown by U.N. secretary-general Kofi Annan for Richard Holbrooke, Clinton's ambassador to the U.N., watched in fascination as the former president talked with Gore's daughter Karenna. "It was so weird," says one person who was there. "They didn't really speak to each other. And then, at the very end, Karenna went over to say good-bye to him, and it was very cordial, but there was sort of this weird tension you were aware of. He's saying, 'How's your dad doing, and how often does he get up to New York?,' and stuff like that. And you're just noticing how strange it is that he has to ask the guy's daughter, in passing."

The following month, Clinton asked another man who has dealings with Gore how the former vice president was doing, making it clear that the two hadn't spoken. "I don't think that relationship has gotten any better," says this source with some amazement. By the same token, Gore apparently sent Clinton no word during the winter and spring, when the former president was enduring his own mud bath of controversy.

Some Gore associates chuckle over the strange irony by which Gore's shunning of Clinton can now be seen as prescient. Clinton's gigantic shadow and his dominance of the Democratic Party have been violently dissipated by the Marc Rich pardon and all the other Milky Way bars the president consumed on his way out of office. "Oddly enough, distancing himself turned out to be a lucky stroke," says a friend—at least in the lower-stakes game of hindsight. "Every story about the bad blood between them sort of disconnects them more." Through Clinton's acts, Gore may finally be getting the separation he wanted.

But, characteristically, it is Gore who has nearly dropped from sight. Clinton—underemployed, alone in the big, underfurnished Chappaqua house that was bought to launch his wife's new career in another city— makes incessant calls to friends, acquaintances, former associates. "Clinton talks to everybody—he's very lonely," says a political associate of both men. "Everywhere I go, I've run into people who have talked to Clinton in the last three or four weeks. And I have trouble thinking of anyone who has heard from Gore, other than sort of a perfunctory call."

Friends say that Gore has thrown himself into the several teaching jobs he accepted in the wake of his defeat, and, with Tipper, into the writing of a book about families. He has gained something like 30 pounds, and has resisted all attempts to draw him into comment on the early acts of the Bush administration. "He's O.K. I wouldn't say he's great," says a friend. "I think about 70 percent of the time he's fine. And the other 30 percent of the time he realizes he's supposed to be president now."

In May, I asked Clinton's spokeswoman, Julia Payne, if the boys on the bus had had any kind of contact with each other. "I know [Clinton] tried to call him on his birthday, but I don't think they connected, and that was back in March," she said. "We weren't too sure where he was staying," she added. The only connection they've made, it appears, is a birthday note Clinton dropped in the mail. As Payne observed, "You never forget someone's birthday."

Hill Climbing
Jennifer Senior

New York magazine | April 2, 2001

After all the sparks Hillary Clinton created as First Lady, a lot of folks were looking for fireworks once she reached the Senate. Yet after running a tightly controlled campaign in which she visited every county in New York State, shrugged off charges of being a carpetbagger, and rolled over her opponent Rick ("Little Ricky") Lazio by a 55 to 43 margin, Hillary's tenure in Congress has been nothing but smooth sailing to date.

How does she do it? The best answer to that riddle can be found in this profile by Jennifer Senior, who caught up with the Empire State's freshman senator a few months into her first term. While Senior doesn't manage to crack Clinton's inscrutable facade, she does manage to tease out a few of her secrets. Number one on the list: charm the pants off your elders. . . .

Just minutes after Strom Thurmond's mortifying guerrilla hug on swearing-in day, Hillary Clinton walked back up the aisle of the Senate chamber and plopped herself down next to John Breaux. If you're going to be strangled by a subsentient nonagenarian on your first day in public office, Breaux's the best man to turn to for comic relief. An easygoing Democrat from the Big Easy, he's a charmer, a bit of a rogue, and one of the few senators who don't take themselves or the pomp of their station all that seriously. Clinton looked at him. Breaux looked at her. "Well, Hillary," he said, shrugging, "welcome to the Senate. Now it's your turn to deal with him."

Even if Thurmond, 98 and still horny as a brass band—he's been known to blurt his admiration for the female form at the most horrific of moments—hadn't ambushed Clinton and squeezed her speechless, it would have been a peculiar afternoon. Ted Kennedy didn't know whether to call our new senator Mrs. Clinton or Hillary, didn't know whether to hug her or to shake her hand. Hours before she took her oath, rumors were whipping through the Capitol that she'd have to be sworn in ahead of the other senators because of Secret Service considerations. And the president—*of the United States*—was sitting in the gallery of the chamber, nearly weeping, surrounded by dozens of Senate wives in updos.

But it was Breaux, a pal of the former president's (both are southern centrists and set on the same devious frequency), who zoomed in on the most awkward part of the proceedings.

"Look at all those Republicans," he whispered as her colleagues rose, one by one, to plant their hands on the Bible and take their oaths. "Lookin' at ya, all wishin', or at least thinkin', that they'd finally gotten rid of the Clintons, and here you are—*they're baaack!*"

And how. After seven years of running Bill Clinton through a steady rinse cycle of hatred and contempt, congressional Republicans are now in the terribly awkward position of seeing his wife—that bungler of health care, that concealer of billing records, that suspicious profiteer from cattle futures!—every day. To them, Hillary was arguably even worse than he was, the very blow-dried embodiment of political turpitude. And now, she's their colleague. Trent Lott, who idly wondered aloud whether she'd be struck by lightning before her arrival, wasn't even the worst of her Senate antagonists. Chuck Grassley, the chairman of the Finance Committee, made several trips to the Senate floor in 1996, decrying the First Lady's involvement in the White House travel office and Whitewater. (And he's one of the Senate good guys: a plainspoken, 67-year-old Iowa farmer, the sort who'd pitch in if your John Deere conked out on you.) And then there was Don Nickles, Lott's deputy. He blithely predicted four years ago on CNN that she'd be indicted.

President Clinton's mad pardon spree in his last 24 hours in office, combined with the revelation that the brothers Rodham had been involved, only managed to confirm what everyone already knew.

"People weren't shocked," said John McCain, charming and outspoken as ever, when I asked him about Marc Rich a couple of weeks ago as he was heading down to the Capitol basement. "Did you see that Clinton's conversations with Monica Lewinsky were taped by the Russians?" He pulled out the *The Hotline*, a Beltway tip sheet summarizing the day's papers, and started to skim. "Accused spy . . . Russian . . . Hanssen . . . *here*: 'Seventy hours of phone sex, some from Air Force One.'" He looked at me helplessly.

So Pardongate pales in comparison?

"I'm saying it's . . . " He shrugged, at a loss for words, and climbed into the Senate Subway. It let out an evocative *clang-clang*, like a San Francisco trolley.

It's what?

"Interesting!" he shouted as the car pulled away.

What he probably meant was that Pardongate was just one more obstacle for Hillary to climb over. A huge obstacle, certainly: forcing her to roll out her plans for New York in a less timely fashion, driving her into hiding, consuming most of her time with the media (at her first press conference, more than half of the eighteen questions were about gifts and pardons, while others were about Giuliani, the Giants, and her hair), and—worst of all—enraging her Democratic colleagues, who once again had to gnash their teeth as she and her husband gaudily dominated the news. (When I recently told Joe Lieberman I was looking for good Hillary anecdotes, unrelated to pardons, he told me: "Good—otherwise I might have had to jump off this escalator.")

But the Senate is a funny place. In some ways, it's a lot like a posh northeastern boarding school: clannish, predominantly male, spilling over with rich people of only middling intelligence. But it is also clubby and self-congratulating and stuffed with large, fragile personalities. Its climate—a neurotic combination of camaraderie and strained formality, comity and vitriol, ego and deference—is, to say the least, sociologically unique. From this tension, strange unions and friendships are born.

Certainly, Hillary's arrival has created some turmoil and irritation. How could it not? She's a goodie-goodie do-gooder but surrounded by a penumbra of scandal and stink; she's opaque but charming, polite but condescending, courtly but stubborn, ingratiating but aloof.

But in the Senate, none of this is a recipe for permanent pariah status. "What is most surprising for people who come here," muses Byron Dorgan, a mild-mannered Democrat from North Dakota, "is that what appears from the outside is not always true on the inside. Inside the institution, people respect each other, generally."

Even Phil Gramm, the Tabasco-tongued Texan who spent years tormenting the Clinton administration, sounds positively expansive when he evaluates Hillary's prospects. "In the Senate," he explains, "if you work hard, and you get things done, nothing else matters. So in the end, it"—meaning Pardongate—"won't matter. That's the fairness of the system."

And Hillary is nothing if not a hard worker. In fact, there has always been a tremendous gulf between Hillary the icon and Hillary the grind. Hillary the icon earned sixteen months of campaign coverage and attracted

50 reporters to her first coffee with the twelve other Senate women. But Hillary the grind went on a listening tour of New York, can dutifully list all the reasons why New York State should be in the Northeast Dairy Compact, and exited a high-speed-railway press conference last month exclaiming to a colleague, "Boy, wasn't Kay Bailey"—Hutchison, Republican of Texas—"terrific? She knew all of those subsidies!"

No one in the Senate likes a show horse. But a workhorse can command admiration, if not warmth, from her colleagues. "I knew my colleagues in the Senate would like Mrs. Clinton once they got to know her," explains Barbara Mikulski, dean of the Senate women and Democrat of Maryland, "because she's *crazy* about homework and briefings."

And a very fast learner, apparently. Hillary has already figured out how to cope with Strom. The next time she ran into Thurmond, notes Breaux, she gave him the "Clinton-Arafat handshake—that is, you take your left hand and grab his shoulder, so he won't get any closer." He demonstrates, his arm outstretched, like a mime desperate to keep a door closed. "She was very nice, very polite . . . and *verrrrry* cautious."

So this is the weird, prep-school hothouse that Hillary has joined: A few weeks ago, I found myself in a senators only elevator, taking a ride down to the basement of the Capitol. Its other occupants were Paul Wellstone, the lefty professor turned senator from Minnesota; Sam Brownback, a conservative Christian who replaced Bob Dole; and Gramm. Wellstone, a full head shorter than either of his two colleagues, tugged at Brownback's sleeve. "I wanted to ask you about your trip!"

Brownback nodded, explaining to Gramm in haiku: "Thailand. Sex trafficking."

Gramm raised his eyebrows suggestively. Wellstone lunged at him. "Phil, don't say anything!" he said, shaking him by both his elbows. "We're in an *elevator* with a *reporter!* I am protecting you, do you understand? I am *saving* you from *yourself!*"

Gramm, grinning, couldn't resist. "Well," he drawled, looking expectantly at Brownback, "how closely did you look into it?"

The official line among Senate Republicans is that Hillary had earned her rightful place in the Senate, and that she is therefore entitled to the benefit of the doubt. In Gramm's words: "She's Hillary Clinton, not Bill Clinton. Judging my wife based on me, that's not fair." He pronounces "wife" *wahf.*

But for the first month of the legislative session, some Republican senators couldn't quite conceal their contempt. In late January, I asked Tim Hutchinson, an Arkansas Republican, whether his new colleague had disarmed him yet with her charm. He looked at me blankly. "No," he said. "But I did have a colleague ask, 'Does she ever smile?' "

Two weeks later, I asked Judd Gregg, a boyish New Hampshire senator who serves on two of the same committees as Hillary, whether he'd spoken to the former First Lady yet. "Uh, we said hello from a distance." Pause. "Over the heads of the Secret Service." Another pause. "She's surrounded by a *cadre*. She's like an aircraft carrier with a task force around her."

McCain, meanwhile, was appalled by the $8 million book deal and the $190,000 worth of gifts she'd made off with—"As the author of the gift ban, it doesn't get her off on the right foot with me"—and Jeff Sessions, the spitfire former Alabama attorney general, was fuming about the pardons for the four crooked rabbis in New Square. "It is troubling," he said. "Very, very troubling. To give a pardon for political votes is *beneath* contempt."

You could really see the hostility on the Senate floor. There were a few moments when Hillary talked to virtually no one—she just stood by herself, awkwardly looking around. A few Republicans seemed to go out of their way to snub her. On the day of her third vote, Nickles spent a good three minutes standing directly in front of Clinton, waiting to approach the desks where votes are tallied. He kept his back to her the entire time.

But it soon dawned on the Senate Republicans: How vindictive could they really afford to be? Most of them realize that tormenting Hillary Clinton— or any female senator, for that matter—usually backfires, because they come across as a bunch of bullying, overbearing husbands. Even Arlen Specter (known among Senate staffers as Mr. Burns) didn't discuss Hillary's brothers at his pardon hearings. "I don't know if it was because she's a fellow senator," says Sessions, who sits on the Judiciary Committee, "or if it was because there was no evidence to show she did anything wrong. I suspect it was both."

As a rule, alienating your Senate colleagues is a pretty bad idea, no matter how much you loathe them or their politics. "Because if one senator decides that there are people he or she won't work with," explains Dorgan, "at some point, somewhere down the road, that senator is going to have legislation. And it's going to wind up in some subcommittee where those people he or she slighted have the opportunity to say, 'Thanks a lot—here's your payback.' "

Getting along is especially important given the Republicans' knife-thin margin. Though no G.O.P. senator dares speak about this directly, Strom Thurmond's health, once actually taken for granted, is now on all of their minds—remarkably, it looks like he may finally surrender to age. ("When Strom sneezes," a top G.O.P. aide ruefully told me a few weeks ago, "49 senators scramble to hand him a Kleenex.") If Thurmond dies, the governor of South Carolina, a Democrat, gets to choose his successor, and the Democrats become the majority party. In the 2002 election, if the Republicans lose so much as one seat—and twenty of them are up for re-election, as opposed to fourteen Democrats—again, Democrats will win control of the chamber. And Hillary, within a couple years (even months!), could be just the subcommittee chairman Dorgan was talking about.

"So you see Republicans come up somewhat sheepishly and shakin' hands with her, sayin' hello," says Breaux. "I saw Shelby"—first name Richard, an early and rather vocal foe of Bill Clinton's—"talkin' to her yesterday. I thought that was good."

"Senator Lott has been gracious in the way he has talked to her personally," adds Tom Daschle, the Democratic leader. "Far more gracious," he ruefully notes, "than what his public comments would have anticipated."

Gramm now brags about how he never *personally* attacked the First Lady. "If you ask people to list who killed her health-care bill," he says, "they'd say me, but *never* did I call it anything but the president's bill. Other people called it 'Hillary Care.' I never did that."

A butcher could not slice baloney this thin. But a senator can.

The day the Starr Report came out, Congressman Pete King saw Hillary. It should have been an excruciating experience. It wasn't. Just a couple of weeks before, the Long Island Republican had been on a trip to Ireland with the First Lady, and she happened to have met his mother—who at the time was in the middle of a logistical nightmare involving her plane ticket home. Now, as King sat awkwardly in the Diplomatic Reception Room of the White House, his head aswarm in the strangeness of the moment, Hillary strolled right up to him. "Your mother ever catch that plane?" she asked.

"That's Hillary," King says. "You see her a month later, and she asks you an obscure question about your last conversation. Unlike her husband, who only listens to about maybe half of what you say to him, she really listens to *everything*. That has to disarm all but the most hard-assed senator.

When she asks, 'What happened to your grandson at Communion?'—that's gonna weaken some of that hatred."

Her charm offensive has already begun. Almost the moment she set foot in the Senate, Hillary greeted Jesse Helms. "She came over to say hello," he marvels, "and she had a hairdo just like everybody else! And I said, 'I believe I read in the newspaper that you're now a United States senator.' She just laughed. I said, 'I hope I see you.' "

The 79-year-old senator, who now scoots around the Capitol on a motorized wheelchair, seems to bear her no grudge. "I always got a kick out of her," he says. "She said I was the head of a vast right-wing conspiracy—on TV! A few weeks after, I was on the receiving line at a State Department dinner, and I said, 'Vast right-wing conspiracy reporting for duty, ma'am.' " He salutes. "It didn't faze her."

Ben Nighthorse Campbell, the Senate's only Native American (he has a long, frizzy ponytail and got special dispensation from the Rules Committee to wear his bolo ties on the Senate floor), offered Hillary a ride on his motorcycle. Chuck Hagel, a handsome, fiftysomething G.O.P. maverick from Nebraska, had Hillary to lunch in the privacy of his office. He says he didn't tell his colleagues. But he didn't keep it a secret from them, either. "I think she, uh, has come into the Senate under a considerable glare," he explains, "and that probably has put her in a bit of an awkward situation with her colleagues, so I figured she probably hasn't had many invitations just to talk a little bit, and just to get acquainted. She certainly is very charming and very gracious and very lovely and very smart."

Charming, gracious, lovely, smart? Good Lord—didn't this man get the *memo*?

Dorgan is right: These people need each other—sort of like the contestants on *Survivor*, another narcissistic group of strangers thrown together under artificial circumstances. So even as the pardon hearings were coming to a boil, and even as he was lamenting Bill Clinton's ethics on TV, Jeff Sessions, perhaps the Clinton family's most rabid Senate foe, was discussing his bankruptcy bill with Hillary, hoping she'd support it.

Does this mean he'd work with her? "Sure," he says.

So he won't filibuster a Clinton bill, just for sport? Or stall it in the cloakroom?

"Oh, no," he says. Beat. "Unless it's a bad bill."

It's nearly noon, and Clinton is sitting in a dull-as-nails Budget Committee hearing on agriculture and energy deregulation, trying valiantly to look interested in what the witnesses are saying. Because she's the most junior Democrat on the committee, she sits all the way at the end of the horse-shoe-shaped table. She writes things down in a spiral notebook occasionally. She cradles her head in her hand.

Because Democrats do not control the Senate, they do not control the agenda at committee hearings, and they can choose few of the witnesses. Yet Clinton still sits through these meetings almost in their entirety, because she knows everyone in the Senate is watching her, wondering how serious she is, wondering whether she's going to be a prima donna or roll up her sleeves and work.

Pete Domenici, the committee chairman, is speaking. He's a friendly man, an old-timer who actually remembers when members stayed in Washington on weekends and had dinner with one another's families. "And then you," he's saying. "Senator Hillary—you're next."

Senator Hillary? Domenici seems to realize he's made a gaffe. He leaps up to whisper something in her ear, throwing his arm around her as he speaks. Whatever he says, it makes both of them grin. She puts her hands to her face, smiles, and stifles a laugh.

I ask him later that week what he whispered to her. Was it to apologize for calling her Senator Hillary? He grins. "I caught that mistake," he says. "It wasn't about that. It was about something else. And I'm not telling you."

The hearing began at 10:30. Senator Hillary got her first chance to speak at 12:20.

Democrats care for Hillary both more and less than Republicans do. A number have always found her more reliable than her husband, who embarrassed them with his lying, lost control of Congress for them with his overreaching, and then, once Republicans took over, habitually betrayed them with his triangulating. She, they believe, is the real deal.

Then along came Pardongate. "A lot of people were concerned that so much of the discussion after the election was about Clinton's last few days in office," concedes Breaux. "It was a distraction, clearly, and, um, I think most people wish it hadn't occurred. But look—I'm sure he wishes the same thing! I mean, I've talked to him since, and he wishes it hadn't all happened, but it did."

So what was Clinton thinking?

"To some extent, he wasn't."

Even before Marc and Denise Rich became household names, though, plenty of Democrats were toting their own satchel of resentments toward Hillary. "She's like what happened when the astronaut John Glenn got elected—cubed," explains Joe Biden, the Delaware Democrat. "And there's a lot of egos in this place. So when any senator walks into a meeting, into a room, into a crowd, with Hillary, all of you in the press are going to immediately go to her, no matter how much more clout or significance the other senator has. And that's obviously going to generate some difficulty with her colleagues."

Like Chuck Schumer—who, at least technically, is still the senior senator from New York. They say the most dangerous place in the Capitol is between Chuck Schumer and a camera, and if Hillary wanted to, she could occupy that place all the time. Though Schumer undeniably campaigned hard for the First Lady, her presence in the Senate, on some level, must kill him. ("I'm sure he finds it galling," says one of his New York colleagues. "Don't get me started," says another. "They'll eat each other up," says a third.)

Of course, many senators from the same state and the same party wind up disliking, if not outright loathing, each other. Barbara Boxer and Dianne Feinstein. Thad Cochran and Trent Lott. Olympia Snowe and Susan Collins. Robert Torricelli and Frank Lautenberg, when the two were still serving together. (Two years ago, at a Democratic retreat at the Library of Congress, the former famously snarled to the latter: "I'm going to cut your balls off.")

Chuck and Hillary will probably get along better than that.

The day she got sworn in, Biden recalls, Hillary addressed her new colleagues in the old Senate chamber and asked them to forgive her for all the media attention she was going to attract, at least initially. "And she's not speaking up in the caucuses," he adds. "Other freshmen are talking a lot more than Hillary is. A *whole* lot more. At least *three* freshmen have talked *ten* times as much as she has. Hillary listens."

But her potential for refracting the limelight requires constant monitoring. Recently, I called the office of a New York Democrat, and his staff had just completed a legislative meeting, going through their bills one-by-one, trying to determine whether Hillary's involvement would help or hurt their boss. At her first coffee with the Senate women, Hillary's colleagues writhed as the cameras focused almost exclusively on her. The first day the freshmen Democrats gave a press conference, Daschle, who introduced them, told the media each senator was only allowed *one* question. "Of course, she took the *first* question," deadpans Tom Carper, formerly the governor of Delaware and easily the funniest guy in the Democratic caucus. He pauses. "And then all the other questions were, 'So, Senator, what do *you* think about Hillary?' "

Perhaps no Democrat needed to be more persuaded of Hillary's virtues than Robert Byrd. Byrd is one of the Senate's living legends. He's a master of parliamentary procedure and an avid history buff, and on a good afternoon, he can work in references to both Socrates and Pliny the Elder in a floor speech. Byrd may be the only sitting senator to speak in standard written English. He wears three-piece suits to work every day. And at 83, he has supposedly shaken the hand of one of every three constituents in the state of West Virginia.

Byrd wields awesome power within the Democratic caucus, most notably because he's the top member of the Appropriations Committee, which determines how much money gets spent on all sorts of federal projects.

This year, Hillary wanted very much to be on the Appropriations Committee. She was turned down. Byrd did not care for her husband in the slightest.

So the first week of Congress, Hillary went to see Robert Byrd. She spent an hour in his gilded Senate office, with its heavy chandelier and silk-lined sofa and giant oil painting of his wife, and asked him how to be a good senator. And he gave her a disquisition worthy of Polonius.

"I told her: 'To be a good senator, you've got to do your committee work and become an expert in legislation,' " he recalls. " 'Don't talk too often; you will have plenty of chances to speak. Make yourself a workhorse, not a show horse. And remember, behind every curtain and every drapery there is a monster called envy. Don't expect any favors; you start at the bottom, just like any other new senator.'

"And she said, 'I don't.' " He nods approvingly. "I was very favorably impressed. I didn't expect her to have this kind of attitude. I expected that she would come in here and she would expect a lot of special treatment. But there was none of that. She even took notes."

The day of Hillary's first vote, she again approached Byrd, this time on the Senate floor. She told him she was supposed to preside over the Senate that day—to whom should she turn for a quick briefing on Senate procedure? He told her about the parliamentarian, Robert Dove. Then she asked if she could round up the other freshmen later that week so that Byrd himself could give them a little lecture on the Senate rules. "Now, wasn't that something?" he marvels, with a breathy twang. "I thought that was exceptional."

I predict: In two years, Hillary will be on the Appropriations Committee.

"There have been any number of people who've come into the Senate over the decades with a strike against them," muses Congressman Jerry Nadler, the Democrat who represents the West Side from Zabar's to Nathan's. "And hard work changed the opinion. Ted Kennedy is the obvious example. When he came in, everybody knew he didn't deserve to be there. And yet he turned out to be one of the best senators of the century."

Actually, Kennedy thinks Hillary's more qualified than he ever was. "She comes in, really, in a different situation," he says. "Because she was already very much involved in many of these issues—like health and education— as First Lady." While he, the implication is, was not. He was merely a Kennedy.

Back at that budget committee hearing, Hillary finally has a chance to speak. She thanks the chairman, Domenici, for having this panel—"and the future panels that are planned, including a panel on coal, Senator Byrd, because I do think it is extremely helpful in forming our decisions when it comes to the budget issues we face."

Byrd smiles, pleased as punch.

"The colloquy between Mr. Simmons and Dr. Penner was of particular interest to me," she continues, and then speaks for about five minutes in a surprisingly relaxed, impassioned way, sounding nothing like she does at her heavily scripted press conferences. Her questions are sharp. The witnesses are impressed. If policy-speak were an aphrodisiac, she'd probably be the most seductive person alive.

She brings up Senator Byrd's pet project again. ("It's always struck me as rather unfortunate that we didn't make even greater investments in helping the market respond to clean coal demands . . .") Domenici thanks her. Then he asks whether everyone's finished with his or her statements and questions. The Democrats say they'd love just a few quick follow-ups, but Hillary has a lunch appointment. Domenici asks Byrd whether he minds if she goes before him.

"Well, actually, I'd wait for Senator Byrd, Mr. Chairman," says Hillary.

Byrd beams like a proud father. "I would suggest that the distinguished senator from New York proceed," he says. "I'd like to hear her, and I know she has a luncheon."

There was talk for a long time of Hillary's being a super-senator—the next Ted Kennedy, taking to the floor whenever Republicans crossed some unthinkable Rubicon—or perhaps even the next president. But for the moment, she has no choice but to focus her energies on New York, not just because of her recent pardon troubles but because her colleagues and constituents are closely, warily watching her to make sure she doesn't use the Senate floor as a glorified launching pad for another Clinton presidency. At least not immediately.

Besides, New York will need her full attention. With the recent departures of Daniel Patrick Moynihan and Alfonse D'Amato, the state has lost two seats on the Finance Committee, arguably the most powerful in the Senate. In the House, we're better off. "But if I have to fight and scratch for New York and not feel that I have anyone on the Finance Committee or the leadership over there," says Charles Rangel, Harlem Democrat and ranking member on the Ways and Means Committee, "it would be a problem."

There's another problem, too. "Maybe I'm being paranoid," says Nadler. But in Congress, "I suspect that there's a lot of anti-New York hostility, and that Hillary'll come across it from time to time, in addition to the hostility to *her*. You know, it's partly anti-Semitic, though I think that's fading. And I think New York also personifies, like Massachusetts, liberal Democrats. I mean, Newt Gingrich used to delight in picking on New York as the image of everything that was wrong."

Unfortunately, this anti-New York sentiment has a way of asserting itself legislatively. Nadler remembers when Dan Burton walked out on the House floor and railed against New York's and Los Angeles's generous helping of funding from the National Endowment for the Arts.

"So I got up," says Nadler, "and said I was shocked, *shocked* to discover the prejudice against New York—that we didn't get a *penny* of the *wheat subsidy!* And how much went to *Indiana!*" He bangs his fist on his desk for emphasis. "Never mind that we don't grow any wheat."

Outside Clinton's Senate office, a sweaty bike messenger suddenly appears. "I just, like, wanted to meet her," he tells one of her aides, who happens to be walking by. "Do you, like, need an appointment or can you just walk in?" The aide graciously explains that the senator is talking with her staff, but he can probably catch her when she leaves to go to a meeting. Inside, a cute kid with floppy hair is working one of the phones. "I will definitely make a note of it," he's saying. "Where are you from . . . ?"

Clinton's three receptionists estimate that they take more than 1,000 calls per day. Her interns open more than 2,000 pieces of mail per week. And the foot traffic outside her suite, located on the fourth floor of the Russell Building, rivals Disney World's. Hillary might be a celebrity. But this new job of hers is by no means glamorous. And it is perhaps this humdrum dimension of the job—the grueling, tiresome, quotidian details that go into helping constituents and making policy—that her colleagues say will be the hardest adjustment for her to make. First Ladies browse for china patterns, choose a few pet issues, and travel all over the world. Senators spend their days raising money, commuting, listening to unhappy constituents, racing to meetings, sitting through four-hour hearings, going to parades in far-flung towns, and raising more money. This time three years ago, Hillary was off on an eleven-day tour of Africa. These days, she's spending her weekends in Schenectady.

"She'll find out how tedious it is," says Pete King. "I don't know if she's prepared for that." He thinks. "I'm also wondering how the disorder will affect her," he says after a moment. "There's no orderly life as a member of Congress. One hundred constituents arrive you have to meet with. Committee meetings abruptly adjourn. You're scheduled for a talk in Syracuse, and suddenly Trent Lott doesn't let the Senate go home.

"That stuff wouldn't bother Bill Clinton," he continues, "because—and I mean this as a compliment—his life is total confusion all the time. But she's more like an appellate lawyer, having structured arguments in structured ways. Which is fine in normal life. But not in the Senate."

Clinton is bending over backward to make it clear that she doesn't expect any special treatment. In spite of what Judd Gregg says, she has taken pains to wear her three-man Secret Service entourage as unostentatiously as possible: They don't accompany her on the Senate floor; they don't cling too closely in the halls. She chats easily with her colleagues. (On the floor, she's a furious gesticulator.) And already, she has a reputation for being one of the best female senators to work for. (Though the competition isn't stiff. They're a difficult lot.)

But some of Hillary's peers, like Ben Nighthorse Campbell, still can't help wondering how certain questions of protocol will be resolved. Campbell is on the Helsinki Commission with Hillary. The other day, he realized he had no idea what'll happen when they take their first trip overseas.

"Usually, there's a special section of the plane, a private stateroom, for the chairman," he explains. "And then another section with reserved seats for senior senators—it has tables and headphones and even cots for sleeping. And then the freshmen sit in the back, in regular coach seats, with the staff."

He throws up his hands. "The old bulls, they're not used to being upstaged. But if she gets special seating with her Secret Service people, I don't know how they'll take to it. Then again . . . " He hesitates. "Well, it's a little awkward to have the ex-First Lady in the back, with her knees up by her chin, all cramped up, after traveling on Air Force One. Don'tcha think?"

Back in the White House, Clinton could also keep the media at arm's length. But the Capitol provides its press corps with uncommon access to elected officials. Reporters can trap Hillary outside her office in the Russell Building, in the private subway that takes her from Russell to the Capitol, and even right off the Senate floor. The public has almost as much access, and people pretty much stop her every ten feet or so—to take pictures, to say hello, to talk about issues of concern to them.

In one of its cattier moments, the *Washington Times* recently conjectured that Hillary looks worse in photographs these days because she lost her stylist when she left the White House. But I doubt that's the case. I think the reason is because her time is less stage-managed now than it was in the past. Today, there are plenty of random opportunities to catch Clinton staring unbecomingly into space or looking harried as she flies through the halls.

"She's gotta get used to bags under her eyes, her makeup coming off," sighs Congresswoman Carolyn Maloney, the Democrat who represents the East Side. "My constituents have seen me that way. Because I tell you, you spend four hours at these hearings, you have eighteen-hour days, you're running to meetings . . . that's how you *look*."

Two weeks ago, I revisited some of Hillary's biggest skeptics. Predictably, they were singing a different tune. Pardon hearings seem much less interesting to them, for one thing. "Senator Clinton's on my subcommittee," said Hutchinson, who doubtless has seen her smile by now. "I've got to work with her every day. There's just . . . " He stammered. "I'm with President Bush: Just let it go away."

Gregg, presumably, found a way to approach her, in spite of her Secret Service cadre. "This is a person I deal with," he said. "Because when I do business on the Senate floor, I need 51 votes, or 61 votes, and she's certainly one of them. We're negotiating on a couple things right now—I hope to have her join myself and Senator Carper on the charter-school bill."

"Getting to know somebody on a human level can eliminate a lot of misconceptions." That's Hillary herself talking. I caught up with her that day, too, briefly, as she was making her way back to her office after a vote. "I feel that a lot of my colleagues are really—not only polite, but interested in what I really believe in and what kind of senator I'll be. And I think that's good." As we headed toward the subway, four teenage girls stopped her and started to squeal.

"Oh, Mrs. Clinton! Can we take your picture?"

"Sure, though I'm late—"

"Please?"

One nestled herself under the senator's arm. *Flash.*

"Thanks!"

"Bye, girls. Thanks, thanks." We missed the subway.

"Shoot." We started to walk down the long, underground corridor toward her office building.

"You know what's surprising?" she continued. "How much goes on at one time." She started recounting a harrowing day when she had to attend two committee markups simultaneously.

"But there's a lot of humorous asides that kind of cut the tension and keep people from taking any of this personally," she said. "Senator Lott came up to me on the floor the other day and said, 'What is it about our *hair?* Why is it that your hair and my hair draw all this attention?'" She gave a weary smile. Lightning didn't strike; she's a senator now. "I suggested we start a hair caucus."

How Jeffords Got Away

Douglas Waller
with reporting by Matthew Cooper, John Dickerson and Karen Tumulty

Time | June 4, 2001

In late May 2001, one story dominated the news: The rumor that Senator Jim Jeffords of Vermont (nicknamed "Jeezum Jim" for his straight-arrow aversion to profanity), was about to quit the Republican Party and declare himself an independent. The famously quirky Jeffords—who holds a black belt in tae kwon do and once lived out of a van—had apparently grown tired of being rejected by his fellow Republicans, and was thinking of jumping ship.

In and of itself, his threatened defection wasn't that earth-shattering—registered independents do consitutute Vermont's largest political bloc, after all. But with the Senate divided 50-50, the G.O.P. held power by the slim margin of veep Dick Cheney's tie-breaking vote. Jeffords' defection would shift the balance to 50–49 in favor of the Democrats, giving them control of the Senate and the committee chairmanships that went with it. Here, Time *magazine reveals the inside dope on the reluctant Vermonter's fateful decision. . . .*

The defection of Jim Jeffords may be remembered as one of the most successful covert operations in American political history, with Democratic leader Tom Daschle as the mastermind and Jeffords as the spy who came in from the cold. But when Jeffords helped blow his own cover, the scene was like something out of *Ally McBeal.* By last Tuesday morning, rumors had been swirling for days that the Vermont senator was thinking about leaving the Republican Party. That morning Jeffords stood in a rest room off the Senate floor staring at his haggard face in the mirror.

Republican Senator Pat Roberts sidled up to him at the next sink. "Jim, how you doing?" Roberts asked. Jeffords just shook his head.

"Well, I hope some of the stories I've been hearing are not accurate," said Roberts, trying to get Jeffords to open up.

"I've got to do what's in my heart and mind," Jeffords replied, and that's all he would say. He walked out. But Roberts knew what it meant. He found majority leader Trent Lott and warned him that "it's pretty doggone serious." Lott had been getting similar reports and sounded the alarm to the White House and the Senate's G.O.P. leadership. But he was too late. The defector had already slipped past the gate.

White House aides were dumbfounded. "The horizon was clear; there were no clouds," says one. "No one saw it, and then it poured." As Republicans from Bush to Dick Cheney to party hacks in Vermont tried everything they could think of to lure Jeffords back, Daschle and his top lieutenant, minority whip Harry Reid, sat in their offices hiding broad grins from the rest of the world. They knew something else that Lott was in the dark about. The Jeffords deal had been practically sealed a full week before. In fact, for almost a month, Daschle and Reid had conducted their secret negotiations under Lott's nose, with the Republican leader clueless that he was the victim of a silent, slow-motion fleecing.

The recruitment of Jim Jeffords had no code names, no dead drops, no encrypted communications, but it followed all the rules of a classic CIA operation. Democrats had targeted Jeffords as a possible party switcher practically from the day he came to Congress 26 years ago. Daschle, a former Air Force intelligence officer, knew that spymasters don't have a chance of bagging a high-value defector unless he is eager to defect. Even then, he has to be slowly and carefully cultivated. By last month, Jeffords seemed ready to come over. His disenchantment with the Republican Party had been building for months.

Moderates don't survive in the Republican Party without a thick skin. Over the years, the proud, laconic Jeffords had endured countless arm twistings, cold shoulders and petty slights for taking stands at odds with his party— against Ronald Reagan's 1981 tax cut and Clarence Thomas' Supreme Court nomination, for the Clintons' health-care reform, minimum-wage hikes and more money for the National Endowment for the Arts. But by last year, the hostility had begun to wear him down. He was chairman of the Health, Education, Labor and Pensions Committee, a post that could be powerful in promoting his passion for schools, but conservative G.O.P. upstarts on the panel, such as New Hampshire Senator Judd Gregg, were constantly maneuvering to undercut Jeffords' authority, doing things like convening private meetings of the committee's Republicans and not inviting him. Jeffords complained to Lott, but the majority leader didn't rein in the right-wingers.

When Bush was elected President, Jeffords hoped that this "new kind of Republican," as the Texan liked to call himself, was actually an old kind of Republican—a closet progressive in the mold of Nelson Rockefeller. Jeffords soon realized Bush was nothing of the kind, as the president catered to his Republican base by appointing such right-wingers as John Ashcroft as Attorney General and Gale Norton as Interior Secretary. By January, Jeffords was no longer ignoring the casual entreaties that came from the other side. At that point, Daschle, Reid and other Democrats made them half jokingly to keep things low key, even though they were hungry for a defector to break the fifty-fifty split in the Senate.

Jeffords began withdrawing from his Republican colleagues and finding Democratic friends more appealing. Some of the "Mod Squad"—moderate G.O.P. Senators Olympia Snowe, Lincoln Chafee, Susan Collins and Arlen Specter—found Jeffords increasingly quiet at the private lunches they held each week. After Senator Hillary Clinton sat down from delivering an impassioned floor speech about education funding, Jeffords stopped at her desk. "I really agree with you," he said. "We've got to fight harder, so don't get discouraged." But Jeffords was becoming gloomy.

"The past couple of months just brought everything into focus," he told *Time*. In April, his budget negotiations with Lott and the White House about boosting education money for disabled students ended in a bitter stalemate. The White House was furious with him. Jeffords wasn't satisfied with the Administration's proposals, and Bush aides felt that Jeffords backed away every time they were ready to nail down a compromise. Lott was irritated as well. He had fended off conservatives who wanted to steal Jeffords' chairmanship, and put him on the prestigious Finance Committee. Lott had even invited Jeffords into the Singing Senators vocal quartet. Yet all he seemed to get from Jeffords was obstinacy.

Ultimately, Republicans stripped other school funds from the budget. Jeffords knew more feuds were coming over the environment, Bush's pro-drilling energy policy, health care and conservative nominees to the Supreme Court. On a Friday afternoon after most Senators headed back to their home states, Jeffords slipped into Connecticut Democratic Senator Chris Dodd's office and began venting. "This doesn't seem to be working," he confided. Education "is the biggest thing for me. But I'm not sure what to do from here."

Dodd smiled and said softly, "Look, Jim, there's room for you over here." "Hmm," Jeffords answered—first mulling the possibility, then catching himself. "Gee, I would never be a Democrat." Maybe an independent, he said, but not a Democrat. Dodd smiled and didn't push.

But the White House and Senate Republicans were pushing, in ways they would come to regret. Angry over Jeffords' opposition to Bush's $1.6 trillion tax-cut plan, Bush aides didn't invite him to a White House ceremony honoring a Vermont teacher, a minor slight of the kind Jeffords had grown used to over the years. Others were more serious. The Administration began hinting that a program aiding Vermont dairy farmers might be in jeopardy. Jeffords was getting the silent treatment in the Finance Committee, and Gregg announced that he would be "spearheading" the education bill for the G.O.P.

On the prowl for disgruntled Republicans, Reid thought Chafee was the ripest target. But after a chance encounter with Jeffords in April, Reid became convinced Jeffords would bolt. Daschle was skeptical but put Reid in charge of the recruitment. Reid and Jeffords had similar personalities— taciturn, press shy, not given to windy speeches in public or private. Reid knew Jeffords hated confrontation and horse trading, so he stuck to high principles in their conversations and never, ever asked him directly to defect. "The issues you stand for are the ones we believe in in the Democratic Party," Reid told him. "Jim, this is beyond you and me. This is for the country." But early on, sources say, Reid dangled the possibility that Jeffords could chair the Environment and Public Works Committee under Democratic rule. Jeffords has denied making such a deal.

Everyone leaks on Capitol Hill, but the two men somehow managed to keep their talks secret. Reid told only one top aide about them. Sometimes the two lawmakers ducked into a private office; at other times, figuring the best place to hide was in plain sight, they talked on the Senate floor with colleagues milling about and reporters watching from the press gallery above. On Tuesday morning, May 15, Daschle, Reid and Jeffords slipped away to Jeffords' Capitol hideaway near the Senate press gallery to negotiate the offer. "Here's what we can do for you if you decide to put us in the majority," Daschle said. The Vermonter was ready to jump but had to discuss the decision with family and close friends. By Friday night, CNN was reporting rumors that Jeffords was mulling a switch. Daschle panicked; Bush would surely helicopter Jeffords to Camp David for a weekend charm blitz that could unravel the deal. But Jeffords' allies and Vermont G.O.P. officials assured the president's people that there was nothing to the report.

The G.O.P. was sorely misinformed. Last Monday night on the Senate floor, during a long debate about tax cuts, Jeffords told Olympia Snowe that he was seriously considering switching. Snowe placed a frantic call to White House chief of staff Andrew Card, but Card had already gone home. Snowe left a message saying the matter was "sensitive and urgent." She tried Card again in the morning, but his aides said he wouldn't be available until noon.

Interrupt him now, Snowe demanded, "even if he's in with the president." Card phoned back minutes later, and the White House finally knew.

The cement was hardening by the time Cheney huddled with Jeffords around midday on Tuesday in the vice president's ceremonial office off the Senate floor. The meeting did not go well. Sources say Jeffords told Cheney the Democrats had offered him a chairmanship. The vice president walked Jeffords through the ramifications of a defection but had no answers for his complaints. "You better talk to him," Cheney told Bush.

On Tuesday afternoon, Jeffords walked into the Oval Office. Bush summoned all his charm. "I'd like you to stay in our party," he pleaded. Has the White House done anything to push you out? No, Jeffords replied politely, but the party is ignoring the moderates. On important issues like education and the environment, conservatives are running the show, Jeffords warned, and if Bush didn't move to the center, he would be a one-term President. "I hear you, I hear you," Bush answered. Jeffords promised to ponder, but Bush suspected the decision had been made. "I don't think I was very persuasive," the president told Lott afterward.

On Wednesday morning, half a dozen G.O.P. colleagues sat Jeffords down in a room off the Senate floor for a last stab at changing his mind. "Jim, do you really believe you can further your dreams and aspirations by doing this?" Senator Chuck Hagel asked plaintively. "We can fix this. Give us a chance." Jeffords agreed only to meet later that day. When they reconvened at 4:15, the senators had a sweet offer for him. The White House promised more money for education, Lott would give him a seat at the Senate leadership table as the moderates' representative, and Jeffords could chair the Health and Education Committee for as long as he wanted. For the rest of the 90-minute session, the arguments got personal. Hundreds of G.O.P. staff members would be fired if the Democrats took control. Senators who had worked long and hard to become committee chairmen would have the prize yanked away. Senator Charles Grassley, who had chaired the Finance Committee for just four months, was in tears.

Jeffords was moved. "That's the worst emotional experience I've been through," he told *Time*. "These are all wonderful friends of mine. They were frustrated, as I had been over the years, but they nevertheless wanted to stay with the party." Wait a few days, the senators begged, and make this decision after a good night's rest.

But Jeffords had committed to holding a press conference the next day in Vermont. On the flight home that evening, he decided once and for all to become an independent and vote with the Democrats, giving them control of the Senate. "I became a Republican not because I was born into the party but because of the kind of fundamental principles Republicans stood for—moderation, tolerance, fiscal responsibility," he told the press in Montpelier the next day. "Our party was the party of Lincoln," but conservatives now dominate it, so "it has become a struggle for our leaders to deal with me and for me to deal with them."

As Jeffords made his announcement, Air Force One was streaking west to Cleveland, where Bush was scheduled to promote his faith-based-charities initiative. Stewards passed out earphones so that the Congressmen and Senators on board could hear a CNN audio feed of Jeffords' press conference. Aides say Bush didn't bother to listen to the broadcast. That may not have been wise. Look what happened the last time he ignored Jeffords.

The Centrist Does Not Hold
Margaret Carlson

Time | June 4, 2001

Every event of note in Washington gets closely scrutinized for its underlying political meaning. In the following article, Time columnist Margaret Carlson suggests that Jim Jeffords' defection may be an indication that the Bush administration is showing its true colors. . . .

Isn't it amazing how one low-key defector put the lie to the "new" G.O.P.?

In the eyes of Washington, Senator Jim Jeffords took on a whole new identity last week. Switching parties is a big deal here, akin to a sex-change operation. But in Vermont, the Jeffords of this week seems little different from last week's—independent, pro-tree, pro-choice, pro-special ed. In the eyes of the country, it's George Bush's identity—consummate professional, protean charmer, reasonable conservative—that has become mottled. Bush campaigned as an adult who would restore not only honor but also professionalism to the White House. No all-night sessions strewn with pizza boxes. He would institute appropriate dress, muted cell phones and meetings that started—and ended—on time.

So how did this smooth Bush operation lose Jeffords? First, by its simple failure to recognize that Bush needed him more than he needed Bush. Grownups know that little things matter (Newt Gingrich shut down the government when he didn't like his seat on Air Force One) and that relationships are based on respect and reciprocity. Enamored of the corporate model, the Bushies treated Jeffords like some fungible account executive who could be replaced at will instead of recognizing that in a fifty-fifty Senate, every senator is king. White House staff rarely saved Jeffords a seat at the table, and even tried to end-run him on the committee he chaired. He wasn't invited to a routine Rose Garden ceremony for a Vermonter named Teacher of the Year, and was reportedly denied his ration of West Wing tour passes. If it was just an oversight (their explanation), they hardly look like management geniuses. If it was a hamhanded snub (everyone else's explanation), it showed how petty they could be.

Even in middle age, White House aides can be full of themselves. But where was the mythical Bush charm, so potent it tamed the entire Texas legislature? In the Oval Office—the most seductive room on earth—with the stakes as high as they get, Bush couldn't persuade the senator to stay with the party the Jeffords family had thrived in for three generations. It turns out that Bush reserves his charm for those who agree with him or are outright opponents. Wooing those who, by rights, should already be under your thumb looks wimpish. For them, how about the silent treatment or a bust in the chops? Thus Vernon Jordan gets a nickname (V.J.), whereas Jeffords barely gets a hello. Not for Jeffords a dinner in the private quarters or one of those coveted invitations to dine on chicken cacciatore and see the latest movie. Forget a call to the ranch.

In six months, Democrats hadn't been able to define Bush as bent on satisfying his right wing at the cost of the center. Jeffords did that in one press conference. The debate shifted overnight to whether Bush could continue to govern from the right. Already, moderates are getting more attention: John McCain was invited for dinner, Olympia Snowe got her calls returned, Arlen Specter got a leadership post.

Bush aides tried to dress Jeffords in a Yankee clown suit, portraying him as addled from living among oddballs fond of natural fibers, gay marriage and socially-conscious ice cream.

"It's difficult to address all the quirks of someone who is self-described quirky, and I mean that with all respect," Karen Hughes said, adding, "There's something funny there." Aides described Jeffords, who has never met a camera he would preen for or a cheap shot he would take, as a powermonger seduced by Democrats with the promise of a committee chairmanship. This, although Republicans last week were offering to waive Senate rules and make him chair for life of the Education Committee if only he would.

Bush values most that which he can finesse. At Yale's commencement, the charming C student boasted (again) of winning the presidency despite napping through college. What charming thing could Bush say to a man in his seventh decade who hailed from the greatest generation of Republicans and wasn't leaving because of "something funny" but for something principled? Finding a way to work with those like Jeffords, who saw him ruling from the right when he had promised to govern from the middle, would have taken the kind of effort Bush is loath to expend. The White House expressed no remorse. And on Wednesday, when Jeffords was with his colleagues and was about to go it alone, the eyes of all in the ceremonial room off the Senate floor filled with tears; not only would they be losing the majority, but they would be losing a friend. Jeffords is a serious man. It's why he got away.

What Bush Has to Learn

Howard Fineman,
with Martha Brant, T. Trent Gegax, Matt Bai, and Michael Isikoff

Newsweek | June 4, 2001

So—what should the Bush administration have done to try and placate Senator Jeffords? Or more to the point, how do they pick up the pieces and move forward? Howard Fineman and the political staff of Newsweek *offer the fledgling president some free advice. . . .*

It was the kind of invitation Andy Card probably should have issued earlier. Last Monday the White House chief of staff called Senator John McCain. Would he like to dine—alone—with the president the following Thursday? McCain accepted. But by Wednesday the world had changed: Senator Jim

Jeffords was leaving the Republican Party. McCain called Card back. Since the Senate would be working late on Thursday, the senator said, shouldn't they reschedule? Yes, Card agreed, it would be too hectic. But there were other, unspoken, reasons for the postponement. McCain didn't want to look like a prop in an emergency post-Jeffords outreach program, or like the next man about to leave the G.O.P. He's not—at least not yet. As for Card, he didn't want Bush to look desperate. He's not—at least not yet.

As governor of Texas, George W. Bush managed to become the master of all he surveyed. But Jeffords' departure dramatized a message the president has yet to hear and seems not to want to accept: Washington isn't Austin, and he isn't LBJ. In fact, Bush isn't even Tony Soprano. He can't afford to be smug or arrogant or dictatorial—or caught by surprise, as he was by Jeffords. The capital's Democrats are far more powerful, shrewd and well funded than the ones in Texas, and Republicans in D.C. aren't all of a predictably conservative stripe. The media are omnipresent and harder to tame, and interest groups are more massive and entrenched. There are far more people to be stroked and far less time to do it. Even a president can't slow the driving pace of the place.

Are there lessons to be learned from the loss of Jeffords? Inside the White House, they tend to think not. They point out that the president got his big tax cut—the centerpiece of his campaign agenda—as well as the biggest increase in education funding the House has approved in 36 years. They put Jeffords' departure down to a mixture of liberalism and personal ambition, not a failure of attention. "If the president had reached out any more, his arms would have fallen off," said a senior White House aide. Aides insist legislative strategy will change little. Handling the Senate, after all, is always like herding cats. "It's a disappointment to everybody, sure," said a top aide, "but nothing changes the fact that he is the president, and he will lead the way he was elected to lead."

Still, with the relatively easy wins behind him—and the wily Senator Tom Daschle confronting him—the president must do what he's reluctant to do: become adept at the Washington inside game. Ironically, he now must dig back into his own family roots, mimicking the dealmaking, compromising career of his own Yankee father, who thrived on Hill gossip and owned a fan-jet-size Rolodex of Washington contacts. It's a pattern that the Texas-bred Bush the Younger had hoped to avoid—because it cost his father a secure conservative base. But 43 may now be destined to repeat it. At least that's the sum of the advice from wise guys busy examining what (and who) went wrong, and how Bush can do better. For starters, everyone agrees he has to work nights and weekends. The rest of their collective wisdom:

Get better intel. Bush shouldn't have been blindsided by Jeffords. "This was a long process, and the scuttlebutt was around for weeks," said Democratic Senator Chris Dodd. Democrats began a systematic effort to woo Republican moderates more than a month ago. Democratic elders, from Daschle to Ted Kennedy to Dodd, huddled privately with Jeffords, McCain and Senator Lincoln Chafee. McCain was invited to what he thought was a health-care meeting with Kennedy, who it turned out wanted to ask him to become a Democrat. A month ago Vice President Dick Cheney's own legislative liaison got wind of Jeffords' terminal displeasure, and passed on the info. But no one acted on it—and Bush didn't get the word until last Tuesday, well after the first published hints surfaced in Vermont.

Expand the charm circle. It's easy to be ingratiating in your own fraternity. Bush, a frat president at Yale, is good at it. His challenge now is to befriend the quirky and uncool, for, as one of his aides says, the Senate is "100 kings." Jeffords is a lost cause, but opportunities remain. One is Senator Olympia Snowe of Maine, who was close to Bush the Elder, but she doesn't have regular conversations with the current president. "She could help Bush a lot," said one Democratic colleague. "She's smart and wired. He should be talking to her all the time." Indeed, it was Snowe who warned Card that Jeffords was about to quit the party. Maybe Bush is paying more attention: he is scheduled to have dinner soon after the recess with Senator Chafee.

All politics is personal. LBJ made it his business to know every whim and want of his allies and enemies. The Bush White House produces statistics that show that the president has "met" with a record number of legislators. But the Hill remains largely terra incognita to him. It may be more important to reach out to enemies than friends. McCain's aides were amused when the White House called to ask if McCain would like to smoke cigars after the postponed dinner. The senator is one of the Hill's leading anti-tobacco crusaders, and hasn't touched the stuff himself in decades.

Don't count on Cheney. The vice president tends to be more comfortable in the role of tough-guy enforcer than favor-dispensing father confessor. G.O.P. moderates call his office just off the Senate floor the "Torture Chamber." "When you get called in there it means you're going to get your arm twisted," said one G.O.P. senator. Cheney, who learned a bare-knuckle style as a member of an oppressed G.O.P. minority in the House, simply isn't good at schmoozing with the enemy. He and Senator Joe Lieberman played to good reviews, and met after the Florida finale to exchange good wishes. But the veep hasn't called since, sources close to the senator say.

Rein in Rove. In public, Karl Rove, the president's political guru-for-life, obliquely questioned whether Jeffords' motive was a better chairmanship. Privately, other G.O.P. insiders trash the senator as an unreliable hypocrite. Rove's conservative allies in the Americans for Tax Justice, meanwhile, will launch a jihad against the New England Dairy Compact. It's a "stupid little compact," says ATJ director Grover Norquist. G.O.P. moderates plead for the White House to lay off, or risk offending others of their number. "That kind of thing is not going to be helpful," said Snowe. Indeed, the First Father was so upset by Jeffords' decision that he privately asked another Vermont friend, former senator Robert Stafford, to make a last-minute plea to their mutual old friend.

Learn to love the chaos. Bush and his closest aides—Rove and counselor Karen Hughes—are control freaks. They believe above all in loyalty and long-term planning. Bush's initial legislative agenda was, in effect, written in Austin in 1999, when Bush assembled his campaign platform in a series of meetings with issue advisers. But that plan has lost much of its value now, like the scripted plays for the opening drive of a football game. "Party loyalty" is becoming an oxymoron, as each new issue draws a new coalition of support. Now Bush has to go with the flow, looking for the best-available deals on issues such as the patient's bill of rights. The White House must begin following Bush's own be-humble dictum. "If you hear it from one you hear it from 30 guys up here," said Dodd, the Democratic son of a senator and a student of the Hill game. "They come off as arrogant in the extreme."

Look for the silver lining. Some White House advisers see benefit in the Senate's switch to Democratic control. They ruefully recall how the G.O.P. takeover in the House in 1994 drove Bill Clinton to the middle on issues such as welfare reform—and helped get him re-elected in 1996. Now, says one adviser, Bush will "have to be more moderate. On the environment, on his judges. This frees him up from the more conservative wing. In the end, it'll be a good thing." In other words, by acting more like his father Bush may win the second term his father never could.

Bush's Trillions
Nicholas Lemann

The New Yorker | February 19 & 26, 2001

Over the years, The New Yorker *magazine has produced some of the nation's most insightful political reporting. In the following pair of articles, staff writer Nicholas Lemann looks at the first year of George W. Bush's presidency at two very different stages: Early in 2001, as Bush was poised to push through his big tax cut; and again in the lazy, ranch-vacation days of late summer, just before the thunder clap of September 11.*

In this first selection, Lemann reveals how the Bush agenda fits in very neatly with the Republicans' longterm strategy. . . .

A few weeks ago in Washington, I went to see a very junior Republican congressman from South Carolina named Jim DeMint, who, I'd been told, is considered a comer in the party. (He'd better make his move quickly, because he just started his second term and he has promised to step down after three.) DeMint, a polished, handsome man who was previously in the marketing business, was practically on fire about a theory he has developed, which is that the country—and the Republican Party in particular— is facing a decisive moment.

"I think we've got a major crisis in democracy," DeMint said, in the slightly abashed tone of an amiable man who is expressing a concern that he knows may sound exaggerated, but, damn it, that was how he saw things. "We assume that voters will restrain the growth of government because it becomes burdensome to them personally. But today fewer and fewer people pay taxes, and more and more are dependent on government, so the politician who promises the most from government is likely to win. Every day, the Republican Party is losing constituents, because every day more people can vote themselves more benefits without paying for it. The tax code will destroy democracy, by putting us in a position where most voters don't pay for government."

Usually, when people talk about "dependency" in connection with government, they're talking about welfare payments to poor people. DeMint had something more in mind—the entire bargain between state and citizen. Income taxation, he said, has been shifting, so that a relatively small number of people at the very top pay for much of government, while middle-class benefits, like old-age pensions, health care, and public schooling, have become ever more generous. Soon, unless something is done, most people will have no reason not to keep voting for more government, because they won't be paying for it. And that will be dangerous for the Republicans. "The Reagan message"—tax cuts—"won't work anymore, because the number of people dependent on government has risen dramatically," DeMint said. "This presidential election was the last chance to salvage our freedom."

Later, DeMint sent me a lot of statistics supporting his ideas, as well as a four-color printout of a PowerPoint presentation called "Is America Losing Its Freedom?," which he had recently delivered to a group of congressional Republicans. One chart showed that in 1986 the wealthiest one percent had begun paying more in individual income tax than the bottom seventy-five percent, and that by 1998 the share of the one percent had risen to approximately double the share of the seventy-five percent.

DeMint's theory has some obvious flaws. Social Security and Medicare taxes, which are paid much more evenly by all workers, aren't in his calculations. Still, there is definitely something to it. Until Bill Clinton became President, the electorate was assumed to be so exquisitely sensitive to federal taxation that, if you were a national politician, to raise taxes, or even to entertain the possibility publicly, was to perish. A prime example was the first President Bush, who was elected on a promise never to raise taxes, delivered in language lifted from action-adventure movies, and was then defeated because he broke it.

Clinton altered the social compact. If you divide the country into fifths by income, during his presidency the federal tax rate, and the share of taxes paid, went up substantially for the top fifth, especially for the top one percent, and down for the other four-fifths. Clinton didn't take from the rich and give to the poor, he took from the rich and gave to the broad middle class. He raised the top income-tax rate from 31 percent to 39.6, and he cut taxes for working people through measures like the child credit and the earned-income-tax credit, which come out to about twenty billion dollars and thirty billion dollars a year, respectively. The top one percent now pay about a quarter of all federal taxes, and the top five percent about two fifths. (The reason these fortunate folks haven't been more up in arms about their taxes increasing is that during the Clinton years their incomes rose much more than their taxes did.) "This progressive trend is probably one reason most of the public seems so indifferent to G.O.P. calls for big tax cuts," Robert McIntyre, Washington's leading liberal tax expert, wrote last summer—exactly Jim DeMint's position. Clinton also created the impression that, if you're middle class, the government, in return for your taxes, will give you what you need—family leave, more police officers and teachers—instead of giving your hard-earned money away to poor people. DeMint is right. Clinton moved most Americans in the direction of thinking of government more as a giver of benefits and less as a taker of taxes. That is not good for the Republican Party.

When a new president from a different party takes office, he has an opportunity to alter the political correlation of forces in the United States by rearranging what government does. If this doesn't begin to happen in the first six months of the new administration, it probably won't happen at all. Right now, President George W. Bush has a much better opportunity than you'd expect—given his nonexistent margin of victory, his inexperience, and his soothing, unambitious campaign rhetoric—to remake the Republican Party in national politics.

Social Security, the biggest federal program, makes for a good example. From a Republican point of view, an ideal relationship between the government and the people might look like this: Social Security, although it is packaged as insurance, is really a welfare program; workers pay taxes to the government, which sends the money on to retirees. Instead, workers could have individual retirement accounts, whose managers they could designate themselves. Then they would become members of what conservatives like to call "the investor class," which is to say that, as they enter senior-citizenhood, they would care more about how the markets are doing than about the level of government benefits. As John Goodman, the head of a conservative think tank in Dallas and an occasional adviser to Bush over the last few years, puts it, "They would tend to resist government actions that reduce the value of their investments."

The same principle of loosening the bond between voters and government could be applied elsewhere. In the case of the second-biggest program, Medicare, the government could give states a lump sum that people could use to buy private health insurance. Public education could be financed more through individual vouchers and less through direct government support of schools. The tax system could be made less progressive, with fewer brackets, so that the non-rich would bear a greater share of the burden and would therefore begin to think of government programs, with newly awakened suspicion, as costing them money. A program of tax cuts stretching out over many years would make it more difficult for the Democrats to launch new programs that would increase voters' loyalty to them. All these changes would have the collateral benefit of strengthening Republican interest groups, like stockbrokers, and weakening Democratic interest groups, like public-employees' unions.

Bringing this conservative dream world into being is exceedingly tricky. The main services that government provides in America—Social Security, Medicare, and public schooling—have tens of millions of high-voter-turnout beneficiaries, so a proposal to alter them fundamentally is a political risk. For a candidate who was rarely very far ahead in the polls, Bush was unusually willing to take a first poke at these basic provisions of American governance. During the presidential campaign, he proposed creating individual retirement accounts in Social Security, a federal school-voucher program, and a big, across-the-board, ten-year tax cut. The Gore campaign was practically gleeful about these positions, because of their presumed unpopularity. But now Bush, having taken them and having (barely) survived, has some room to maneuver in the direction of building up his party's strength for the long term.

The main event in Washington this year is going to be Bush's tax cut. If it passes, it will be more significant than any single piece of legislation that Clinton was able to achieve in eight years. Clinton's health-care plan, which was even more ambitious, would have moved the polity strongly in a Democratic direction by creating a major new middle-class-benefit program; the Bush tax cut could have an effect of similar magnitude, but one that would be helpful to the Republicans.

While Bush was tied up for the months of November and December with the post-election controversy, he was also getting a couple of enormously lucky breaks. When the economy slowed down over the holidays, it created a rationale for cutting taxes which he hadn't used during the campaign: the economy needed goosing. At the same time, the Office of Management and Budget and the Congressional Budget Office were gift-wrapping a wonderful present for Bush: projections, now public, that show the federal-budget surplus to be hundreds of billions of dollars bigger than everybody thought. Another, less visible break was that Election Day exit polls, which circulated widely among Democrats in Congress, showed voters favoring across-the-board tax cuts rather than cuts aimed at lower-to-middle-income people. This time last year, Bush's tax-cut proposal looked like bothersome baggage, something to which he had committed himself in anticipation of a strong challenge from the billionaire flat-taxer Steve Forbes. Al Gore was going to use it against him. Today, all Washington, from Alan Greenspan on down, is for a deep tax cut.

During the first working week of the Bush administration, I went to see Senator Kent Conrad, of North Dakota, who has just become the ranking Democrat on the Senate Budget Committee. The size of Bush's tax cut will probably be decided in a budget resolution, which means that Conrad's committee will be the place where its fate is determined. What Conrad thinks matters a lot.

Conrad, a careful, meticulous man who spent most of his early career working in the North Dakota Tax Department, handed me a printout of a presentation called "Budget Surplus Considerations" (presentation software seems to have become the lingua franca of the United States Congress), and led me through it. The Senate Budget Committee staff had tentatively set the surplus through the year 2011 at $5.7 trillion. But if you took out estimates of the portions that ought to go into the Social Security and Medicare trust funds the number would come down to $2.6 trillion. Then if you subtracted to account for the passage of a few seemingly inevitable legislative items, such as a new prescription-drug benefit, you'd be down to $2 trillion.

That was page 1 of the presentation. On page 2, Conrad reestimated the cost of Bush's tax cut, to account for various items that had been too low, and came up with $2.2 trillion—ahead of Bush's own estimate of $1.6 trillion, and more than the surplus as Conrad figured it, in other words. Page 3 was labelled "Possible Compromise." It suggested setting aside the portions of the surplus meant for Social Security and Medicare and dividing the remainder into three portions, each worth eight hundred and fifty billion dollars: a tax cut, a series of new domestic programs, and a "strategic reserve" in case the federal-budget situation became less rosy, which would happen quickly if there was a recession. The new, higher budget-surplus projections assume that, starting next year, the economy will grow at a rate of more than three percent a year over the next decade. In the last quarter of last year, it grew at a rate of only 1.4 percent.

"Every indication is that Bush will push hard for his full proposal," Conrad said. "It's a mistake. It's a serious mistake. It's a very serious constraint on the federal government, because there is very little money left over: little for Social Security, nothing for other domestic programs, nothing as a hedge. He's used up all the money. There is nothing left for other priorities. It just doesn't make sense to put all our eggs in one basket that way."

Fine, but isn't the news here not that Kent Conrad thinks the Bush tax cut is irresponsibly large but that he is now in favor of an eight-hundred-and-fifty-billion-dollar tax cut? Conrad even said that he was willing to see the top rate of 39.6 percent come down. In 1999, just after the federal budget surplus had materialized, most Democrats on Capitol Hill were willing to support tax cuts in the range of three hundred billion dollars over ten years. Last year, Gore got only as high as five hundred billion. Now, just three months after Election Day, the Democrats have gone up by well over fifty percent. The idea of making the tax cut retroactive to the beginning of the year, so that people's pay checks will get a little bigger as soon as the bill passes, began floating around Washington after the election. That was not something that Bush had proposed during the campaign, but early this month he endorsed it.

When Bush was governor of Texas, his style was to become buddies with the leaders of the legislature and to compromise on his proposals if they told him it was necessary. (Nonetheless, he wound up cutting taxes so much that the Texas legislature will be spending most of its 2001 session figuring out how to avoid a budget deficit.) He was good at getting part of what he wanted and declaring victory. A similar outcome is the most likely in Washington this year. Bush is already doing well in the friendship-with-legislators department. He can lower the range of his tax-cut proposal to a figure closer to Kent Conrad's and still be able to say, accurately, that he delivered the biggest tax cut since Ronald Reagan's, in 1981—and his, unlike Reagan's, won't instantly produce big deficits. He is the first Republican president since Eisenhower to have control in both houses of Congress. He seems to be in an awfully good position.

A little while after I met with Kent Conrad, I spoke on the phone with Karl Rove, who has been the chief political strategist for Bush's entire career in elected office. Obviously, Rove was thinking past the tax cut, to a whole first-year program for Bush that could strengthen the Republican Party considerably. "Take a look at our agenda," Rove said. "Education. This year, we picked up seven points in the suburbs over '96. Our education plan allows us to make further gains in the suburbs. It will also allow us to make gains with Hispanics and African-Americans. The tax cuts will make the economy grow. As people do better, they start voting like Republicans— unless they have too much education and vote Democratic, which proves there can be too much of a good thing. Look at the course of the campaign. There's a lot of data. If you give people the choice between a tax cut and more government services, they'll choose the tax cut. The more Bush talked about an across-the-board cut, the more support for it grew. People do have a desire for basic services—schools, helping the less fortunate—but not for unrestricted government."

Rove can't show too many cards right now, but it's easy to imagine Bush's next few moves. With a little skill, Bush can work his way around the most unpopular parts of the Republican agenda, as Clinton was able to do with the most unpopular parts of the Democratic agenda. Bush can signal the right-to-life movement, through language and appointments and minor initiatives, that he is on its side, without having to speak personally on the subject or propose anything significant. Education vouchers, which, according to polls, are not popular in the all-important big-city suburbs, where almost all kids go to public school, are contained in Bush's educa- tion proposal, but members of the administration, including Bush himself, in his first Saturday radio address, have been signalling that they might be willing to drop vouchers in the negotiations over the bill. I've heard that Bush has also said this privately to Democrats in Congress. Without vouchers, yearly testing in the basic subjects would be left as the most obvious fea- ture of the bill, which will alienate teachers (but they're Democrats anyway) and may win over suburban parents. On Social Security, Bush can put off—at least until after the tax cut—another potentially explosive issue by appointing a commission to draft a plan for individual private accounts, rather than immediately proposing legislation. (Rove put this forward as a likely scenario.)

Bush can try to provide the one new government service that the public most wants, a prescription-drug benefit, through private insurance com- panies rather than through Medicare, thus preventing that program from growing or becoming more popular. Then he might plausibly claim to have delivered important new programs in education and health, taking away the Democrats' exclusive claim to those issues in the way Clinton took reducing crime away from the Republicans. Bush's initiative to promote faith-based social programs takes away the Democrats' monopoly on caring about helping the poor while also, by creating a tax credit for donations to such programs, redirecting money from the government to evangelicals. Bush can also try to diminish the influence of some of the main Democratic interest groups by pushing "tort reform" (hurts trial lawyers) and "paycheck protection" (cuts union dues), and by resisting campaign-finance reform of the kind John McCain wants (reduces the power of individual contributors in politics more than that of organized labor). In each of these cases, Bush can try to find a Democratic co-sponsor for his legislation, to create an aura of bipartisanship. And has anybody noticed that Bush's Cabinet includes former elected officials from four big states—Wisconsin, Michigan, Illinois, and New Jersey—that usually vote Republican but went for Gore in 2000?

If all this happened, Bush not only would have passed a popular tax cut but would have made it difficult for the Democrats to offer voters more government services; instead, they'd have to be the party of fiscal restraint, because all the money for services would have been removed from the federal budget for at least the next ten years. The tax code would be left looking more the way Jim DeMint wants it to look. Under Bush's campaign tax-cut proposal, the share of the federal-tax burden borne by almost everyone would rise slightly, and the share borne by those in the top one percent would fall significantly. But this wouldn't be obvious to the middle class, because people's actual tax payments would go down. (A family whose income is in the middle fifth would pay $453 a year less in federal taxes; a family in the top one percent would pay $46,072 less.) Bush can return to the partial privatization of Social Security, Medicare, and public schools in the fall, or next year. Alternatively, he can remind us of his often-repeated campaign line—"I want to do a few things and do them well"— and, after the tax cut passes, start spending a lot of time at his ranch.

Nothing ever goes as well in the event as it does prospectively. Some unexpected crisis, or scandal, or mistake by Bush could suddenly take away the new administration's momentum. Like Al Gore during the campaign, the Democrats could stop calling Bush's tax cut a risky scheme and start pointing out how heavily it benefits the top one percent. I asked Karl Rove about this, and he said, "What's interesting is, I'm not certain people believe it. They get those statistics by including the abolition of the death tax." That's Republican for the estate tax, which the United States passed in 1916, which only two percent of estates pay, and which Bush will surely propose phasing out.

Right now, the most obvious problem for Bush seems to be that conservative Republicans, especially in the House, will want to cut taxes more than Bush originally promised, and will also want him to stand firm on political-capital-depleting causes like Social Security privatization. Bush's most ambitious initiative in Texas, a 1997 overhaul of the tax system, was killed by Republicans and lobbyists, not by Democrats, and the same thing could happen now in Washington. Twenty years ago, Reagan's budget director, David Stockman, delivered to the journalist William Greider that memorable line about Reagan's tax cut "The hogs were really feeding." Once the idea of big changes in federal taxes and spending is in play, Washington comes to life. Everybody wants something. Already, the advocates of a cut in the capital-gains tax, not satisfied with the substantial reductions that they got in 1997, are bestirring themselves. They may soon be joined by the powerful lobbies for more favorable tax treatment of pensions and heavy machinery—boring and not generally noticed but big-dollar budget items. If Bush's first budget resolution gets overloaded to the point where it will obviously throw the federal government back into deficit, that could sink it.

If, on the other hand, Bush manages to leverage the tiniest imaginable election victory into a big tax cut, rich in Republican-majority-building potential, it will be just the latest example of the endlessly complicated nature of his relationship with his father. George H. W. Bush has done two politically stupid things in his life. The first was moving, in 1948, to a state dominated by the Democratic Party. That helps to explain why Bush twice failed to win statewide office in Texas. The second, in 1990, was breaking his no-new-taxes pledge. Both these things now look like paternal sacrifices for the sake of the son, although that couldn't have been apparent to either of them at the time. George W. Bush was able to grow up in Texas, absorb the middle-American conservative culture that had always eluded his father, and come into middle age when the wilderness decades for Texas Republicans has ended. Like his father, he twice ran for statewide office in Texas, but he won both times. The elder Bush's budget deal terminally alienated the conservative wing of his party, but it paved the way for the process (furthered by Clinton) of bringing the government's revenues up to the level of its spending. Without it, we might not have had the surplus that may be about to pay off politically for the younger Bush, big time.

William Jennings Bush

Nicholas Lemann

The New Yorker | September 10, 2001

In this piece, Lemann travels with President Bush to the heartland and discovers that living in Washington, D.C. hasn't affected the ex-Texas governor's common touch. . . .

On the last Sunday in August, I went to Pennsylvania to watch President Bush wind up his "Home to the Heartland" tour, which wasn't so much a tour as a series of short forays that punctuated the month he spent at his ranch, in Crawford, Texas. This time, on his way to being inducted into the Little League Hall of Excellence, in Williamsport, Bush stopped at a steel mill in the Monongahela Valley to attend a picnic for steelworkers and their families. There are probably more sylvan spots for a summer picnic; this one was held in an asphalt interior courtyard surrounded by long battleship-gray corrugated-steel industrial structures out of a Charles Sheeler painting. But the picnickers' real purpose was not recreation, it was lobbying—for strict limits on imported steel, a cause on which labor and management are in agreement. U.S. Steel sponsored the event, and a procession of company and United Steel Workers' officials and politicians warmed up the crowd for Bush by issuing calls from the podium for a "level playing field" for the steel industry.

As usual, Bush arrived precisely on time, at the head of an entourage that included his wife, Laura, two Cabinet secretaries, and the governor of Pennsylvania, Tom Ridge. The president was the most informally dressed and the most suntanned member of the group. He spent an hour and a half at the picnic—an eternity in the realm of presidential scheduling—and most of that time he devoted to one of the primal activities of politics, moving along the edge of a surging crowd shaking hands, hugging, holding babies, signing autographs, and posing for pictures. Bush's quotient of charisma is below that of a rock star—it was possible for people to sit eating heaping plates of fried chicken and sausages while he was shaking hands fifty feet away—but he appeared to be enjoying himself, and people seemed to come away thinking, You know, he's a good guy. Ross McClellan, Sr., the union-local president at the factory, who sat next to Bush at lunch, left the president's company positively aglow. "He told me he puts on his pants the same way I do," he reported to his friends.

The speakers reminded the crowd that in June Bush had ordered up an investigation of unfair trade practices by foreign steel manufacturers. This seems like a modest favor, since no one knows its outcome, but because Bill Clinton had declined to do the same thing Bush could plausibly appear in hero's guise at a steelworkers' picnic. At the podium, he presented himself as a humble, decent, uxorious, God-fearing, unpretentious man, perhaps a little rascally, who stands in opposition to the federal government over which he presides. "Congress is on vacation," he said. "The country's never run better." And, a little later, "Washington passes laws, but it doesn't pass values legislation. Values exist in the hearts and souls of our citizens."

Where presidents travel domestically is determined according to the political art called targeting; a location is never accidental. Bush and the people close to him have got to be exquisitely aware that he lost the popular vote in 2000 and, through the defection of Jim Jeffords, lost the Senate in 2001 and that his advantage in the House will be lost in 2002 if the Democrats get the traditional off-year gain for the party that doesn't control the White House. Political wisdom is that after taking office you nail down your base and repay your contributors, and then you switch your attention to winning converts. That is what Bush has to do now.

If union steelworkers in the Monongahela Valley (many of them Catholic gun owners) are an example of the hoped-for new Bush voter, that's interesting. Al Gore is eternally consigned to be the answer to the trivia question "Which presidential candidate lost his home state?" It's worth noting that Bush lost to Gore by a wide margin in the state where he was born, Connecticut. Although Bush moved to Texas as a toddler, his connection to his birthplace is not faint. His grandfather was a United States senator from Connecticut. Gerald Ford carried Connecticut in 1976, Ronald Reagan carried it in 1980 and 1984, and George H. W. Bush carried it in 1988. Not only did George W. Bush lose Connecticut in the general election; he lost the Connecticut Republican primary, to John McCain. McCain even carried the Bush family seat, Greenwich.

In earlier generations, states like Connecticut and Vermont, Jim Jeffords' home, made up the heart of the Republican Party in presidential politics, while places like Tennessee and West Virginia, the site of another surprising Bush victory last fall, belonged to the Democrats. The historic shifts in regional political loyalties, which between the late nineteen-sixties and the late nineteen-eighties seemed to be running in a strongly Republican direction, now seem to be bidirectional. The South, the agricultural Midwest, and the mountain West are the Republican base. Clinton, during his time as the head of the Democrats, nailed down the Northeast, the Great Lakes states, and the West Coast for his party. Hence the striking electoral map of the 2000 presidential election, which, as it became familiar from constantly being projected on television screens, represented a shorthand way of thinking about the country: there's Red America, the Bush-voting center; and Blue America, the Gore-voting perimeter.

Bush seems to feel his Red Americaness deeply. The more relaxed he is, the more he talks about it. When he arrived in Crawford in early August, a reporter asked him a question indicating dissatisfaction with the hundred-degree heat, and Bush shot back, "This is Texas. I know a lot of you wish you were in the East Coast, lounging on the beaches, sucking in the salt air, but when you're from Texas, and love Texas, this is where you come home; this is my home. We built a house in the Crawford area; it'll be the house where I live in for the rest of my life." (A couple of weeks later, when a reporter teased Bush by saying he'd been away "sucking up salt air on the West Coast," Bush's instant comeback was "Brie and cheese?"—which was not only funny but message-reinforcing, since it communicated that Bush is too country to know that Brie *is* cheese.) In public statements during the month, Bush favorably compared Crawford with Washington, which he usually called "Washington, D.C.," the city where people would rather take positions than get things done, like in Texas. Whenever Bush left town, it was always to go to regular-folks venues, such as a Harley-Davidson plant in Menomonee Falls, Wisconsin, a Target store in Kansas City, and the steel mill where I caught his act—in states with no ocean frontage, where the last election had been very close.

For the past couple of years, Karl Rove, who has functioned as chief adviser to Bush throughout his political career, has been fond of comparing the 2000 and 1896 presidential elections. In 1896, William McKinley beat William Jennings Bryan by putting together a coalition of the rising industrial regions of the country, which wound up becoming the geographic basis of a Republican majority that dominated national politics until the Great Depression. What's interesting about Rove's comparison now—as John Milton Cooper, Jr., a University of Wisconsin historian, observes in a forthcoming book of essays on the 2000 election—is that Bush's territory resembles Bryan's, not McKinley's. McKinley took all the Northeastern and Great Lakes states, plus California and Oregon—Blue America—and Bryan got the South and the West.

I don't think this is entirely a coincidence. Like Bryan, Bush is a populist—an unlikely populist, given his background, but evidently a sincere one. As a politician, he appeals, as Bryan did, far more to the middle of the country than to the coasts, and more to the small towns and farms than to the metropolitan areas. Like Bryan, he seems to stand more with religion than with science, more with what the Populists called "producers" than with financiers, and more for the United States operating solo in the world than for its being entwined in a system of international entanglements. Bryan was florid and Bush is straightforward, but the rhetoric of both contains a large dose of resentment of the fancy people in the sophisticated areas. It would be hard to find a purer example of the proposition that the same thought can be expressed in quite different ways than by placing Bush's Crawford pronouncements next to this one of Bryan's, from the "Cross of Gold" speech:

> Ah, my friends, we say not one word against those who live upon the Atlantic coast, but the hardy pioneers who have braved all the dangers of the wilderness, who have made the desert to blossom as the rose—the pioneers away out there, who rear their children near to Nature's heart, where they can mingle their voices with the voices of the birds—out there where they have erected school-houses for the education of their young, churches where they praise their Creator, and cemeteries where rest the ashes of their dead—these people, we say, are as deserving of the consideration of our party as any people in this country. It is for these that we speak.

Bush, in his public self-presentation, glorifies simplicity and "heart"; without using specifically religious language, he traffics in the evangelical Christian ideal of leadership by a simple, good man. As he reminded the press several times during August, he is going to deal with Vladimir Putin by bringing him to Crawford and talking man to man—pointing to this rather than to their official summit meeting in Shanghai, where they would be surrounded by diplomatic experts. The dramatic climax of Bush's month in Crawford, his speech on stem cell research, may have represented his making a compromise, but it also underscored his Bryanism. Of the hundreds of things a president works on, he decides which issues to elevate to primary national importance. Bill Clinton chose not to draw attention to stem cell research. Bush made it the subject of his only televised prime time address as president so far. The next morning, his aides gave a lavish supplementary briefing to explain in detail how he had reached his position, as they have done on no other issue since he became president. The impression Bush created was that he shares the basic premises of the right-to-life movement about the rights of the unborn, and that he and the people around him consider the moral compass, as opposed to some more advanced and technical instrument, to be his most important piece of equipment.

There is a connection between Bush's Bryanism and the search for new Republican voters. One might think that Bush, the tax cutter and regulation lifter, would look for them in affluent, traditionally Republican suburbs. Instead, if I am reading the signals correctly, he appears to believe that the most promising course is to push the boundaries of Red America just a little farther outward, by persuading middle-class, small-town heartlanders who have traditionally been Democrats to switch. That is what he was doing in the Monongahela Valley. Trying to raid Democratic territory demonstrates a certain strategic bravado on Bush's part, but it also raises a question: Why is the old Republican Northeast and Midwest such a tough sell for him?

I got only one real chance to suck in salt air with those who live upon the Atlantic Coast this summer, and that was when I interviewed Representative Christopher Shays on the deck of his house in Bridgeport, Connecticut, which overlooks a pretty little sailboat-filled cove of Long Island Sound. I had made a small project of checking in with moderate Republican congressmen, who are a strikingly regionalized group. Their home territory is the Northeast, with outposts in the midwestern suburbs and in coastal California. Not much had been heard from them as a group for decades, as their party's base moved relentlessly south and west following Barry Goldwater's presidential campaign in 1964, but after Jeffords left his party this spring, they seemed to be reemerging. Moderates voted against the Bush administration and their leadership in the House on a series of issues: drilling in the Arctic National Wildlife Refuge, faith-based social programs, air-quality standards, the patients' bill of rights, and, the most dramatic example—with Shays leading a revolt that barely failed—campaign-finance reform. (Shays has gathered the signatures of more than two hundred House members on a petition for the reintroduction of his bill in the fall.)

The scene at Shays's residence—a neat, white Colonial house with chintz sofas and a copy of *Millie's Book,* by Barbara Bush on the coffee table; the slender, polite, prematurely white-haired Shays; an American flag flying next to the front door; sailboats in the Sound—bespoke Republicanism, and Shays insisted that he is a real Republican. He told me that his introduction to politics was riding his bike, as a small boy, down to the Republican headquarters in Darien to get an "I Like Ike" button.

"What's happened in my district is this," he said. "The Democratic Party isn't stronger. The Republican Party is weaker. Independents predominate." Shays's district is the one that the Bush family came from, by the way. "The more the Republican Party becomes the party of the South, the Southwest, and the West, the less relevant the Republican Party will be in New England. The more Jesse Helms, Strom Thurmond, Trent Lott, Dick Armey, and Tom DeLay are viewed as representing the party, the harder it is for me to win elections. George W. Bush is a Texan. He is proud of it. He doesn't think like somebody from Greenwich, Connecticut. Here's a great example: George W. went to Europe *once* before he became president. That's mind-boggling to somebody from this district, especially considering his family background."

Most of the moderates have a similar story about their districts to tell. Mike Castle, of Delaware, who heads the Republican Main Street Partnership, a three-year-old organization of House and Senate moderates whose most prized recent recruit is John McCain, told me that the first time he ran for the state legislature, in 1966, rural downstate Delaware was Democratic and the suburbs of Wilmington were Republican. Now downstate is the Republican base and the suburbs swing (though not the way they did in *The Ice Storm,* which was set in Christopher Shays's district). "Even the corporate chieftains aren't Republican anymore," Castle said. Beginning in 1952, Delaware voted for the winner in every presidential election until 2000, when it voted for Gore.

The moderates' distance from their party is cultural as much as political. Evangelicals are not a strong presence in their districts today, and even when they were, in the nineteenth century, they were a liberal pressure group, not a conservative one. The moderates, and their constituents, are uncomfortable with politics and religion blending together. The moderates have a different style from that of the House leadership. They don't use ideological rhetoric. They don't rail against liberals. The government shutdown engineered by Newt Gingrich, the former speaker, and the impeachment of Clinton played poorly in their districts. The moderates even look different from the conservatives, being more likely to resemble reedy country parsons than prosperous automobile dealers.

They are heirs to the Progressive tradition, with its view of government as an honorable profession to be practiced by experts, and of business interests as a corrupting force. One aide to a moderate Republican congressman told me, horrified, about a meeting he and his boss had held with a lobbyist for Peabody Coal about legislation to renew the federal Clean Coal Technology Program, a perfect example of an initiative born in a reform spirit which has evolved into a subsidy for an industry. "I wrote that bill!" the lobbyist proclaimed, showing a wounded author's pride at the idea that a member of the legislative branch of government would presume to alter it.

Politicians have to think first about being reelected, and therefore the moderates are less worried about incurring the displeasure of their party leadership than about the possibility of facing Democratic opponents who would be pro-choice and pro-environment but conservative on budget and spending issues, and who would try to identify them with the national Republican leadership. I asked another of the moderates, Rob Simmons, who represents a district in eastern Connecticut, how one would run against him. "You link me to Bush and Cheney," he said. "I'm a toady of President Bush. I'm in league with the oil industry. None of that is true, but truth matters less in politics than it used to." Simmons, a freshman, barely won in a district that had been represented by Democrats for the preceding twenty-six years. What if Bush offered to come to the district next fall and campaign for him? Simmons did not leap at the possibility. "Hopefully he would come to discuss something relevant to the district, like the military, or infrastructure," he said. "Prescription drugs would have a lot of currency. If he came to talk about his position on stem cell research, or about, perhaps, even faith-based programs, I don't think there'd be much enthusiasm."

What the moderates see as self-preservation has, however, incurred the wrath of the right wing of their party. The year after Mike Castle and his colleagues created the Republican Main Street Partnership, a young supply-sider named Stephen Moore set up a lobbying group in Washington called the Club for Growth, which finances conservative primary opponents of moderate Republicans. "The enemy isn't so much Dick Gephardt"—the House minority leader—"as it is Mike Castle," Moore told me with a grin. In the 2000 elections, its first cycle, the Club for Growth targeted the ten-term incumbent Marge Roukema, of New Jersey, but she beat back her primary challenger and is still in the House. In 2002, Moore told me, he plans to target two more Republican moderates. (He once wrote an article in *The American Spectator* called "Who Needs the Northeast?") This spring, Moore sent a letter to all the Republican moderates in the House vowing to find primary opponents for them if they voted against Bush's tax cut. After telling me this, he held up his thumb and index finger to form a circle. "Zero. Nobody voted against us. We sent the letter to thirty people. None of them wanted to suffer the same near-death experience as Marge Roukema. We did the same thing in the Senate, but it didn't work as well, because we hadn't been involved in races and they weren't afraid of us. We ran ads attacking the senators who voted against the tax cut in their states. Not too long after that, Jeffords defected. That was a bad thing. If I'd known that might happen, I wouldn't have run the ad in Vermont."

In theory, the leadership and the administration should be afraid of the moderates, who number at least twenty in a House that has a Republican majority of ten. Instead, the moderates, for all their rebellions of the spring and summer, have not yet won a single battle. Part of their problem, if it is a problem, is precisely that they are moderate—they tend to be loyal and well mannered. John Podesta, who was Clinton's chief of staff and now teaches at Georgetown Law School, recently told me, "I used to say, when I was in the White House, anybody who came into my office with a strategy built around the House moderates, I'd throw them out. Because they always collapsed." That is one reason Bush has been able to govern as if he had a mandate, when he doesn't. But what he probably is not going to be able to do is pick up political support in the moderates' territory. The moderates themselves may be holding for Bush, but their districts are long gone.

Earlier this year, Congress passed President Bush's budget for fiscal 2002, based on revenue estimates that now appear to have been far too optimistic. The main action in Washington this fall will have to do with numbers—in particular with Social Security, which is the rare federal program that has its own tax. These days, Social Security takes in far more in taxes than it pays out in benefits. When the baby-boom generation retires, that will no longer be the case.

In his State of the Union message in 1998, Bill Clinton, by unveiling the slogan "save Social Security first," introduced the idea that whatever was left over of the Social Security tax monies after benefits had been paid should be put into a trust fund for the baby boomers' retirement. By the time Al Gore ran for president, the trust fund had metaphorically morphed into the "ironclad lockbox" that Darrell Hammond made fun of on *Saturday Night Live*. There is no actual Social Security trust fund—it's only a construct, which didn't exist until the sixty-sixth year of the program and has no legislative authority behind it. But Clinton saw it as a way to make Republican tax cuts seem like tampering with the sacrosanct Social Security program, and Bush, during the campaign, appeared to accept the trust-fund idea.

A few days before Bush got back to Washington from Crawford, the Congressional Budget Office issued numbers indicating that, with the tax cut and the bad economy, the federal government won't be taking in enough money to avoid dipping slightly into the Social Security trust fund. This signaled the start of a giant game of chicken. Gephardt and Senator Tom Daschle, the Democratic leaders in their respective houses, who are both thinking about running for president in 2004, will try to force Bush into a choice between cutting the budgets of the two government departments he wants to spend more on, Education and Defense, and picking the ironclad lockbox. If it's the latter, the Democrats will accuse him of having raided Social Security in order to cut taxes for the rich. Bush will counter by accusing the Democrats of being irresponsible big spenders. (Both sides have fired opening salvos already, in the form of brief negative advertising campaigns; the Democrats' ad aired in Crawford, the Republicans' in Daschle's and Gephardt's home towns.)

The whole routine is deeply fake—Social Security isn't in imminent danger, and the budget-balancing Democrats are anything but big spenders—but it represents a real question, which is whether the federal government should be nourished, so that it can stand ready to solve national problems, or starved, so it cannot grow. As the game plays out, it will present Bush with choices that will reveal more about his political intentions. He has very efficiently got rid of all the extra money available to the federal government, by cutting taxes so much. If he accepts the current Democratic formulation, in which fiscal prudence generally and the Social Security surplus in particular are sacred, it will suggest that he wants to fight for the unlikely new Democratic political territory in the sophisticated suburbs. That's what a legatee of William McKinley would do. But, if he's really William Jennings Bush, the president of Red America, he'll just let the numbers go out of whack, keep his new programs for the school kids and our brave men in uniform, and say that anybody who disagrees with him is just stuck in that old way of thinking that they have up in Washington, D.C.

The National Conversation:
The Bush Tax Cut

Surprise, Surprise, He Meant It

Fred Barnes

The Weekly Standard | February 19, 2001

In May 2001, at the urging of President Bush, Congress passed the largest tax cut since the days of Ronald Reagan—an estimated reduction of some $1.6 trillion, to be phased in over the next ten years. Before and since, experts have continued to debate its wisdom: Was the tax cut a prudent and important shift in govermental philosophy—or a fiscally irresponsible boondoggle, guaranteed to bring back the days of huge federal deficits?

The conservative Weekly Standard *favored the Bush tax cut as a matter of simple fairness. The bigger question, according to executive editor Fred Barnes, was whether Bush had the will and the political clout to make it happen. . . .*

George W. Bush drafted his $1.6 trillion tax cut, with help from Larry Lindsey and a band of conservative economists, in the summer of 1999 and unveiled it later that year. During 2000, the proposal was zinged in the Republican presidential primaries by Senator John McCain, then trashed in the general election by Al Gore. Bush never wavered, stubbornly sticking with every element of his plan, including a 17 percent reduction in the top rate on individual income. Now we see the result. His tenacity has been rewarded: The Bush tax cut is popular.

This trend in Bush's direction doesn't mean we have another Ronald Reagan in the White House. But it does suggest three things about Bush as a national leader. The first is that the conservative side of his compassionate conservatism is more appealing than the media or even some of his aides let on. Second, he does have a Reagan-like determination to stick with an unpopular idea for months until it begins to generate public approval. And third, he has benefited from a presidential effect. Bush is viewed far more favorably by the public as president (62 percent approval in the Fox Dynamics Poll) than he was as a candidate, and his agenda, including the tax cut, has picked up support as well.

Okay, the Bush tax cut isn't wildly popular. Pollster John Zogby points out its backing has risen only from "a high plurality to a low majority." Last

September, a Gallup poll found the public preferred Gore's tax cut—whatever it was—to Bush's by 45 percent to 37 percent.

Zogby gave Bush a slight edge on taxes then, but by mid-January, approval of the Bush proposal had jumped to 53 percent, with 34 percent opposed. The Fox poll after 20 days of the Bush presidency came up with roughly the same finding: The tax cut was favored by 54 percent to 29 percent. If those numbers hold, the Bush tax cut or something similar is bound to pass Congress.

The popularity of the tax cut confirms that, as a pure political matter, Bush was wise to follow his ideological instincts. From the beginning, his complaint was that "the federal government is overcharging people," Karen Hughes, Bush's White House counselor, says. According to Lindsey, Bush "believes it's the people's money. That's pretty basic."

To Bush, a federal tax bite at its highest point in a half-century is simply unfair. And from the 1999 discussions, Bush came up with a principle of taxation that he now routinely mentions in speeches: No one should pay more than one-third of their income in federal taxes. Thus, his cut lowers the top rate from 39.6 percent to 33 percent. The one-third principle puts Bush close to what the public thinks about taxation—closer than Democrats, anyway. Their notion of "targeted tax cuts" has fallen into disfavor. A poll for congressional Democratic leaders in January discovered the public views these cuts as ones they won't get.

Bush's persistence in sticking with his tax cut is, well, surprising, though Bush aides insist no one should have been shocked that the proposal he sent to Congress on February 8 was the same exact one he announced 14 months ago. "He never considered giving it up or even altering it," says Lindsey. Twice, however, he was under strong pressure to do so. The first episode came after McCain humiliated Bush in the New Hampshire primary. McCain claimed Bush would devote too much of the surplus to tax cuts and not enough to debt relief. But when Bush vanquished McCain in South Carolina and later on Super Tuesday, the pressure subsided. Then Gore created a new pressure point by relentlessly assailing Bush for giving most of his tax cut to the "top one percent." Bush never flinched.

What did change, however, was the way Bush promotes the tax cut. Initially he paid little attention to its potential economic effects, except to call it an "insurance policy against an economic downturn." Now, he stress the economic impact. Many Americans "are beginning to actually feel what it means to be in an economic downturn," Bush said in transmitting his tax bill to Congress last week. "A warning light is flashing on the dashboard of our economy. And we just can't drive on and hope for the best. We must act without delay." This argument, says Zogby, has helped build support, changing the broad public attitude about the tax cut from "Why?" to "Why not?"

Another adjustment in the tax message has also helped—tax families. When Gore was pounding Bush on taxes last summer, Hughes came up with an answer. Bush would appear with low- and middle-income families, explain how much of a cut they'd get, and rebut Gore's charge that his plan was chiefly "a tax cut for the rich." Hughes suggested the idea to Karl Rove, Bush's chief strategist, who liked it. So first in an appearance in Georgia and then everywhere he campaigned, Bush put families on stage with him.

Bush liked the ploy so much he recruited four new families to join him in the Diplomatic Room of the White House when he formally announced his tax proposal on February 5. Each represented a tax bracket. Bush said he, with his $400,000 a year presidential salary, represents the top bracket. Two days later, Bush held a reunion of 21 tax families from the campaign as part of his week-long drive to promote his tax cut.

All this might have seemed hokey if Bush had still been a candidate. Actually, it was a bit hokey even in the White House. But there was a difference. Before, meeting with tax families was a gimmick to win an election. Now, tax families are soldiers in a presidential drive to reduce taxes and spur the economy. Same families, same George W. Bush, but a higher purpose and a glow of significance, That's how the presidential effect works. And for Bush, it's working quite well indeed.

Surely He Jests

Molly Ivins

Dallas-Fort Worth Star-Telegram | March 1, 2001

Texas-based columnist Molly Ivins is famous for her barbed wit and for her common-sense perspective on politics. She's also spent more years than anyone observing the George Bushes—both 41 and 43—at close range. Here Ivins cuts through the rhetoric surrounding the Bush tax cut to ask a basic question: What's it going to cost us?

President Bush's maiden address to the nation was classic Dubya: He talks moderate and governs right. And this is never more true than on economic issues.

Again, with Bush, what you see is not what you get. What you hear is not what you get. What you get is what you get.

One is tempted to conclude, "Surely he jests."

The man cannot possibly want us to sign off on an enormous tax cut designed to benefit the rich without telling us what will be cut in return. Houston, we have a problem. Earth to Karl Rove: Beam me up, Scotty.

In budgets, as in bridges, the devil is in the details—and the details of the amorphous plan that Bush presented are grim indeed.

Just the other day, I had occasion to cite one of the Great Questions of government, which is: What the Hell Will They Do to Us Next? Dubya's maiden speech before Congress brought up another always-timely query: How Dumb Do They Think We Are?

This tax cut is carefully back-loaded: We won't fully feel its effects until 10 years into the future, yet we have to start cutting already to accommodate the little wedge of it that will affect this budget.

To use one of the great legislative clichés of all time, this year's tax cut is the head of the camel under the tent. And if you think the head causes problems, wait'll you see what the rest of the beast does when it's inside.

For all the size of the federal budget, the amount available for discretionary spending is relatively small, and within that small portion are most of the efforts to use government flexibly and intelligently.

Again, to cut basic scientific research is sheer folly. To cut job-training programs is not only cruel but stupid. To cut health and human service programs is to abandon investments in people; as we have long known, the earlier we can invest in a child's health and education, the more money we save in the long run.

Bush's budget is irrefutably the work of old Reaganites who do not like government and believe that the best way to deal with it is to starve it to death.

According to *The Wall Street Journal*, the chief architects of Bush's budget are John Cogan of the ultra-conservative Hoover Institution at Stanford, and Mitch Daniels, a former executive at Eli Lilly & Co., newly named head of the Office of Management and Budget.

Relying on the wide range of opinion available from such sources at the Heritage Foundation and Citizens Against Government Waste, a span that covers the gamut from A to B, Cogan and his team noodled the numbers.

Bush so clearly represents a change of rhetoric without a change of intent that it's almost painful. Ronald Reagan used to go around saying, "Government is not the solution; government is the problem." Newt Gingrich thought so little of the institution that he shut it down twice.

I say that government is neither the problem nor the solution. It is just a tool. Whether you put the tool to good use or bad, whether you use it wisely or carelessly, is not the fault of the tool.

I can't say that I see we're better off for paying for a $1.5 million statue of the Roman god Vulcan in honor of Alabama steelworkers—one of the splendid items of pork spotted by Cogan's team—but it's certain that some Alabama steelworkers are going to need job retraining if we keep making trade pacts with no labor or environmental floors.

Perhaps the single funniest argument I have heard in favor of Bush's tax cut for the rich is from CNN's Tucker Carlson, who crossly announced that it is vulgar—vulgar—to point out that the rich are going to get ever so much more out of this tax cut than everybody else. Quite, quite vulgar to point out that in a society already deeply scarred by the dramatically growing gap between the rich and everyone else, a tax cut that transfers yet more wealth into the hands of the rich while shifting more of the burden of taxation to everyone else is a truly bad idea.

However, I believe it is even more vulgar—in fact, crass, stupid, and greedy—to actually pass such a tax cut.

I believe it is vulgar that this tax cut is proposed by the wealthiest Cabinet in history; seven of them are worth more than $10 million, and 11 of the remaining 12 are worth at least $1 million apiece. (Ag Secretary Ann Veneman is the pauper in the bunch, worth only $680,000, according to *The Guardian* of London.)

One of Bush's "ordinary" couples, Paul and Debbie Peterson, will get a tax cut of $1,100 a year. Bush himself will get more than 60 times that. I find that a little vulgar.

According to the Census Bureau, 3.7 million Americans suffer from hunger as a result of being unable to buy basic foods. About 9 million households have "uncertain access to food." I find that truly vulgar.

Et tu, Alan?
Paul Krugman

The New York Times | January 28, 2001

There must have been times over the past couple of years when economist Paul Krugman felt like the only American capable of doing simple arithmetic. Beginning back in the presidential campaign, Krugman used his twice-weekly column in The New York Times *to point out again and again that George Bush's numbers didn't add up—and that his fiscal proposals would inevitably mean dipping into the funds earmarked for Social Security and Medicare, and probably plunge the federal budget back into deficit as well.*

These predictions turned out to be right—but what really bothered Krugman was the way the Bush administration's rationale for the tax cut kept shifting. In this famous column, he sharply criticizes one of Washington's most revered figures, Federal Reserve chief Alan Greenspan, for going over to the dark side. . . .

Despite his legendary obscurity, what Alan Greenspan has to say is usually quite clear and intellectually coherent once translated into English. But his testimony last Thursday before the Senate Budget Committee was evasive and often inconsistent. It was hard to avoid the impression that Mr. Greenspan's intent was to give aid and comfort to the new administration, while retaining plausible deniability.

True, Mr. Greenspan explicitly rejected the administration's argument that we must immediately cut taxes to prevent a recession. While conceding that the economy may grow little if at all this quarter, he suggested that a recovery would probably be underway before tax cuts could have any impact. By the way, new evidence suggests that manufacturing, which suffered a nasty downturn in the last few months, has already started to rebound.

Nonetheless, the headlines were all about Mr. Greenspan's endorsement of tax cuts—something the Fed chairman must have known would happen. And when you look at the tortured logic by which Mr. Greenspan arrived at that endorsement, you have to wonder whether those headlines weren't exactly what he wanted.

His argument went as follows: given its projected surpluses over the next decade, the federal government may not only pay off its debt, but actually find itself using surplus cash to buy private assets. This could cause problems, he suggested, because it would be "difficult to insulate the government's investment decisions from political pressures." So we should engage in "pre-emptive smoothing of the glide path," which turns out to mean cutting taxes enough so that the federal government never does pay off its debt, after all.

Now I would quarrel with those surplus projections. I would also point out that in declaring "it is far better . . . that the surpluses be lowered by tax reductions than by spending increases," Mr. Greenspan was out of bounds. Since when is it the Fed's business to say that we should have a tax cut rather than, say, a new prescription drug benefit—or for that matter a missile defense system? (Neither program is factored into those surplus projections.) Mr. Greenspan himself seemed aware that he was on shaky ground, offering the very inadequate excuse that "I speak for myself and not necessarily for the Federal Reserve."

But the really strange thing about his argument was that he seemed to ignore the fact that the main reason the federal government will one day become an investor is the buildup of assets in the hands of the Social Security and Medicare systems—and those funds must accumulate assets to prepare for the future demands of the baby-boom generation. Indeed, by all estimates even the huge projected surpluses of those trust funds will be inadequate to the task. "Certainly," Mr. Greenspan declared, "we should make sure that Social Security surpluses are large enough to meet our long-term needs." Well, I'm sorry, but you can't do that without allowing the federal government to become an investor.

So if that prospect was what was really worrying Mr. Greenspan, he should have focused on the problem of how to prevent the government's position as an investor from being abused. And there are many ways to do that—including, by the way, realistic plans for partial privatization of Social Security, which (unlike the fantasy promises of the Bush campaign) would require the federal government to ante up trillions of dollars to pay off existing obligations, solving the "problem" of excessive surpluses quite easily.

But Mr. Greenspan seemed determined to arrive at tax cuts as an answer. After dismissing the argument that we need a tax cut to fend off a recession now, and conceding that tax cuts have historically "proved difficult to implement in the time frame in which recessions have developed and ended," he waffled: "Should current economic weakness spread beyond what now seems likely, having a tax cut in place may, in fact, do noticeable good." But by the same token, if the economy is strong again by the time a tax cut goes into effect, won't that tax cut do noticeable harm? Mr. Greenspan declined to answer questions along those lines.

When a man who is usually a clear thinker ties himself in intellectual knots in order to find a way to say exactly what the new president wants to hear, it's not hard to guess what's going on. But it's not a pretty sight.

Better, Simpler, Fairer
William Raspberry

The Washington Post | February 12, 2001

Just to keep us all honest, Washington Post *columnist William Raspberry passes along this alternative tax cut proposal, devised by Representative Bernie Sanders of Vermont. Sanders' aim was a basic one: to provide the maximum benefit for the most people. (Don't worry, we know it can't ever work—if only because it's so easy to understand. . . .)*

The same day President Bush sent his tax-cut proposal to Congress, Rep. Bernie Sanders (I-Vt.) and the Congressional Progressive Caucus unveiled a tax-cut plan that Sanders says will do everything the president's will do, only better, more simply and more fairly. The funny thing is, he may be right.

The proposal: A $300 tax cut for every man, woman and child in America—provided the surplus is for real.

That's it. If you're an American, you get the $300 cut (or tax credit) each year for the next 10 years. A family of four gets a $1,200 cut, no matter whether the family's income is $20,000 or $200,000 a year.

But simplicity is just the starting point. "If you cross-reference our proposal with the *Wall Street Journal*'s analysis," says Sanders spokesman David Sirota, "you'll find ours gives more tax relief than the president's for 80 percent of American families. That is, families in the first through 80th percentiles get a bigger tax reduction under our plan—at least during the five years before the president's increased child credit kicks in.

"Families in the 81st to 95th percentiles get an average cut of $1,447 under Bush's plan, which is in the same ballpark as our $1,200 for a family of four."

It's only the top earners, Sirota says, who would do better under Bush. Families in the 96th to 99th percentiles (with an average income of $183,000 a year) get a $2,330 cut under Bush, and the top one percent (average income of $915,000) get their taxes slashed by more than $46,000 under the Bush plan.

"It's a travesty," says Sanders, "that the president would put forward a tax plan that provides a millionaire family with over $40,000 in tax relief while a family earning $40,000 will only get around $600."

The president's argument, of course, is that the rich deserve to get more benefit from the budget surplus because they contributed substantially more to it—both in taxes and in their investments in, and leadership of, the economy.

Sanders, an avowed socialist, sees it another way. "The factory workers, sales people and clerical workers contributed to the boom as surely as Bill Gates did," he says. "The rich already have benefited from the economic boom. My proposal would help those who have pretty much been bypassed by the boom."

There's more yet. The Sanders plan would be triggered only by an actual surplus and could expand or shrink depending on the size of the surplus. Says Sirota:

"The Bush people are saying he won't even consider a trigger. His rationale is that we can afford his big tax cut because of the projected surplus—a projection based on the Congressional Budget Office's assumption of a 3 percent annual growth in the economy. We believe that's too rosy. [Federal Reserve Board Chairman] Alan Greenspan says we're at about a zero growth rate right now."

But at the same time Bush is saying that we can afford the cut because of the surplus produced by the economic boom, he's also saying to be on the lookout for a recession. Indeed the newest rationale for the tax cut (which he first proposed while the economy was doing well) is to prevent a recession.

It makes for a tricky argument. If the economy is in such trouble that we need a $1.6 trillion tax cut to forestall a recession, then how can he count on an economy-generated surplus as the source of the cut?

Bernie Sanders avoids the problem. If there's no surplus, there's no tax cut. But if Bush is right, and there is a surplus, then everybody gets a $300 tax cut.

The Vermonter (and former Brooklyn hippie) figures his plan would cost about $900 billion. "If the president thinks that's too little to stimulate the economy sufficiently, then he could take our plan and bump it up to his $1.6 trillion. That would give every man, woman and child almost $600."

In fact, though, the Sanders approach might prove more of an economic stimulus than the president's. Rich people might decide to salt their tax-break money into savings or splurge on European vacations. With poor people, the one certainty is that they'll spend the money and most likely close to home.

Part Three: (Not) Politics As Usual

Punditry for Dummies

James Wolcott

Vanity Fair | February 2001

Who needs the headache of writing about politics, when a journalist can make a whole lot more money shooting the breeze on television? In this piece, Vanity Fair's *James Wolcott reveals the origin of the word "pundit," and tells how you too can learn to be one in ten easy lessons. . . .*

Nothing puts more of a damper on a writer's day than actually having to drop anchor and write. Civilians think a writer's life is taking sips of coffee in your bathrobe while the rest of the world reports for work, but from the writer's perspective it's more like being in perpetual summer school, stuck indoors while everyone else is out playing. All of the time-honored delay tactics and sorry excuses for missed deadlines handed down through generations of hacks—from the coffeehouse wits of 18th-century London to the Josh Freelantzovitzes of our own day, bent over their laptops in the window seats at Starbucks—only postpone the inevitable anticlimax of having to put away the newspaper, mute the TV, and coax a few dinky paragraphs out of one's inner blah. Nonfiction writers have discovered that there is a lucrative way to lighten this overhanging chore. It's called punditry, taken from the Hindi term for a "learned man," and it can be the ticket out of the tedium of trying to make every word count. Once one can parlay a byline into a TV I.D.-tag, the quality craftwork of journalism—constructing paragraphs as if they were fine cabinets, filigreeing the sentences with a wry touch here, a bass note there—becomes a Victorian enterprise that no longer need weigh one down. Being granted the license to blab on TV permits the writer to blab in print, since it all becomes part of the same shtick. Grooming a loftier persona on the page will only confuse your new fans! Now that so many journalists are hanging out their shingles on the Internet (Mickey Kaus, Andrew Sullivan, and Joshua Micah Marshall all have their own busy Web sites), the old Walter Lippmann formalities have gone kaput. Chat is king.

Sure, punditry looks easy, doubters will scoff. Because it is! Do you think

Tweety Birds such as Margaret Carlson (*Time*) or Tucker Carlson (no relation, *The Weekly Standard*) could do it if it weren't? Moreover, job prospects
have never been riper. Everyone grouches about tracking polls, photo ops,
and "Sabbath gasbags" (Calvin Trillin's pungent phrase) to equally futile
effect: the expansion of cable news coverage of the latest hoo-ha—what
Frank Rich has christened the "Mediathon"—requires a full roster of
rotating faces, some fresh, others old-reliable. (The cable channels often
stack four pundits at once in a *Brady Bunch* grid.) But if instant analysis
seems like an E-ZPass lane to fame, highway-robbery speaking fees, and
unctuous phone calls from senior officials close to the president, beware.
The spiral staircase of punditry is strewn with the twisted remains of
writers who couldn't quite make the climb to the top. Scant years ago, Ruth
Conniff of *The Progressive* surfaced on CNN talk shows, so young, so full of
peppy, socialist idealism. She's supposedly a regular commentator on the
Fox News Channel, but I didn't spot her once during the election-crisis
coverage—where were they hiding this breath of spring? Where is sourpuss
Washington Times columnist Mona Charen, a once familiar presence? Her
conservative parking spot seems to have been delegated to Kate O'Beirne
of the *National Review* (a regular on CNN's *The Capital Gang*), leaving
Charen in limbo. Of the blonde-witch coven that boiled Clinton in a pot
over Monica Lewinsky, Laura Ingraham (author of *The Hillary Trap*) is still
making the rounds while Ann Coulter (author of *High Crimes and Misde-
meanors: The Case Against Bill Clinton*) seems to have fallen by the wayside,
no longer enticing viewers with the *Basic Instinct* ride of her miniskirts and
Fatal Attraction stare.

   To assist my brethren in their ruthless climb to the hospitality suite of
celebrity journalism, I have devised a 10-point program that will help
prospective pundits not only get to the top, but stay there.

1. Abandon Your Ideals

They're only holding you back. You'll feel so much better, so much *lighter*,
once you let go. There was a time when your role model might have been
Bobby Kennedy in rolled-up shirtsleeves wading into a sea of outstretched
hands in Harlem; or perhaps—shudder—it was Newt Gingrich standing
like the Pillsbury Doughboy before the billboard-size copy of the Contract
with America on the steps of the Capitol. Treasure these images in your
scrapbook for their inspirational value, but don't let them mist your mind.
To be a successful pundit is to forgo quixotic crusades for a hard-boiled

cynicism and sarcasm worthy of a *film noir* detective in some fancy joint. Henceforth, you must patronize politicians (aside from a few personal pets) as used-car salesmen, dismiss civil servants as "faceless bureaucrats," and regard foreign partners as America's puny chess pieces. Consider Chris Matthews, host of MSNBC's *Hardball*, and Lawrence O'Donnell Jr., MSNBC's senior political analyst and a panelist on *The McLaughlin Group*: Matthews worked for former House Speaker Tip O'Neill, O'Donnell for Senator Daniel Patrick Moynihan, yet you'll seldom hear them crooning about the glory days of Democratic liberalism, mourning the loss of sweeping social initiatives. They see through their former allies and cronies, saving their most fire-breathing scorn for liberals who pad their ambitions in soft, pandering baby fat. Their favorite target is Bill Clinton, who symbolizes the damp underbelly of the Kennedy legacy of public jauntiness, private debauchery. They beat up on him like a couple of rogue cops. (The liberal pundit who has kept the faith is Doris Kearns Goodwin, wrapping her rooting interest for a return to New Deal/Great Society big-government rollout in warm nostalgia.) On the Republican side, Tony Blankley, Gingrich's former mouthpiece and also a panelist on *The McLaughlin Group*, can barely recite the conservative mantra of less regulation, lower taxes without his lips betraying a smile. He dresses like a dapper riverboat gambler, as if to signal to the audience, "Don't kid yourself, folks—it's all a game."

2. Dress the Part

Tony Blankley can get away with a Jackie Gleason ensemble—a portly dandy can carry off a carnation in the lapel. You, buster, probably can't. The moody Mafia hit-man dark shirts and electric ties of *Salon*'s Jake Tapper are a singular statement, as is the casual Gap-ad attire of Andrew Sullivan, which telegraphs a nonconformist message consonant with his gay-Catholic-conservative identity. (Michael Kinsley in the same outfit would look as if he forgot to change.) One fashion option is the popular bow tie. The pre-eminent bow-tie pundit is, of course, George Will (ABC's *This Week with Sam Donaldson and Cokie Roberts*), on whom this puckish accessory achieves an odd sobriety. It seems to fasten his gravitas in place. On Thomas Oliphant (*The NewsHour with Jim Lehrer*) and Tucker Carlson (the rising star of CNN's *Late Edition* and *The Spin Room*), it serves a more traditional function as a twerp accessory. But for most male pundits, standard business attire is the safest bet.

Female pundits such as Margaret Carlson employ Susie Student eye-glasses for that sorority look, but most choose a sedate, borderline-matronly wardrobe and a coif that might be called Hillary lite. The balancing act for women is looking attractively telegenic without coming on too overtly sexy, arousing the resentment of other women and impure thoughts in the horny hosts (a mistake made by Ruth Shalit, who, before she gave up political reporting for advertising, appeared on *Politically Incorrect with Bill Maher* in do-me shoes and baby-doll makeup). Sparky blondes such as Laura Ingraham, who posed on the cover of *The New York Times Magazine* in a leopard-print miniskirt, have learned to lower their wattage and adopt a tamer junior-law-partner getup that makes their polit-ical cheap shots sound like feisty advocacy.

3. Bury Your Nose in Don Imus

The view isn't pretty, but it'll pay off down the line.

The successful pundit understands that punditry begins at dawn, with a quick on-line skim of the buzzworthiest sites (Drudge, *Salon, Slate*) and a mental download of the *New York Times* op-ed page to find out the smarty-pants line to take as laid down by Gail Collins or Maureen Dowd. Then it's time to tune into *Imus in the Morning*, a syndicated radio show simulcast on MSNBC, the breakfast club of the punditry. Although Imus has lost audience share in recent years, his appeal to the Northeast Corridor media elite has never been stronger. The I-man stamp of grumpy approval ("Bernie, see if you can get that lying weasel Paul Begala on the phone") means that the pundit has well and truly arrived. Tim Russert, Jeff Green-field, Laura Ingraham, Jonathan Alter, Howard Fineman, Frank Rich, Chris Matthews, Cokie Roberts, Mary Matalin, Mike Barnicle, George Stephanopoulos, Bob Schieffer, even the reclusive Maureen Dowd—all take their spin at the mike as members of the Imus all-star squad. To make it onto the Imus show, however, his people must call you. Being pushy will only earn you Imus's leather-tongued wrath. While waiting for this sum-mons to the majors, familiarize yourself with every aspect of his big-deal life. His bossy wife, Deirdre. His son, Wyatt. His ramshackle brother, Fred. Become conversant on I-man topics such as Joseph Abboud neckwear and custom-made cowboy boots; listen to Delbert McClinton, read Kinky Friedman mysteries, catch Rob Bartlett in the play *Tabletop*. Prepare your-self, grasshopper, for the trial ahead, always keeping in mind the message of hope enunciated by Johnny Carson, who, after a particularly obsequious compliment from sidekick Ed McMahon, turned to the camera and pronounced, "Sucking up *does* work."

The danger of dealing with Imus is sucking up to excess. Even the most vain monarch doesn't want his courtiers to drool. An Imus rookie must be a dignified toady, making exaggerated bows to his exalted status ("Yes, Your Lordship, the Dixie Chicks indeed rock"), extracting from his incoherent ramblings a pithy nugget of received wisdom, and accepting his teasing as part of the hazing process. Once you've passed the Imus initiation, proceed carefully. Don't get too chummy. Work in the fawning references to Deirdre, Wyatt, and the Imus Ranch slowly, judiciously, raising yourself from a prostrate position by imperceptible degrees. A sudden swagger will only provoke Imus to pop open a can of salsa-flavored whupass. I-man regulars such as CNN's Jeff Greenfield and radio host Mike Francesca enjoy the privilege of flinging darts at Imus's expense, targeting his temper and turkey neck, but insult humor from a relative newcomer is a risky proposition. Err on the side of caution. Above all, never presume to call him "Don," an honor reserved for media equals (Russert, Tom Brokaw) and longtime pals (sports writer Mike Lupica). The deference you pay will yield lifelong dividends. Because once you're inducted into the Imus fraternity, you're set. The Cosa Nostra couldn't be tighter.

Consider the case of columnist Mike Barnicle. Accused of plagiarism and fictionalizing sources, this stale-beer, man-of-the-people Mike Royko pretender was bounced from *The Boston Globe* and could have easily joined fellow miscreants Janet Cook and Stephen Glass in journalism's leper colony. Almost anyone else would have had to slink off into anonymity. But braced by Imus and Tim Russert, who kept throwing him on the air despite the leaky holes in his reputation, Barnicle managed to win back his badge and completely recharge his blowhard batteries. He has a new soapbox in New York's Sunday *Daily News* and has survived his own perfect storm. So take heart: pundits are loyal to their own kind, once they make the cut.

4. Master the Snappy Patter of Pop Culture

Many of the eulogies for Lars-Erik Nelson, the *Daily News* columnist and *New York Review of Books* contributor, whose death in November left an unfillable gap of candor and integrity, quoted a complaint he had lodged against his colleagues in the press—that what they were practicing these days wasn't political analysis but "theater criticism." Shrewd owls such as

Nelson and Jack Germond represent a diminishing breed. In the past a prospective pundit could pass inspection by mouthing a rosary of political clichés. The New Hampshire primary: "retail politics." Social Security: "the third rail of American politics:" Ronald Reagan: "the Great Communicator." Today's pundit, raised in front of the TV and the computer screen, doesn't have the luxury of dismissing political theatrics as so much mascara. She or he has to be not merely a theater critic but an insatiable pop-culture sponge, putting an *Entertainment Weekly* face on every political player (Katherine Harris as Cruella De Vil). It is not enough to trot out the same tired line from *Casablanca* ("The Republicans were shocked, shocked, to discover pork in the House appropriations bill"), or to evoke *Wayne's World* ("It looks as if Ralph Nader will be forgiven by the Democrats— NOT"). Keeping tabs on current pop-culture fluff is hard work, requiring constant scanning, a cement butt, and the ability to turn attention deficit to your advantage. Let Maureen Dowd be your *Love Boat* guide. She and *New York Times* colleague Frank Rich are the ones most responsible for chasing politics through the cineplex. A recent Dowd column on George W. Bush began, "President-elect (?) Mini-Me has not yet started gnawing on his cat, as the 'Austin Powers' Mini-Me did to the hairless Mr. Bigglesworth"—a wisecrack that was cited that week by Al Hunt on *The Capital Gang*, much to Robert Novak's unamusement.

5. Pick a Side, Then Stick with It

Crucial to the career prospects of the aspiring pundit is deciding which team to play on. Committing to conservatism based on a close reading of Edmund Burke, the Federalist Papers, and the criticism of T. S. Eliot has become as passé as subscribing to liberalism after repeated exposure to John Stuart Mill and Arthur Schlesinger Jr.'s *The Age of Roosevelt*. Unless you've undergone strict Jesuit training, having too much intellectual ballast will only load you down and hamper your agility to dance around the truth when it comes time to defend Tom DeLay without gagging. No, today one's political loyalty is mostly a brand preference, like choosing Coke over Pepsi, Apple over Wintel. (Or a negative brand-selection rooted in antipathy, a way of signing up for any posse hounding Hillary Clinton.) Once your political label is chosen, however, it's pinned to your hide. Idiosyncratic political commentators who attack issues from unpredictable angles, such as the brilliant Kevin Phillips, who went from crafting Nixon's southern strategy to being the pin-striped populist of the books *Arrogant*

Capital and *Boiling Point*, perplex talk-show programmers trying to book a simple Punch-and-Judy act. Similarly, sage elders who transcend partisan bickering, such as *The Washington Post's* David S. Broder, the anointed egghead of Washington correspondents, function as sedatives during periods of national uncertainty and unrest. As long as Broder retains the title of the press corps's most respected calmer-downer, no one else need apply. Your task is not to hold complex problems up to a prism or to allay the anxiety of a troubled nation; your job is to dig a foxhole on one side of the liberal-conservative divide and fight like a breezy fanatic, giving no ground.

But which side? Eight years of Clinton scandal and the insurgence of Fox News have created openings for conservative nasties, but the saturation level may have been reached. Radio gripefests are dominated almost entirely by filibustering reactionaries like Sean Hannity and Bill O'Reilly (both Fox hosts). Unadulterated liberals have become so rare that the stars of Fox's *The Beltway Boys*, Mort Kondracke and Fred Barnes, are forced to collude in the laughable fiction that a lukewarm moderate like Kondracke consorts like a French hussy with the left. (When not crossing his arms and pouting, Fred makes ho-ho references to Mort's "liberal buddies on the Hill.") If I were you, I'd seize the opportunity of a possible liberal swing-back and try out for the underdog team. Unless, of course, you feel that would violate your "principles."

6. Once You Stake Out a Position, Feel Free to Abandon It

Dramatic flip-flops, which can be fatal to the health of a political career ("Read my lips—no second term"), are integral items in a pundit's acrobatic repertoire, along with the Palestinian-state pommel-horse straddle, the whoopee cartwheel, and the indignant whipback. Logical inconsistencies— lauding Anita Hill as a brave voice speaking truth to power, then diagnosing Kathleen Willey as a hysteric; asserting "the rule of law" until the rule of law rules against you—can be tucked into the larger consistency of sticking to the game plan. Twenty-twenty hindsight and a dose of amnesia allow even the most myopic opinion-maker to smooth out bad calls into the clean horizon of history. (Pundits who pronounced Clinton "political dead meat" during the Monica craze now marvel at his Houdini escape as if it were an outcome any fool could have foreseen.) Maintaining a fluid line of logical inconsistency means that the old debating-society rules no longer apply. In the early years of *Firing Line*, which was broadcast from 1966 to 1999, host William F.

Buckley Jr. had a feline ability to tease out the weak threads of an opponent's presentation until the entire case seemed to unravel. Today no one has the TV patience for such slow, methodical cross-exams. Constant interruptions and high-contrast personalities have miniaturized political debates into karate catfights, midair duels of catchphrases.

He/She says, "Chinese money-laundering!"

You say, "Iran-contra!"

He/She says, " 'No controlling legal authority!' "

You say, " 'Subliminable!' "

He/She says, "Class warfare!"

You say, "Top 1 percent!"

In the future, the transcripts of pundit squabbles will come to resemble snippets from e. e. cummings, chunks of concrete poetry.

doorpound of miami mob!
             dimpled ballot bingo.
     Katherine Harris's red-red lipstick
             —democracy's deathkiss
gore (sigh)/bush . . . hidebehinddaddy
    How dja lk yr
        willofthepeople
   now?
        mr chad

7. Learn to Modulate

Each pundit must turn himself into a one-man or -woman rapid-response machine, a compact version of the Clinton-Gore model. But the necessity to speak fast doesn't entail the necessity to speak LOUD. A pundit can raise his voice on occasion as long as it doesn't become a persistent foghorn.

The decline of John McLaughlin is instructive. A former speechwriter and special assistant to Presidents Nixon and Ford and an editor and columnist for the *National Review*, McLaughlin launched *The McLaughlin Group* in 1982. From the outset his band of pundits—which included the Prince of Darkness, Robert Novak—buffaloed through the modest compunctions and courtesies that characterized stodgier public-affairs shows such as *Washington Week in Review* and *Agronsky & Company* (whose verbal foot-dragging was hilariously lampooned by Michael Kinsley in *The*

New Republic). McLaughlin redefined the genre, and the panel itself took their act on the road, playing corporate events. The group's recognition factor peaked when *Saturday Night Live* parodied the show, with Dana Carvey imitating McLaughlin's stentorian boom and gavel-rapping verdicts (*"Wrong!"*), asking absurd round-robin questions, and ringing innumerable bananafana changes on Kondracke's name ("Mort-on Salt, when-it-rains-it-pours . . . what say you? . . . *Wrong!*"). McLaughlin took the wrong lesson from the satire. He seemed to believe that the skit's whopping success signified that audiences found his excesses endearing: he became even more of a caricature after Carvey's send-up, as if to show he was in on the joke and, what's more, could top it. For a man already riddled with hubris, priding himself as a mirth-maker was the folly of follies. As the show grew into a franchise, *The McLaughlin Group* began to drown in its host's chicken fat. Mc Laughlin's introductions became longer and fuller of thunderation, his choice of topics even more arbitrary and capricious; he imperiously played musical chairs with the panelists, antagonizing Novak and Germond until they finally defected. In Germond's memoir, *Fat Man in a Middle Seat*, he recalls how McLaughlin assumed the airs of a self-appointed caesar in the studio and on the road, hogging the money and sliding into a chauffeured limo while the other panelists had to pile into a van. His top-heavy ego eventually took its toll. In recent years, ratings for *The McLaughlin Group* have sunk like a damaged submarine, McLaughlin himself becoming a rusty relic, a dull roar.

His mouth has been supplanted by Chris Matthews's on *Hardball*. It's Matthews who is now the alpha-male master at talking over his guests, tackling their responses in mid-sentence, and free-associating like Dutch Schultz on his deathbed. But Matthews may have heeded the warning of McLaughlin's meltdown. In November, *Saturday Night Live* did a parody of him, mocking his outboard-motor manner and compulsion to ratchet up every discussion into a screaming meemie. Unlike McLaughlin, Matthews didn't interpret the parody as a popular mandate. It seems to have chastened him. Since then he's toned down his demeanor, becoming a reasonable facsimile of a rational person. On *Charlie Rose* recently, he seemed almost . . . calm. If he can continue to adapt, he'll be able to dodge the nickname of "Old Yeller."

8. Don't Merely Give Advice—Help Gum Up the Works!

"I can speak to almost anything with a lot of authority," Fred Barnes is quoted as saying with fathead complacency in Eric Alterman's *Sound and Fury: The Making of the Punditocracy.* Speaking with authority on everything from global warming to the ripple effects of Viagra is vital to a pundit's aura of offhand infallibility. A pundit is someone who knows exactly how hard Alan Greenspan should tap on the brakes to glide the economy to a soft landing, what the price of gas should be at the pump, where and how NATO forces should be stationed, and whether Microsoft should be compelled to unbundle its browser. You'll never hear a pundit confess, "Man, the Mideast, what a mess—glad it's not my problem." But sometimes it isn't enough to be a nimble know-it-all. Crucial moments in the course of human events require a more active meddling.

On Election Night, NBC and *Newsweek's* Jonathan Alter boldly stepped forward to help ball everything up. Only a week and a half earlier, Alter had told viewers of the *Today* show, "As many Americans know, the person with the most votes doesn't necessarily win. The election is decided by the electoral college." But on Election Night he flabbergasted Tom Brokaw (not an easy thing to do) and Tim Russert at the anchor desk by contending, "If it turns out that Al Gore wins the popular vote nationally, there will be intense pressure in this country to have him become the president. Most people think the guy with the most votes wins. The political pressure would mount quickly to certify Al Gore as the winner." Whoa! cried Brokaw and Russert, quickly dismissing this scenario and reasserting the primacy of the electoral college. "Yet in that moment, as his seniors smacked him down," wrote John J. Miller in the *National Review*, "Alter laid out what has become Gore's post-election strategy: denigrating an outcome in which Bush wins by the rules but not by a popular vote. Alter was on-message, even before there was a message to be on." And thus served as the advance scout guiding the Gore mule team and the electoral process into the Florida swamps and the morass of multiple lawsuits and political stalemate.

Way to go, guy!

9. Insulate Yourself from "the Little People"

Sometimes, sadly, to make new friends you must leave old friends behind. To become a successful pundit means saying good-bye to all "the little people" you used to know, those superfluous souls who aren't on TV and fill in the space in the fly-over zone lying between the power triangle of D.C.-N.Y.-L.A. From now on the average American belongs to a vast, vague abstraction known as "the American people," which is subdivided into cardboard-cutout cartoons such as soccer moms, former Reagan Democrats, and urban Bobos, and whose domestic concerns fall under the patronizing category of "kitchen-table topics." (Pundits love to picture families gathering around the kitchen table to discuss prescription-drug benefits.) These residents of Munchkin Land need not concern you, since you'll never have to meet them in the flesh, except in airports or town meetings where the caste system has broken down. Once you've joined the journalistic in-crowd and done your first of many E-mail chats on *Slate*, it's time to draw the curtain in the first-class compartment. Where a reporter like Haynes Johnson used to take palm readings of the masses to support his woolly platitudes (in Kinsley's parody of *Agronsky & Company*, he was Haynes Underwear, solemnly pronouncing, "For me to pass among the American people at this fleeting yet crucial moment in history, touching an outstretched hand here, accepting a gentle kiss on the foot there, was as stirring and moving for me as a journalist as it was for them as the American people"), today such dirty work can be shunned through the mediation of polls. Every pundit must be as conversant with polls and pollsters as a market analyst is with support levels and significant tops, able to divine the deeper booga-booga of conflicting numbers issuing from Zogby and Rasmussen. "Well, as you know, Brit, polls taken on Friday nights skew Democratic since more Democrats are likely to be home watching *The Fugitive*." ("Skew"—a key verb in the pundit's vocabulary.)

Polling data are the white noise of political discourse, a jamming device to make public opinion seem decisive when it's corporate money calling the shots. It's not a conspiracy, this nonstop numbers babble, but a collusion, a nexus of converging interests. Corporate sponsors underwrite the pundit's affluenza; they're the ones buying the ads (where would Sunday-morning Washington talk shows be without those G.E. spots?), hosting the business conventions and expos, and sharing the skybox with your media bosses. It's only natural that the pundit class would eventually gravitate to management's point of view while offering lip service to "the mood of the people." How can you align yourself with the workers when they keep losing your luggage? Led by Robert Novak, sneers at labor bosses have become a common slur in the pundit libretto. Germond states that McLaughlin was furious when he refused to cross a union picket line to tape the show. A fellow panelist, the supposed neo-liberal Kondracke, had no qualms about crossing the line (or sneaking around it), claiming the unions were "way out of control." Anything that inconveniences Mort is clearly the mark of anarchy.

10. Always End with a Hearty Chuckle

Pundit spats should never be taken personally. Ripping off your lapel mike and stomping out of the studio may feel good and look macho, but it will tend to cut down on future invitations. Remember, you and your fellow panelists belong to the same V.I.P club—practice collegiality; tease but don't torment. Nearly every broadcast of *Crossfire* and *The Capital Gang* ends with everyone enjoying a no-hard-feelings chuckle as the credits roll. Chuckling isn't as easy as it looks: to convey the shallows of phony bonhomie calls for a relaxed diaphragm and a nice twinkle. (Note the evident strain of the guests on *Washington Week in Review* laughing gamely at one another's toothless whimsies.) Pundits incapable of producing a fade-out chuckle—such as Joe Conason, who was the Michael Corleone to Jack Newfield's Godfather at *The Village Voice*, or the humorless tax-cut militant Grover Norquist—aren't as welcome in the banquet hall as more congenial spirits. They're booked, but not asked to join the regular roundtable. And then someday they won't be asked back anymore, and they'll sit in their lonely apartments, cursing the darkness.

A question from the floor:

—Are there any pundits you can recommend? Ones I could emulate without hating myself?

Yes. William Kristol of *The Weekly Standard*. He's civil, sheepishly self-deprecating (as befits Dan Quayle's former chief of staff), willing to depart from the Republican script and entertain doubts and contrary findings (unlike his associate at *The Weekly Standard*, Fred Barnes, who's squandered the journalistic credibility he built up at *The New Republic*), and he doesn't need to be grilled over an open flame to admit he's made a bum prediction. Whoever made the decision to drop him from the lineup of ABC's *This Week* deserves a dunce cap. James Warren of the *Chicago Tribune* has a sardonic, deadpan delivery. Bill Press started promisingly as the left side of *Crossfire*, but seems to be cashing in his brain cells as co-host of CNN's *The Spin Room*, where he and the self-enamored Tucker Carlson (who yips at his own jokes) field phone calls and E-mails from ignoramuses. *Newsweek's* Anna Quindlen and *The Nation's* editor, Katrina vanden Heuvel, were quite forceful on *Charlie Rose's* coverage of the second presidential debate. And of course there's our own excoriating Christopher Hitchens.

That's about it.

Any other questions? Good. Now go out there and hit the hair spray!

Washington
Meg Greenfield

from *Washington*

In her dual role as Newsweek *columnist and editorial page editor of* The Washington Post, *Meg Greenfield developed a well-deserved reputation as one of the country's canniest (and wittiest) observers of the national political scene. When she died of cancer in 1999 at the age of 68,* Post *publisher Donald Graham honored her as "a unique woman: wise and honest, skillful and brave—and funny."*

It turns out that Greenfield had one last, posthumous wisecrack up her sleeve—a book on Washington politics, which she began in the early 1990s and hadn't quite finished at the time of her death. The book was finally published last year, thanks to an editing assist from historian Michael Beschloss, and it garnered rave reviews. In the following excerpt, Greenfield lays out her principal thesis: That politics, as practiced in our nation's capital, resembles nothing so much as a latter-day high school, populated by chronic overachievers living in perpetual fear of the next election. . . .

Every derogatory comparison you can think of has been invoked to show how political Washington works and thus to explain its least endearing ways. The city and its inhabitants have been likened to a boring, elitist men's club; a recklessly run business; and a den of every known public and private vice, including lechery, larceny, pride, sloth, dissembling, and, above all, the lust for acquiring power and wielding it cruelly and carelessly.

I can understand what has given rise to each of these unflattering analogies. But I don't think any of them quite gets it right. The analogy I favor is to high school. . . .

High school is a preeminently nervous place. Never mind that high school students everywhere are known for adopting a pose of "What, me worry?" nonchalance so extreme as to border on an appearance of being dead. And why shouldn't high school be such a place? These are the years in which young people first encounter a make-or-break, peer-enforced social code that calculates worth as popularity and popularity as a capacity to please and be associated with the right people (no matter how undeserving they may be), as well as to impress and be admired by the vast, undifferentiated rest.

Even in today's most anarchic high schools, with cops and metal detectors, the basic social code and the imperatives to conform seem to be the same. Some version of these imperatives exists in other group settings as well, from kindergarten to the nursing home. But nowhere are they so intensely and continuously and unforgivingly present as in high school and Washington, D.C.

In saying this, I go against one fairly settled idea of the nation's capital as the quintessential company town. Under that reading, Washington is just one more of those familiar American settlements whose social as well as economic life is tightly organized around a single industry—in this case government, not cars or clothing or insurance.

The Washington I am talking about is not really a town at all, let alone an entire city. I am not thinking of the actual, physical District of Columbia, surrounded by Maryland and Virginia suburbs. The smaller, political/governmental Washington of which I write merely nests within that larger jurisdiction.

This other, lesser Washington is a relatively interconnected segment of the capital area's population, numbering only a few tens of thousands, there to manage, staff, study, lobby, or report on the federal government. Many of these people will have come to the city from somewhere else, some for a brief tour of duty, others for most of their working lives. They will have left behind the familiar, comforting landmarks and supports of their previous lives: the schools they attended, the churches, the friends, the parents and grandparents and cousins and rest of the extended family. They will create new lives from scratch in Washington without any of that automatic grounding or affirmation.

Practically all will still be vaguely planning to go back sometime to the place that was home, wherever it is, to be buried when the time comes. This will be true of some who have lived in the capital long enough to raise a family, buy a house, and pay off the mortgage. Although over long stretches of time they may be productively engaged and even happy, they are still only provisional citizens of the city or the region in which they live. Even as personal strangers, they tend to know a lot about one another. As individuals and groups who are often working politically at cross-purposes, they think of themselves nonetheless as a kind of shaggily coherent whole.

This population of long-term squatters is attuned to its own purposes, answers to its own code, administers its own rewards and punishments, and has its own distinctive conception of what constitutes winning and losing. On the basis of some unfathomable combination of all these factors, it maintains its own separate social and professional pecking order as well. More than any other pecking order on earth, I suspect, including the real kind, thought up in the barnyard by chickens, this one is given to continuous updating, downgrading, and overall revision of who or what ranks as the celebrity or urgency of the hour. For those who take the code seriously, it permits no rest. Gaming it is like trying to game the ooze of a lava lamp.

Now consider this settlement's profoundly high school nature. It is psychologically fenced off from the larger community within which it makes its home, free—like irresponsible youth—of all but the minimal obligations of citizenship to that community, and absorbed to the exclusion of all else in its own eccentric aims and competitions. And the high-school-like feel political/governmental Washington takes on by virtue of all of this is intensified by certain givens of its existence.

One is the only-passing-through nature of so much time spent here. I know that nowadays other cities also have more transient populations than they used to and that Americans as a whole have become remarkably mobile. I know too that other enterprises that employ large numbers of people have rigid hierarchies and fixed advancement schedules and a scale of increasing perks to mark the ascension to power and glory. But here in Washington—unlike in Detroit, say, or Hartford or Fort Worth—the entire experience tends to be structured and spoken of and often even thought about in ways strongly suggesting school.

Those other cities' reigning industries, for example, surely don't have "freshmen," as we do. Nor is this some semantic fluke: The words retain their conventional implications in Washington. "Freshman," for instance, is a congressional designation that is taken very seriously, entailing if not exactly hazing at least some initiation rites and put-downs by the big kids and expectations of deference to the elders while one is being tested and looked over and kept busy learning the place's protocols and taboos.

Note the astonishment that greeted newly installed Speaker Newt Gingrich's decision in 1995 to give a number of just-elected House freshmen seats on desirable committees. Traditionally, the most a congressional freshman could hope for in Washington was to eventually become a "sophomore," a second-termer, who is by custom accorded slightly more freedom of action, office space, and respect. The fact is that senators as well as representatives all consider themselves members of some class or other, dating from their election—the "class of 1972," they will say, for instance, or "the class of 1986." They establish a special relationship with their "classmates" across party lines and have "class" pictures taken.

In addition to classes, we have "terms," underscoring the fixed period of time for which people in both the legislative and executive branches have been sent to do their jobs. We also have Christmas, spring, and summer vacations, when a considerable part of the working population is out all at the same time and not, as in more normal adult working settings, on staggered personal vacation schedules. During such periods, much of the workforce that is technically not on vacation is nevertheless vaguely off-duty too—or at least partially idled and catching up on backlogged paperwork while waiting for the unruly bunch to return and the next hellacious, semester-like session to begin. . . .

Finally, and most important, since we have, effectively, underclassmen, so too we have upperclassmen and thus the ultimate sadistic joys of seniority. When the Republicans retook Congress in 1994, as with other previous upheavals like 1964 and 1974 and 1980, it was said that this time seniority had been dealt a mortal blow, that the young rebels who came to Congress were really going to break the old-guy mystique now, once and for all.

A lot does change on these occasions, but don't be misled: A lot also doesn't change. That is because too many Washington veterans of both parties have too much vested in the status they have acquired as a group. They have as well the advantage of knowing their way around the mine-strewn terrain that is federal-government Washington much better than any upstart, would-be supplanters could.

Seniority in Washington means more than merely having managed to get elected for fifty increasingly authoritarian years on the Hill, or having ascended the prescribed "grade-steps" in the career civil and foreign service, or having hung around long enough to be accorded among journalists the old-walrus-like honorific of "dean." It means having acquired the sway and savvy and special privilege of upperclassmen. And since not everybody leaves at the end of a few congressional terms or an administrative tour of duty or a rotating journalism assignment, some become more or less upperclassmen in perpetuity. They are hazers for life.

Traditionally the arbiters of the Washington scene are these big guys who set the rules. They select promising freshmen who are singled out for special advancement as protégés. These few lucky newcomers, on the basis of their talent and willingness to accept a period of apprenticeship and work within the peculiar spirit of the place, suddenly find themselves being mentioned everywhere as the freshmen "to watch."

The "seniors," it is true, can lose some altitude that they can't later regain when there is an upheaval by the voters. But they fight hard to retain their authority, and owing to the vast web of indebtedness and camaraderie they have spun and their known ability to inflict punishment when they are really angry, they have over the years been able to retain clout. This can even be true of big hitters who actually lose their jobs in Congress, the executive branch, or the press, for that matter. They may hang around in some new capacity, poshly headquartered in an office where they can show off their autographed power pictures and other evidence of recent glory, work their rich and bursting Rolodexes, and generally for much more pay than they ever got before, continue to influence public business—until those Rolodexes become pitifully out-of-date.

All this is, in the most cynical sense of the term, bipartisan. Even though the power of appointment and an ability to monopolize the agenda and the news belong to whichever party wins at the polls, there is a sense in which ideology, political party, and majority or minority status are irrelevant to the internal workings and power relationships of this Washington. And it is precisely these relationships that people start to cultivate, worry about, and protect when they have been here awhile. Once within the confines of the Capitol complex, most people come to accept its standards, live by its rules, honor its imperatives, treat its freshmen as they themselves once were treated, and—a telltale sign of embattled, bipartisan solidarity—start referring to the rest of the country (without quite realizing what the term conveys) as "out there."

Those two words say it all. "Out there" is the near equivalent of the schoolkid's term "the real world." It means where everybody else is, where we have to go some day when this is over, where we'll have to settle down and take "out-there" kinds of jobs, becoming just like all the rest. Both terms connote a less rewarding and more onerous environment in which to live, even if you are feeling oppressed by your homework and your tests or by your political pressures or gargantuan departmental workload. Like "the real world," "out there" seems less sympathetic and less exciting.

• • •

The outsider must be mystified that any mature, self-respecting adult would go along with the archaic and often degrading demands made on those who come to Washington—the schoolish, because-I-said-so rules, the layered-on customs and traditions that have something like the force of law and yet no longer seem related to the kind of subject matter they govern.

The answer begins with the particular nature of so many of the people who come here. Leave aside the demographics and the social science surveys and the analyses of median income, consumption habits, and religious background. The key index is this: Political/governmental Washington is an adult community made up largely of people who were extremely successful children. I don't say happy children or wealthy children or godly children. I mean only people who, as children, were good at being children.

Many of them continue to think of themselves as successful children and pursue their ambitions in the manner of the successful child. I'm not talking about the fabled "inner child" here but the "outer child" (if there can be such a term)—the invincibly pushy, precocious, overachieving-kid-like personas of a Clinton, a Gingrich, a Jack Kemp, for example, or the stylistically different personas of others who embody a different version of the childhood success story.

Such figures will have kept much of the outlook and mode of operating that served them so well in childhood. Why change an approach that from the beginning enabled them to flourish in a grown-up-imposed system that seemed to other kids pointless, unfair, and impossible to master or escape? We don't get many of the unsuccessful children here—almost none of the outright kid losers and not even all that big a population of the middling, muddle-through nondescript. On the contrary, what we tend to get are the hall monitors. In truth, we get many more than any one city should have to tolerate.

Washington also gets the teachers' pets; the most likely to succeed; the ones who got excellent grades; the ones who were especially good-looking in an old clothing-ad way; the ones who mowed the neighbor's lawn and were pronounced "fine young people"; the ones who got the Chamber of Commerce Boy or Girl of the Year Award; or the ones who figured out how to fake it and still make it—that whole range of smiling but empty-faced youth leaders who were universally admired, though no one could have told you for exactly what.

We get 4-H Club and Boy's Nation and Debating Society officers, along with some who made the all-star football team; we get the ingratiators and the operators and the grinds. And most notably, we get a small but steady stream of amazing prevailers, men and women who were able to overcome horrendous adversity of some kind in childhood to get here—the determined, express-train kids who knocked down all the obstacles and were the first in their families to do practically everything.

• • •

They may be very different from one another in lots of ways, including their varying tickets to success—good looks, good mind, pure grit. But from their early, formative experiences they will share one thing: They don't just like to prevail; they need to and expect to. Prevailing in this context means securing their place at the very top of whatever social collectivity it happens to be and becoming an influential, leading member of it, a praised person.

I don't mean to suggest that everyone in political/governmental Washington comes here as a queen bee and continues to function as one. Like most hives, this one owes plenty to its large complement of worker bees. But the people in Washington you've read about are likely to have come here at the end of a pretty well uninterrupted ascent to leadership of some kind that began, to much acclaim and gratification, in childhood. Partly because, to their consternation, they will unexpectedly find themselves surrounded in Washington by others who have followed the same trajectory and are equally accustomed to being number one, and partly because it is in the very nature of politics, there turns out to be no respite from the competition once they get here.

That is the big surprise. They are astonished to learn that they have not, after all, reached some triumphant resting place in their career where they can sit back and savor the rewards of their effort. On the contrary, they are immediately propelled into a way of life characterized by unremitting worry that some other aggressive, prize-winning mama's darling or some utterly unmanageable political catastrophe is about to overtake them. This turns out to be a daily consideration, never absent, always commanding some portion of their attention, and, by definition, never laid to rest. For as soon as they have disposed of one such anxiety, another will turn out to have been patiently waiting to take its place.

Here you have a defining horror of life in the capital. Its impact slowly dawns on those who come here. Like professional athletes, to whom they bear no other obvious resemblance, Washington political people are compelled to see themselves as holders of coveted jobs that are continuously at risk. They feel in constant danger not just of being suddenly tackled by an opponent—that much was to be expected—but of suddenly losing their title altogether or being benched for the rest of the season because someone better has turned up.

Washington figures are always, except for a privileged, ensconced, senior few, on professional probation. They feel driven to establish anew, every day of their working lives, their basic claim to be where they are. This they do through press leaks, self-promoting statements, grandstanding gestures, and subtle (of course, routinely denied) preemptive strikes at real, potential, and wholly imagined rivals.

• • •

This is not the prescription for a grounded, serene life, let alone an ethically irreproachable one. And it gets worse. Professional athletes can at least protect their position by doing what they get paid to do on the field. But for those in politics and government in Washington, this whole preoccupation is something that must be handled as an add-on to their day job. It's not what they are paid to do, not what most of them want to spend their time doing, and, worse, not the kind of concern they can easily confess to others. They must pretend that the grand and petty struggles for place, which consume so much of their attention, never happened.

They will, as a rule, respond to press inquiries or opposition attacks concerning such activities with an I-can't-imagine-what-you-are-talking-about protestation of innocence, which nobody believes. But they are more or less obliged to keep up the fiction. Many are here, after all, for the purpose of conducting public business at taxpayer expense, and that, in the public's view, is meant to be about something other than their own personal political fortunes or their rising and falling rank within the hive.

Yet the only people who can function effectively in Washington are those who have figured out how to integrate these two concerns—that of doing the substantive job and that of staying politically vital, ahead or at least abreast of all the other Little Rollos. The two efforts cannot be separated but must be in some right relation to each other. Officials who spend the bulk of their time serving mainly the requirements of personal ambition clearly will not get much governmental work of substance done and will in any case lack the influence needed to bring others along on such work as they do, since people will sneer at them as full-time self-servers. But, equally, officials who are all substance and no political maneuver, who are either indifferent to or contemptuous of the need to keep up in the wearing rank-and-status and base-building game, will fare no better. They may have the best intentions and the greatest ideas in the world, but they will probably soon be speaking into dead telephones.

Whether or not it should be the case, it is true that maintaining one's standing in political/governmental Washington is a condition of getting anything to happen. The rare political kamikaze flight or unexpected, electrifying breakout from the pack in a tell-all speech or defiant vote can have a tremendous impact. But it is generally a onetime impact, and a onetime impact for which its perpetrator will be made to pay plenty by offended colleagues at a later date, when the TV cameras aren't running and the public is looking the other way. To be productive over the long haul in Washington jobs of consequence, government people must establish and maintain strong political positions inside the governing complex.

This cannot usually be done simply by dictate or compulsion or intimidation or other strong-arm methods. It also cannot be done strictly on merit, that is, simply by being very proficient at something. Neither superior force nor sheer excellence, in other words, is sufficient. This can be categorically stated as a law: All durable success in political/governmental Washington—all "winning," all achieving—is derivative and dependent.

For finally what a winner must win is not anything that can be mechanically scored, like the outcome of a bowling match or a pie-eating contest, or anything that can be achieved on one's own, like a perfect half-gainer from the thirty-two-foot board. What a winner must win is the consent of others, whether out of respect or admiration or political agreement or mere expediency, to get something done. To get the machinery going at all, it is necessary first to elicit the cooperation—active or passive, freely or grudgingly given—of many other players.

Without this, one can only make speeches or rack up minor victories—obstructing a bill or an appointment or the implementation of a policy, for example, strictly by virtue of the delaying powers that go with a job. Even these will almost always eventually be undone by the larger group, and they only add to the disfavor in which the obstructors are held. On the Hill, their influence will wane. In the executive branch, they will be isolated, circumvented, and generally made the subject of ghastly, "authoritative" press leaks that will weaken them and, in good time, probably force them out.

The point is that loners may be able to sell themselves electorally at home and perhaps even nationwide in today's television-driven personality politics. But they cannot win in Washington, no matter how bad or good they are. Winning here means winning people over—sometimes by argument, sometimes by craft, sometimes by obsequiousness and favors, sometimes by pressure, and sometimes by a chest-thumping, ape-type show of strength that makes it seem prudent to get with the ape's program.

Every couple of years, when the parties choose their new congressional leaders, or from time to time, when someone is summarily kicked out of government or another high Washington post and someone unexpected is installed, you will be able to see the principle at work. This is how a dour, unpersonable, but favor-doing fellow like Senator Bob Byrd of West Virginia could ace out a personable but then self-involved and inattentive Ted Kennedy for Senate Democratic whip in 1971.

This explains how Newt Gingrich worked his way into a hostile, resisting, more moderate House Republican leadership and eventually to the office of speaker. It explains why some of the most dedicated and brilliant people who have come to the capital in recent years, like Senators Jacob Javits and Bill Bradley, may have engineered certain important pieces of legislation but were never really able to fulfill their awesome potential as powerful leaders in Congress. And the same principle explains how any number of seeming "stars" who have come to any number of presidential administrations wound up being axed in favor of the less talented, less celebrated, less charismatic souls backstage who were doing the greasing and making the trade-offs necessary to prevail.

One way or another, and no matter what else they may seem to be up to at any given moment, successful political people in Washington will be engaged in some form of this activity: Operation Make Them Love You, Operation Pay Them Off, Operation Watch Your Flank. It may not be attractive to behold, but it is not disreputable. On the contrary, it is indispensable to their work.

On Politics and the Art of Acting
Arthur Miller

from *On Politics and the Art of Acting*

The kinship between politics and show business has been part of our accepted wisdom since long before Ronald Reagan strode onto the national stage. Still, no one has elucidated the interplay of the two art forms as brilliantly as playwright Arthur Miller does here. Fittingly enough, this piece of writing originated as a speech—the 30th annual Jefferson Lecture in the Humanities, which Miller gave last year at the John F. Kennedy Center for the Performing Arts in Washington, D.C. In his essay, Miller describes how an effective political performance is like a good play—and explains why a well crafted persona is key to a politician's success. . . .

Political leaders everywhere have come to understand that to govern they must learn how to act. No differently than any actor, Al Gore apparently rummaged through several changes of costume before finding the right mix to express the personality he thought it profitable to project. Up to the campaign he seemed an essentially serious man with no great claim to merry humor, but the presidential-type character he felt he had to play was apparently happy, upbeat, with a kind of Bing Crosby mellowness. I daresay that if he seemed so awkward it was partly because the adopted image was not really his, he had cast himself in a role that was wrong for him, as not infrequently happens to unlucky actors cast in films and theater. The original production of *Death of a Salesman*, for example, veered very close to disaster because the director and I were trying to be too faithful to a stage direction I had written into the script describing Willy as a small man. We proceeded to audition every small actor we could find, some very good ones among them, but the role in their hands seemed to be diminished into a kind of complaint, far from what was intended. In fact, there was a heroic aspect to the part which a Lee Cobb—over six feet tall and weighing nearly two hundred pounds—could effortlessly bring out, at least in rehearsal. Of course once an audience takes its seats these effects are extremely difficult to predict. I think this is so because, fundamentally, a play is trying to create an individual out of a mob, a single unified reaction out of a thousand individual ones whose interactions are mysterious. The political leader faces the same task and uncertainty, neither more nor less. Whether calculatedly or instinctively, he has to find the magnetic core that will draw together a fragmented public, and is thus obliged to try to avoid sending signals that might alienate significant sectors of his audience. Inevitably, this kind of management of an audience requires acting.

The difficult question of sincerity, therefore, arises from the very nature of persuasion itself, and with it, inevitably, the question of lying or shaving the edges of inconvenient truths. Hence, the resort to acting, to performing a role. I would like to believe—and often do—that most American congressmen and senators most of the time are probably saying in public what they also say in private, if only because consistency costs them little when they have few listeners anyway and little to lose. But the burning white light focused on the American presidential candidate is of a very different order when his election may mean a new direction for the country and a threat or reassurance to business and government in many other parts of the world. Thus the television lens becomes a microscope with the world at the eyepiece. Now the candidate's self-control, his steadiness under fire, is dangerously magnified and becomes as crucial to his success as it is to the actor facing a thousand critics as he stands alone in a spotlight surrounded by darkness on a stage.

Power, of course, changes how people act, and George W. Bush, now that he is president, seems to have learned not to sneer quite so much, and to cease furtively glancing left and right when leading up to a punch line, followed by a sharp nod to flash that he has successfully delivered it. This is bad acting, because all this dire overemphasis casts doubt on the text. Obviously, as the sparkly magic veil of actual power has descended upon him, he has become more relaxed and confident, like an actor after he has read some hit reviews and knows the show is in for a run.

At this point I suppose I should add something about my own bias toward acting and actors. I recall the day, back in the fifties, during Eisenhower's campaign against Adlai Stevenson, when I turned on my television and saw the general who had led the greatest invasion force in history lying back under the hands of a professional makeup woman preparing him for his TV appearance. I was far more naive then, and so I still found it hard to believe that henceforth we were to be wooed and won by rouge, lipstick, and powder rather than ideas and positions on public issues. It was almost as though he were getting ready to go on in the role of General Eisenhower instead of simply *being* him. In politics, of course, what you see is rarely what you get, but in fact Eisenhower was not a good actor, especially when he ad-libbed, disserving himself as a nearly comical bumbler with the English language when in fact he was actually a lot more literate and sophisticated than his fumbling public-speaking style suggested. As his biographer, a *Life* editor named Emmet John Hughes, once told me, Eisenhower, when he was still a junior officer, was the author of all those smoothly euphonious, rather Roman-style speeches that had made his boss, Douglas MacArthur, seem on the verge of donning a toga. Then again, I wonder if Eisenhower's syntactical stumbling in public made him seem more convincingly sincere.

Watching some of our leaders on TV has made me wonder if we really have any idea what is involved in the actor's art, and I recall again a story once told me by my old friend the late Robert Lewis, director of a number of beautiful Broadway productions, including the original *Brigadoon*. Starting out as an actor in the late twenties, Bobby had been the assistant and dresser of Jacob Ben-Ami, a star in Europe and in New York as well. Ben-Ami, an extraordinary actor, was in a Yiddish play, but despite the language and the location of the theatre far from Times Square, on the Lower East Side of Manhattan, one of its scenes had turned it into a substantial hit with English-speaking audiences. Experiencing that scene had become the in thing to do in New York. People who had never dreamed of seeing a Yiddish play traveled downtown to watch this one scene, and then left. In it Ben-Ami stood at the edge of the stage staring into space and, with tremendous tension, brought a revolver to his head. Seconds passed, whole minutes. Some in the audience shut their eyes or turned away, certain the shot was coming at any instant. Ben-Ami clenched his jaws. Sweat broke out on his face. His eyes seemed about to pop out of his head; his hands trembled as he strove to will himself to suicide. More moments passed. People in the audience were gasping for breath and making strange asphyxiated noises. Finally, standing on his toes now as though to leap into the unknown, Ben-Ami dropped the gun and cried out, *"Ikh ken nit!"* I can't do it! Night after night he brought the house down; Ben-Ami somehow compelled the audience to suspend its disbelief and to imagine his brains splattered all over the stage.

Lewis, aspiring young actor that he was, begged Ben-Ami to tell him the secret of how he had created this emotional reality, but the actor kept putting him off, saying he would only tell him after the final performance. "It's better for people not to know," he said, "or it'll spoil the show."

Then at last the final performance came, and at its end Ben-Ami sat in his dressing room with the young Lewis.

"You promised to tell me," Lewis said.

"All right, I'll tell you. My problem with this scene," Ben-Ami explained, "was that I personally could never blow my brains out. I am just not suicidal, and I can't imagine ending my life. So I could never really know how that man was feeling, and I could never play such a person authentically. For weeks I went around trying to think of some parallel in my own life that I could draw on. What situation could I be in where, first of all, I am standing up, I am alone, I am looking straight ahead, and something I feel I must do is making me absolutely terrified, and finally that whatever it is I can't do it?"

"Yes," Lewis said, hungry for this great actor's key to greatness. "And what is that?"

"Well," Ben-Ami said, "I finally realized that the one thing I hate worse than anything is washing in cold water. So what I'm really doing with that gun to my head is, I'm trying to get myself to step into an ice-cold shower."

Now if we transfer this situation to political campaigns, who are we really voting for: the self-possessed character who projects dignity, exemplary morals and forthright courage enough to lead us in war or depression, or is he simply good at characterizing a counterfeit with the help of professional coaching, executive tailoring, and that whole array of technological pretense which the grooming of the president can now employ? Are we allowed anymore to know what is going on not in the candidate's facial expression and his choice of suit but in his head? Unfortunately, as with Ben-Ami, this is something we are not told until he is securely in office and his auditioning ends. During the campaign, for example, Mr. Bush made much of his interest in supporting education, child-protective measures, as well as the environmental protections, but within days of his administration's accession he moved to weaken one environmental protection after another, his budget shortchanged education and slashed the budget of child-protection agencies. After spending tens of millions of dollars, both candidates—at least for me—never managed to create that unmistakable click of recognition as to who they really were and it may well be that at least in Mr. Bush's case he knew the agenda he really had in mind would lose him votes, if revealed too soon, and this very possibly was why one had so much trouble locating him as a real individual. As for Gore, it is impossible to know how true to his programs he would have turned out to be, but his surprising announcement of support during the campaign for the Florida Cubans in their refusal to turn over Elian Gonzalez to the boy's father may well have signaled a more general opportunism; we will never know. In any case, that the Cubans' votes would ever go to a Democrat was so unlikely that the gesture toward them seemed inept even as politics, especially when for many of his followers it put Gore's integrity into question.

But stepping back from all this one has to wonder if it is simply silly to expect consistency or even coherence in candidates for national office when they are obliged to placate interests that in fact are in direct conflict with one another.

The so-called Stanislavsky system came into vogue at the dawn of the twentieth century, when science was recognized as the dominating force of the age. Objective scientific analysis promised to open everything to human control, and the Stanislavsky method was an attempt to systematize the actor's vagrant search for authenticity as he works to portray a character different from his own. Politicians do something similar all the time; by assuming personalities not genuinely theirs—let's say six-pack, lunch-box types—they hope to connect with ordinary Americans. The difficulty for Bush and Gore in their attempts to seem like regular fellas was that both were scions of successful and powerful families. Worse yet for their regular-fella personae, both were in effect created by the culture of Washington, D.C., but since you can't hope to be president without running against Washington they had to run against themselves, something which surely did not add reality to either of them. The problem for Gore was that Washington meant Clinton, whom he dared not acknowledge lest he be challenged on moral grounds. As for Bush, he was forced to impersonate an outsider pitching against dependency on the federal government, whose payroll, however, had helped feed two generations of his family. There's a name for this sort of cannonading of Washington; it is called acting. To some important degree both gentlemen had to act themselves out of their real personae into freshly begotten ones. The reality, of course, was that the closest thing on the political stage to a man of the people was Clinton the Unclean, the real goods with the six-pack background, whom it was both dangerous and necessary to disown. This took a monstrous amount of acting.

Digital Disjuncture
Ted Halstead and Michael Lind

from *The Radical Center: The Future of American Politics*

Is the current two-party system failing the average American voter? That's the conclusion of this provocative tract, born out of a new think tank called the New American Foundation whose stated mission is "to bring exceptionally promising new voices and new ideas to the fore of our nation's public discourse." In this excerpt from their book The Radical Center, *Halstead and Lind (NAF president and senior fellow, respectively) explain how the Republican and Democratic parties have gotten off track, and what can be done to remedy the situation. . . .*

In December 2000, in the wake of the closest presidential election in U.S. history, the Gallup Organization asked Americans, in a national poll, about their political affiliation. The result: More Americans (42 percent) identified themselves as independents than as either Democrats or Republicans. Astonishing as it may seem, a clear plurality of Americans have become so hostile to the two parties that have defined our nation's politics for the past century that they preferred "neither of the above," even in the absence of a serious alternative. Political analysts like to talk about electoral "realignments" in favor of one party or another, but what is occurring here is something altogether different—we are experiencing a large-scale political "dealignment."

This striking dealignment suggests that our Democratic and Republican parties have failed the two most important tests of American politics: the ability to unite a majority of citizens in a lasting coalition, and the ability to find workable solutions to the problems of our time. Having been captured by their own extremes, both parties are increasingly incapable of promoting majority views across a wide range of issues. Second, both remain so wedded to the ideas and institutions of the last century that neither has proven itself capable of rising to the challenges of the next. Our nation's politics are dominated by two feuding dinosaurs that have outlived the world in which they evolved.

Let us consider each of these shortcomings of our two-party cartel in turn.

• • •

Despite concerted efforts over the past decade, both the Democratic and Republican parties have failed to build new majority coalitions. Instead of expanding their voter bases, both parties have allowed themselves to be taken hostage by narrow pressure groups on certain defining issues. These groups include social conservatives and economic libertarians in the case of the Republican Party, and a constellation of aggrieved minority groups and public employee unions in the case of the Democratic Party. Naturally, this consolidation of power at the extremes has further alienated growing numbers of Americans from either party.

The ascendancy of these well-organized factions in their respective parties has given them a level of political power far out of proportion to their actual numbers in the general electorate. In the 2000 presidential primaries, for instance, it was clear that no candidate who dared defy the religious Right could gain the Republican nomination, as Senator John McCain discovered. By early 2001, McCain had nevertheless become the most popular politician in the United States, further crystallizing the disconnect between the views of the electorate and those of his own party, where he remained relatively unpopular. The same minority veto power was at play on the Democratic side, where vice presidential candidate Joseph Lieberman was forced to abandon his principled positions on school choice and affirmative action in order to qualify for the ticket. This is not to suggest that the parties do not espouse centrist positions on other issues, or that neither has centrist members; to the contrary, McCain and Lieberman are both leaders among the centrist wings of their respective parties. But these centrists are constantly overshadowed and overpowered by the more extreme elements of their own camp.

This basic reality leads to a fundamental disjuncture between what the American people want and what the leading parties offer. As Harvard political scientist David C. King explains, "Both political parties have been growing more extreme . . . they are increasingly distant in their policies from what the average voter would like." While the conservative wing of the Republican Party and the liberal wing of the Democratic Party have become ever more powerful, the American people themselves have become ever more moderate in their views. During the 2000 election, for instance, a national poll revealed that only 29 percent of Americans actually view themselves as conservatives, and an even smaller number, 20 percent, view themselves as liberals, with a full 50 percent describing themselves as moderates.

It is this moderate majority of Americans—composed of self-identified independents, along with significant numbers of centrist Republicans and Democrats—who feel most alienated by today's increasingly dogmatic two-party system. Although their numbers in the electorate far outweigh those of the special interest groups on the Right and Left, the latter nevertheless continue to wield more political power as a result of the archaic design of our electoral process, which in effect limits political choices to an option between two extremes. This not only fuels popular resentment against the political system as a whole, it perpetuates the illusion of a sharply divided nation when in fact the alienated majority of Americans are far more interested in finding common ground than in fighting culture wars.

Further fueling this sense of political alienation, our current two-party cartel forces many voters to sacrifice one important value for another. Suppose that, like many Americans, you believe in reproductive choice as well as school choice. In an ideal world, you could vote for a presidential candidate and political party that reflects both of these positions. In today's political system, however, any American holding these two views must confront the uncomfortable dilemma of choosing one at the expense of the other. Likewise, voters are now routinely forced to choose between the party that stands for treating all citizens equally regardless of racial origin and the party that stands for treating all citizens equally regardless of sexual orientation; between the party in favor of tax fairness and the party in favor of tax simplification; and between the goal of a more competitive marketplace and that of a more sustainable environment. In addition to imposing these artificial trade-offs on the public, several items most Americans say they favor—such as genuine campaign finance reform or amending our electoral system to increase voter choice—are not on offer from the major parties, which are less interested in pleasing voters than in colluding to maintain rules that preserve their comfortable cartel.

Given the degree to which our major parties are captured by their extremes, is it really that surprising that an unprecedented number of Americans feel they no longer have a party to call their own? This striking political dealignment has not escaped the attention of politicians. Indeed, during the 2000 presidential race, analysts from both parties agreed that the election would turn on a candidate's ability to win the support of the growing pool of undecided and independent-minded swing voters. But this presented presidential aspirants with a genuine dilemma, given the stark dichotomy between their increasingly rigid parties and an increasingly heterodox electorate. In an effort to escape from this dilemma, recent presidential candidates and victors have developed the dubious art of political triangulation.

The two-term presidency of Bill Clinton from 1992 to 2000 was unusual in that Clinton, a Democrat, borrowed heavily from the ideas of the Republican establishment, often to the consternation of his own party's rank and file. His dominant strategy, which came to be known as triangulation, was premised on applying what were widely seen as conservative policy ideas to achieve progressive ends. George W. Bush used the same strategy in reverse during the 2000 presidential race: In an effort to appropriate what are traditionally viewed as Democratic issues (such as concern about poverty and education) to his advantage, he coined the clever campaign slogan of "compassionate conservatism."

With the benefit of hindsight, it seems clear that this two-way triangulation, far from providing a genuine alternative to conservative Republicans or liberal Democrats, only reinforced the shortcomings of our two-party system, and will accelerate the political dealignment already under way. Interestingly, Clinton's and Bush's versions of triangulation failed for different reasons.

To his credit, President Clinton did forge a new middle ground on some issues, such as fiscal policy and welfare reform, though he often had difficulty bringing the Democratic Party along with him. Yet the more fundamental fact is that Clinton never so much as tried to challenge his party's most powerful special interest groups, which have maintained their lock on issues like affirmative action, Social Security, and education policy. After eight years of Clintonian triangulation, then, the Democratic Party remains as dominated as ever by its most-entrenched interest groups.

President Bush's early experimentation with triangulation was also a failure, but mostly because it was disingenuous. Indeed, to Bush, triangulation appears to have been little more than a game of bait and switch. During the campaign, he promised the American people that he would be a different kind of Republican, tear down the walls that kept America divided, and even fight to reduce our emissions of carbon dioxide (the main culprit in the global warming equation). Yet during his first months in office Bush did just the opposite: He angered many centrist voters by tapping a far-right conservative, John Ashcroft, as his attorney general; he pushed for a large tax cut that would overwhelmingly benefit the well-to-do; and he reversed himself completely on his global warming pledge. As a result, Bush not only alienated many Americans but also alienated Senator

James Jeffords, whose defection from the Republican Party turned over control of the U.S. Senate to Democrats.

For all the talk of bipartisan cooperation and moderation during the 2000 campaign, it became clear within the first months of the new administration that neither party had really changed, and that the alienated majority of Americans, once again, had nowhere to turn.

If the first way in which our two-party duopoly has failed the American people is by succumbing to extremes, then its second and more profound failure is its imprisonment in the past. . . .

Many of the tenets of Democratic liberalism, now commonly called progressivism, were developed during the New Deal era, beginning in the 1930s, while most of the orthodoxies of today's Republican conservatism were developed during the 1960s or 1970s. Both ideologies are vestiges of the Second Industrial Revolution of the twentieth century and are ill suited to the new challenges and opportunities of the information era. . . .

All of this suggests that it is high time for a new political program, one tailored to the new realities of Information Age America yet anchored in our nation's timeless values.

We call our new political program the Radical Center. We chose this name to differentiate our principles and policies from those of the Democratic Left and the Republican Right. To us, it seems obvious that the familiar varieties of liberalism and conservatism, developed as they were in response to the Second Industrial Revolution, are largely irrelevant in the fundamentally different environment of the first half of the twenty-first century. "Centrism" itself has become something of a shallow mantra in recent American politics. It is usually invoked in a tactical effort to bridge the differences between the existing Left and Right—yielding a "Squishy Center" that lies between Left and Right, rather than a "Radical Center." We use the word *radical*—in keeping with its Latin derivation from "radix," or "root"— to emphasize that we are interested not in tinkering at the margin of our inherited public, private, and communal institutions but rather in promoting, when necessary, a wholesale revamping of their component parts.

The underlying purpose of this Radical Centrist program is to further expand America's perennial goals of individual liberty, equality of opportunity, and national unity in the new circumstances of the Information Age.

• • •

What then should be the organizing principle of an Information Age political program? In redesigning our nation's public, private, and communal institutions once again for the new conditions of the early twenty-first century, we believe that one design criterion above all others should guide us: increasing the amount of choice available to individual citizens. So far, the information era has enabled most Americans to enjoy newfound choices only as consumers in the economic and entertainment spheres. Any new political program worthy of the Information Age must be capable of translating this so far narrow expansion of choices to many other spheres of society: voting choices, educational choices, medical choices, retirement choices, lifestyle choices, and career choices.

Our Radical Centrist philosophy therefore begins from the premise that American citizens in the twenty-first century deserve more choices in—and discretion over—the decisions that shape their lives. While this emphasis on expanding individual choices may seem obvious, its implications are profound. For one thing, if individual citizens are to be empowered with greater decision-making authority, then many of today's institutions must be redesigned so as to become citizen-based. For example, today's employer-based programs (such as health care), group-based programs (such as Social Security), and place-based programs (such as locally financed public schools) must undergo a radical reinvention if the locus of decision making is to be transferred to the individual. Such a shift would not only empower individuals but also protect them from many of the uncertainties associated with relying on intermediary institutions that are themselves at the whim of today's fast-changing economy.

• • •

A second guiding principle of Radical Centrism is that the citizens of the twenty-first century can and should be held to a higher personal standard. In this new era of big citizenship, greater choice and freedom must go hand in hand with greater responsibility. Formerly, civic duty was identified primarily with military service, jury duty, and the act of voting. But the definition of civic duty now needs to be expanded, especially in a society in which most citizens receive transfer payments or subsidies from their fellow taxpayers. In such a society, self-reliance must become a civic duty as well as a private virtue. If Americans want more discretion over the decisions that affect their lives, then they will need to be more self-sufficient. For example, if our health care and pension systems are to become citizen-based and personally managed, then it seems only reasonable to require those who can to pay for their own health care insurance and save for their own retirement. Doing otherwise would inhibit personal freedom at the broadest level, by forcing our least fortunate citizens to subsidize the irresponsibility of those who are capable of fending for themselves. Likewise, certain types of personal freedom—the ability to use genetic engineering to create designer babies, for example—must be limited when they risk undermining the broader common good. In short, freedom and responsibility must expand in tandem.

Implicit in this Radical Centrist philosophy is a new conception of the role of government. There are, in essence, two models through which a government can provide basic economic security to its citizens: the safety net model and the universal provider model. The former assumes that public benefits should only go to help the neediest, while the latter assumes that public benefits should accrue to all citizens, regardless of need. The New Deal philosophy, in its most familiar version—epitomized by programs like Social Security and Medicare—is based on the universal provider model. The Radical Centrist philosophy, by contrast, is premised on the safety net model.

At this stage in our nation's history, the universal provider model not only inhibits personal choice and responsibility, but economic security as well. For instance, the very design of our Social Security system creates a powerful disincentive for personal savings, which is the exact opposite of what the nation needs as the retirement of the baby boom generation approaches. Meanwhile, many of today's youngest workers fear for the future of our Social Security system. More worrisome still is the threat that the rapidly escalating costs of Social Security and Medicare will turn our government into little more than an intergenerational transfer agency, while crowding out government's ability to fund and invest in other critical public functions, ranging from education to infrastructure to national defense.

To criticize the New Deal welfare model that is routinely defended by today's Democratic Party is not to side with today's Republican Party, which has established a troubling record of slashing funds to the neediest and youngest Americans. The Radical Centrist alternative is a true safety net model, under which public benefits would be provided to those who need them the most, while those who can afford to pay their own way would be required to do so. The overwhelming advantage of this approach is that it would enable our nation to increase individual choice, responsibility, and security simultaneously.

A final implication of this new emphasis on individual choice relates to our notion of federalism, or the balance between state and federal authority. Typically, debates over federalism are viewed as zero-sum games pitting the power of local or state bureaucracies against those of federal bureaucracies. Ensuring greater individual choice in public policy, however, will sometimes require a greater federal role at the expense of local or state governments. For example, any equitable plan for nationwide school choice would require nationwide equalization of school funding on a per pupil basis, which in turn can only be accomplished through greater federal involvement in school funding. Interestingly, however, the terms of such a debate would not so much pit federal control against local control as they would pit control by local bureaucracies against control by individual citizens (in this particular case, parents). Hence a final principle of Radical Centrism is cooperative federalism: the principle that local and state jurisdictions should sometimes cede authority to federal jurisdictions in cases where the outcome is the expansion of individual freedoms and choices. As we shall see, this principle has strong precedents in U.S. Constitutional thought.

Combined, these various principles for a Radical Centrist public philosophy for Information Age America—expanding individual choices and responsibilities through citizen-based programs, the notion of big citizenship, a safety net approach to public benefits, and cooperative federalism—serve as unifying threads that weave together the various proposals that animate these pages.

In the realm of the market, if American citizens are to welcome a highly dynamic global economy and tolerate continuous waves of technology-driven change, then the prerequisite will be a new citizen-based social contract. In the twenty-first century, the flexibility of business and the security of individuals alike require severing the traditional link between employers and the provision of benefits, and doing away with the old distinctions between full-time and contingent workers altogether. Done correctly, this would free businesses from the burden of benefit administration, and give rise to a very dynamic new workforce able to enjoy the freedoms of today's contingent workers and the security of today's full-time employees. Specifically, we propose a mandatory private health care system for all Americans that would ensure that the poorest and least healthy are fully covered.

In the area of retirement policy, we recommend "progressive privatization" of our Social Security system, to be based on mandatory retirement savings for all workers, public subsidies to top off the personal savings accounts of low-income workers, and a guaranteed safety net for those who fall through the cracks. Both reforms—severing health care insurance from employment, and increasing reliance on personal savings accounts for retirement—embody the principles of citizen-based policies, of big citizenship and greater self-reliance, and of a safety net approach to public benefits.

In the twentieth century, the objective of our basic social contract was to protect all Americans from destitution. In the twenty-first century, however, we must go one step further by adding a major new clause: universal capitalism. The key to upward mobility and personal wealth creation in the so-called new economy is ownership of capital assets, which explains why the gap between the very wealthy (who own most of our nation's financial assets) and the rest of Americans (who rely primarily on their wages for income) is growing to frightening heights. The solution is to broaden the ownership of financial capital so that all Americans can benefit directly from our growing economy, and have access to the resources required to invest in their own skills development and futures. We therefore propose endowing every American child with individual financial assets from birth.

When it comes to our public sector, the challenge is not so much to shrink or expand government as it is to radically modernize it. As we have seen, much of the popular resentment against government and elected officials stems from our lack of true electoral choices. We therefore propose overhauling our political system via changes that would provide more options to voters, whether they choose to support our existing parties or new parties. Most modern democracies have upgraded their electoral systems in the past half century, and there is no reason why the United States shouldn't follow suit. No less important would be modernizing and revising some of the internal procedures of the House and Senate.

Next, we turn to the one feature of the government that most impacts the daily lives of all Americans: the tax code. In order to solve the Internet sales tax problem and boost national savings rates, we propose eliminating the antiquated patchwork of state sales taxes altogether and replacing it with a simple and progressive national consumption tax, whose revenues would be rebated to all states. The centerpiece of our proposed new federal tax structure is a radically simplified progressive income tax. By eliminating virtually all the tax deductions, expenditures, and loopholes that render our current system so unwieldy, we could create a much fairer tax system for the twenty-first century that is so simple and transparent that most Americans could file their tax returns in a matter of minutes.

As for the all-important task of educating future generations, we favor various ways to broaden school choice and, in the process, increase accountability. But for this to be done in an equitable manner, we argue for the national equalization of school funding on a per pupil basis, and for doing away once and for all with the archaic link between school financing and state and local taxation. This fundamental change could dramatically improve the quality of public education across our land, and pave the way for numerous educational improvements to follow. . . .

In the absence of a crisis, new alliances and new ideas have not always proved to be sufficient. We are cautiously optimistic, however, for several reasons. First and foremost, the dissatisfaction of the American electorate in recent years has given rise to a broad and diverse base of independent-minded voters who, we argue, might be particularly receptive to the principles and programs of the Radical Center. Next, a new generation and a new elite are ascending in America. Both lack a well-formed political worldview, and could prove to be a ready audience for the institutional and ideological metamorphosis that we propose. In addition, the sheer speed and magnitude of the technological revolution under way could further destabilize today's archaic political and institutional arrangements far sooner than many of us might expect.

Already, the current coalitions that form the bases of the Democratic and Republican Parties are beginning to fissure, perhaps irreparably. For Democrats, the issue of school choice is pitting two of the party's core constituencies against one another: teachers unions, which are overwhelmingly opposed to school choice, and African-Americans, who are overwhelmingly in support. The emerging biotech revolution may have much the same effect on the Republican side, pitting social conservatives, who tend to oppose the genetic modification of human beings, against the free-market libertarian camp, which views genetic technology as the next big commercial bonanza.

Each of these developments suggests that America's next major political realignment may not be far off. That realignment may take the form of the emergence of one or more new national parties. More likely, however, it will result from the transformation of either or both of today's leading parties. The future of American politics may well belong to the major party that is first to renounce its more extreme positions, and embrace a new Radical Centrist agenda.

What We Must Overcome
Lani Guinier

The American Prospect | March 12, 2001

Most Americans remember Lani Guinier best from her short-lived nomination in 1993 for the post of U.S. Attorney General—a nomination that President Bill Clinton (in an early sign of his readiness to abandon liberal positions when politically necessary) swiftly withdrew after Guinier drew fire from conservatives for her writings on election law.

Since then, Guinier has been managing just fine in her day job as professor of law, first at the University of Pennsylvania Law School and currently as a member of the faculty at Harvard Law School. She has also continued to write eloquently about her primary interest: How to provide a better electoral process and fairer access to the voting booth for all Americans.

In the following essay, Guinier reflects on the U.S. Supreme Court's role in the 2000 presidential election—and suggests that the high court's decision in Bush v. Gore *may spur a new "citizens' movement" in the pursuit of a more representative voting system. . . .*

For years many of us have been calling for a national conversation about what it means to be a multiracial democracy. We have catalogued the glaring flaws inherent in our winner-take-all form of voting, which has produced a steady decline in voter participation, underrepresentation of women and racial minorities in office, lack of meaningful competition and choice in most elections, and the general failure of politics to mobilize, inform, and inspire half the eligible electorate. Still, nothing changed. Democracy was an asterisk in political debate and the diagnosis for what ailed it was encompassed in vague references to "campaign finance reform." But the harm was not just in the money and its sources; the problem has been the rules of American democracy itself.

Now, in light of its dramatic and unavoidably political resolution of the 2000 presidential election, no less an authority than the U.S. Supreme Court calls on us to consider what it means to be a multiracial democracy that has equal protection as its first principle. On December 12, 2000, in *Bush v. Gore,* the Supreme

Court selected the next president when, in the name of George W. Bush's rights to equal protection of the laws, it stopped the recounting of votes. Excoriated at the time for deciding an election, the Court majority's stout reading of equal protection could nevertheless become an invitation not just to future litigation but to a citizens' movement for genuine participatory democracy. At minimum, the Court's decision—and the colossal legal fight that preceded it—should now spark a real debate about the rules of democracy on an even larger scale than we previously imagined.

The decision invites future litigants to rely on the Court's newfound equal protection commitments to enforce uniform standards for casting and tabulating votes in federal elections from state to state, county to county, and within counties. The conservative majority found that the source of the fundamental nature of the right to vote "lies in the equal weight accorded to each vote and the equal dignity owed to each voter." We have not heard such a full-throated representation of the equal protection clause in many years, at least not with regard to the rights of voters to do more than cast a ballot. This language harkens back to the broad commitment we once heard from the 1960s-era Warren Court, which affirmed the people's fundamental right to exercise their suffrage "in a free and unimpaired manner." Concerned that the lack of uniform standards for a manual recount would lead to "arbitrary and disparate treatment" of the members of the Florida electorate, the majority relied on two expansive Supreme Court decisions, *Harper v. Virginia Board of Election* and *Reynolds v. Sims*. These cases, from the salad days of the Warren Court, explicitly affirm Lincoln's vision of government of the people, by the people, for the people. Perhaps—in the name of restoring "voter confidence in the outcome of elections"—the conservative majority will now welcome, as it did in *Bush v. Gore*, other lawsuits that seek to challenge the very discretion the five-vote majority found so troublesome when exercised by local Florida county officials. Perhaps not.

It seems unlikely, of course, that the conservative majority will act in the future to rehabilitate our partial democracy. Some undoubtedly will argue that the *per curiam* decision only addresses the remedial power of a state court seeking a statewide remedy. Others will point to the great irony that the Court has shown itself more deeply committed to safeguarding the rights of a major-party candidate than to protecting disenfranchised voters across the board.

The *Bush v. Gore* majority, which went out on a limb to protect the rights of a single litigant, George W. Bush, has been noticeably less exercised about arbitrary or disparate treatment when such considerations are raised by voters who are racial minorities. Indeed, in a 1994 concurring opinion, when the claim to a meaningful and equally valued vote was raised by black litigants, Justice Clarence Thomas declared that the Court should avoid examining "electoral mechanisms that may affect the 'weight' given to a ballot duly cast." Even where congressional statutes, such as the Voting Rights Act, explicitly define the term "voting" to "include all action necessary to make a vote effective," Justice Thomas urged the Court to ignore the actual text of the statute.

The *Bush v. Gore* invitation to value votes equally, in order to "sustain the confidence that all citizens must have in the outcome of elections," should be heeded, but not in the form of legal wrangling before a judge. That it is time for political agitation rather than judicial activism may be the most important contribution of the *Bush v. Gore* opinion. In fact, that is already happening, at least in the law schools. *The New York Times* reported on February 1, 2001—almost three months after the election—that the decision continues to generate a beehive of activity among law professors furious at the Supreme Court's role. The debate in law schools already has the "flavor of the teach-ins of the Vietnam War era, when professors spurred their students to political action." As during the movements for abolition, women's suffrage, and black voting rights, we, the people, must take up the burden.

Indeed, the Court's choice of language explicitly valuing "no person's vote over another's" ought to launch a citizens' movement similar to the 1960s civil rights marches that led to the Voting Rights Act, demonstrations in which citizens carried banners with the "one person, one vote" slogan. One vote, one value—meaning that everyone's vote should count toward the election of someone he or she voted for—should be the rallying cry of all who wish to restore the confidence that even the conservative Court majority agrees "all citizens must have in the outcome of elections." This movement, let's recall, began in the streets, was cautiously then boldly embraced by liberal politicians, and eventually led to both raised grass-roots consciousness and national legislation. That is how democratic movements change the course of events—and in the process enrich and renew democracy.

Where's the Outrage?

Certainly many people outside the legal academy continue to feel alienated by the outcome of this presidential election. A survey released in early December from the Harvard Vanishing Voter project suggests that large majorities of the American people believe election procedures have been "unfair to the voters." Not surprisingly, nationwide those most likely to feel disenfranchised are blacks. In December 2000, 86 percent of black voters felt that way. One out of 10 blacks reported that they or someone in their family had trouble voting, according to a national report produced by Michael Dawson and Lawrence Bobo, of the Center for the Study of Race, Politics and Culture, and the W.E.B. DuBois Institute. A CBS News poll, made public on the eve of the inauguration, found that 51 percent of the respondents said they considered Bush's victory a legitimate one, but only 19 percent of Democrats and 12 percent of blacks said so.

The anger over what happened in Florida has only been reinforced by the failure of the Democratic Party leadership to move quickly and seriously to engage the legitimacy issue. Right after November 7, when the perception first emerged that the election was being hijacked, the Gore campaign actively discouraged mass protest. On January 12, when Al Gore presided over the counting of the electoral college votes, it was only members of the Congressional Black Caucus (CBC) who rose, one by one, to protest the filing of Florida's votes. They could not get a single Democratic senator (from a body that includes not a single black representative) to join their objection. The silence of the white Democrats in Congress turned the CBC demonstration into an emphatic recapitulation of the election drama. As the presiding officer, Al Gore overruled the protests. The moment was especially poignant, because the Black Caucus members, in speaking out for Floridians whose votes were not counted, were speaking out for all Americans, while even their progressive white colleagues sat in awkward silence. E.J. Dionne, a columnist for *The Washington Post*, watched the drama unfold on television. Turning to his eight-year-old son, seated next to him, Dionne explained, "They are speaking out for us too."

"It was the Black Caucus, and the Black Caucus alone," James Carroll wrote in *The Boston Globe*, "that showed itself sensitive to . . . what is clearly true about the recent presidential election in Florida." That truth is the gap between what the rules permit and what democracy requires. Florida made it obvious that our winner-take-all rules would unfairly award all of Florida's electoral college votes to one candidate even though the margin of victory was less than the margin of error. Yet our elected officials in Washington are committed to those rules and, even more, to maintaining civility between those adversely affected by the rules and those who benefited. As Carroll wrote, "Those who sit atop the social and economic pyramid always speak of love, while those at the bottom always speak of justice."

The CBC protest shows that outrage over the election continues. But the CBC protest also speaks to the fact that the conversation about the true meaning of democracy is not happening yet, at least not at the highest levels of government. There is talk, of course, about fixing the mechanics of election balloting; but it is the rules themselves, and not just the vote-counting process, that are broken. Which is all the more reason that this conversation, which needs to address issues of justice, not just compassion, also needs to rise up from communities and a citizens' movement.

Those who were disenfranchised—disproportionately black, poorer, and less well educated—were not asking for pity; they wanted democracy. Stories of long lines at polling places, confusing ballots, and strict limitations on how long voters could spend in the voting booth help explain why turnout numbers are skewed toward those who are wealthy, white and better educated. We are a democracy that supposedly believes in universal suffrage, and yet the differential turnout rates between high-income and low-income voters are far greater than in Europe, where they range from 5 to 10 percent. More than two-thirds of people in America with incomes greater than $50,000 voted, compared with one-third of those with incomes under $10,000. Many poor people are also less literate; for them, time limits and complex ballots proved disabling when they were organized around lists of individuals rather than easily identified icons for political parties. Indeed, more ballots were "spoiled" in the presidential race than were cast for "spoiler" Ralph Nader. The shocking number of invalid ballots is a direct result of antiquated voting mechanics, an elitist view of the relationship between education and citizenship, and an individualistic view of political participation that would shame any nation that truly believes in broad citizen participation.

Class, Race, and Balloting

In addition to class, the window into the workings of Florida's balloting allowed us to see how race affects—and in turn is affected by—voting rules and procedures. The election debacle revealed gaps not just in our democracy, but in the way our democracy racializes public policy and then disenfranchises the victims of those policies. Old voting machines, more likely to reject ballots not perfectly completed, were disproportionately located in low-income and minority neighborhoods. These problems contributed to stunning vote-rejection numbers. According to *The New York Times*, black precincts in Miami-Dade County had votes thrown out at twice the rate of Cuban (and primarily Republican) precincts and at close to four times the rate of white precincts. In that county alone, in predominantly black precincts, the *Times* said, one in 11 ballots were rejected . . . a total of 9,904—thousands more than Bush's margin of victory.

The balloting rules in Florida did not just incidentally disenfranchise minority voters, but apparently resulted from what many think were aggressive efforts to suppress black turnout. *The New York Times* also reported that county officials in Miami-Dade gave certain precincts—mostly the Hispanic (that is, Cuban and Republican) ones—laptop computers so that they could check names against the central county voter file. In black precincts, where there were a lot of recently registered voters whose names didn't appear on the local list, the precinct workers were not given computers and were supposed to call the county office to check the list—but no one answered the phones or the lines were busy, so thousands of actually registered voters, were just sent away.

Florida's minority residents and many others faced another structural hurdle to having their voices heard. Anyone convicted of a felony is permanently banned from voting in Florida and 12 other states (disproportionately from the old Confederacy) even after they have paid their debt to society. As a result, 13 percent of black men nationwide and in some southern states as many as 30 percent of black men are disenfranchised. In Florida alone, more than 400,000 ex-felons, almost half of them black, could not vote last November. Also worth noting is that before the election Florida's secretary of state hired a firm to conduct a vigorous cleansing of the voting rolls—not just of Florida's felons, but also of ex-offenders from other states whose rights had been restored in those states and who were thus still legally eligible to vote in Florida. The Hillsborough County elections supervisor, for example, found that 54 percent of the voters targeted by the "scrub" were black, in a county where blacks make up 11 percent of the voting population. While Canada takes special steps to register former prisoners and encourage citizenship, Florida and other states ostracize them.

One short-term solution to the problem of the disenfranchised ex-offender population is to lobby state legislators to abolish the permanent disenfranchisement of felons. Alternatively, Congress could pass a statute providing voting rights for all ex-felons in federal elections.

The Soul of a Democracy Movement

Unfortunately, in pursuit of bipartisan civility, the Democratic Party leadership appears to be marching to a false harmony—being charmed by compassionate conservatism and conscious of the conflict aversion of middle-of-the-road swing voters, while ignoring issues of justice and the troubling disenfranchisement of many of the party's most loyal supporters. If we learn anything from the Supreme Court's role in the election fiasco, it must be that when the issue is justice, the people—not the justices of the Court or the Democratic leadersship in Washington—will lead. And if anything is true about the fiasco in Florida, it is the need for new leadersship that is willing to challenge rather than acquiesce to unfair rules. Such leadership will not come from a single, charismatic figure orchestrating deals out of Washington, D.C.; nor will it be provided by a group devoted only to remedying the disenfranchisement of black voters. What is needed instead is a courageous assembly of stalwart individuals who are willing to ask the basic questions the Black Caucus members raised—questions that go to the very legitimacy of our democratic procedures, not just in Florida but nationwide. These are likely to be individuals organized at the local level, possibly even into a new political party that is broadly conceived and dedicated to real, participatory democracy. Such a movement could build on the energy of black voter participation, which between 1996 and last year went from 10 percent to 15 percent in Florida and from 5 percent to 12 percent in Missouri.

But while black anger could fuel a citizens' movement or a new, European-style political party that seeks reforms beyond the mechanics of election day voting, the danger is that whites will be suspicious of the struggle if they perceive that its aim is simply to redress wrongs done to identifiable victims or to serve only the interests of people of color. And people of color can alienate potential supporters if they focus exclusively on vindicating the rights of minority voters and fail to emphasize three dramatic distortions in our present rules that undermine the ability of low-income and working people, women, and progressives, as well as racial minorities, to participate in a genuinely democratic transformation. These rules (1) limit voting to 12 hours on a workday and require registration weeks or even months in advance; (2) disenfranchise prisoners for the purpose of voting but count them for the purpose of allocating legislative seats; and (3) waste votes through winner-take-all elections. A pro-democracy movement has a good chance to succeed if it focuses on unfair rules whose dislocations may be felt first by blacks but whose effects actually disempower vast numbers of people across the country.

A pro-democracy movement would need to build on the experience of

Florida to show how problems with disenfranchisement based on race and status signify systemic issues of citizen participation. Such mobilization would seek to recapture the passion in evidence immediately after the election as union leaders, civil rights activists, black elected officials, ministers, rabbis, and the president of the Haitian women's organization came together at a black church in Miami, reminded the assembly of the price their communities had paid for the right to vote, and vowed never to be disfranchised again. "It felt like Birmingham last night," Mari Castellanos, a Latina activist in Miami, wrote in an e-mail describing the mammoth rally at the 14,000-member New Birth Baptist Church, a primarily African-American congregation.

> "The sanctuary was standing room only. So were the overflow rooms and the school hall, where congregants connected via large TV screens . . . . The people sang and prayed and listened. Story after story was told of voters being turned away at the polls, of ballots being allegedly destroyed, of NAACP election literature being allegedly discarded at the main post office, of Spanish-speaking poll workers being sent to Creole precincts and vice-versa."

Although not encouraged by Democratic Party leaders, by joining their voices these Florida voters were beginning to realize their collective potential—as ordinary citizens—to become genuine democrats (with a small d). By highlighting our nation's wretched record on voting rules and practices, these impassioned citizens were raising the obvious questions: Do those in charge really want large citizen participation, especially if that means more participation by poor people and people of color? Even more, do Americans of all incomes and races realize that everyone loses when we tolerate disenfranchisement of some? And how can we tolerate the logjam of winner-take-all two-party monopoly, especially at the local level?

Enriching Democratic Choice

As the Florida fiasco suggests, the problem includes mechanical defects, but it is the rules themselves, not just old technology, that limit the political clout of entire communities. Weak democracy feeds on itself. There are some technical fixes worth pursuing. But reform of voting mechanisms—while important—is not enough. The circumstances of this last election call for a larger focus on issues of representation and participation. A longer-term and more-far-ranging solution to the problems in Florida as well as those around the country would be to enrich democracy by broadening ways of reflecting and encouraging voter preferences.

For example, in South Africa, where the black majority now shares political power with the white minority, there is a successful system of proportional representation. Voters cast their ballots for the political party they feel most represents their interests, and the party gets seats in the legislature in proportion to the number of votes it receives. Instead of a winner-take-all situation in which there are losers who feel completely unrepresented when their candidate doesn't capture the top number of votes, each vote counts to enhance the political power of the party of the voters' choice. Under South Africa's party-list system, the party that gets 30 percent of the vote gets 30 percent of the seats. Or if the party gets only 10 percent of the vote, it still gets 10 percent of the seats in the legislature. Only because of this system does South Africa's white minority have any representation in the national legislature. Ironically, South Africa, only seven years out of apartheid, is more advanced in terms of practicing democratic principles than the United States is 150 years after slavery and 40 years after Jim Crow.

As June Zeitlin, executive director of the Women's Environment and Development Organization points out, proportional representation systems also benefit women. In a letter that *The New York Times* declined to publish, Zeitlin wrote: "Women are grossly underrepresented at all levels of government worldwide. However, women fare significantly better in proportional representation electoral systems . . . . The 10 countries with the highest percentage of women in parliament have systems that include proportional representation." Zeitlin, who spearheads a campaign—*50/50 Get the Balance Right*—aimed at increasing women's participation in government, has noticed that proportional representation mechanisms work in many countries in tandem with the deliberate political goals of progressive parties.

Proportional representation reforms for legislative bodies, even Congress, would not even require an amendment to the U.S. Constitution. Nothing in the Constitution says that we have to use winner-take-all single-member districts. Since seizing the initiative in 1995, two Democratic members of the Congressional Black Caucus, Representatives Cynthia McKinney of Georgia and Mel Watt of North Carolina, have repeatedly introduced legislation called the Voter Choice Act, which provides for states to choose proportional representation voting. It's a system that should have great appeal not just for African Americans but for every group that has ever felt disenfranchised.

A pro-democracy movement would look seriously at forms of proportional representation that could assure Democrats in Florida, Republicans in Democratic-controlled states, and racial minorities and women in all states fair representation in the state legislatures. It would focus renewed attention on the importance of minority voters—racial, political, and urban minorities—gaining a more meaningful voice as well as a real opportunity to participate throughout the democratic process and not just on election day. The five-member Supreme Court majority allowed the interests of the Florida legislature (in obtaining the safe-harbor benefits of a congressional statute for certifying electors) to trump any remedy to protect the rights of the voters, about whom it was ostensibly so solicitous.

If legislatures are to enjoy such power to speak for all citizens, it is imperative that voters' voices be reflected in fully representative legislative bodies. Florida voters are closely divided along party lines, but in the legislature they are represented by an overwhelmingly Republican leadership. And the partisan acts of the Florida legislature in the 2000 election should focus renewed attention on how the winner-take-all system in a state legislature can fail to recognize the will of racial and political minorities: It wastes the votes of those whose ballots are cast and tabulated but don't lead to the election of any candidate they selected.

If we are not to abolish the electoral college, we might at least mitigate its winner-take-all effect and apportion electoral votes based on the popular split. In Florida, where all of the state's 25 electoral votes went to the Republican candidate, Bush could have gotten 13 votes and Gore 12 (or vice versa!). Such a system is perfectly constitutional and can be readily enacted by the state legislature. Two states do this already, although they use unfairly gerrymandered congressional districts rather than statewide proportions to allocate electoral college votes.

Proportional representation voting, which is used in most of the world's democracies, ensures that each voter's ballot counts when it is cast. Voters essentially "district" themselves by how they mark their ballots. The method thus eliminates the problem of gerrymandering by incumbents protecting their seats. Proportional voting could also encourage the development of local political organizations to educate and mobilize voters. Only when voters are vigilant, even after the votes are counted, shall we return to a government of, by, and for the people. Developing local grass-roots organizations that can monitor not only elections but also legislative actions is especially important in 2001, a year when every state legislature will be engaged in the decennial task of redistricting. The spread of such organizations—which a proportional representation system makes possible because the participants actually have a chance to win elections—could also fuel a new era of issue-centered politics in which people exercise their political views through advocacy groups focused on issues of concern to them. As Richard Berke has written in *The New York Times:*

> "The first half of the last century was dominated by party-centered politics. Then came candidate-centered politics. Now, some foresee an era where the power moves to activists, who create local coalitions around specific issues. That could happen because, with the rise of the Internet, activists have far greater access to communication and organizing tools—and no longer have to rely on help from campaigns or party committees."

Local grass-roots and issue-centered coalitions are more likely if we adopt proportional representation because it rewards those who mobilize directly with seats in the local collective-decision-making body. And local multiparty organizing could effectively generate citizen engagement and meaningful participation not merely on election day but in between elections, too.

Of course, there are downsides to a politics that depends primarily on activists building multiple coalitions of overlapping constituencies through issue-oriented organizing. Creating such coalitions requires enormous energy; they often have to be built from scratch, and for every one that gets it together, dozens will fall short. Moreover, they can encourage a fragmentation of progressive energy and what Urvashi Vaid, the gay rights activist who is now at the Ford Foundation, memorably called "a misuse of powerlessness."

But the upside is that coalitions that start with narrowly focused issues and then engage multiple constituencies can create sustainable alliances even after an election. They can grow into institutions that use their aggregated power again and again—getting organized labor to join fights that affect Latinos and gays, civil rights groups to join labor, and so forth. These coalitions can also aspire to an electoral strategy and nurture leaders who can eventually become candidates.

Over time, the best of these permanent coalitions might begin to look a little bit like parties: presumably they would have broad platforms, sizable but loose constituencies, and candidates and elected officials allied to them. Proportional representation would lower the bar to successful cross-constituency and multiracial-coalition organizing. But even with a proportional voting system, realizing a fully democratic movement would still require us to fight fragmentation and to aggregate, rotate, and share power among progressive interests in a lasting and sustainable way.

"One vote, one value," a notion underscored by the conservative Supreme Court majority, ironically could become the rallying cry of a multiracial and multi-issue grass-roots movement of voters throughout the nation. It could herald a new era of issue-centered rather than candidate-centered politics. Black leaders may be key in some communities; union activists or environmentalists in others. But in the end, an aroused and engaged citizenry—one committed to a broad, multiracial democracy—will be our best, indeed our only protection to ensure that every vote counts and that every citizen can truly vote. Mobilizing citizens requires local, grass-roots political organizations accountable to the people themselves instead of ad hoc candidate machines that are too often driven by money. Voting should not be an obstacle course of arbitrary deadlines, lousy lists, untrained poll workers, and outdated ballot technology. Rather, voting should be just the first step in a democratic system by which we, the people—through democratic institutions that are accountable to all of us—actually rule.

The National Conversation:
Stem Cell Research and Cloning

The Genius of George W. Bush

Frank Rich

The New York Times | August 18, 2001

Prior to 9/11, the single toughest decision of President Bush's stewardship (according to the press and his own aides, anyway) involved the question of whether or not to allow government funding for stem cell research. Stem cells have the wonderful ability to grow into replacement cells for virtually any part of the body, offering new hope for a huge array of illnesses. The most valuable type of stem cells, however, are derived from human embryos (typically the unused byproducts of in vitro fertilization procedures). This poses a moral dilemma: Are we sacrificing one human life to save another?

After a much-publicized deliberation process, Bush emerged in mid-August to proclaim his solution: Federally-funded research could go forward, but only on existing stem cell lines. The announcement left scientists scratching their heads (no one was sure exactly how many viable stem cell lines were out there), and had some commentators crying "Waffle!" But as Frank Rich explains, what looked to many observers like a cop-out was actually a classic display of political tight-rope walking. . . .

After months of deriding the president as an idiot, Democrats have to face the fact that he is at the very least an idiot savant—and just possibly a genius.

The final proof is The Great Stem Cell Compromise. "This is way beyond politics," said George W. Bush while pondering his verdict. What's more, he told the nation, he had found a solution to please everyone. His plan will at once "lead to breakthrough therapies and cures" and do so "without crossing a fundamental moral line."

In fact, everything Mr. Bush said is false. His decision was completely about politics. It will slow the progress to breakthrough therapies and cures. It did force the pro-life movement he ostensibly endorses to cross a fundamental moral line. And yet the politics were so brilliantly handled— and exquisitely timed, for the August dog days—that few vacationing Americans bothered to examine the fine print, which didn't arrive until the final seconds of an 11-minute speech. Few have noticed, at least not yet, that the only certain beneficiary of this compromise is George W. Bush.

Denigrated as a lightweight and a slacker, he seized on the stem cell debate to transform his image into that of our philosopher king—grappling mightily with the science and ethics of an issue he and his handlers hyped as "one of the most profound of our time"—even as he induced religious-right political leaders to sell out their principles and sent Alzheimer's, Parkinson's and juvenile diabetes patients to the back of the medical research bus. As an act of self-serving political Houdinism, this is a feat worthy of Mr. Bush's predecessor, another master at buying time when caught in a political corner with no apparent way out.

If you spend a week talking to scientists actively involved with stem cells, which I did, the most enthusiasm you can find for Mr. Bush's compromise is lukewarm. "It could have been better, it could have been worse," as Sloan Kettering's Harold Varmus, the former head of the National Institutes of Health, puts it. Jerome Groopman, a Harvard Medical School professor who has worked on bone marrow stem cells, calls the president's decision "unprecedented" in the way "it ignores the fundamental needs and process of experimental medicine" by "holding research hostage to private companies" that own many of the 60 stem cell lines that Mr. Bush has approved for federal study. "No company has the kind of resources that can match the N.I.H. for the kind of free scientific inquiry that might bear fruit," says Dr. Groopman. Besides, he adds: "There isn't a soul alive who can testify that these 60 lines can give us what we need. The success of science depends on a string of failures, and no one can work at a laboratory bench with his hands shackled behind him."

"Where are those lines? Are they any good? Are they available?" asks Doug Melton, a leading stem cell scientist who had a 45-minute meeting with the president, Karl Rove and other political operatives in July. It's not enough, Dr. Melton says, "to say there are cells at Singapore at this phone number and go get them." Since there has been no firsthand scientific investigation of the quality of these far-flung lines, some of them could prove stale, unstable or insufficiently varied for research purposes.

But even if by some miracle they're all just what the doctors ordered, Dr. Melton fears delays of many months for all the lawyering required to sort out the intellectual property rights of the Bush-blessed cells before their private owners ("who have now been given a mini-monopoly") will transfer them to academic researchers. It was only four days after Mr. Bush's speech that the Wisconsin Alumni Research Foundation, allied with the pioneering stem cell scientist James Thomson, sued its biotech partner, the Geron Corporation, over who controls which commercial rights. Evan Snyder, another prominent stem cell researcher at Harvard, fears that some owners of Bush-approved stem cells could restrict their intellectual property as zealously as "Coca-Cola and its secret formula or a computer company that won't give out the secrets of its latest chip."

Dr. Snyder also points out that the administration is "scientifically naive," since some of its approved cells may have been extracted by already outdated mid-1990's technology. "We can now get stem cell lines that are more efficacious and heartier," he says. "Would we fight new infections only with penicillin and sulfa and not the new antibiotics?" He also worries about a potential brain drain beyond the well-publicized decision by Dr. Roger Pedersen of the University of California to decamp to Cambridge University in pursuit of scientific freedom. It's possible that "new intellects and talents we'd like to see jump into the game" will go into other fields, given the roadblocks to stem cell work.

As if these barriers to the expeditious pursuit of life-and-death research weren't enough, the Bush administration has also yet to appoint its new director of the N.I.H.—the person needed to run all the bureaucratic and legal gauntlets separating researchers from the approved stem cell lines. Will that appointee have to pass an ideological litmus test, and if so, will there be a lengthy Senate confirmation fight?

The president's new council on stem cells, headed by the bioethicist Leon Kass, may add further confusion and delays. No one seems to know its precise role, including the White House, which has yet to delineate any of its specific stem cell duties. If the panel's point is to rule on the ethical questions, didn't the president already do that? If it's to add another layer of guidelines as to how the research can proceed, "it could add another year to the process," says Harold Varmus.

Yet if scientists—not to mention patients desperately hoping for stem-cell therapies—got at best a half-loaf out of the Bush compromise, the anti-abortion absolutists got snookered.

The pro-life cause (and the Republican platform that parrots it) has staked its moral rectitude on the belief that life begins at conception. As Douglas Johnson of the National Right to Life Committee said in July,

"We're opposed to federal funding of research if it kills embryos, whether the killing took place yesterday or today."

Well, that was yesterday. By the time the president gave his go-ahead for federal funds to underwrite research on previously killed embryos, the White House had smartly romanced the National Right to Life Committee to the point where it declared itself "delighted" with the news. A few spoil-sports who disagreed with this retreat—such as the U.S. Conference of Catholic Bishops—were drowned out and marginalized by pro-life politicos like James Dobson of Focus on the Family and Jerry Falwell, who also enthusiastically endorsed the Bush speech. Pat Robertson went so far as to dismiss "ethical dilemmas" as secondary to the "practical reality" of a "very useful science."

Pro-choicers should welcome all these former pro-lifers into the fold. Their position—that it's O.K. to sacrifice embryos to the greater good of potentially ending the suffering of living juvenile diabetes and Alzheimer's patients—is at one with the pro-choice view that in pregnancy embryos sometimes must be sacrificed for the health of the mother.

What gives the scientists I spoke with some guarded hope despite the strictures placed on their work by the president's policy is that Mr. Bush moved just enough to convince them that the policy isn't permanent. Though Mr. Bush said he wouldn't change his mind, they predict that if the 60 stem cell lines aren't accessible or scientifically useful, the political pressure from patients' advocacy groups and Congress will force inevitable concessions from the White House. And now they have the added boon that not just pro-life senators like Orrin Hatch and Bill Frist but also the nation's loudest pro-life leaders will be in the president's pocket when he next capitulates.

Thanks to the sudden national fixation on stem cells, the entire country now knows that there are between 100,000 and 200,000 frozen embryos currently in storage at fertilization clinics, most of them slated to be killed anyway, most of them with greater potential for saving lives than becoming lives. As Christopher Reeve has noted, long before anyone had heard of stem cells there was never any "outrage that these unwanted fertilized embryos are being thrown in the garbage." When Mr. Bush inevitably finds another ingenious "compromise" to make more of them available to med-ical research, there won't be outrage either—only votes.

Ban Stand

Leon Kass and Daniel Callahan

The New Republic | August 6, 2001

When he made his stem cell decision public, President Bush also announced he would appoint a new Presidential Council on Bioethics, to be headed by Dr. Leon Kass, a widely respected bioethicist from the University of Chicago. In this article for The New Republic, *Kass and coauthor Daniel Callahan argue that the greatest moral danger facing mankind is not, in fact, stem cell research—but rather the prospect of for cloning human embryos for research purposes. . . .*

Everyone has been arguing for weeks about whether President Bush should authorize funding for research on human embryonic stem cells. But few have noticed the much more momentous decision now before us: whether to permit the cloning of human beings. At issue in the first debate is the morality of using and destroying human embryos. At issue in the second is the morality of designing human children.

The day of human cloning is near. Reputable physicians have announced plans to produce a cloned child within the year. One biotech company (Advanced Cell Technology) just announced its intention to start producing embryonic human clones for research purposes. Recognizing the urgent need for action, Congress is considering legislation that would ban human cloning. Last Tuesday the House Judiciary Committee approved a tough anti-cloning bill, H.R. 2505, the Human Cloning Prohibition Act of 2001. Introduced by Republican Dave Weldon of Florida and Democrat Bart Stupak of Michigan, and co-sponsored by more than 120 members from both parties, the bill is scheduled for a vote on the House floor as early as this week. But the House is also considering a much weaker "compromise" bill that would ban reproductive cloning but permit cloning for research. It is terribly important that the former, and not the latter, passes. First, because cloning is unethical, both in itself and in what it surely leads to. Second, because the Weldon-Stupak bill offers our best—indeed, our only—hope of preventing it from happening.

The vast majority of Americans object to human cloning. And they object on multiple grounds: It constitutes unethical experimentation on the child-to-be, subjecting him or her to enormous risks of bodily and developmental abnormalities. It threatens individuality, deliberately saddling the clone with a genotype that has already lived and to whose previous life its life will always be compared. It confuses identity by denying the clone two biological parents and by making it both twin and offspring of its older copy. Cloning also represents a giant step toward turning procreation into manufacture; it is the harbinger of much grizzlier eugenic manipulations to come. Permitting human cloning means condoning a despotic principle: that we are entitled to design the genetic makeup of our children.

So how do we stop it? The biotech industry proposes banning only so-called reproductive cloning by prohibiting the transfer of a cloned embryo to a woman to initiate a pregnancy. But this approach will fail. The only way to effectively ban reproductive cloning is to stop the process from the beginning, at the stage where the human somatic cell nucleus is introduced into the egg to produce the embryo clone. That is, to effectively ban any cloning, we need to ban all human cloning.

Here is why: Once cloned embryos exist, it will be virtually impossible to control what is done with them. Created in commercial laboratories, hidden from public view, stockpiles of cloned human embryos could be produced, bought, and sold without anyone knowing it. As we have seen with in vitro embryos created to treat infertility, embryos produced for one reason can be used for another: Today, "spare embryos" created to begin a pregnancy are used—by someone else—in research; and tomorrow, clones created for research will be used—by someone else—to begin a pregnancy. Efforts at clonal baby-making (like all assisted reproduction) would take place within the privacy of a doctor-patient relationship, making outside scrutiny extremely difficult.

Worst of all, a ban only on reproductive cloning will be unenforceable. Should the illegal practice be detected, governmental attempts to enforce the ban would run into a swarm of practical and legal challenges. Should an "illicit clonal pregnancy" be discovered, no government agency is going to compel a woman to abort the clone, and there would be understandable outrage were she fined or jailed before or after she gave birth. For all these reasons, the only practically effective and legally sound approach is to block human cloning at the start—at producing the embryonic clone.

The Weldon-Stupak bill does exactly that. It precisely and narrowly describes the specific deed that it outlaws (human somatic cell nuclear transfer to an egg). It requires no difficult determinations of the perpetrator's intent or knowledge.

It introduces substantial criminal and monetary penalties, which will deter renegade doctors or scientists as well as clients who would bear cloned children. Carefully drafted and limited in scope, the bill makes very clear that there is to be no interference with the scientifically and medically useful practices of animal cloning or the equally valuable cloning of human DNA fragments, the duplication of somatic cells, or stem cells in tissue culture. And the bill steers clear of the current stem-cell debate, limiting neither research with embryonic stem cells derived from non-cloned embryos nor even the creation of research embryos by ordinary in vitro fertilization. If enacted, the law would bring the United States into line with many other nations.

Unfortunately, the House is also considering the biotech industry's favored alternative: H.R. 2608, introduced by Republican Jim Greenwood of Pennsylvania and Democrat Peter Deutsch of Florida. It explicitly permits the creation of cloned embryos for research while attempting to ban only reproductive cloning. But that's not something it is likely to achieve. It licenses companies to manufacture embryo clones, as long as they say they won't use them to initiate a pregnancy or ship them knowing that they will be so used.

It therefore guarantees that there will be clonal embryo-farming and trafficking in clones, with many opportunities for reproductive efforts unintended by their original makers. And the bill's proposed ban on initiating pregnancy is, as already argued, virtually impossible to enforce.

There are further difficulties. The acts the Greenwood-Deutsch bill bans turn largely on intent and knowledge—hard matters to discern and verify. The confidentiality of the called-for Food and Drug Administration registration of embryo-cloning means that the public will remain in the dark about who is producing the embryo clones, where they are being bought and sold, and who is doing what with them. A provision preempting state law would make it impossible for any state to enact any other—and more restrictive— legislation. A sunset clause dissolving the prohibition after ten years would leave us with no ban at all, not even on reproductive cloning. Most radically, the bill would create two highly disturbing innovations in federal law: It would license for the first time the creation of living human embryos solely for research purposes, and it would make it a felony not to ultimately exploit and destroy them. The Greenwood-Deutsch legislation reads less like the Cloning Prohibition Act of 2001 and more like the "Human Embryo Cloning Registration and Industry Protection Act of 2001."

It is possible that embryo-cloning will someday yield tissues derivable for each person from his own embryonic twin clone, tissues useful for the treatment of degenerative disease. But the misleading term "therapeutic cloning" obscures the fact that the research clone will be "treated" only to exploitation and destruction and that any future "therapies" are, at this point, purely hypothetical. Besides, we have promising alternatives—not only in adult stem cells but also in non-cloned embryonic stem-cell lines— that do not open the door to human clonal reproduction. Happily, these alternatives will not require commodifying women's ovaries in order to provide the vast number of eggs that would be needed to give each of us our own twin embryo when we need regenerative tissue. Should these alternatives fail, or should animal-cloning experiments someday demonstrate the unique therapeutic potential of stem cells derived from embryo clones, Congress could later revisit and lift the ban.

The Weldon-Stupak bill has drawn wide support across the political spectrum; feminist health writer Judy Norsigian and liberal embryologist Stuart Newman joined Catholic spokesman Richard Doerflinger and political theorist Francis Fukuyama in testifying in its favor. Health and Human Services Secretary Tommy Thompson, a proponent of research with embryonic stem cells, has endorsed it. Thoughtful people understand that human cloning is not about pro-life versus pro-choice. Neither is it a matter of right versus left. It is only and emphatically about baby design and manufacture, the opening skirmish of a long battle against eugenics and the post-human future. Once embryonic clones are produced in laboratories, the eugenic revolution will have begun. Our best chance to stop it may be on the House floor next week.

Editor's note: The proposed federal ban on all cloning for reproduction or medical research was passed overwhelmingly by the House of Representatives in the summer of 2001, but stalled in the Senate in the spring of 2002. A less-restrictive Senate bill is currently under consideration.

Part Four:
The View from Main Street

Carpe Dems
Michael Tomasky

New York magazine | November 19, 2001

New York City's 2001 mayoral election should have been one of the hottest local political stories of the year—but given the impact of the 9/11 disaster and outgoing mayor Rudy Giuliani's concomitant ascension to near-mythic status, it was hard for New Yorkers or anyone else to get too excited about the race. Flying largely beneath the media's radar, billionaire (and nominal Republican) Michael Bloomberg spent an estimated $60 million of his own money to edge out the favored candidate, Democrat Mark Green, by 40,000-odd votes.

Bloomberg's record-setting expenditures were clearly the biggest factor in the contest. But Michael Tomasky, New York magazine's "City Politic" columnist, sees something more than deep pockets at work here. In his election post-mortem, he asks: Does Bloomberg's victory signal the demise of the old-fashioned Democrat?

In the days leading up to the election, I received some e-mails from a few readers who, broadly speaking, fell into the category of Democrats for Bloomberg. They were not, they assured me, quislings or disloyalists. One woman came from a family in which the occasion of her 16th birthday was marked by a gift from her father not of *Abbey Road* or *Frampton Comes Alive!* but of a subscription to *The Nation*—among other things, the magazine to which a frequent contributor over the years, alone among New York politicians, had been Mark Green.

My correspondents weren't closet right-wingers. But they were persuaded that Mike Bloomberg's independence from the local political infrastructure made him, as one put it, not "an excellent choice, just a better choice." I wrote back to all of them: Didn't the way these two men arrived at this point count for anything? One had done obviously impressive things in the private sector, but his involvement in the life of the city was largely built around the act of opening his checkbook. The other had graduated from Harvard Law in 1970 with good enough grades that he could have joined any white-shoe firm he'd chosen and contented himself with some nice pro bono work; instead, at considerable financial sacrifice, he spent 30

years fighting for the things—granted, sometimes unsuccessfully, sometimes artlessly—in which he believed.

I got exactly nowhere with this argument. At first, I confess, I was shocked.
In the home in which I was raised, and in the milieu of friends and associates with whom I have surrounded myself now, this argument is virtually
an automatic deal-closer. But my readers' responses, and the election's
result, made me start thinking this through a little more deeply. When did
$4 billion and no civic track record become better credentials—to
Democrats!—than years of salaried public service spent aiming a sword at
mobbed-up garbage carters and the tobacco lobby?

For all the talk about how September 11 transformed things, and it did,
this change occurred long before then. Thirty years ago, or even ten,
Green's credentials would have defeated Bloomberg's money. But in the
past decade or so, the universe of people for whom this liberal ideal of
public service would have made Green the better choice has contracted,
and the vineyards in which Green has toiled have come to smell, to too
many citizens, of rotten grapes. This has happened for some reasons that
are the fault of Democrats, and some reasons that aren't. But if the local
Democratic Party is to pick up its thoroughly shattered pieces and move
forward from here, it needs to understand and do something about them.

It was striking to me that the last full week of this mayoral campaign was
the same week that anti-government rhetoric in Washington was on
unprecedentedly frank display. Tom DeLay and his charges said quite
openly that they were opposed to an airline-security bill, which no less a
conservative than Jesse Helms had voted for in the Senate, because it
would add 28,000 unionized employees to the federal workforce. The
argument—by hook or by crook, but that's politics—won the day.

Obviously, it would be absurd to say there's a direct link between that legislation and Bloomberg's victory. But there is, perhaps, a historical one. The
DeLay position on that bill was just a more transparent version of an argument that has been the beating heart of national Republican ideology since
Ronald Reagan's victory 21 years ago: The less government, the better.
Clearly, this argument hasn't taken hold in New York City in the way it has
in DeLay's Texas, or in the fifteen other states Al Gore lost by landslide proportions last year. But so many people have been saying it with such ferocity
for so long that, even here, the message has seeped in like gas through the
crevices. Rudy Giuliani, in his 1993 campaign and in his governance, has

offered a version of the argument tuned finely to a New York wavelength; his rhetoric about "old thinking," and about actually feeling sorry for people stuck in some befogged, Marxian past, helped shift public perception dramatically. The old, reform-era default position for most New York Democrats was one of reflexive respect for a life spent in liberal politics. The new position is that of automatically looking askance at such a life.

Changes in the media over the past ten years have contributed to the shift as well. I think first and foremost of the cable-television screaming shows, on which a superficial, lunch-bucket populism (of millionaire hosts!) has become the guiding ethos. These shows have transformed the discourse—I would say disfigured it—into a language of emotionalism that denigrates qualities once associated with leadership and preparation for public life. In this lexicon, by far the worst sin is that of elitism, which is defined by three criteria: having gone to a fancy-pants university (Bloomberg has a Harvard MBA, just as W. went to Yale, but it somehow doesn't count against Republicans, who are understood to have escaped Cambridge or New Haven without having been indoctrinated); being intelligent in a wonkish and admittedly sometimes proselytizing way; and, usually, espousing liberal politics. To meet those criteria, as Al Gore learned to his woe, is to be condemned as "out of touch" with the regular Joes. It was Gore, of course, who was for a higher minimum wage and for giving those Joes more generous prescription-drug benefits, but never mind.

In New York, the tabloids carry forward with that emotionalist-populist ethos, and the effect is to frame debate in a way that rewards the candidate who can connect with the voters' visceral skepticism about public affairs. Bloomberg did this well—not on the stump, where he never did anything very well, but in his ads (fortunately for him, far more people saw the ads). The pseudo-populist response to his spending—"Hey, it's his money"— ended up insulating him from a rigorous examination by the media of where, and I mean specifically into whose pockets, some of that money may have gone. Then, of course, there's another face of New York journalism, which is populism's antipode but which sits cheek-by-jowl with it in the pages of the very same newspapers—the cult of celebrity and wealth. Advantage, Bloomberg on this front as well; in many respects it's no surprise at all that a mogulocracy should take root in the city that the richest and most powerful people in America call home.

Mark Green and his party are not responsible for any of the foregoing, but they are responsible for the way they have answered those shifts. And this, I think, is what my e-mailers were getting at.

Forget, for the moment, the improbable events of the past two months. Forget the World Trade Center, forget Bloomberg's $50 million, forget Green's inferior—and, at the end, quite dubious—ad campaign. Forget even the racial anthrax thrown into the election by Al Sharpton and Roberto Ramirez, about whom I will have a great deal to say in the near future. In those and other particulars, this campaign followed a script no one could have written.

But on another level, the campaign followed a script that any reasonably knowledgeable observer of city politics could have written with ease. Once again, the Democratic Party's standard-bearer ended up a captive of the party's constituent elements; once again, the party nominated a person who had respectably—I'd say more than respectably—paid his dues, at a historical moment when dues-paying strikes even many Democrats as tinkering under the hood of a car that hasn't been roadworthy for years. Bloomberg's perceived strength—and only time will tell whether it's an actual strength—was exactly Green's perceived weakness. In a word, *management*. In more than a word, it's about giving voters the sense that new things will be tried, that risks will be taken, that entrenched interests will be shaken, and that time-servers and Mau-Mauers of various stripes will be told that the rules have changed.

That's not easy to do. While recognizing that Green didn't manage it, I nevertheless felt sympathy for him on that score. In part it's a function of just how diverse and cantankerous this party is—Al Sharpton to Dov Hikind and everything in between. Impossible to keep peace in that jungle. I spoke to Green briefly off the record the Saturday before the vote, and again on Election Night when it still seemed he might win. I know exactly how hamstrung he felt, not only by Sharpton but also by the dozens of local sultans and suzerains playing out their infuriating, secret agendas.

If New York's Democratic Party is going to recapture the loyalty of voters like my correspondents and return some nobility to the idea of public service, it's going to have to do it by showing people that public service is producing a creative government that's doing them some tangible good. Bill Clinton understood this on a national level. He embraced welfare reform and free trade and the death penalty, and attacked Sister Souljah, but he still had white liberals, blacks, and Latinos eating out of his hand. He defended, at crucial moments, the things that were really important; he basically kept alive the notions of activist government and public service while modifying them to adjust to the forces I cited above; and his political will was such that his party changed according to his designs.

Some of the things Clinton did, you simply couldn't do in New York. But just as Giuliani tailored Reaganism to suit his circumstances, the Democrats need someone who can create a New York brand of Clintonism. There's no heir apparent to that on the scene. Maybe Bill and Hillary can move to Sutton Place in time for the next election. Or maybe the Democrats, about whom I wrote essentially this same article during the mayoral debacle of 1997, can finally start figuring all this out.

The Triumph of Robust Tokenism
Randall Kennedy

The Atlantic Monthly | February 2001

Among other things, 2001 was a time for looking back on now ex-President Bill Clinton's tenure in office. Clinton's record on race relations is a particularly tough topic to get a handle on. While he was consistently popular among African-Americans and other minority group members, his backing of the 1996 welfare-reform bill also disappointed many of his minority supporters. At the same time, no one has forgotten Clinton's "Sister Souljah moment" during the 1992 campaign, when he publicly attacked a black artist's lyrics to shore up his own centrist credentials.

In this Atlantic Monthly *article, Harvard Law School professor Randall Kennedy considers whether Clinton's racial legacy is more or less than the sum of its parts. . . .*

What has William Jefferson Clinton, the master of American electoral politics over the past decade, done to and for race relations? The record, of course, is as mixed as the rest of his legacy.

To his great political benefit, Clinton managed simultaneously to appeal to Reagan Democrat whites who were impatient with ongoing complaints about racial injustice and to Maxine Waters-style blacks who were insistent that more must be done to redress past and present racial inequities. This political balancing act played a large role in enabling him to win the White House in 1992, to outlast the Gingrich Revolution of 1994, to overcome the Bob Dole challenge of 1996, and to weather the Monica Lewinsky embarrassment of 1998.

Clinton's strategy was two-pronged. One prong entailed assuaging fears that "progressive" politicians who attempt to be sensitive to the wrongs of racism will give away too much to racial minorities, particularly blacks. Clinton took this approach in his 1992 campaign when he decided to upstage Jesse Jackson at a forum Jackson had organized—a meeting of the Rainbow Coalition, his personal fiefdom. One of Jackson's guests was a young rap artist, Sister Souljah, who had made remarks to the press suggesting that it would be preferable for black criminals to prey on whites rather than on their racial kin. Clinton seized the opportunity to condemn Sister Souljah. Although he did so before an immediate audience that was mainly black, the audience he plainly had in mind was impressionable whites. He wanted to show them that he could stand up to blacks on their own turf and rebuff black guilt-tripping and mau-mauing. An array of black politicians and commentators assailed Clinton for "disrespecting" his host. But their highly public anger played right into Clinton's strategy: the more vociferous their denunciation, the more credibly Clinton could signal to white Reagan Democrats that he was courageously willing to offend his black allies, even if doing so cost him politically—though, of course, standing up to them was precisely the politic thing to do.

As President, Clinton made sure to insulate himself periodically against the charge that on matters of race he was too soft. This largely explains his sermons in black churches castigating illegitimacy, criminality, and other moral failings (this from the man who would give us the infamous blue dress); his signing of a welfare bill that was overwhelmingly opposed by the Congressional Black Caucus; and his refusal to speak up in favor of relaxing the draconian drug laws that have had an egregiously disproportionate and destructive impact on black communities. This calculation also explains Clinton's continuing support for capital punishment even though it is obvious that racial selectivity plays a major (albeit subtle) role in determining who are the unlucky few the state deems fit to kill.

The second prong of Clinton's strategy involved persuading influential black leaders—the CBC, the NAACP, black preachers—that ultimately he was on their side, that he felt their pain and shared their aspirations, that he sincerely liked them and was willing to display a fond association with them before the white American public. To accomplish this aim Clinton did several important things.

He defended affirmative action—the one program that black activists see as indispensable and non-negotiable. He appointed blacks to high office, including positions above those commonly associated with African-Americans. He made it clear to everyone—through attendance at black churches, walks in black neighborhoods, highly public friendships with black people—that he enjoys the presence and ways of black folk. He visited Africa. And he created and hosted occasions aimed at making amends for America's past racial sins. These occasions generated enormously moving (and politically safe) moments, such as the one in which he apologized for the infamous Tuskegee syphilis experiment and the one in which he awarded Medals of Honor to black veterans whose heroism had previously been ignored. It is because of these measures and because of the paucity of such gestures from political rivals that Clinton has won the enthusiastic loyalty and deep affection of many blacks.

Though Clinton's racial strategy has been good for him, has it, on balance, been good for the country? The answer is by no means clear. For all of Clinton's much-expressed concern about social justice in general and racial justice in particular, his programs, policies, and gestures have done painfully little to help those whom Professor William Julius Wilson calls "the truly disadvantaged"— impoverished people, disproportionately colored, who are locked away in pestilent and crime-ridden inner cities or forgotten rural or small-town wastelands, people who are bereft of the money, training, skills, or education needed to escape their plight. True, Clinton had to contend with a reactionary, Republican-led Congress for much of his presidency. But even before the Gingrichian deluge of 1994 he had made it plain that his sympathies lay predominantly with "the middle class." For those below it, he offered chastising lectures that legitimated the essentially conservative notion that the predicament of the poor results primarily from their own conduct and not from the deformative deprivations imposed on them by a grievously unfair social order that is in large part a class hierarchy and in smaller part a pigmentocracy.

In 1997 Clinton initiated a "conversation on race" and created a commission chaired by Professor John Hope Franklin to oversee the envisioned discussions. Rather quickly, however, the initiative displayed the parochial, shallow self-servingness that besmirches all too much of Clinton's talk about race relations. Portrayed as an effort at dialogue, the president's conversation was from the beginning a tightly scripted monologue that regurgitated familiar nostrums while avoiding discussion of real problems. Compared with the reports and agendas on race relations produced by commissions established by Harry Truman in 1946 and Lyndon Johnson in 1967, the report and agenda produced by Clinton's commission are laughable. Does this matter? Any highly public action taken by a president matters. Because of Clinton's conversation and its embarrassing end, a long time will have to pass before another president invests personal and political capital in pressing for public education about the American race question.

Clinton's main bequest to race relations is that he helped to sustain and accelerate the desegregation of the higher circles of American life. On the psychological plane he has gently pushed the white American public to accept something that for many whites is still more in question than one would like to believe: that blacks really can be equal or even superior to whites in performing the most crucial and difficult tasks demanded by our society. President George Bush contributed to this process in a major way when he selected General Colin Powell to be chairman of the Joint Chiefs of Staff. Through his appointment of blacks and genuine friendships with blacks, Clinton has deepened this tendency in American life. To a large extent, desegregation remains at the primitive level of mere tokenism. But compared with exclusion, robust tokenism, though far from enough, is a step in the right direction.

The Return of the "Undeserving Poor"
Glenn Loury

The Atlantic Monthly | February 2001

In the following essay, Boston University economist Glenn Loury focuses on the 1996 welfare-reform act and its consequences as an example of the price Clinton and the Democrats have paid in distancing themselves from traditional liberal politics. As Loury observes, just because a position is politically popular doesn't mean it's right. . . .

The successful two-term Clinton presidency has left the Democratic Party in a position to compete effectively with Republicans over the next decade in the ongoing struggle to define our nation's agenda for collective action. That is its most significant political legacy. After the ideological shift rightward during the Reagan years, and in the wake of humiliating national defeats for Walter Mondale and Michael Dukakis, Bill Clinton managed to recast the Democratic message so that it once again resonates with the sentiments of a majority of American voters. He moved the party toward the center, for the most part quieted its radical left wing, and, using a combination of center-right social-policy initiatives (on welfare and crime, for instance), clearly signaled the Democrats' endorsement of values widely held in the electorate at large.

To be sure, this strategy was aided by the good fortune of an unprecedented economic expansion. And it was powerfully abetted by the incompetence of Clinton's political opponents, who failed to understand that this country is far less ideological and (thank God!) much less self-righteous than is the right wing of the Republican Party. Even so, this repositioning of the unwieldy coalition of interests that constitutes the national Democratic Party has been a very impressive act to watch.

There is, however, an obvious problem in such repositioning. When not tempered by an uncompromising adherence to core principles, efforts to co-opt conservative rhetoric on social issues are not very different from capitulating to conservative values on social issues. That the death penalty is popular does not make it right. That middle-class taxpayers resent the giving of public money to unwed, unemployed, uneducated young mothers does not mean that such resentment is justified in the richest country on earth. That parents fear the prospect of drug use by their children does not make the War on Drugs good social policy. The Clinton presidency, while beating a full retreat from the "liberal ideology" that so plagued the Democrats in national politics during the 1980s, has also managed to confer an undeserved legitimacy on some widely held but not commendable notions about American social life. This, too, is a part of its legacy: self-consciously progressive political rhetoric has been essentially banished from the top of the Democratic Party.

As one example of this process, consider the public discussion of welfare policy. Clinton campaigned in 1992 on a promise to "end welfare as we know it." In this way he inoculated himself against the charge of being an old-style liberal Democrat seeking to protect the welfare status quo. Clinton's original plan was, in my view, a good one—but it never had a chance. When, after a protracted struggle with Republican majorities in Congress, a welfare-reform act was passed and signed into law in 1996, it initiated one of the most far-reaching conservative shifts in social policy in the post-New Deal era. The federal entitlement of indigent children to public support was terminated. Strict work requirements for recipients of assistance were put in place, and time limits were imposed on eligibility for assistance. Such a policy seemed to abandon the most vulnerable of our fellow citizens. Peter Edelman, one of several Clinton appointees to resign in protest over the signing of that bill, made a crucial point: much of welfare policy is really better thought of as disability policy. One third of the welfare case load involves some disability in either mothers or children; a third to a half of adult recipients seem to be unemployable, given that in the best "supported work" experiments many were still jobless despite three years of concerted searching. A great number of these folks are socially, psychologically, physically, or mentally impaired. Young children are involved. Why should our response to them properly be conceived along the single dimension of work?

This policy was due neither to historical inevitability nor to intellectual necessity. Rather, it was the result of political expediency. "Workfare" became the salable rejoinder to conservatives' anti-welfare rhetoric. The Democrats' mantra became "If you work hard and play by the rules, you shouldn't be poor." But where does that leave the great number of people who are unable (or unwilling) to "work hard and play by the rules"? By implication, they (and their children) deserve to be poor. In other words, the conservative distinction between "deserving" and "undeserving" poor people has now been written into national policy—and by a Democratic administration. A line of argument that started with the idea that everyone should pull his or her own weight has ended with a five-year lifetime limit on receipt of federal support for millions of indigent families incapable of supporting themselves.

Of course, defenders of the reform process can cite declining welfare rolls and relatively high employment rates among previous recipients. But here, again, the sheer good luck of an extraordinary economic climate must be kept in mind. Clinton has presided over a huge change in the structure of our anti-poverty policy. Much greater importance is now being placed on earnings relative to transfers. Little remarked is the fact that this policy shift has left low-income American families much more vulnerable to an inevitable rise in unemployment.

All of this leads me to regret the diminution of ideological (as distinct from partisan political) fervor that one must, I think, associate with the Clinton presidency. Crime rates are down, and the president takes due credit. Be it noted, however, that incarceration rates have continued to soar over the past eight years, growing at roughly the same rate during Clinton's presidency as during Ronald Reagan's. (The number of people in local, state, and federal custody on a given day has essentially quadrupled since 1980.) We are fast becoming a nation of jailers. Our major public outreach to impoverished, ill-educated young men occurs within this vast corrections establishment. Now, defenders of President Clinton would no doubt deny that the vast expansion of imprisonment that has taken place on his watch, alongside a comparable growth in our economic well-being, should be counted as part of his legacy. The point is debatable. What is beyond doubt, however, is that he has done precious little to awaken in the American people a sense of disquiet about it. Indeed, to the contrary, and in keeping with his grand political strategy, he has on occasion pandered to base public sentiments. That most certainly is a part of his legacy. And it does not look like progress to me.

Nickel and Dimed
Barbara Ehrenreich

from *Nickel and Dimed: On (Not) Getting By in America*

In her best-selling book Nickel and Dimed, *reporter Barbara Ehrenreich makes a bold attempt to put economic theory into practice by working at a series of low-paying jobs in three different regions of the United States. The following selection contains excerpts from her stints as a waitress/housekeeper in Key West, Florida, a housecleaner in Portland, Maine, and a Wal-Mart employee in a Minneapolis suburb—along with her sobering conclusions about the uphill battle to make ends meet in low-income America. . . .*

Part I—Serving In Florida

You might imagine, from a comfortable distance, that people who live, year in and year out, on $6 to $10 an hour have discovered some survival stratagems unknown to the middle class. But no. It's not hard to get my coworkers talking about their living situations, because housing, in almost every case, is the principal source of disruption in their lives, the first thing they fill you in on when they arrive for their shifts. After a week, I have compiled the following survey:

Gail is sharing a room in a well-known downtown flophouse for $250 a week. Her roommate, a male friend, has begun hitting on her, driving her nuts, but the rent would be impossible alone.

Claude, the Haitian cook, is desperate to get out of the two-room apartment he shares with his girlfriend and two other, unrelated people. As far as I can determine, the other Haitian men live in similarly crowded situations.

Annette, a twenty-year-old server who is six months pregnant and abandoned by her boyfriend, lives with her mother, a postal clerk.

Marianne, who is a breakfast server, and her boyfriend are paying $170 a week for a one-person trailer.

Billy, who at $10 an hour is the wealthiest of us, lives in the trailer he owns, paying only the $400-a-month lot fee.

The other white cook, Andy, lives on his dry-docked boat, which, as far as I can tell from his loving descriptions, can't be more than twenty feet long. He offers to take me out on it once it's repaired, but the offer comes with inquiries as to my marital status, so I do not follow up on it.

Tina, another server, and her husband are paying $60 a night for a room in the Days Inn. This is because they have no car and the Days Inn is in walking distance of the Hearthside. When Marianne is tossed out of her trailer for subletting (which is against trailer park rules), she leaves her boyfriend and moves in with Tina and her husband.

Joan, who had fooled me with her numerous and tasteful outfits (hostesses wear their own clothes), lives in a van parked behind a shopping center at night and showers in Tina's motel room. The clothes are from thrift shops.*

It strikes me, in my middle-class solipsism, that there is gross improvidence in some of these arrangements. When Gail and I are wrapping silverware in napkins—the only task for which we are permitted to sit—she tells me she is thinking of escaping from her roommate by moving into the Days Inn herself. I am astounded: how can she think of paying $40 to $60 a day? But if I was afraid of sounding like a social worker, I have come out just sounding like a fool. She squints at me in disbelief: "And where am I supposed to get a month's rent and a month's deposit for an apartment?" I'd been feeling pretty smug about my $500 efficiency, but of course it was

---

* I could find no statistics on the number of employed people living in cars or vans, but according to a 1997 report of the National Coalition for the Homeless, "Myths and Facts about Homelessness," nearly one-fifth of all homeless people (in twenty-nine cities across the nation) are employed in full- or part-time jobs.]

made possible only by the $1,300 I had allotted myself for start-up costs when I began my low-wage life: $1,000 for the first month's rent and deposit, $100 for initial groceries and cash in my pocket, $200 stuffed away for emergencies. In poverty, as in certain propositions in physics, starting conditions are everything.

There are no secret economies that nourish the poor; on the contrary, there are a host of special costs. If you can't put up the two months' rent you need to secure an apartment, you end up paying through the nose for a room by the week. If you have only a room, with a hot plate at best, you can't save by cooking up huge lentil stews that can be frozen for the week ahead. You eat fast food or the hot dogs and Styrofoam cups of soup that can be microwaved in a convenience store. If you have no money for health insurance—and the Hearthside's niggardly plan kicks in only after three months—you go without routine care or prescription drugs and end up paying the price. Gail, for example, was doing fine, healthwise anyway, until she ran out of money for estrogen pills. She is supposed to be on the company health plan by now, but they claim to have lost her application form and to be beginning the paperwork all over again. So she spends $9 a pop for pills to control the migraines she wouldn't have, she insists, if her estrogen supplements were covered. Similarly, Marianne's boyfriend lost his job as a roofer because he missed so much time after getting a cut on his foot for which he couldn't afford the prescribed antibiotic.

My own situation, when I sit down to assess it after two weeks of work, would not be much better if this were my actual life. The seductive thing about waitressing is that you don't have to wait for payday to feel a few bills in your pocket, and my tips usually cover meals and gas, plus something left over to stuff into the kitchen drawer I use as a bank. But as the tourist business slows in the summer heat, I sometimes leave work with only $20 in tips (the gross is higher, but servers share about 15 percent of their tips with the busboys and bartenders). With wages included, this amounts to about the minimum wage of $5.15 an hour. The sum in the drawer is piling up but at the present rate of accumulation will be more than $100 short of my rent when the end of the month comes around. Nor can I see any expenses to cut. True, I haven't gone the lentil stew route yet, but that's because I don't have a large cooking pot, potholders, or a ladle to stir with (which would cost a total of $30 at Kmart, somewhat less at a thrift store), not to mention onions, carrots, and the indispensable bay leaf. I do make my lunch every day—usually some slow-burning, high-protein combo like frozen chicken patties with melted cheese on top and canned pinto beans on the side. Dinner is at the Hearthside, which offers its employees a choice of BLT, fish sandwich, or hamburger for only $2. The burger lasts longest, especially if it's heaped with gut-puckering jalapeños, but by midnight my stomach is growling again.

So unless I want to start using my car as a residence, I have to find a second or alternative job. I call all the hotels I'd filled out housekeeping applications at weeks ago—the Hyatt, Holiday Inn, Econo Lodge, HoJo's, Best Western, plus a half-dozen locally run guest houses. Nothing. Then I start making the rounds again, wasting whole mornings waiting for some assistant manager to show up, even dipping into places so creepy that the front-desk clerk greets you from behind bullet-proof glass and sells pints of liquor over the counter. But either someone has exposed my real-life house-keeping habits—which are, shall we say, mellow—or I am at the wrong end of some infallible ethnic equation: most, but by no means all, of the working housekeepers I see on my job searches are African-Americans, Spanish-speaking, or refugees from the Central European post-Communist world, while servers are almost invariably white and monolingually Eng-lish-speaking. When I finally get a positive response, I have been identified once again as server material. Jerry's—again, not the real name—which is part of a well-known national chain and physically attached here to another budget hotel, is ready to use me at once. The prospect is both exciting and terrifying because, with about the same number of tables and counter seats, Jerry's attracts three or four times the volume of customers as the gloomy old Hearthside.

[After one day of trying to hold down both full-time jobs, the author quits the Hearthside when she is chastised for trying to eat a cup of clam chowder on the job.]

I make the decision to move closer to Key West. First, because of the drive. Second and third, also because of the drive: gas is eating up $4–$5 a day, and although Jerry's is as high-volume as you can get, the tips average only 10 percent, and not just for a newbie like me. Between the base pay of $2.15 an hour and the obligation to share tips with the busboys and dishwashers, we're averaging only about $7.50 an hour. Then there is the $30 I had to spend on the regulation tan slacks worn by Jerry's servers—a setback it could take weeks to absorb. (I had combed the town's two downscale department stores hoping for something cheaper but decided in the end that these marked-down Dockers, originally $49, were more likely to survive a daily washing.) Of my fellow servers, everyone who lacks a working husband or boyfriend seems to have a second job: Nita does something at a computer eight hours a day; another welds. Without the forty-five-minute commute, I can picture myself working two jobs and still having the time to shower between them.

So I take the $500 deposit I have coming from my landlord, the $400 I have earned towards the next month's rent, plus the $200 reserved for emergencies, and use the $1,100 to pay the rent and deposit on trailer number 46 in the Overseas Trailer Park, a mile from the cluster of budget hotels that constitute Key West's version of an industrial park. Number 46 is about eight feet in width and shaped like a barbell inside, with a narrow region—because of the sink and the stove—separating the bedroom from what might optimistically be called the "living" area, with its two-person table and half-sized couch. The bathroom is so small my knees rub against the shower stall when I sit on the toilet, and you can't just leap out of the bed, you have to climb down to the foot of it in order to find a patch of floor space to stand on. Outside, I am within a few yards of a liquor store, a bar that advertises "free beer tomorrow," a convenience store, and a Burger King—but no supermarket or, alas, Laundromat. By reputation, the Overseas park is a nest of crime and crack, and I am hoping at least for some vibrant multicultural street life. But desolation rules night and day, except for a thin stream of pedestrians heading for their jobs at the Sheraton or the 7-Eleven. There are not exactly people here but what amounts to canned labor, being preserved between shifts from the heat.

In line with my reduced living conditions, a new form of ugliness arises at Jerry's. First we are confronted—via an announcement on the computers through which we input orders—with the new rule that the hotel bar, the Driftwood, is henceforth off-limits to restaurant employees. The culprit, I learn through the grapevine, is the ultraefficient twenty-three-year-old who trained me—another trailer home dweller and a mother of three. Something had set her off one morning, so she slipped out for a nip and returned to the floor impaired. The restriction mostly hurts Ellen, whose habit it is to free her hair from its rubber band and drop by the Driftwood for a couple of Zins before heading home at the end of her shift, but all of us feel the chill. Then the next day, when I go for straws, I find the dry-storage room locked. It's never been locked before; we go in and out of it all day—for napkins, jelly containers, Styrofoam cups for takeout. Vic, the portly assistant manager who opens it for me, explains that he caught one of the dishwashers trying to steal something and, unfortunately, the miscreant will be with us until a replacement can be found—hence the locked door. I neglect to ask what he had been trying to steal but Vic tells me who he is—the kid with the buzz cut and the earring, you know, he's back there right now.

I wish I could say I rushed back and confronted George to get his side of the story. I wish I could say I stood up to Vic and insisted that George be given a translator and allowed to defend himself or announced that I'd find a lawyer who'd handle the case pro bono. At the very least I should have testified as to the kid's honesty. The mystery to me is that there's not much worth stealing in the dry-storage room, at least not in any fenceable quantity: "Is Gyorgi here, and am having 200—maybe 250—catsup packets. What do you say?" My guess is that he had taken—if he had taken anything at all—some Saltines or a can of cherry pie mix and that the motive for taking it was hunger.

So why didn't I intervene? Certainly not because I was held back by the kind of moral paralysis that can mask as journalistic objectivity. On the contrary, something new—something loathsome and servile—had infected me, along with the kitchen odors that I could still sniff on my bra when I finally undressed at night.

[Continuing to wait tables at Jerry's, the author lands a second job as a house-keeper in the adjoining hotel.]

I can do this two-job thing, is my theory, if I can drink enough caffeine and avoid getting distracted by George's ever more obvious suffering.* The first few days after the alleged theft, he seemed not to understand the trouble he

---

* In 1996 the number of persons holding two or more jobs averaged 7.8 million, or 6.2 percent of the workforce. It was about the same rate for men and for women (6.1 versus 6.2). About two-thirds of multiple jobholders work one job full-time and the other part-time. Only a heroic minority—4 percent of men and 2 percent of women—work two full-time jobs simultaneously (John F. Stinson Jr., "New Data on Multiple Jobholding Available from the CPS," *Monthly Labor Review,* March 1997).

was in, and our chirpy little conversations had continued. But the last couple of shifts he's been listless and unshaven, and tonight he looks like the ghost we all know him to be, with dark half-moons hanging from his eyes. At one point, when I am briefly immobilized by the task of filling little paper cups with sour cream for baked potatoes, he comes over and looks as if he'd like to explore the limits of our shared vocabulary, but I am called to the floor for a table. I resolve to give him all my tips that night, and to hell with the experiment in low-wage money management. At eight, Ellen and I grab a snack together standing at the mephitic end of the kitchen counter, but I can only manage two or three mozzarella sticks, and lunch had been a mere handful of McNuggets. I am not tired at all, I assure myself, though it may be that there is simply no more "I" left to do the tiredness monitoring. What I would see if I were more alert to the situation is that the forces of destruction are already massing against me. There is only one cook on duty, a young man named Jesus ("Hay-Sue," that is), and he is new to the job. And there is Joy, who shows up to take over in the middle of the shift dressed in high heels and a long, clingy white dress and fuming as if she'd just been stood up in some cocktail bar.

Then it comes, the perfect storm. Four of my tables fill up at once. Four tables is nothing for me now, but only so long as they are obligingly staggered. As I bev table 27, tables 25, 28, and 24 are watching enviously. As I bev 25, 24 glowers because their bevs haven't even been ordered. Twenty-eight is four yuppyish types, meaning everything on the side and agonizing instructions as the chicken Caesars. Twenty-five is a middle-aged black couple who complain, with some justice, that the iced tea isn't fresh and the tabletop is sticky. But table 24 is the meteorological event of the century: ten British tourists who seem to have made the decision to absorb the American experience entirely by mouth. Here everyone has at least two drinks—iced tea *and* milk shake, Michelob *and* water (with lemon slice in the water, please)—and a huge, promiscuous orgy of breakfast specials, mozz sticks, chicken strips, quesadillas, burgers with cheese and without, sides of hash browns with cheddar, with onions, with gravy, seasoned fries, plain fries, banana splits. Poor Jesus! Poor me! Because when I arrive with their first tray of food—after three prior trips to refill bevs—Princess Di refuses to eat her chicken strips with her pancake and sausage special since, as she now reveals, the strips were meant to be an appetizer. Maybe the others would have accepted their meals, but Di, who is deep into her third

Michelob, insists that everything else go back while they work on their starters. Meanwhile, the yuppies are waving me down for more decaf and the black couple looks ready to summon the NAACP.

Much of what happens next is lost in the fog of war. Jesus starts going under. The little printer in front of him is spewing out orders faster than he can rip them off, much less produce the meals. A menacing restlessness rises from the tables, all of which are full. Even the invincible Ellen is ashen from stress. I take table 24 their reheated courses, which they immediately reject as either too cold or fossilized by the microwave. When I return to the kitchen with their trays (three trays in three trips) Joy confronts me with arms akimbo: "What *is* this?" She means the food—the plates of rejected pancakes, hash browns in assorted flavors, toasts, burgers, sausages, eggs. "Uh, scrambled with cheddar," I try, "and that's—" "*No*," she screams in my face, "is it a traditional, a super-scramble, an eye-opener?" I pretend to study my check for a clue, but entropy has been up to its tricks, not only on the plates but in my head, and I have to admit that the original order is beyond reconstruction. "You don't know an eye-opener from a traditional?" she demands in outrage. All I know, in fact, is that my legs have lost interest in the current venture and have announced their intention to fold. I am saved by a yuppie (mercifully not one of mine) who chooses this moment to charge into the kitchen to bellow that his food is twenty-five minutes late. Joy screams at him to get the hell out of her kitchen, *please*, and then turns on Jesus in a fury, hurling an empty tray across the room for emphasis.

I leave. I don't walk out, I just leave. I don't finish my side work or pick up my credit card tips, if any, at the cash register or, of course, ask Joy's permission to go. And the surprising thing is that you *can* walk out without permission, that the door opens, that the thick tropical night air parts to let me pass, that my car is still parked where I left it. There is no vindication in this exit, no fuck-you surge of relief, just an overwhelming dank sense of failure pressing down on me and the entire parking lot.

Part II—Scrubbing In Maine

In my interview, I had been promised a thirty-minute lunch break, but this turns out to be a five-minute pit stop at a convenience store, if that. I bring my own sandwich—the same turkey breast and cheese every day—as do a couple of the others; the rest eat convenience store fare, a bagel or doughnut salvaged from our free breakfast, or nothing at all. The two older married women I'm teamed up with eat best—sandwiches and fruit. Among the younger women, lunch consists of a slice of pizza, a "pizza pocket" (a roll of dough surrounding some pizza sauce), or a small bag of chips. Bear in mind we are not office workers, sitting around idling at the basal metabolic rate. A poster on the wall in the office cheerily displays the number of calories burned per minute at our various tasks, ranging from about 3.5 for dusting to 7 for vaccuming. If you assume an average of 5 calories per minute in a seven-hour day (eight hours minus time for travel between houses), you need to be taking in 2,100 calories in addition to the resting minimum of, say, 900 or so. I get pushy with Rosalie, who is new like me and fresh from high school in a rural northern part of the state, about the meagerness of her lunches, which consist solely of Doritos—a half bag from the day before or a freshly purchased small-sized bag. She just didn't have anything in the house, she says (though she lives with her boyfriend and his mother), and she certainly doesn't have any money to buy lunch, as I find out when I offer to fetch her a soda from a Quik Mart and she has to admit she doesn't have eighty-nine cents. I treat her to a soda, wishing I could force her, mommy-like, to take milk instead. So how does she hold up for an eight- or even nine-hour day? "Well," she concedes, "I get dizzy sometimes."

How poor are they, my coworkers? The fact that anyone is working this job at all can be taken as prima facie evidence of some kind of desperation or at least a history of mistakes and disappointments, but it's not for me to ask. In the prison movies that provide me with a mental guide to comportment, the new guy doesn't go around shaking hands and asking, "Hi there, what are you in for?" So I listen, in the cars and when we're assembled in the office, and learn, first, that no one seems to be homeless. Almost everyone is embedded in extended families or families artificially extended with housemates. People talk about visiting grandparents in the hospital or sending birthday cards to a niece's husband; single mothers live with their own mothers or share apartments with a coworker or boyfriend. Pauline, the oldest of us, owns her own home, but she sleeps on the living room sofa, while her four grown children and three grandchildren fill up the bedrooms.

But although no one, apparently, is sleeping in a car, there are signs, even at the beginning, of real difficulty if not actual misery. Half-smoked cigarettes are returned to the pack. There are discussions about who will come up with fifty cents for a toll and whether Ted can be counted on for prompt reimbursement. One of my teammates gets frantic about a painfully impacted wisdom tooth and keeps making calls from our houses to try to locate a source of free dental care. When my—or, should I say, Liza's—team discovers that there is not a single Dobie in our buckets, I suggest that we stop at a convenience store and buy one rather than drive all the way back to the office. But it turns out I haven't brought any money with me and we cannot put together $2 between the four of us.

The Friday of my first week at The Maids is unnaturally hot for Maine in early September—95 degrees, according to the digital time-and-temperature displays offered by banks that we pass. I'm teamed up with the sad-faced Rosalie and our leader, Maddy, whose sullenness, under the circumstances, is almost a relief after Liza's relentless good cheer. Liza, I've learned, is the highest-ranking cleaner, a sort of supervisor really, and said to be something of a snitch, but Maddy, a single mom of maybe twenty-seven or so, has worked for only three months and broods about her child care problems. Her boyfriend's sister, she tells me on the drive to our first house, watches her eighteen-month-old for $50 a week, which is a stretch on The Maids' pay, plus she doesn't entirely trust the sister, but a real day care center could be as much as $90 a week. After polishing off the first house, no problem, we grab "lunch"—Doritos for Rosalie and a bag of Pepperidge Farm goldfish for Maddy—and head out to the exurbs for what our instruction sheet warns is a five-bathroom spread and a first-timer to boot. Still, the size of the place makes us pause for a moment, buckets in hand, before searching out an appropriately humble entrance. It sits there like a beached ocean liner, the prow cutting through swells of green turf, windows without number. "Well, well," Maddy says, reading the owner's name from our instruction sheet, "Mrs. W. and her big-ass house. I hope she's going to give us lunch."

Mrs W. is not in fact happy to see us, grimacing with exasperation when the black nanny ushers us into the family room or sunroom or den or whatever kind of specialized space she is sitting in. After all, she already has the nanny, a cooklike person, and a crew of men doing some sort of finishing touches on the construction to supervise. No, she doesn't want to take us around the house, because she already explained everything to the office on the phone, but Maddy stands there, with Rosalie and me behind her, until she relents. We are to move everything on all surfaces, she instructs during the tour, and get underneath and be sure to do every bit of the several miles, I calculate, of baseboards. And be mindful of the baby, who's napping and can't have cleaning fluids of any kind near her. . . .

It's hotter inside than out, un-air-conditioned for the benefit of the baby,

I suppose, but I do all right until I encounter the banks of glass doors that line the side and back of the ground floor. Each one has to be Windexed, wiped, and buffed—inside and out, top to bottom, left to right, until it's as streakless and invisible as a material substance can be. Outside, I can see the construction guys knocking back Gatorade, but the rule is that no fluid or food item can touch a maid's lips when she's inside a house. Now, sweat, even in unseemly quantities, is nothing new to me. I live in a subtropical area where even the inactive can expect to be moist nine months out of the year. I work out, too, in my normal life and take a certain macho pride in the Vs of sweat that form on my T-shirt after ten minutes or more on the StairMaster. But in normal life fluids lost are immediately replaced. Everyone in yuppie-land—airports, for example— looks like a nursing baby these days, inseparable from their plastic bottles of water. Here, however, I sweat without replacement or pause, not in individual drops but in continuous sheets of fluid soaking through my polo shirt, pouring down the backs of my legs. The eyeliner I put on in the morning—vain twit that I am—has long since streaked down onto my cheeks, and I could wring my braid out if I wanted to. Working my way through the living room(s), I wonder if Mrs. W. will ever have occasion to realize that every single doodad and *objet* through which she expresses her unique, individual self is, from another vantage point, only an obstacle between some thirsty person and a glass of water. . . .

I rush home to the Blue Haven at the end of the day, pull down the blinds for privacy, strip off my uniform in the kitchen—the bathroom being too small for both a person and her discarded clothes—and stand in the shower for a good ten minutes, thinking all this water is *mine*. I have paid for it, in fact, I have earned it. I have gotten through a week at The Maids without mishap, injury, or insurrection.

Part III—Selling In Minnesota

Our job, it emerges in fragments throughout the day, is to keep ladies' wear "shoppable." Sure, we help customers (who are increasingly called "guests" here as well), if they want any help. At first I go around practicing the "aggressive hospitality" demanded by our training videos: as soon as anyone comes within ten feet of a sales associate, that associate is supposed to smile warmly and offer assistance. But I never see a more experienced associate do this— first, because the customers are often annoyed to have their shopping dazes interrupted and, second, because we have far more pressing things to do. In ladies' wear, the big task, which has no real equivalent in, say, housewares or lawn and garden, is to put away the "returns"—clothes that have been tried on and rejected or, more rarely, purchased and then returned to the store. There are also the many items that have been scattered by customers, dropped on the floor, removed from their hangers and strewn over the racks, or secreted in locations far from their natural homes. Each of these items, too, must be returned to its precise place, matched by color, pattern, price, and size. Any leftover time is devoted to zoning. When I relate this to Caroline on the phone, she commiserates, "Ugh, a no-brainer."

But no job is as easy as it looks to the uninitiated. I have to put clothes away—the question is, Where? Much of my first few days is devoted to trying to memorize the layout of ladies' wear, one thousand (two thousand?) square feet of space bordered by men's wear, children's wear, greeting cards, and underwear. Standing at the fitting rooms and facing toward the main store entrance, we are looking directly at the tentlike, utilitarian plus sizes, also known as "woman" sizes. These are flanked on the left by our dressiest and costliest line (going up to $29 and change), the all-polyester Kathie Lee collection, suitable for dates and subprofessional levels of office work. Moving clockwise, we encounter the determinedly sexless Russ and Bobbie Brooks lines, seemingly aimed at pudgy fourth-grade teachers with important barbecues to attend. Then, after the sturdy White Stag, come the breezy, revealing Faded Glory, No Boundaries, and Jordache collections, designed for the younger and thinner crowd. Tucked throughout are nests of the lesser brands, such as Athletic Works, Basic Equipment, and the whimsical Looney Tunes, Pooh, and Mickey lines, generally decorated with images of their eponymous characters. Within each brand-name area, there are of course dozens of items, even dozens of each *kind* of item. This summer, for example, pants may be capri, classic, carpenter, clam-digger, boot, or flood, depending on their length and cut, and I'm probably leaving a few categories out. So my characteristic stance is one of rotating slowly on one foot, eyes wide, garment in hand, asking myself, "Where have I seen the $9.96 Athletics Works knit overalls?". . .

• • •

With competence comes a new impatience: *Why does anybody put up with the wages we're paid?* True, most of my fellow workers are better cushioned than I am; they live with spouses or grown children or they have other jobs in addition to this one. I sit with Lynne in the break room one night and find out this is only a part-time job for her—six hours a day—with the other eight hours spent in a factory for $9 an hour. Doesn't she get awfully tired? Nah, it's what she's always done. The cook at the Radio Grill has two other jobs. You might expect a bit of grumbling, some signs here and there of unrest—graffiti on the hortatory posters in the break room, muffled guffaws during our associate meetings—but I can detect none of that. Maybe this is what you get when you weed out all the rebels with drug tests and personality "surveys"—a uniformly servile and denatured workforce, content to dream of the distant day when they'll be vested in the company's profit-sharing plan. They even join in the "Wal-Mart cheer" when required to do so at meetings, I'm told by the evening fitting room lady, though I am fortunate enough never to witness this final abasement. . . .

The only thing to do is ask: Why do you—why do *we*—work here? Why do you stay? So when Isabelle praises my work a second time (!), I take the opportunity to say I really appreciate her encouragement, but I can't afford to live on $7 an hour, and how does she do it? The answer is that she lives with her grown daughter, who also works, plus the fact that she's worked here two years, during which her pay has shot up to $7.75 an hour. She counsels patience: it could happen to me. Melissa, who has the advantage of a working husband, says, "Well, it's a job." Yes, she made twice as much when she was a waitress but that place closed down and at her age she's never going to be hired at a high-tip place. I recognize the inertia, the unwillingness to start up with the apps and the interviews and the drug tests again. She thinks she should give it a year. *A year?* I tell her I'm wondering whether I should give it another week.

Part IV—Evaluation

How did I do as a low-wage worker? If I may begin with a brief round of applause: I didn't do half bad at the work itself, and I claim this as a considerable achievement. You might think that unskilled jobs would be a snap for someone who holds a Ph.D. and whose normal line of work requires learning entirely new things every couple of weeks. Not so. The first thing I discovered is that no job, no matter how lowly, is truly "unskilled." Every one of the six jobs I entered into in the course of this project required concentration, and most demanded that I master new terms, new tools, and new skills—from placing orders on restaurant computers to wielding the backpack vaccuum cleaner. None of these things came as easily to me as I would have liked; no one ever said, "Wow, you're fast!" or "Can you believe she just started?" Whatever my accomplishments in the rest of my life, in the low-wage work world I was a person of average ability—capable of learning the job and also capable of screwing up. . . .

But the real question is not how well I did at work but how well I did at life in general, which includes eating and having a place to stay. The fact that these are two separate questions needs to be underscored right away. In the rhetorical buildup to welfare reform, it was uniformly assumed that a job was the ticket out of poverty and that the only thing holding back welfare recipients was their reluctance to get out and get one. I got one and sometimes more than one, but my track record in the survival department is far less admirable than my performance as a jobholder. On small things I was thrifty enough; no expenditures on "carousing," flashy clothes, or any of the other indulgences that are often smugly believed to undermine the budgets of the poor. True, the $30 slacks in Key West and the $20 belt in Minneapolis were extravagances; I now know I could have done better at the Salvation Army or even at Wal-Mart. Food, though, I pretty much got down to a science: lots of chopped meat, beans, cheese, and noodles when I had a kitchen to cook in; otherwise, fast food, which I was able to keep down to about $9 a day. But let's look at the record.

In Key West, I earned $1,039 in one month and spent $517 on food, gas, toiletries, laundry, phone, and utilities. Rent was the deal breaker. If I had remained in my $500 efficiency, I would have been able to pay the rent and have $22 left over (which is still $78 less than the cash I had in my pocket at the start of the month). This in itself would have been a dicey situation if I had attempted to continue for a few more months, because sooner or later I would have had to spend something on medical and dental care or drugs other than ibuprofen. But my move to the trailer park—for the purpose, you will recall, of taking a second job—made me responsible for $625 a month in rent alone, utilities not included. Here I might have economized by giving up the car and buying a used bike (for about $50) or walking to work. Still, two jobs, or at least a job and a half, would be a necessity, and I had learned that I could not do two physically demanding jobs in the same day, at least not at any acceptable standard of performance.

In Portland, Maine, I came closest to achieving a decent fit between income and expenses, but only because I worked seven days a week. Between my two jobs, I was earning approximately $300 a week after taxes and paying $480 a month in rent, or a manageable 40 percent of my earnings. It helped, too, that gas and electricity were included in my rent and that I got two or three free meals each weekend at the nursing home. But I was there at the beginning of the off-season. If I had stayed until June 2000 I would have faced the Blue Haven's summer rent of $390 a week, which would of course have been out of the question. So to survive year-round, I would have had to save enough, in the months between August 1999 and May 2000, to accumulate the first month's rent and deposit on an actual apartment. I think I could have done this—saved $800 to $1,000—at least if no car trouble or illness interfered with my budget. I am not sure, however, that I could have maintained the seven-day-a-week regimen month after month or eluded the kinds of injuries that afflicted my fellow workers in the housecleaning business.

In Minneapolis—well, here we are left with a lot of speculation. If I had been able to find an apartment for $400 a month or less, my pay at Wal-Mart—$1,120 a month before taxes—might have been sufficient, although the cost of living in a motel while I searched for such an apartment might have made it impossible for me to save enough for the first month's rent and deposit. A weekend job, such as the one I almost landed at a supermarket for about $7.75 an hour, would have helped, but I had no guarantee that I could arrange my schedule at Wal-Mart to reliably exclude weekends. If I had taken the job at Menards and the pay was in fact $10 an hour for eleven hours a day, I would have made about $440 a week after taxes—enough to pay for a motel room and still have something left over to save up for the initial costs of an apartment. But were they really offering $10 an hour? And could I have stayed on my feet eleven hours a day, five days a week? So yes, with some different choices, I probably could have survived in Minneapolis. But I'm not going back for a rematch.

All right, I made mistakes, especially in Minneapolis, and these mistakes were at the time an occasion for feelings of failure and shame. I should have pulled myself together and taken the better-paying job; I should have moved into the dormitory I finally found (although at $19 a night, even a dorm bed would have been a luxury on Wal-Mart wages). But it must be said in my defense that plenty of other people were making the same mistakes: working at Wal-Mart rather than at one of the better-paying jobs available (often, I assume, because of transportation problems); living in residential motels at $200 to $300 a week. So the problem goes beyond my personal failings and miscalculations. Something is wrong, very wrong, when a single person in good health, a person who in addition possesses a working car, can barely support herself by the sweat of her brow. You don't need a degree in economics to see that wages are too low and rents too high.

AIDS—The Epidemic Continues
Bob Herbert

The New York Times | May 31 & June 4, 2001

Whether critiquing the fairness of the death penalty or probing relations between the police and the citizens they serve, Bob Herbert's op-ed column in The New York Times *is a consistent voice for the forgotten segments of the U.S. and world communities. In a series of memorable columns last summer, Herbert addressed the exploding AIDS crisis in China and sub-Saharan Africa, and also shone a spotlight on the resurgence of AIDS in our own backyard. . . .*

It Hasn't Gone Away

The scourge came upon us rather quietly. In the late spring of 1981 a new president, Ronald Reagan, was rounding up votes for his tax-cut package. Americans were fascinated by Prince Charles's fairy-tale courtship of Lady Diana Spencer, who was routinely referred to as the next queen of England. Al Pacino was starring in David Mamet's *American Buffalo* at the Circle in the Square. And an enormous ad campaign was touting a new movie from the creators of *Jaws* and *Star Wars*, an old-fashioned cliffhanger called *Raiders of the Lost Ark.*

It was then, almost exactly 20 years ago, that the first hint of a serious problem was detected. On June 5, 1981, the Centers for Disease Control and Prevention published an article in its *Morbidity and Mortality Weekly Report* that began as follows:

"In the period October 1980-May 1981, 5 young men, all active homosexuals, were treated for biopsy-confirmed Pneumocystis carinii pneumonia at 3 different hospitals in Los Angeles, California. Two of the patients died."

A month later, on July 3, *The New York Times* ran an article by Lawrence K. Altman that said:

"Doctors in New York and California have diagnosed among homosexual men 41 cases of a rare and often rapidly fatal form of cancer. Eight of the victims died less than 24 months after the diagnosis was made.

"The cause of the outbreak is unknown, and there is as yet no evidence of contagion. But the doctors who have made the diagnoses, mostly in New York City and the San Francisco Bay Area, are alerting other physicians who treat large numbers of homosexual men to the problem in an effort to help identify more cases and to reduce the delay in offering chemotherapy treatment."

The cancer was Kaposi's sarcoma. AIDS was upon us, and the progression of the disease from that early mystifying period would be swift and horrible. But the reaction to the disease, both in the United States and elsewhere, was tragically slow.

Ronald Reagan's biographer, Lou Cannon, wrote: "Reagan's response to this epidemic was halting and ineffective. In the critical years of 1984 and 1985, according to his White House physician, Brigadier General John Hutton, Reagan thought of AIDS as though 'it was measles and it would go away.' "

By the end of 1988, nearly 90,000 Americans had been diagnosed with AIDS and nearly 50,000 had died. By the mid-90's, the peak of the epidemic in the U.S., more than half a million Americans had been diagnosed with AIDS, and more than half of them had died.

Elsewhere the news has been worse. What is happening in Africa is beyond hideous, maybe even beyond comprehension. According to the World Health Organization, more than 25 million people in sub-Saharan Africa are infected with the human immunodeficiency virus, H.I.V., and AIDS. More than 12 million African children have been orphaned by AIDS. Nearly four million Africans were infected with H.I.V. last year.

Worldwide, more than 36 million people are infected with the AIDS virus, and in some places much, much worse is yet to come.

Twenty years after the first scientific paper on the disease we now call AIDS, the world is still not ready to properly fight the epidemic that has already killed more than 23 million people and will soon surpass the lethal toll of the bubonic plague of the Middle Ages.

The countries that have been hit hardest by the disease do not, in many cases, have the money, the medical resources or the sociopolitical infrastructure necessary to fight the disease. (In much of Africa it is still taboo to even talk about AIDS.) And there is no real plan among the wealthier nations to fight AIDS globally.

In the U.S., where AIDS deaths have been reduced dramatically by the use of protease inhibitors and other drugs, a dangerous sense of complacency seems to have settled in. But there are 40,000 new cases of H.I.V. infection each year, and no one knows, really, how long individuals taking the drugs can survive, or whether the virus will mutate, or become resistant to the drugs.

Twenty years later the epidemic is still with us. There is no cure. There is no vaccine. And in a world as interconnected as ours has become, there is no cause for complacency.

• • •

A Black AIDS Epidemic

The warning sirens are wailing, but young black men who are gay don't seem to be listening. And so the march into self-destruction continues.

The AIDS virus is being detected in gay black men at stunning rates, comparable to some of the hardest-hit sections of Africa.

A study released last week by the Centers for Disease Control and Prevention showed an annual H.I.V. infection rate of nearly 15 percent among young black men who were gay or bisexual. The study, which focused on six cities, was conducted by researchers who reported in February that 30 percent of all young, gay black men were already infected with the virus that causes AIDS.

The researchers described the latest findings as "alarming," which was an understatement. And yet there's been no tremendous outcry over these developments, from blacks or anyone else.

"Why aren't we outraged?" asked Phill Wilson, executive director of the African American AIDS Policy and Training Institute in Los Angeles. "Why aren't we marching in the streets? This is a major health catastrophe."

I am waiting for the so-called leaders of the black community—the politicians, the heads of civil rights organizations, the preachers—to step forward and say, in thundering tones, that it's time to bring an end to the relentlessly self-destructive behavior that has wrecked so many African-American families and caused so much suffering and death.

Gay black men have been hit the hardest, but the problem goes much deeper. The AIDS virus is being spread through the black community by people who are having intercourse without condoms, by drug users who contract the virus by sharing needles and then pass it on to others through sexual contact, by men who have sex with both men and women, and by poor judgment in general about sexual behavior, including unprotected sex with multiple partners and the common practice of trading sex for drugs.

It is time to shatter the taboos that have prevented blacks from speaking plainly and constructively about homosexuality, about H.I.V. and AIDS, and about drugs and other destructive practices that have inflicted grue-some damage on one generation after another of young black Americans.

The messages delivered to date have obviously not worked. AIDS is the leading cause of death for African-Americans between the ages of 25 and 44. While blacks are just 13 percent of the U.S. population, more than half of all new H.I.V. infections occur among blacks. Blacks are 10 times more likely than whites to be diagnosed with AIDS, and 10 times more likely to die from it.

Those would seem to be good reasons for blacks to be significantly more careful than whites about avoiding the virus.

The Centers for Disease Control believes 1 in every 50 black American men is infected with H.I.V. One in 50! It believes 1 in every 160 black women is infected. By comparison, 1 in every 250 white men is infected, and 1 in 3,000 white women.

One of the biggest obstacles to controlling the spread of the AIDS virus among young blacks is denial. There is still a widespread belief among blacks that AIDS is a disease primarily of gay white men. And there is the widespread belief that the disease is easily controlled, and perhaps even cured, by drugs.

Joe Pressley, an official with the New York AIDS Coalition, told me about a 15-year-old girl who said: "Don't tell me nothin' about no AIDS 'cause that won't impact me. And if I was to get it, all I'd have to do is take a pill in the morning and I'll be O.K."

The denial runs so deep—and the stigma surrounding homosexuality is still so strong among blacks—that many black men who have sex with other men nevertheless think of themselves as heterosexual, not gay or bisexual. These men, while attempting to present a heterosexual image to the outer world, frequently engage in compulsive, high-risk sex with men while engaged in ongoing sexual relationships with one or more women. This is behavior that puts girlfriends and wives in grave danger.

A new and intense and creative effort—led by black Americans—will be required to reclaim the lives of the thousands upon thousands of young blacks succumbing to the ravages of destructive sexual behavior, drug use and (in so many of these cases) the emotional pain of self-loathing, depression and despair.

If ever there was a need for tough love, this is it.

One America, Slightly Divisible

David Brooks

from *The Atlantic Monthly* | December 2001

*If compassionate conservativism has a face, it belongs to David Brooks. In wearing his several hats as author (*Bobos in Paradise, *his book on America's new bourgeois-bohemians, is considered a classic), senior editor at* The Weekly Standard *magazine, and commentator on* PBS's NewsHour with Jim Lehrer, *Brooks represents his right-of-center viewpoint with a politeness that's increasingly rare these days.*

In this excerpt from an Atlantic Monthly *article, Brooks commutes between his own upper-class Maryland town and a rural Pennsylvania county, in an attempt to find out what separates the inhabitants of the "Red" and the "Blue" states—and what binds them together. . . .*

Sixty-five miles from where I am writing this sentence is a place with no Starbucks, no Pottery Barn, no Borders or Barnes & Noble. No blue *New York Times* delivery bags dot the driveways on Sunday mornings. In this place people don't complain that Woody Allen isn't as funny as he used to be, because they never thought he was funny. In this place you can go to a year's worth of dinner parties without hearing anyone quote an aperçu he first heard on *Charlie Rose*. The people here don't buy those little rear-window stickers when they go to a summer-vacation spot so that they can drive around with "MV" decals the rest of the year; for the most part they don't even go to Martha's Vineyard.

The place I'm talking about goes by different names. Some call it America. Others call it Middle America. It has also come to be known as Red America, in reference to the maps that were produced on the night of the 2000 presidential election. People in Blue America, which is my part of America, tend to live around big cities on the coasts. People in Red America tend to live on farms or in small towns or small cities far away from the coasts. Things are different there.

Everything that people in my neighborhood do without motors, the people in Red America do with motors. We sail; they powerboat. We cross-country ski; they snowmobile. We hike; they drive ATVs. We have vineyard tours; they have tractor pulls. When it comes to yard work, they have rider mowers; we have illegal aliens.

Different sorts of institutions dominate life in these two places. In Red America churches are everywhere. In Blue America Thai restaurants are everywhere. In Red America they have QVC, the Pro Bowlers Tour, and hunting. In Blue America we have NPR, Doris Kearns Goodwin, and socially conscious investing. In Red America the Wal-Marts are massive, with parking lots the size of state parks. In Blue America the stores are small but the markups are big. You'll rarely see a Christmas store in Blue America, but in Red America, even in July, you'll come upon stores selling fake Christmas trees, wreath-decorated napkins, Rudolph the Red-Nosed Reindeer collectible thimbles and spoons, and little snow-covered villages.

We in the coastal metro Blue areas read more books and attend more plays than the people in the Red heartland. We're more sophisticated and cosmopolitan—just ask us about our alumni trips to China or Provence, or our interest in Buddhism. But don't ask us, please, what life in Red America is like. We don't know. We don't know who Tim LaHaye and Jerry B. Jenkins are, even though the novels they have co-written have sold about 40 million copies over the past few years. We don't know what James Dobson says on his radio program, which is listened to by millions. We don't know about Reba or Travis. We don't know what happens in mega-churches on Wednesday evenings, and some of us couldn't tell you the difference between a fundamentalist and an evangelical, let alone describe what it means to be a Pentecostal. Very few of us know what goes on in Branson, Missouri, even though it has seven million visitors a year, or could name even five NASCAR drivers, although stock-car races are the best-attended sporting events in the country. We don't know how to shoot or clean a rifle. We can't tell a military officer's rank by looking at his insignia. We don't know what soy beans look like when they're growing in a field.

Crossing the Meatloaf Line

Over the past several months, my interest piqued by those stark blocks of color on the election-night maps, I have every now and then left my home in Montgomery County, Maryland, and driven sixty-five miles northwest to Franklin County, in south-central Pennsylvania. Montgomery County is one of the steaming-hot centers of the great espresso machine that is Blue America. It is just over the border from north-western Washington, D.C., and it is full of upper-middle-class towns inhabited by lawyers, doctors, stockbrokers, and establishment journalists like me—towns like Chevy Chase, Potomac, and Bethesda (where I live). Its central artery is a burgeoning high-tech corridor with a multitude of sparkling new office parks housing technology companies such as United Information Systems and Sybase, and pioneering biotech firms such as Celera Genomics and Human Genome Sciences. When I drive to Franklin County, I take Route 270. After about forty-five minutes I pass a Cracker Barrel—Red America condensed into chain-restaurant form. I've crossed the Meatloaf Line; from here on there will be a lot fewer sun-dried-tomato concoctions on restaurant menus and a lot more meatloaf platters.

Franklin County is Red America. It's a rural county, about twenty-five miles west of Gettysburg, and it includes the towns of Waynesboro, Chambersburg, and Mercersburg. It was originally settled by the Scotch-Irish, and has plenty of Brethren and Mennonites along with a fast-growing population of evangelicals. The joke that Pennsylvanians tell about their state is that it has Philadelphia on one end, Pittsburgh on the other, and Alabama in the middle. Franklin County is in the Alabama part. It strikes me as I drive there that even though I am going north across the Mason-Dixon line, I feel as if I were going south. The local culture owes more to Nashville, Houston, and Daytona than to Washington, Philadelphia, or New York.

• • •

Some of the biggest differences between Red and Blue America show up on statistical tables. Ethnic diversity is one. In Montgomery County 60 percent of the population is white, 15 percent is black, 12 percent is Hispanic, and 11 percent is Asian. In Franklin County 95 percent of the population is white. White people work the gas-station pumps and the 7-Eleven counters. (This is something one doesn't often see in my part of the country.) Although the nation is growing more diverse, it's doing so only in certain spots. According to an analysis of the 2000 census by Bill Frey, a demographer at the Milken Institute, well over half the counties in America are still at least 85 percent white.

Another big thing is that, according to 1990 census data, in Franklin County only 12 percent of the adults have college degrees and only 69 percent have high school diplomas. In Montgomery County 50 percent of the adults have college degrees and 91 percent have high school diplomas. The education gap extends to the children. At Walt Whitman High School, a public school in Bethesda, the average SAT scores are 601 verbal and 622 math, whereas the national average is 506 verbal and 514 math. In Franklin County, where people are quite proud of their schools, the average SAT scores at, for example, the Waynesboro area high school are 495 verbal and 480 math. More and more kids in Franklin County are going on to college, but it is hard to believe that their prospects will be as bright as those of the kids in Montgomery County and the rest of upscale Blue America.

Because the information age rewards education with money, it's not surprising that Montgomery County is much richer than Franklin County. According to some estimates, in Montgomery County 51 percent of households have annual incomes above $75,000, and the average household income is $100,365. In Franklin County only 16 percent of households have incomes above $75,000, and the average is $51,872.

• • •

The two counties vote differently, of course—the differences, on a nationwide scale, were what led to those red-and-blue maps. Like upscale areas everywhere, from Silicon Valley to Chicago's North Shore to suburban Connecticut, Montgomery County supported the Democratic ticket in last year's presidential election, by a margin of 63 percent to 34 percent. Meanwhile, like almost all of rural America, Franklin County went Republican, by 67 percent to 30 percent.

However, other voting patterns sometimes obscure the Red-Blue cultural divide. For example, minority voters all over the country overwhelmingly supported the Democratic ticket last November. But—in many respects, at least—blacks and Hispanics in Red America are more traditionalist than blacks and Hispanics in Blue America, just as their white counterparts are. For example, the Pew Research Center for the People and the Press, in Washington, D.C., recently found that 45 percent of minority members in Red states agree with the statement "AIDS might be God's punishment for immoral sexual behavior," but only 31 percent of minority members in Blue states do. Similarly, 40 percent of minorities in Red states believe that school boards should have the right to fire homosexual teachers, but only 21 percent of minorities in Blue states do.

From Cracks to a Chasm?

These differences are so many and so stark that they lead to some pretty troubling questions: Are Americans any longer a common people? Do we have one national conversation and one national culture? Are we loyal to the same institutions and the same values? How do people on one side of the divide regard those on the other?

I went to Franklin County because I wanted to get a sense of how deep the divide really is, to see how people there live, and to gauge how different their lives are from those in my part of America. I spoke with ministers, journalists, teachers, community leaders, and pretty much anyone I ran across. I consulted with pollsters, demographers, and market-research firms.

Toward the end of my project the World Trade Center and the Pentagon were attacked. This put a new slant on my little investigation. In the days immediately following September 11 the evidence seemed clear that despite our differences, we are still a united people. American flags flew everywhere in Franklin County and in Montgomery County. Patriotism surged. Pollsters started to measure Americans' reactions to the events. Whatever questions they asked, the replies were near unanimous. Do you support a military response against terror? More than four-fifths of Americans said yes. Do you support a military response even if it means thousands of U.S. casualties? More than three-fifths said yes. There were no significant variations across geographic or demographic lines.

A sweeping feeling of solidarity was noticeable in every neighborhood, school, and workplace. Headlines blared, "A NATION UNITED" and "UNITED STATE." An attack had been made on the very epicenter of Blue America— downtown Manhattan. And in a flash all the jokes about and seeming hostility toward New Yorkers vanished, to be replaced by an outpouring of respect, support, and love. The old hostility came to seem merely a sort of sibling rivalry, which means nothing when the family itself is under threat.

But very soon there were hints that the solidarity was fraying. A few stray notes of dissent were sounded in the organs of Blue America. Susan Sontag wrote a sour piece in *The New Yorker* about how depressing it was to see what she considered to be a simplistically pro-American reaction to the attacks. At rallies on college campuses across the country speakers pointed out that America had been bombing other countries for years, and turnabout was fair play. On one NPR talk show I heard numerous callers express unease about what they saw as a crude us-versus-them mentality behind President Bush's rhetoric. Katha Pollitt wrote in *The Nation* that she would not permit her daughter to hang the American flag from the living-room window, because, she felt, it "stands for jingoism and vengeance and war." And there was evidence that among those with less-strident voices, too, differences were beginning to show. Polls revealed that people without a college education were far more confident than people with a college education that the military could defeat the terrorists. People in the South were far more eager than people in the rest of the country for an American counterattack to begin.

It started to seem likely that these cracks would widen once the American response got under way, when the focus would be not on firemen and rescue workers but on the Marines, the CIA, and the special-operations forces. If the war was protracted, the cracks could widen into a chasm, as they did during Vietnam. Red America, the home of patriotism and military service (there's a big military-recruitment center in downtown Chambersburg), would undoubtedly support the war effort, but would Blue America (there's a big gourmet dog bakery in downtown Bethesda) decide that a crude military response would only deepen animosities and make things worse?

So toward the end of my project I investigated Franklin County with a heightened sense of gravity and with much more urgency. If America was not firmly united in the early days of the conflict, we would certainly not be united later, when the going got tough.

"The People Versus the Powerful"

There are a couple of long-standing theories about why America is divided. One of the main ones holds that the division is along class lines, between the haves and the have-nots. This theory is popular chiefly on the left, and can be found in the pages of *The American Prospect* and other liberal magazines; in news reports by liberal journalists such as Donald L. Barlett and James B. Steele, of *Time;* and in books such as *Middle Class Dreams* (1995), by the Clinton and Gore pollster Stanley Greenberg, and *America's Forgotten Majority: Why the White Working Class Still Matters* (2000), by the demographer Ruy Teixeira and the social scientist Joel Rogers.

According to this theory, during most of the twentieth century gaps in income between the rich and the poor in America gradually shrank. Then came the information age. The rich started getting spectacularly richer, the poor started getting poorer, and wages for the middle class stagnated, at best. Over the previous decade, these writers emphasized, remuneration for top-level executives had skyrocketed: now the average CEO made 116 times as much as the average rank-and-file worker. Assembly-line workers found themselves competing for jobs against Third World workers who earned less than a dollar an hour. Those who had once labored at well-paying blue-collar jobs were forced to settle for poorly paying service-economy jobs without benefits.

People with graduate degrees have done well over the past couple of decades: their real hourly wages climbed by 13 percent from 1979 to 1997, according to Teixeira and Rogers. But those with only some college education saw their wages fall by nine percent, while those with only high school diplomas saw their wages fall by 12 percent, and high school dropouts saw a stunning 26 percent decline in their pay.

Such trends have created a new working class, these writers argue—not a traditional factory-and-mill working class but a suburban and small-town working class, made up largely of service workers and low-level white-collar employees. Teixeira and Rogers estimate that the average household income for this group, which accounts for about 55 percent of American adults, is roughly $42,000. "It is not hard to imagine how [recent economic trends] must have felt to the forgotten majority man," they write.

As at least part of America was becoming ever more affluent, an affluence that was well covered on television and in the evening news, he did not seem to be making much progress. What could he be doing wrong to be faring so poorly? Why couldn't he afford what others could? And why were they moving ahead while he was standing still?

Stanley Greenberg tailored Al Gore's presidential campaign to appeal to such voters. Gore's most significant slogan was "The People Versus the Powerful," which was meant to rally members of the middle class who felt threatened by "powerful forces" beyond their control, such as HMOs, tobacco companies, big corporations, and globalization, and to channel their resentment against the upper class. Gore dressed down throughout his campaign in the hope that these middle-class workers would identify with him.

Driving from Bethesda to Franklin County, one can see that the theory of a divide between the classes has a certain plausibility. In Montgomery County we have Saks Fifth Avenue, Cartier, Anthropologie, Brooks Brothers. In Franklin County they have Dollar General and Value City, along with a plethora of secondhand stores. It's as if Franklin County has only forty-five coffee tables, which are sold again and again.

When the locals are asked about their economy, they tell a story very similar to the one that Greenberg, Teixeira, Rogers, and the rest of the wage-stagnation liberals recount. There used to be plenty of good factory jobs in Franklin County, and people could work at those factories for life.

But some of the businesses, including the textile company J. Schoeneman, once Franklin County's largest manufacturer, have closed. Others have moved offshore. The remaining manufacturers, such as Grove Worldwide and JLG Industries, which both make cranes and aerial platforms, have laid off workers. The local Army depot, Letterkenny, has radically shrunk its work force. The new jobs are in distribution centers or nursing homes. People tend to repeat the same phrase: "We've taken some hits."

And yet when they are asked about the broader theory, whether there is class conflict between the educated affluents and the stagnant middles, they stare blankly as if suddenly the interview were being conducted in Aramaic. I kept asking, Do you feel that the highly educated people around, say, New York and Washington are getting all the goodies? Do you think there is resentment toward all the latte sippers who shop at Neiman Marcus? Do you see a gulf between high-income people in the big cities and middle-income people here? I got only polite, fumbling answers as people tried to figure out what the hell I was talking about.

When I rephrased the question in more-general terms, as Do you believe the country is divided between the haves and the have-nots?, everyone responded decisively: yes. But as the conversation continued, it became clear that the people saying yes did not consider themselves to be among the have-nots. Even people with incomes well below the median thought of themselves as haves.

What I found was entirely consistent with the election returns from November of last year. Gore's pitch failed miserably among the voters it was intended to target: nationally he lost among non-college-educated white voters by 17 points and among non-college-educated white men by 29 points. But it worked beautifully on the affluent, educated class: for example, Gore won among women with graduate degrees by 22 points. The lesson seems to be that if you run a campaign under the slogan "The People Versus the Powerful," you will not do well in the places where "the people" live, but you will do fantastically well in the places where "the powerful" live. This phenomenon mirrors, on a larger scale, one I noted a couple of years ago, when I traveled the country for a year talking about *Bobos in Paradise*, a book I had written on upscale America. The richer the community, the more likely I was to be asked about wage inequality. In middle-class communities the subject almost never came up.

Hanging around Franklin County, one begins to understand some of the reasons that people there don't spend much time worrying about economic class lines. The first and most obvious one is that although the incomes in Franklin County are lower than those in Montgomery County, living expenses are also lower—very much so. Driving from Montgomery County to Franklin County is like driving through an invisible deflation machine. Gas is thirty, forty, or even fifty cents a gallon cheaper in Franklin County. I parked at meters that accepted only pennies and nickels. When I got a parking ticket in Chambersburg, the fine was $3.00. At the department store in Greencastle there were racks and racks of blouses for $9.99.

The biggest difference is in real-estate prices. In Franklin County one can buy a nice four-bedroom split-level house with about 2,200 square feet of living space for $150,000 to $180,000. In Bethesda that same house would cost about $450,000. (According to the Coldwell Banker Real Estate Corporation, that house would sell for $784,000 in Greenwich, Connecticut; for $812,000 in Manhattan Beach, California; and for about $1.23 million in Palo Alto, California.)

Some of the people I met in Franklin County were just getting by. Some were in debt and couldn't afford to buy their kids the Christmas presents they wanted to. But I didn't find many who assessed their own place in society according to their income. Rather, the people I met commonly told me that although those in affluent places like Manhattan and Bethesda might make more money and have more-exciting jobs, they are the unlucky ones, because they don't get to live in Franklin County. They don't get to enjoy the beautiful green hillsides, the friendly people, the wonderful church groups and volunteer organizations. They may be nice people and all, but they are certainly not as happy as we are.

• • •

On my journeys to Franklin County, I set a goal: I was going to spend $20 on a restaurant meal. But although I ordered the most expensive thing on the menu—steak au jus, "slippery beef pot pie," or whatever—I always failed. I began asking people to direct me to the most-expensive places in town. They would send me to Red Lobster or Applebee's. I'd go into a restaurant that looked from the outside as if it had some pretensions—maybe a "Les Desserts" glass cooler for the key-lime pie and the tapioca pudding. I'd scan the menu and realize that I'd been beaten once again. I went through great vats of chipped beef and "seafood delight" trying to drop twenty dollars. I waded through enough surf-and-turfs and enough creamed corn to last a lifetime. I could not do it.

No wonder people in Franklin County have no class resentment or class consciousness; where they live, they can afford just about anything that is for sale.

(In Montgomery County, however—and this is one of the most striking contrasts between the two counties—almost nobody can say that. In Blue America, unless you are very, very rich, there is always, all around you, stuff for sale that you cannot afford.) And if they sought to improve their situation, they would look only to themselves. If a person wants to make more money, the feeling goes, he or she had better work hard and think like an entrepreneur.

• • •

In sum . . . I found no evidence that economic differences explain much of anything about the divide between Red and Blue America.

Ted Hale, a Presbyterian minister in the western part of the county, spoke of the matter this way: "There's nowhere near as much resentment as you would expect. People have come to understand that they will struggle financially. It's part of their identity. But the economy is not their god. That's the thing some others don't understand. People value a sense of community far more than they do their portfolio." Hale, who worked at a church in East Hampton, New York, before coming to Franklin County, said that he saw a lot more economic resentment in New York.

Hale's observations are supported by nationwide polling data. Pew has conducted a broad survey of the differences between Red and Blue states. The survey found that views on economic issues do not explain the different voting habits in the two regions. There simply isn't much of the sort of economic dissatisfaction that could drive a class-based political movement. Eighty-five percent of Americans with an annual household income between $30,000 and $50,000 are satisfied with their housing. Nearly 70 percent are satisfied with the kind of car they can afford. Roughly two thirds are satisfied with their furniture and their ability to afford a night out. These levels of satisfaction are not very different from those found in upper-middle-class America.

The Pew researchers found this sort of trend in question after question. Part of the draft of their report is titled "Economic Divide Dissolves."

A Lot of Religion but Few Crusaders

This leaves us with the second major hypothesis about the nature of the divide between Red and Blue America, which comes mainly from conservatives: America is divided between two moral systems. Red America is traditional, religious, self-disciplined, and patriotic. Blue America is modern, secular, self-expressive, and discomfited by blatant displays of patriotism. Proponents of this hypothesis in its most radical form contend that America is in the midst of a culture war, with two opposing armies fighting on behalf of their views. The historian Gertrude Himmelfarb offered a more moderate picture in *One Nation, Two Cultures* (1999), in which she argued that although America is not fatally split, it is deeply divided, between a heartland conservative population that adheres to a strict morality and a liberal population that lives by a loose one. The political journalist Michael Barone put it this way in a recent essay in *National Journal:* "The two Americas apparent in the 48 percent to 48 percent 2000 election are two nations of different faiths. One is observant, tradition-minded, moralistic. The other is unobservant, liberation-minded, relativistic."

The values-divide school has a fair bit of statistical evidence on its side. Whereas income is a poor predictor of voting patterns, church attendance— as Barone points out—is a pretty good one. Of those who attend religious services weekly (42 percent of the electorate), 59 percent voted for Bush, 39 percent for Gore. Of those who seldom or never attend religious services (another 42 percent), 56 percent voted for Gore, 39 percent for Bush. . . .

One can feel the religiosity in Franklin County after a single day's visit. Chambersburg and its vicinity have eighty-five churches and one synagogue. The Bethesda-Chevy Chase area, which has a vastly greater population, has forty-five churches and five synagogues. Professors at the local college in Chambersburg have learned not to schedule public lectures on Wednesday nights, because everybody is at prayer meetings.

• • •

David Rawley, a United Brethren minister in Greencastle, spoke for many of the social conservatives I met when he said that looking at the mainstream Hollywood culture made him feel that he was "walking against the current." "The tremendous force of culture means we can either float or fight," Rawley said. "Should you drift or stand on a rock? I tell people there is a rock we can hang on—the word of God. That rock will never give way. That rock's never going to move." When I asked Rawley what he thought of big-city culture, he said, "The individual is swallowed up by the largeness of the city. I see a world that doesn't want to take responsibility for itself. They have the babies but they decide they're not going to be the daddies. I'd really have to cling to the rock if I lived there."

• • •

Life is complicated, however. Yes, there are a lot of churches in Franklin

County; there are also a lot of tattoo parlors. And despite all the churches and bumper stickers, Franklin County . . . has most of the problems that afflict other parts of the country: heroin addiction, teen pregnancy, and so on. Nobody I spoke to felt part of a pristine culture that is exempt from the problems of the big cities. There are even enough spectacular crimes in Franklin County to make a devoted *New York Post* reader happy. During one of my visits the front pages of the local papers were ablaze with the tale of a young woman arrested for assault and homicide after shooting her way through a Veterans of the Vietnam War post. It was reported that she had intended to rob the post for money to run away with her lesbian girlfriend.

If the problems are the same as in the rest of America, so are many of the solutions. Franklin County residents who find themselves in trouble go to their clergy first, but they are often referred to psychologists and therapists as part of their recovery process. Prozac is a part of life.

• • •

Certainly Red and Blue America disagree strongly on some issues, such as homosexuality and abortion. But for the most part the disagreements are not large. For example, the Pew researchers asked Americans to respond to the statement "There are clear guidelines about what's good or evil that apply to everyone regardless of their situation." Forty-three percent of people in Blue states and 49 percent of people in Red states agreed. Forty-seven percent of Blue America and 55 percent of Red America agreed with the statement "I have old-fashioned values about family and marriage." Seventy percent of the people in Blue states and 77 percent of the people in Red states agreed that "too many children are being raised in day-care centers these days." These are small gaps. And, the Pew researchers found, there is no culture gap at all among suburban voters. In a Red state like Arizona suburban voters' opinions are not much different from those in a Blue state like Connecticut. The starkest differences that exist are between people in cities and people in rural areas, especially rural areas in the South.

• • •

The Ego Curtain

The best explanation of the differences between people in Montgomery and Franklin counties has to do with sensibility, not class or culture. If I had to describe the differences between the two sensibilities in a single phrase, it would be conception of the self. In Red America the self is small. People declare in a million ways, "I am normal. Nobody is better, nobody is worse. I am humble before God." In Blue America the self is more commonly large. People say in a million ways, "I am special. I have carved out my own unique way of life. I am independent. I make up my own mind."

In Red America there is very little one-upmanship. Nobody tries to be avant-garde in choosing a wardrobe. The chocolate-brown suits and baggy denim dresses hanging in local department stores aren't there by accident; people conspicuously want to be seen as not trying to dress to impress. . . .

People in Franklin County say they felt comfortable voting for Bush, because if he came to town he wouldn't act superior to anybody else; he could settle into a barber's chair and fit right in. They couldn't stand Al Gore, because they thought he'd always be trying to awe everyone with his accomplishments. People in Montgomery County tended to admire Gore's accomplishments. They were leery of Bush, because for most of his life he seemed not to have achieved anything.

• • •

In survey after survey, residents of conservative Red America come across as humbler than residents of liberal Blue America. About half of those who describe themselves as "very conservative" agree with the statement "I have more ability than most people," but nearly two-thirds of those who describe themselves as "very liberal" agree. Only 53 percent of conservatives agree with the statement "I consider myself an intellectual," but 75 percent of liberals do. Only 23 percent of conservatives agree with the statement "I must admit that I like to show off," whereas 43 percent of liberals do.

A Cafeteria Nation

These differences in sensibility don't in themselves mean that America has become a fundamentally divided nation. As the sociologist Seymour Martin Lipset pointed out in *The First New Nation* (1963), achievement and equality are the two rival themes running throughout American history. Most people, most places, and most epochs have tried to intertwine them in some way.

Moreover, after bouncing between Montgomery and Franklin counties, I became convinced that a lot of our fear that America is split into rival camps arises from mistaken notions of how society is shaped. Some of us still carry the old Marxist categories in our heads. We think that society is like a layer cake, with the upper class on top. And, like Marx, we tend to assume that wherever there is class division there is conflict. Or else we have a sort of *Crossfire* model in our heads: where would people we meet sit if they were guests on that show?

But traveling back and forth between the two counties was not like crossing from one rival camp to another. It was like crossing a high school cafeteria. Remember high school? There were nerds, jocks, punks, bikers, techies, druggies, God Squadders, drama geeks, poets, and Dungeons & Dragons weirdoes. All these cliques were part of the same school: they had different sensibilities; sometimes they knew very little about the people in the other cliques; but the jocks knew there would always be nerds, and the nerds knew there would always be jocks. That's just the way life is.

And that's the way America is. We are not a divided nation. We are a cafeteria nation.... We live our lives by migrating through the many different cliques associated with the activities we enjoy and the goals we have set for ourselves. Our freedom comes in the interstices; we can choose which set of standards to live by, and when.

• • •

What unites the two Americas, then, is our mutual commitment to this way of life—to the idea that a person is not bound by his class, or by the religion of his fathers, but is free to build a plurality of connections for himself. We are participants in the same striving process, the same experimental journey.

Never has this been more apparent than in the weeks following the September 11 attacks. Before then Montgomery County people and Franklin County people gave little thought to one another: an attitude of benign neglect toward other parts of the country generally prevailed. But the events of that day generated what one of my lunch mates in Franklin County called a primal response. Our homeland was under attack. Suddenly there was a positive sense that we Americans are all bound together—a sense that, despite some little fissures here and there, has endured.

On September 11 people in Franklin County flocked to the institutions that are so strong there—the churches and the American Legion and the VFW posts. Houses of worship held spontaneous prayer services and large ecumenical services. In the weeks since, firemen, veterans, and Scouts have held rallies. There have been blood drives. Just about every service organization in the county—and there are apparently thousands—has mobilized to raise funds or ship teddy bears. The rescue squad and the Salvation Army branch went to New York to help. . . .

If the September 11 attacks rallied people in both Red and Blue America, they also neutralized the political and cultural leaders who tend to exploit the differences between the two. Americans are in no mood for a class struggle or a culture war. The aftermath of the attacks has been a bit like a national Sabbath, taking us out of our usual pleasures and distractions and reminding us what is really important. Over time the shock will dissipate. But in important ways the psychological effects will linger, just as the effects of John F. Kennedy's assassination have lingered. The early evidence still holds: although there are some real differences between Red and Blue America, there is no fundamental conflict. There may be cracks, but there is no chasm. Rather, there is a common love for this nation—one nation in the end.

The National Conversation: Global Warming

Hot and Cold

Elizabeth Kolbert

The New Yorker | August 13, 2001

According to the best scientific information available, growing levels of carbon dioxide and other "greenhouse gases" in the atmosphere have apparently caused the average temperature of the earth to rise by about one degree Fahrenheit since the beginning of the 20th century. Should we be worried? Environmentalists and most Democrats say yes. The energy industry and most Republicans say no—a negation underscored by President Bush's curt dismissal of the proposed Kyoto Protocol for controlling global carbon dioxide emissions. In the following New Yorker *piece, Elizabeth Kolbert questions the wisdom of Bush's gamble. . . .*

In 1610, Nicolas de Crans, a deputy commissioner in Savoy, set out to investigate some extraordinary events that had recently been reported in the high Alpine valley of Chamonix. Farmers there were complaining that their land was disappearing; entire fields that had yielded rich harvests of wheat and rye were now under ice. They led Crans up the valley to the Des Bois glacier, which he described as "terrible and frightening to look on." It had, he wrote in a report, "ruined a good part of the land and all the village of Chastellard and quite carried away another little village called Bonnenuict."

The ice was still on the move some thirty years later, according to a second report, which noted that the glacier "advances by over a musket shot every day, even in the month of August." Fearing that the encroachment represented divine retribution for human sins, the local magistrates petitioned a bishop in Geneva, who in June of 1644 led a three-hundred-person procession through the mountains. In the course of three days, the bishop blessed four glaciers, sprinkling them with holy water.

The Des Bois glacier is now called the Mer de Glace. It has withdrawn so far that its closest edge lies a good kilometre from the lost village of Chastellard and it is no longer even visible from the valley it once invaded. As it retreats, along with glaciers all around the world, we find ourselves in the opposite situation of the pious, if unfortunate, citizens of Chamonix—and in much the same one.

Last month, exhausted representatives from a hundred and seventy-eight nations finally signed on to the Kyoto Protocol. The agreement, which was endorsed by all of the world's industrialized nations except the United States, amounts to a remarkable, multicultural expression of fear and, to a somewhat lesser extent, penitence. The participants committed themselves over the next decade to reducing their combined annual green-house-gas emissions to five percent below 1990 levels.

The American refusal to sign on fits a by now familiar pattern. Anything that is in anyway constricting, especially to the Bush administration's allies—energy conservation, tighter water-quality standards, emission limits—is to be viewed with caution: who knows if it'll work? Christie Whitman, the head of the Environmental Protection Agency, defended the Kyoto decision, saying that, given the state of the research, it would be premature to accept that accord, or any other. "We're still a long way from knowing how to solve the problem," she asserted.

This philosophy was also at work last week in the House, when law-makers approved the president's energy bill and rejected an amendment to raise fuel-efficiency standards—something the White House had opposed on the ground that the new standards were arbitrary. (Wariness, however, did not prevent Whitman from ordering a full-scale dredging of the Hudson, a move that actually does carry some risk but which many saw as a crucial boost to the reelection bid of New York's Republican governor, George Pataki.)

Kyoto follows on the research efforts of thousands of physicists, geo-chemists, oceanographers, botanists, limnologists, and paleoclimatolo-gists, who have, with virtual unanimity, established two main points. The first is that human activity is changing the atmosphere in unprece-dented ways; the second is that the earth is warming up. Nonetheless, the link between the two does remain inexact. Five years ago, scientists on the Intergovernmental Panel on Climate Change estimated than the earth's temperature would rise two to six degrees over the coming cen-tury; this past spring, after a reassessment that drew upon hundreds of new studies, the panel both raised its estimate and doubled the range of possibilities, saying that the increase could be anywhere from three to eleven degrees.

This imprecision does not represent a lack of progress. Analysis of lake sediments, glaciers, and deep ocean cores, together with the work of computer modellers, has revealed that the earth's climate, even without human influence, is unstable, given to sudden and violent shifts at unpredictable intervals. This inherent instability makes the impact of global warming that much more difficult to predict, and makes devising a solution that would meet Whitman's standards potentially impossible. At the same time, the ultimate costs of inaction threaten to be that much more catastrophic.

The Kyoto Protocol's measures may well prove ineffective, as the Bush administration fears—so much holy water poured on a vanishing glacier. (Already, our experiment with the earth's atmosphere has raised CO_2 levels higher than they have been for a half-million years, and they're rapidly approaching levels that haven't been seen since the age of the dinosaurs.) But refusing to sign the protocol on scientific grounds reflects a deep misunderstanding—or, more likely, misrepresentation—of what climate science has accomplished. Kyoto is, at the least, a gesture of responsibility and an acknowledgment of an essential condition of ethical action, which is, and always has been, uncertainty.

Building a Better Kyoto
Warwick McKibbin and Peter Wilcoxen

Brookings Institution | June 26, 2001

In this essay, originally published by the Brookings Institution under the title "The Next Step for U.S. Climate Change Policy," two Brookings senior fellows try to formulate a new global warming policy that the United States (and the rest of the world) can live with. . . .

During the recent European Summit, President Bush faced criticism from his European counterparts, from protestors and from much of the world media for his stance on rejecting the Kyoto Protocol. Why is there almost universal criticism despite the fact that the Bush administration has done the world a favor by abandoning the Kyoto Protocol? The approach of fixed targets and timetables for emissions reduction at an unknown economic cost is an infeasible and undesirable approach to climate change. The Protocol never had any chance of ratification. The reason for the outcry is that rather than put in place a better alternative to Kyoto, the Bush administration has so far left a vacuum in place of a climate change response. If the administration moves quickly to put a more realistic policy on the table then the focus of the global reaction can be shifted from outrage to reasoned debate. Abandoning the Kyoto Protocol could be the most important and positive environmental legacy of the Bush administration. The European Summit was the first opportunity to act, but it was lost. The next opportunity is at the COP6(II) negotiations to be held in Bonn in July.

Being realistic means discarding a couple of notions cherished by the ideologically pure at either end of the political spectrum. The first thing to go should be the claim that climate change is not a problem. It is quite clear that human activity is raising global concentrations of carbon dioxide. While climatologists disagree about how much warming will occur and when it will happen, virtually no one seriously suggests that we can emit as much carbon dioxide as we want into the atmosphere without any adverse consequences.

The second notion to go should be the one at the other end of the spectrum: the idea that climate change is such an overwhelming problem that it must be stopped no matter what the cost. Frankly, too little is known about the damages caused by climate change and the costs of reducing emissions to draw this conclusion. To pretend that climate policy doesn't need to take costs into consideration is to guarantee that any climate change treaty will be rejected by the Senate as well as by many other governments.

A good way to think about the climate change problem is by analogy to driving in the rain. Both involve risk: rain increases the chance of being involved in a serious accident and carbon dioxide emissions increase the chance of a serious climate problem. The right response to risks like these is prudence: when it is raining, people drive more carefully and avoid unnecessary trips. Likewise, in the face of a potential climate problem, a sensible thing to do would be to slow the growth of carbon dioxide emissions. In neither case is it practical to escape the risk entirely. Few people would be in favor of a law prohibiting driving in the rain under any circumstances. Similarly, few people would be willing to accept sharp reductions in fossil fuel use today simply because it might cause a problem sometime in the future.

After tossing the ideological baggage overboard, what might prudent and realistic governments do about climate change? The answer is to look for a global warming policy with three key features. First, the policy should slow down carbon dioxide emissions where it is cost-effective to do so. Second, the policy should involve some mechanism for compensating those who will be hurt economically. Third, since climate change is a global problem, any solution will require a high degree of consensus both domestically and internationally. However, consensus is the operative word: it is not realistic to think that a rigid global regulatory regime for greenhouse policy can ever be implemented. Few countries want to relinquish sovereignty over setting their own polices especially when the policies in question can have large economic effects.

We have set out such a policy in a recent Brookings Policy Brief. Our proposed permit trading system is much like the one now used to control sulphur emissions. The main difference would be that the market would include a mechanism that would prevent the price of a permit from exceeding a specified threshold. The threshold price would be set for 10 years at a time. Thus emissions would be allowed to vary over time and not be fixed as under the Kyoto Protocol. There are mechanisms in the detailed proposal that allow medium term targets and a market to price these. The permits would be given freely to each citizen and to existing emitters to grandfather emissions. These would be tradable in an open market. Any additional permits that would be required to keep the price from exceeding the threshold would be sold by the government in that year. By raising the price of carbon, the net effect of the policy would be to discourage increases in emissions, and to encourage reductions where they are cost-effective, but without levying a sudden multi-billion dollar burden on fuel users. This would be a significant, realistic step toward controlling climate change.

A key feature of the policy is that it is flexible. The permit price could be adjusted as needed when better information becomes available on the seriousness of climate change and the cost of reducing emissions.

As a unilateral policy this is feasible. Success would encourage other countries to join a more coordinated system. A country could join a multilateral system by adopting the policy domestically and no international negotiations would be required. If the same permit price were chosen in all countries, the system would reach a very efficient and low cost outcome—very similar to that from a global permit trading system but without the problems associated with international permit trading. Flexibility is crucial because it is clear from current negotiations that only a small subset of countries would agree to be initial participants in a climate change treaty.

It is time for the Bush administration to offer realistic alternatives to the Kyoto Protocol. The debate must move away from ideological battles over impractical goals and un-implementable policies to a discussion of policies that could be concrete but cost-effective steps to slow the growth of carbon dioxide emissions.

Note: The views expressed in this piece are those of the authors and should not be attributed to the staff, officers or trustees of The Brookings Institution.

Part Five: September 11, 2001

President George W. Bush's 9/20 address to Congress

Up until the evening of September 20, 2001, President George W. Bush's first year in office had been spent largely in the shadow of his older, more experienced subordinates, his apparent lack of gravitas reinforced by his image as a friendly but shallow fellow with limited communication skills and a seeming lack of interest in global affairs.

In one hour, all that changed. That night, in the well of the Senate before the assembled branches of the U.S. government, Bush spoke with aplomb and grace— giving voice to the nation's anger at the 9/11 attacks and outlining his administration's plans for a response.

The speech was a group effort that took up most of the preceding week. D.T. Max's article in the October 7, 2001 New York Times Magazine rehashed its genesis in detail: According to Max, the primary authors were Bush's head speechwriter Rich Gerson and his colleagues Matt Scully and John McConnell, with additional input from foreign-policy specialist John Gibson. Communications Director Karen Hughes oversaw the polishing of the later drafts, with Bush and others weighing in. Bush then worked on the speech himself, before sending it around to be vetted by the State Department and other interested parties. After that came a series of teleprompter rehearsals, during which Bush continued to pare and cut. Finally, it came time for him to stand and deliver. . . .

Mr. Speaker, Mr. President Pro Tempore, members of Congress, and fellow Americans, in the normal course of events, presidents come to this chamber to report on the state of the Union. Tonight, no such report is needed; it has already been delivered by the American people.

We have seen it in the courage of passengers, who rushed terrorists to save others on the ground—passengers like an exceptional man named Todd Beamer. And would you please help me welcome his wife, Lisa Beamer, here tonight?

We have seen the state of our Union in the endurance of rescuers, working past exhaustion.

We've seen the unfurling of flags, the lighting of candles, the giving of blood, the saying of prayers in English, Hebrew and Arabic.

We have seen the decency of a loving and giving people who have made the grief of strangers their own.

My fellow citizens, for the last nine days, the entire world has seen for itself the state of our Union—and it is strong.

Tonight, we are a country awakened to danger and called to defend freedom. Our grief has turned to anger and anger to resolution. Whether we bring our enemies to justice or bring justice to our enemies, justice will be done.

I thank the Congress for its leadership at such an important time.

All of America was touched on the evening of the tragedy to see Republicans and Democrats joined together on the steps of this Capitol singing "God Bless America."

And you did more than sing. You acted, by delivering $40 billion to rebuild our communities and meet the needs of our military. Speaker Hastert, Minority Leader Gephardt, Majority Leader Daschle and Senator Lott, I thank you for your friendship, for your leadership and for your service to our country.

And on behalf of the American people, I thank the world for its outpouring of support.

America will never forget the sounds of our national anthem playing at Buckingham Palace, on the streets of Paris and at Berlin's Brandenburg Gate.

We will not forget South Korean children gathering to pray outside our embassy in Seoul, or the prayers of sympathy offered at a mosque in Cairo.

We will not forget moments of silence and days of mourning in Australia and Africa and Latin America.

Nor will we forget the citizens of 80 other nations who died with our own. Dozens of Pakistanis, more than 130 Israelis, more than 250 citizens of India, men and women from El Salvador, Iran, Mexico and Japan, and hundreds of British citizens.

America has no truer friend than Great Britain. Once again, we are joined together in a great cause.

I'm so honored the British prime minister has crossed an ocean to show his unity with America.

Thank you for coming, friend.

On September the 11th, enemies of freedom committed an act of war against our country. Americans have known wars, but for the past 136 years they have been wars on foreign soil, except for one Sunday in 1941. Americans have known the casualties of war, but not at the center of a great city on a peaceful morning.

Americans have known surprise attacks, but never before on thousands of civilians. All of this was brought upon us in a single day, and night fell on a different world, a world where freedom itself is under attack.

Americans have many questions tonight. Americans are asking, "Who attacked our country?"

The evidence we have gathered all points to a collection of loosely affiliated terrorist organizations known as al Qaeda. They are some of the murderers indicted for bombing American embassies in Tanzania and Kenya and responsible for bombing the USS Cole.

Al Qaeda is to terror what the Mafia is to crime. But its goal is not making money, its goal is remaking the world and imposing its radical beliefs on people everywhere.

The terrorists practice a fringe form of Islamic extremism that has been rejected by Muslim scholars and the vast majority of Muslim clerics; a fringe movement that perverts the peaceful teachings of Islam.

The terrorists' directive commands them to kill Christians and Jews, to kill all Americans and make no distinctions among military and civilians, including women and children. This group and its leader, a person named Osama bin Laden, are linked to many other organizations in different countries, including the Egyptian Islamic Jihad, and the Islamic Movement of Uzbekistan.

There are thousands of these terrorists in more than 60 countries.

They are recruited from their own nations and neighborhoods and brought to camps in places like Afghanistan where they are trained in the tactics of terror. They are sent back to their homes or sent to hide in countries around the world to plot evil and destruction. The leadership of al Qaeda has great influence in Afghanistan and supports the Taliban regime in controlling most of that country. In Afghanistan we see al Qaeda's vision for the world. Afghanistan's people have been brutalized, many are starving and many have fled.

Women are not allowed to attend school. You can be jailed for owning a television. Religion can be practiced only as their leaders dictate. A man can be jailed in Afghanistan if his beard is not long enough. The United States respects the people of Afghanistan—after all, we are currently its largest source of humanitarian aid—but we condemn the Taliban regime.

It is not only repressing its own people, it is threatening people everywhere by sponsoring and sheltering and supplying terrorists.

By aiding and abetting murder, the Taliban regime is committing murder. And tonight the United States of America makes the following demands on the Taliban:

—Deliver to United States authorities all of the leaders of Al Qaeda who hide in your land.

—Release all foreign nationals, including American citizens you have unjustly imprisoned.

—Protect foreign journalists, diplomats and aid workers in your country.

—Close immediately and permanently every terrorist training camp in Afghanistan. And hand over every terrorist and every person and their support structure to appropriate authorities.

—Give the United States full access to terrorist training camps, so we can make sure they are no longer operating.

These demands are not open to negotiation or discussion.

The Taliban must act and act immediately. They will hand over the terrorists or they will share in their fate. I also want to speak tonight directly to Muslims throughout the world. We respect your faith. It's practiced freely by many millions of Americans and by millions more in countries that America counts as friends. Its teachings are good and peaceful, and those who commit evil in the name of Allah blaspheme the name of Allah.

The terrorists are traitors to their own faith, trying, in effect, to hijack Islam itself.

The enemy of America is not our many Muslim friends. It is not our many Arab friends. Our enemy is a radical network of terrorists and every government that supports them.

Our war on terror begins with al Qaeda, but it does not end there.

It will not end until every terrorist group of global reach has been found, stopped and defeated.

Americans are asking, "Why do they hate us?"

They hate what they see right here in this chamber: a democratically elected government. Their leaders are self-appointed. They hate our freedoms: our freedom of religion, our freedom of speech, our freedom to vote and assemble and disagree with each other.

They want to overthrow existing governments in many Muslim countries such as Egypt, Saudi Arabia and Jordan. They want to drive Israel out of the Middle East. They want to drive Christians and Jews out of vast regions of Asia and Africa.

These terrorists kill not merely to end lives, but to disrupt and end a way of life. With every atrocity, they hope that America grows fearful, retreating from the world and forsaking our friends. They stand against us because we stand in their way.

We're not deceived by their pretenses to piety.

We have seen their kind before. They're the heirs of all the murderous ideologies of the 20th century. By sacrificing human life to serve their radical visions, by abandoning every value except the will to power, they follow in the path of fascism, Nazism and totalitarianism. And they will follow that path all the way to where it ends in history's unmarked grave of discarded lies.

Americans are asking, "How will we fight and win this war?"

We will direct every resource at our command—every means of diplomacy, every tool of intelligence, every instrument of law enforcement, every financial influence, and every necessary weapon of war—to the destruction and to the defeat of the global terror network.

Now, this war will not be like the war against Iraq a decade ago, with a decisive liberation of territory and a swift conclusion. It will not look like the air war above Kosovo two years ago, where no ground troops were used and not a single American was lost in combat.

Our response involves far more than instant retaliation and isolated strikes. Americans should not expect one battle, but a lengthy campaign unlike any other we have ever seen. It may include dramatic strikes visible on TV and covert operations secret even in success.

We will starve terrorists of funding, turn them one against another, drive them from place to place until there is no refuge or rest. And we will pursue nations that provide aid or safe haven to terrorism. Every nation in every region now has a decision to make: Either you are with us or you are with the terrorists.

From this day forward, any nation that continues to harbor or support terrorism will be regarded by the United States as a hostile regime. Our nation has been put on notice, we're not immune from attack. We will take defensive measures against terrorism to protect Americans. Today, dozens of federal departments and agencies, as well as state and local governments, have responsibilities affecting homeland security.

These efforts must be coordinated at the highest level. So tonight, I announce the creation of a Cabinet-level position reporting directly to me, the Office of Homeland Security. And tonight, I also announce a distinguished American to lead this effort, to strengthen American security: a military veteran, an effective governor, a true patriot, a trusted friend—Pennsylvania's Tom Ridge.

He will lead, oversee and coordinate a comprehensive national strategy to safeguard our country against terrorism and respond to any attacks that may come. These measures are essential. The only way to defeat terrorism as a threat to our way of life is to stop it, eliminate it and destroy it where it grows.

Many will be involved in this effort, from FBI agents, to intelligence operatives, to the reservists we have called to active duty. All deserve our thanks, and all have our prayers. And tonight a few miles from the damaged Pentagon, I have a message for our military: Be ready. I have called the armed forces to alert, and there is a reason.

The hour is coming when America will act, and you will make us proud.

This is not, however, just America's fight. And what is at stake is not just America's freedom. This is the world's fight. This is civilization's fight. This is the fight of all who believe in progress and pluralism, tolerance and freedom.

We ask every nation to join us.

We will ask and we will need the help of police forces, intelligence services and banking systems around the world. The United States is grateful that many nations and many international organizations have already responded with sympathy and with support—nations from Latin America to Asia to Africa to Europe to the Islamic world.

Perhaps the NATO charter reflects best the attitude of the world: An attack on one is an attack on all. The civilized world is rallying to America's side.

They understand that if this terror goes unpunished, their own cities, their own citizens may be next. Terror unanswered can not only bring down buildings, it can threaten the stability of legitimate governments.

And you know what? We're not going to allow it.

Americans are asking, "What is expected of us?"

I ask you to live your lives and hug your children. I know many citizens have fears tonight, and I ask you to be calm and resolute, even in the face of a continuing threat.

I ask you to uphold the values of America and remember why so many have come here.

We're in a fight for our principles, and our first responsibility is to live by them. No one should be singled out for unfair treatment or unkind words because of their ethnic background or religious faith.

I ask you to continue to support the victims of this tragedy with your contributions. Those who want to give can go to a central source of information, Libertyunites.org, to find the names of groups providing direct help in New York, Pennsylvania and Virginia. The thousands of FBI agents who are now at work in this investigation may need your cooperation, and I ask you to give it. I ask for your patience with the delays and inconveniences that may accompany tighter security and for your patience in what will be a long struggle.

I ask your continued participation and confidence in the American economy. Terrorists attacked a symbol of American prosperity; they did not touch its source.

America is successful because of the hard work and creativity and enterprise of our people. These were the true strengths of our economy before September 11, and they are our strengths today.

And finally, please continue praying for the victims of terror and their families, for those in uniform and for our great country. Prayer has comforted us in sorrow and will help strengthen us for the journey ahead.

Tonight I thank my fellow Americans for what you have already done and for what you will do.

And ladies and gentlemen of the Congress, I thank you, their representatives, for what you have already done and for what we will do together.

Tonight, we face new and sudden national challenges. We will come together to improve air safety, to dramatically expand the number of air marshals on domestic flights and take new measures to prevent hijacking.

We will come together to promote stability and keep our airlines flying, with direct assistance during this emergency.

We will come together to give law enforcement the additional tools it needs to track down terror here at home.

We will come together to strengthen our intelligence capabilities to know the plans of terrorists before they act, and to find them before they strike.

We will come together to take active steps that strengthen America's economy and put our people back to work.

Tonight, we welcome two leaders who embody the extraordinary spirit of all New Yorkers: Governor George Pataki and Mayor Rudolph Giuliani.

As a symbol of America's resolve, my administration will work with Congress and these two leaders to show the world that we will rebuild New York City.

After all that has just passed, all the lives taken and all the possibilities and hopes that died with them, it is natural to wonder if America's future is one of fear. Some speak of an age of terror. I know there are struggles ahead and dangers to face. But this country will define our times, not be defined by them.

As long as the United States of America is determined and strong, this will not be an age of terror. This will be an age of liberty here and across the world.

Great harm has been done to us. We have suffered great loss. And in our grief and anger we have found our mission and our moment.

Freedom and fear are at war. The advance of human freedom, the great achievement of our time and the great hope of every time, now depends on us.

Our nation, this generation, will lift the dark threat of violence from our people and our future. We will rally the world to this cause by our efforts, by our courage. We will not tire, we will not falter, and we will not fail.

It is my hope that in the months and years ahead life will return almost to normal. We'll go back to our lives and routines, and that is good.

Even grief recedes with time and grace.

But our resolve must not pass. Each of us will remember what happened that day, and to whom it happened. We will remember the moment the news came, where we were and what we were doing.

Some will remember an image of a fire or a story of rescue. Some will carry memories of a face and a voice gone forever.

And I will carry this: It is the police shield of a man named George Howard, who died at the World Trade Center trying to save others.

It was given to me by his mom, Arlene, as a proud memorial to her son. It is my reminder of lives that ended, and a task that does not end.

I will not forget this wound to our country or those who inflicted it. I will not yield, I will not rest, I will not relent in waging this struggle for freedom and security for the American people. The course of this conflict is not known, yet its outcome is certain. Freedom and fear, justice and cruelty, have always been at war, and we know that God is not neutral between them.

Fellow citizens, we'll meet violence with patient justice, assured of the rightness of our cause and confident of the victories to come.

In all that lies before us, may God grant us wisdom, and may He watch over the United States of America. Thank you.

Tuesday, and After
Hendrik Hertzberg

The New Yorker | September 24, 2001

If The New Yorker *were a baseball team, Hendrik Hertzberg would be their all-star leadoff hitter. His "Comment" slot typically heads the magazine's opening "Talk of the Town" section, setting the tone for the rest of the publication's fine political coverage.*

In the following piece, written shortly after September 11, Hertzberg joins with his fellow New Yorkers—and the rest of America—in trying to grasp what happened, and where it will take us. . . .

The catastrophe that turned the foot of Manhattan into the mouth of Hell on the morning of September 11, 2001, unfolded in four paroxysms. At a little before nine, a smoldering scar on the face of the north tower of the World Trade Center (an awful accident, like the collision of a B-25 bomber with the Empire State Building on July 28, 1945?); eighteen minutes later, the orange and gray blossoming of the second explosion, in the south tower; finally, at a minute before ten and then at not quite ten-thirty, the sickening slide of the two towers, collapsing one after the other. For those in the immediate vicinity, the horror was of course immediate and unmistakable; it occurred in what we have learned to call real time, and in real space. For those farther away—whether a few dozen blocks or halfway around the world—who were made witnesses by the long lens of television, the events were seen as through a glass, brightly. Their reality was visible but not palpable. It took hours to begin to comprehend their magnitude; it is taking days for the defensive numbness they induced to wear off; it will take months—or years—to measure their impact and meaning.

New York is a city where, however much strangers meet and mix on the streets and in the subways, circles of friends are usually demarcated by work and family. The missing and presumed dead—their number is in the thousands—come primarily from the finance, international trade, and government service workers in the doomed buildings, and from the ranks of firefighters and police officers drawn there by duty and courage. The umbra of personal grief already encompasses scores or even hundreds of thousands of people; a week or two from now, when the word has spread from friend to colleague to relative to acquaintance, the penumbra will cover millions. The city has never suffered a more shocking calamity from any act of God or man.

The calamity, of course, goes well beyond the damage to our city and to its similarly bereaved rival and brother Washington. It is national; it is international; it is civilizational. In the decade since the end of the Cold War, the human race has become, with increasing rapidity, a single organism. Every kind of barrier to the free and rapid movement of goods, information, and people has been lowered. The organism relies increasingly on a kind of trust—the unsentimental expectation that people, individually and collectively, will behave more or less in their rational self-interest. (Even the anti-globalizers of the West mostly embrace the underlying premises of the new dispensation; their demand is for global democratic institutions to mitigate the cruelties of the global market.) The terrorists made use of that trust. They rode the flow of the world's aerial circulatory system like lethal viruses.

With growing ferocity, officials from the President on down have described the bloody deeds as acts of war. But, unless a foreign government turns out to have directed the operation (or, at least, to have known and approved its scope in detail and in advance), that is a category mistake. The metaphor of war—and it is more metaphor than description—ascribes to the perpetrators a dignity they do not merit, a status they cannot claim, and a strength they do not possess. Worse, it points toward a set of responses that could prove futile or counterproductive. Though the death and destruction these acts caused were on the scale of war, the acts themselves were acts of terrorism, albeit on a wholly unprecedented level. From 1983 until last week, according to the *Times*, ten outrages had each claimed the lives of more than a hundred people. The worst—the destruction of an Air-India 747 in 1985—killed three hundred and twenty-nine people; the Oklahoma City bombing, which killed a hundred and sixty-eight, was the seventh worst. Last week's carnage surpassed that of any of these by an order of magnitude. It was also the largest violent taking of life on American soil on any day since the Civil War, including December 7, 1941. And in New York and Washington, unlike at Pearl Harbor, the killed and maimed were overwhelmingly civilians.

The tactics of the terrorists were as brilliant as they were depraved. The nature of those tactics and their success—and there is no use denying that what they did was, on its own terms, successful—points up the weakness of the war metaphor. Authorities estimated last week that "as many as" fifty people may have been involved. The terrorists brought with them nothing but knives and the ability to fly a jumbo jet already in the air. How do you take "massive military action" against the infrastructure of a stateless, compartmentalized "army" of fifty, or ten times fifty, whose weapons are rental cars, credit cards, and airline tickets?

The scale of the damage notwithstanding, a more useful metaphor than war is crime. The terrorists of September 11th are outlaws within a global polity. They may enjoy the corrupt protection of a state (and corruption, like crime, can be ideological or spiritual as well as pecuniary in motive). But they do not constitute or control a state and do not even appear to aspire to control one. Their status and numbers are such that the task of dealing with them should be viewed as a police matter, of the most urgent kind. As with all criminal fugitives, the essential job is to find out who and where they are. The goal of foreign and military policy must be to induce recalcitrant governments to cooperate, a goal whose attainment may or may not entail the use of force but cannot usefully entail making general war on the peoples such governments rule and in some cases (that of Afghanistan, for example) oppress. Just four months ago, at a time when the whole world was aware both of the general intentions of the terrorist Osama bin Laden and of the fact that the Afghan government was harboring him, the United States gave the Taliban a forty-three-million-dollar grant for banning poppy cultivation. The United States understands that on September 11th the line between the permissible and the impermissible shifted. The Taliban must be made to understand that, too.

As for America's friends, they have rallied around us with alacrity. On Wednesday, the NATO allies, for the first time ever, invoked the mutual-defense clause of the alliance's founding treaty, formally declaring that "an armed attack" against one—and what happened on September 11th, whether you call it terrorism or war, was certainly an armed attack—constitutes an attack against all. This gesture of solidarity puts to shame the contempt the Bush administration has consistently shown for international treaties and instruments, including those in areas relevant to the fight against terrorism, such as small-arms control, criminal justice, and nuclear proliferation. By now, it ought to be clear to even the most committed ideologues of the Bush administration that the unilateralist approach it was pursuing as of last Tuesday is in urgent need of reevaluation. The world will be policed collectively or it will not be policed at all.

The Waking Nightmare—and the Dawn of Life in Wartime

Michael Wolff

New York magazine | September 24, 2001

Whether he's dissing Tina Brown, deconstructing Mike Bloomberg's $60-million-dollar mayoral run ("We assume, I sense, that everything is somehow going to be of a much higher order, fancier, and classier, when we elect a rich man"), or griping that "dumb is the new smart," Michael Wolff's "Media Life" department in New York *magazine invariably offers an entertaining, fresh take on the overlapping worlds of media and politics. In this post-9/11 column, however, Wolff finds the right words are in short supply and uncertainty is the order of the day. . . .*

You could easily have mistaken the daze in the city in the hours after the attack for a snow-day feeling. Traffic had disappeared, pedestrians had spread into the road, most city noises had subsided, and strangers spoke openly to strangers. Basic services—cell phones and mass transit—were no longer working. The task of getting somewhere was the outward focus.

But the main preoccupation for most of us in those first hours was interior: to circle around our own feelings, to keep them at bay. If you knew someone in the towers or in the area, the challenge was to arrive at no conclusions. Never before had so many people witnessed the real-time occasion of such mass destruction. The collapse, the falling away of the two tallest buildings in the city before everyone's eyes, would become part of perceptual history, as well as the history of warfare.

Even if it had been possible, I don't think anyone wanted to start to comprehend; there was protection in the inconceivableness of the event. The media, always obsessing about numbers—right numbers, wrong numbers, estimates no matter how guessed at—could not say what was obvious: Almost everyone in New York would know someone who had died a violent and macabre death. The obvious was unsayable, which meant that through the day there was a strange, limbo-ish refusal to quantify or to frame the scope of the disaster. It was possible, it even seemed, that some old-time civil-defense plan was in use: Get as many people as possible home and off the streets before letting on to the magnitude of the horror.

There were the unfathomable, even beautiful, pictures of the planes penetrating the towers, then the magnificent plumes, then the heaving and condensing of the buildings themselves—they seemed to drip away—but not many pictures from the ground. There were few instant images of the carnage—the iconic twisted steel, bloody people, and terrible screams that have become standard in a terrorist attack.

It was this very lack of information that began to hint at the truth: No screams are worse than screams.

Within a few hours, the city was divided into two, carefully separated sectors. The one sector, above Canal Street, the other sector, below—an instant dead zone, populated by hundreds of firemen, police, medical personnel, and emergency volunteers.

There was an army of ambulances at ground zero plus three or four blocks—none of them going anywhere. Nobody was coming out. Volunteers—former military personnel, people with medical training, good Samaritans—were sent from post to post, across one street and then another, from fire department command to police command to the EMTs. But there would be no rapid response. What response there was had already engulfed a significant part of the fire department. There was nothing to do. Everything was dust. So much of the World Trade Center—Sheetrock, glass, insulation—had simply vaporized. ("Where are the bodies?" was the unasked question.)

There. And then not there.

The catastrophe was so complete that the rescue phase, for all practical purposes, passed immediately to aftermath and cleanup.

Unavoidably, there was awe and amazement. The coordination of the attack, the complexity of the logistics, the appalling cleverness of the concept itself—to use a plane fueled up for a transcontinental flight as a bomb—demanded some kind of awful respect. Here was an example not just of our unexpected and striking vulnerability but of their bizarre and breathtaking audacity, skill, and, certainly, single-mindedness. (It damaged the president's credibility to have called these people cowards—they may have been many things, but they were not cowards.)

The obsessiveness of the plot—involving possibly as much as eight years of planning since the truck bomb failed to bring down the towers in 1993— is one of the things that is most terrifying. To have come back again—to have succeeded in what must be one of the most far-fetched enterprises in the history of warfare—starts to seem like some supernatural act.

What strange, incomprehensible hatreds and unfathomable strategies drew them here? These towers were, obviously, so much more symbolic to them than to us. These too-large, too-square real-estate gimmicks (for much of their 30 years, white elephants) stood, it would seem, for our gigantism and arrogance and dominance. We might accept those faults, but hardly that symbol. ("Twin Towers" is not even a name used by New Yorkers—it's out-of-towner nomenclature; the tallest-building thing is for tourists.) But this time it was, surely, not just the symbolic satanism of the towers that drew the suicide bombers, but also the matter of proving their resolve: They will not be dissuaded; they will not accept their own failures; they will be back.

It is all about what they are capable of—the lengths to which they will go.

Only the most foolish of us would not now acknowledge that anything is possible, that, necessarily, there are even worse horrors to be afraid of.

You couldn't watch the television pictures without being acutely conscious of the nature of the island where the calamity was happening—that we were alone, cut off, not in any way part of the main—and more afraid because of it.

Confoundingly, it is not just the United States that has been attacked, but the world's greatest liberal city. The greatest cosmopolitan city ever to exist—as far from American gung-ho-ism as any place can be. As any New Yorker knows, New York really isn't America. It is as well, of course, the world's greatest Jewish city—who can doubt that that is not a part of the message here? And Gomorrah on the Hudson—is that also the point?

The irony is great: All the redneck militarism out there in America becomes part of the New York way of thinking now.

A double irony: The redneck president scurrying and hiding, heading for safety to the heartland before getting ahold of himself and reversing course. Then, emerging suddenly from the ruins, having been under fire, there was New York's mayor—unafraid, unscripted, levelheaded, strong. Practically an American war hero.

It will be a further, supreme irony if now, after generations of disenfranchisement, New York City becomes the great symbol of Americanism. Certainly, the president, in his scripted, tense, TelePrompTer-challenged way, wasn't synchronized with the feelings here. He offered in his initial, hurried address no example or even notion of bravery and supplied no palliative words. (Giuliani, on the other hand, seemed entirely in sync with the city's emotions.) But this is, perhaps, only partly the president's fault. The language of war, of national threat, and hence of bravery and resolve, has been out of use for so long that it isn't immediately available.

We were stuck using the language of crime. There were "perpetrators." There were guilty parties. There were the people who would be held responsible. The president would give them a "whipping." We would hunt them down wherever they were. The FBI was going to find the culprits. The FBI was already amassing evidence against them.

The talk was about individuals, about conspirators, about terrorists (almost as a professional designation) who can be taken out of the equation—even brought to justice! These are bad guys who do bad things.

But then, clearly, there was the dawning sense that in the era of terrorism, we may have been expressing the threat all wrong. This isn't, we began to conclude, about suicide bombers, nor is it just about Osama bin Laden. Soldiers are fungible. Enmity this vast must be structural, institutional.

You could begin to chart the transformation of the word war—state of war, declaration of war, going to war—from metaphor to a new culture.

It is all so un-New York. the weepiness is so hugely out of character. The timbre of the voices, the eyes that lock and then break away, the neediness of the children in the house—everyone's neediness—makes this a vastly different city.

And then somewhere there are the dead. But as the days go by, the dead are hardly more identifiable or decipherable or calculable than they were in the first moments.

The dread keeps increasing. The emotion becomes heavier and thicker. And it will get worse. It will be the time of the 5,000 or the 10,000 funerals. It is indescribable and unutterable.

The media language fails, too—as much as the political language. THE BASTARDS! said the *Village Voice* on its cover. But such feistiness seemed far from what anyone was feeling. The *Post's* tabloidism—its overeager voyeurism—was tonally way off; this wasn't about other people. The *Times* seemed to be covering events in another place—with its foreign-desk voice. It was the *Daily News*, which found some forties-style sense of war and disaster, that perhaps came closest to the experience—tough, straightforward, aptly New York.

The shared, and as yet unanswered, question is: What comes next?

There's the fear. The bomb threats and the succession of evacuations. Bags found on the street. Suspicious cars. Unidentified noises.

There's the fate of New York itself. Does this become who we are? Is this an inescapable new identity? Does this mean, in some real way, the end of the city? The sense that many New Yorkers always have of being so incredibly lucky to have ended up in New York is, at the very least, on hold—it is now, more than at any other time, more than the worst crime years, a terrifying place.

And then there's the change, the inevitable change, that comes to our expansive, indulged, polymorphous culture. We are who we are, not inconsiderably, because so many of us have never lived—and by all rights have assumed we would never live—in a time of war.

Now we must wait to see what kind of war it will be.

What Went Wrong
Seymour Hersh

The New Yorker | October 8, 2001

The debate over the intelligence breakdowns surrounding the September 11 terrorist attacks has focused mainly on the F.B.I.'s failure to heed warnings from their own agents. But according to a number of people in the intelligence community, the bigger problem may lie on the other side of our border, with the Central Intelligence Agency. A few weeks after 9/11, Seymour Hersh explored this theme in the following article. For Hersh—the reporter who broke the My Lai massacre story during the Vietnam War and, more recently, raised questions about misconduct on the part of the U.S. military in the Gulf War—this and his subsequent New Yorker *pieces showed he is still in top form.*

One other media note: In his piece, Hersh refers to a prescient Atlantic Monthly *article by Reuel Marc Gerecht, "The Counterterrorist Myth," published in July of*

2001. In that article, Gerecht, an ex-C.I.A. operative, warned that until the agency beefed up its counterterrorist efforts, "I don't think Osama bin Ladin and his allies will be losing much sleep around the campfire". . . .

After more than two weeks of around-the-clock investigation into the September 11th attacks on the World Trade Center and the Pentagon, the American intelligence community remains confused, divided, and unsure about how the terrorists operated, how many there were, and what they might do next. It was that lack of solid information, government officials told me, that was the key factor behind the Bush administration's decision last week not to issue a promised white paper listing the evidence linking Osama bin Laden's organization to the attacks.

There is consensus within the government on two issues: the terrorist attacks were brilliantly planned and executed, and the intelligence community was in no way prepared to stop them. One bureaucratic victim, the officials said, may be George Tenet, the director of the Central Intelligence Agency, whose resignation is considered a necessity by many in the administration. "The system is after Tenet," one senior officer told me. "It wants to get rid of him."

The investigators are now split into at least two factions. One, centered in the F.B.I., believes that the terrorists may not have been "a cohesive group," as one involved official put it, before they started training and working together on this operation. "These guys look like a pickup basketball team," he said. "A bunch of guys who got together." The F.B.I. is still trying to sort out the identities and backgrounds of the hijackers. The fact is, the official acknowledged, "we don't know much about them."

These investigators suspect that the suicide teams were simply lucky. "In your wildest dreams, do you think they thought they'd be able to pull off four hijackings?" the official asked. "Just taking out one jet and getting it into the ground would have been a success. These are not supermen." He explained that the most important advantage the hijackers had, aside from the element of surprise, was history: in the past, most hijackings had ended up safely on the ground at a Third World airport, so pilots had been trained to cooperate.

Another view, centered in the Pentagon and the C.I.A., credits the hijackers with years of advance planning and practice, and a deliberate after-the-fact disinformation campaign. "These guys were below everybody's radar—they're professionals," an official said. "There's no more than five or six in a cell. Three men will know the plan; three won't know. They've been 'sleeping' out there for years and years." One military planner told me that many of his colleagues believe that the terrorists "went to ground and pulled phone lines" well before September 11th—that is, concealed traces of their activities. It is widely believed that the terrorists had a support team, and the fact that the F.B.I. has been unable to track down fellow conspirators who were left behind in the United States is seen as further evidence of careful planning. "Look," one person familiar with the investigation said. "If it were as simple and straightforward as a lucky one-off oddball operation, then the seeds of confusion would not have been sown as they were."

Many of the investigators believe that some of the initial clues that were uncovered about the terrorists' identities and preparations, such as flight manuals, were meant to be found. A former high-level intelligence official told me, "Whatever trail was left was left deliberately—for the F.B.I. to chase."

In interviews over the past two weeks, a number of intelligence officials have raised questions about Osama bin Laden's capabilities. "This guy sits in a cave in Afghanistan and he's running this operation?" one C.I.A. official asked. "It's so huge. He couldn't have done it alone." A senior military officer told me that because of the visas and other documentation needed to infiltrate team members into the United States a major foreign intelligence service might also have been involved. "To get somebody to fly an airplane—to kill himself," the official added, further suggests that "somebody paid his family a hell of a lot of money."

"These people are not necessarily all from bin Laden," a Justice Department official told me. "We're still running a lot of stuff out," he said, adding that the F.B.I. has been inundated with leads. On September 23rd, Secretary of State Colin Powell told a television interviewer that "we will put before the world, the American people, a persuasive case" showing that bin Laden was responsible for the attacks. But the widely anticipated white paper could not be published, the Justice Department official said, for lack of hard facts. "There was not enough to make a sale."

The administration justified the delay by telling the press that most of the information was classified and could not yet be released. Last week, however, a senior C.I.A. official confirmed that the intelligence community had not yet developed a significant amount of solid information about the terrorists' operations, financing, and planning. "One day, we'll know, but at the moment we don't know," the official said.

"To me," he added, "the scariest thing is that these guys"—the terrorists—"got the first one free. They knew that the standard operating procedure in an aircraft hijacking was to play for time. And they knew for sure that after this the security on airplanes was going to go way up. So whatever they've planned for the next round they had in place already."

The concern about a second attack was repeated by others involved in the investigation. Some in the F.B.I. now suspect that the terrorists are following a war plan devised by the convicted conspirator Ramzi Ahmed Yousef, who is believed to have been the mastermind of the 1993 World Trade Center bombing. Yousef was involved in plans that called for, among other things, the releasing of poisons in the air and the bombing of the tunnels between New York City and New Jersey. The government's concern about the potential threat from hazardous-waste haulers was heightened by the Yousef case.

"Do they go chem/bio in one, two, or three years?" one senior general asked rhetorically. "We must now make a difficult transition from reliance on law enforcement to the preemptive. That part is hard. Can we recruit enough good people?" In recent years, he said, "we've been hiring kids out of college who are computer geeks." He continued, "This is about going back to deep, hard dirty work, with tough people going down dark alleys with good instincts."

Today's C.I.A. is not up to the job. Since the breakup of the Soviet Union, in 1991, the C.I.A. has become increasingly bureaucratic and unwilling to take risks, and has promoted officers who shared such values. ("The consciousness of kind," one former officer says.) It has steadily reduced its reliance on overseas human intelligence and cut the number of case officers abroad—members of the clandestine service, now known formally as the Directorate of Operations, or D.O., whose mission is to recruit spies. (It used to be called the "dirty tricks" department.) Instead, the agency has relied on liaison relationships—reports from friendly intelligence services and police departments around the world—and on technical collection systems.

It won't be easy to put agents back in the field. During the Cold War, the agency's most important mission was to recruit spies from within the Soviet Union's military and its diplomatic corps. C.I.A. agents were assigned as diplomatic or cultural officers at American embassies in major cities, and much of their work could be done at diplomatic functions and other social events. For an agent with such cover, the consequence of being exposed was usually nothing more than expulsion from the host country and temporary reassignment to a desk in Washington. Today, in Afghanistan, or anywhere in the Middle East or South Asia, a C.I.A. operative would have to speak the local language and be able to blend in. The operative should seemingly have nothing to do with any Americans, or with the American embassy, if there is one. The status is known inside the agency as "nonofficial cover," or NOC. Exposure could mean death.

It's possible that there isn't a single such officer operating today inside Islamic-fundamentalist circles. In an essay published last summer in *The Atlantic Monthly*, Reuel Marc Gerecht, who served for nearly a decade as a case officer in the C.I.A.'s Near East Division, quoted one C.I.A. man as saying, "For Christ's sake, most case officers live in the suburbs of Virginia. We don't do that kind of thing." Another officer told Gerecht, "Operations that include diarrhea as a way of life don't happen."

At the same time, the D.O. has been badly hurt by a series of resignations and retirements among high-level people, including four men whose names are little known to the public but who were widely respected throughout the agency: Douglas Smith, who spent thirty-one years in the clandestine service; William Lofgren, who at his retirement, in 1996, was chief of the Central Eurasia Division; David Manners, who was chief of station in Amman, Jordan, when he left the agency, in 1998; and Robert Baer, an Arabic speaker who was considered perhaps the best on-the-ground field officer in the Middle East. All left with feelings of bitterness over the agency's procedures for running clandestine operations.

"We'll never solve the terrorism issue until we reconstitute the D.O.," a former senior clandestine officer told me. "The first line of defense, and the most crucial line of defense, is human intelligence." Baer, who was awarded a Career Intelligence Medal after his resignation, in late 1997, said, "You wouldn't believe how bad it is. What saved the White House on Flight 93"—the plane that crashed in Pennsylvania—"was a bunch of rugby players. Is that what you're paying thirty billion dollars for?" He was referring to the federal budget for intelligence. He and his colleagues aren't surprised that the F.B.I. had no warning of the attack. "The bureau is wonderful in solving crimes after they're committed," one C.I.A. man said. "But it's not good at penetration. We've got to do it."

Today, the C.I.A. doesn't have enough qualified case officers to man its many stations and bases around the world. Two retired agents have been brought back on a rotating basis to take temporary charge of the small base in Karachi, Pakistan, a focal point for terrorist activity. (Karachi was the site of the murder, in 1995, of two Americans, one of them a C.I.A. employee, allegedly in retaliation for the arrest in Pakistan of Ramzi Ahmed Yousef.) A retired agent also runs the larger C.I.A. station in Dacca, Bangladesh, a Muslim nation that could be a source of recruits. Other retirees run C.I.A. stations in Africa.

One hard question is what lengths the C.I.A. should go to. In an interview, two former operations officers cited the tactics used in the late nineteen-eighties by the Jordanian security service, in its successful effort to bring down Abu Nidal, the Palestinian who led what was at the time "the most dangerous terrorist organization in existence," according to the State Department. Abu Nidal's group was best known for its role in two bloody gun and grenade attacks on check-in desks for El Al, the Israeli airline, at the Rome and Vienna airports in December, 1985. At his peak, Abu Nidal threatened the life of King Hussein of Jordan—whom he called "the pygmy king"—and the king responded, according to the former intelligence officers, by telling his state security service, "Go get them."

The Jordanians did not move directly against suspected Abu Nidal followers but seized close family members instead—mothers and brothers. The Abu Nidal suspect would be approached, given a telephone, and told to call his mother, who would say, according to one C.I.A. man, "Son, they'll take care of me if you don't do what they ask." (To his knowledge, the official carefully added, all the suspects agreed to talk before any family members were actually harmed.) By the early nineteen-nineties, the group was crippled by internal dissent and was no longer a significant terrorist organization. (Abu Nidal, now in his sixties and in poor health, is believed to be living quietly in Egypt.) "Jordan is the one nation that totally succeeded in penetrating a group," the official added. "You have to get their families under control."

Such tactics defy the American rule of law, of course, and the C.I.A.'s procedures, but, when it comes to Osama bin Laden and his accomplices, the official insisted, there is no alternative. "We need to do this—knock them down one by one," he said. "Are we serious about getting rid of the problem—instead of sitting around making diversity quilts?"

A few days after the attacks, Vice-President Dick Cheney defended the C.I.A.'s director, George Tenet, on television, saying that it would be a "tragedy" to look for "scapegoats." President Bush subsequently added a note of support with a visit to C.I.A. headquarters. In an interview last week, one top C.I.A. official also defended Tenet. "We know there's a lot of Monday-morning quarterbacking going on, but people don't understand the conditions that George inherited," he told me. "You can't penetrate a six-man cell when they're brothers and cousins—no matter how much Urdu you know." The official acknowledged that there was much dissatisfaction with the C.I.A.'s performance, but he said, "George has not gotten any word other than that the president has full confidence in him." He went on, "George wouldn't resign in a situation like this."

I was informed by other officials, however, that Tenet's days are numbered. "They've told him he's on his way out," one official said. "He's trying to figure it out—whether to go gracefully or let it appear as if he's going to be fired." A White House adviser explained Cheney's public endorsement of Tenet by saying, "In Washington, your friends always stab you in the chest. Somebody has to take the blame for this." It was his understanding, he added, that "after a decent interval—whenever they get some traction on the problem—he will depart. I've heard three to six months." Even one of Tenet's close friends told me, "He's history."

Tenet's standing was further undermined, after September 11th, by what proved to have been a series of wildly optimistic claims about the effectiveness of the C.I.A.'s Counter Terrorism Center, which was set up in 1986 after a wave of international bombings, airplane hijackings, and kidnappings. The idea was to bring together experts from every American police agency, including the Secret Service, into a "fusion center," which would coordinate intelligence data on terrorism. In October, 1998, after four men linked to bin Laden were indicted for their role in the bombings at the American embassies in Tanzania and Kenya, reporters for *Newsweek* were given a tour of the center. The indictments, *Newsweek* reported, "were intended as a clear message to bin Laden and his fugitive followers: the United States knows who they are and where to find them. . . . The story of how the C.I.A. and F.B.I., once bitter bureaucratic rivals, collaborated to roll up bin Laden's elusive network is a tale of state-of-the art sleuthing—and just plain luck."

But in fact the C.T.C. was not authorized to recruit or handle agents overseas—that task was left to the D.O. and its stations in the Middle East, which had their own priorities. The C.T.C. was bolstered with more money and more manpower after the World Trade Center bombing in 1993, but it remained a paper-shuffling unit whose officers were not required to be proficient in foreign languages. Many of the C.I.A.'s old hands have told me that the C.T.C., despite its high profile, was not an assignment of choice for a young and ambitious D.O. officer. The C.T.C. and two of the other major intelligence centers—dealing with narcotics and nuclear-nonproliferation issues—are so consumed by internecine warfare that the professional analysts find it difficult to do their jobs. "They're all fighting among each other," said one senior manager who took early retirement and whose last assignment was as the director of one of the centers. "There's no concentration on issues."

In 1986, Robert Baer, freshly arrived as a case officer from Khartoum, was drafted into the Counter Terrorism Center, a few months after it was set up, by its director, Duane (Dewey) Clarridge. A draft of a memoir Baer wrote, which will be published by Crown this fall, depicts what happened next:

> The first few months was about as exhilarating as it can get in the spy business. Dewey had authority to pretty much do any thing he wanted against the terrorists. He had all the money he wanted. . . . It wasn't long, though, before the policies of intelligence undermined everything Dewey tried to do. . . . It was too risky. A botched—or even a successful—operation would piss off a friendly foreign government. Someone would be thrown out of his cushy post. Someone could even get killed. . . .
>
> You'd ask [the C.I.A. station in Bonn] to recruit a few Arabs and Iranians to track the Middle East émigré community in West Germany, and it would respond that it didn't have enough officers. You'd ask Beirut to meet a certain agent traveling to Lebanon, and it would refuse because of some security problem. It was nothing but bureaucratic foot-dragging, but it effectively hamstrung anything Dewey tried to do. After six months, Dewey could put his hands on only two Arabic speakers—another officer and me.

Many people in the intelligence community, in their conversations with me, complained bitterly about how difficult it was to work with the Directorate of Operations, even during a crisis. "In order to work on a problem with D.O.," a former senior scientist told me, "you have to be in D.O." Similarly, a congressional observer of the C.I.A. came to understand the bureaucratic power of the D.O. "To succeed as director of Central Intelligence," he said, "you have to ingratiate yourself with the D.O." Other intelligence sources have told me that the D.O.'s machinations led, at one point, to a feud with the National Security

Agency over who would control the Special Collection Service, a joint undertaking of the two agencies that deploys teams of electronics specialists around the world to monitor diplomatic and other communications in moments of crisis. The S.C.S.'s highly secret operations, which produced some of the Cold War's most valuable data, are usually run from secure sites inside American embassies. Competence and sophistication were hindered by an absurd amount of bickering. A military man who in 1998 was involved in a Middle East signals-intelligence operation told me that he was not able to discuss the activity with representatives of the C.I.A. and the N.S.A. at the same time. "I used to meet with one in a safe house in Virginia, break for lunch, and then meet with the other," the officer said. "They wouldn't be in the same room."

If the current crisis does lead to an overhaul of the agency, the Senate and House intelligence committees are not likely to be of much help. Lofgren, Smith, Manners, and Baer, among others, repeatedly met with legislators and their staffs and testified before Congress in an effort to bring about changes. But nothing was done.

Not surprisingly, Republicans and Democrats have differing explanations for what went wrong. One Republican staff member said that Senator Richard C. Shelby, of Alabama, who was the committee's chairman until early this year, understood that the problem was at the top of the agency. "We do have guys in the field with great ideas who are not supported by the establishment," the staff member said. But none of the senior Democrats, he said, wanted to embarrass the director, George Tenet, by holding an inquiry or hearings into the various complaints. (Tenet had spent years working for the Democrats on the committee staff, and had served as a member of Bill Clinton's National Security Council staff before joining the C.I.A.'s management team.)

One Democrat, however, blamed the process within the Senate committee, which, he said, neglected terrorism in favor of more politically charged issues. "Tenet's been briefing about bin Laden for years, but we weren't organized to consider what are threats to the United States. We're chasing whatever the hell is in the news at the moment."

Former Senator Bob Kerrey, of Nebraska, who served for four years as the Intelligence Committee's ranking Democrat and is now the president of the New School, in New York, is one of Tenet's defenders. But Kerrey also acknowledges that he no longer knows "how well we did our job" of legislative oversight. "Nobody with any responsibility can walk away from this. We missed something here."

Kerrey remains angry about the U.S. policy toward Afghanistan in the years after its defeat of the Soviet Union. "The Cold War was over, and we shut down Afghanistan"—that is, ceased all intelligence operations. "From Bush to Clinton, what happened is one of the most embarrassing American foreign-policy decisions, as bad as Vietnam," Kerrey said. He cited a botched 1996 C.I.A plot to overthrow President Saddam Hussein of Iraq: "We also had a half-baked Iraqi operation and sent a signal that we're not serious."

Last June, Shelby, after a tour of the Persian Gulf and a series of intelligence briefings, told a *Washington Post* reporter that bin Laden was "on the run, and I think he will continue to be on the run, because we are not going to let up." He went on, "I don't think you could say he's got us hunkered down. I believe he's more hunkered down." After the bombing, however, Shelby was among the first to suggest publicly that it was time for Tenet to go. "I think he's a good man, and he's done some good things, but there have been a lot of failures on his watch," Shelby told *USA Today*. Tenet, he said, lacked "the stature to control all the agencies. In a sense, he is in charge, but in reality he's not."

One friend and former colleague of Tenet's says that his refusal to urge the Senate leadership to deal with the hard issues was symptomatic of his problems as C.I.A. director. "He's a politician, too," that person said of Tenet. "That's why he shouldn't have been there, because he had no status to tell the senators, 'You don't know what you're talking about.'"

In his memoir, Robert Baer describes the "fatal malaise" that came over the Paris station of the C.I.A. in the early nineties: "Case officers weren't recruiting new agents. The agents already on the books were old. They'd lost their access. And no one seemed to care." Many in the agency were shocked in early 1992 when Milton Bearden, the head of the Soviet-East European division— he had also played a major role in the C.I.A.'s support for the Afghan rebels in their brutal war against the Soviet Union—informed his overseas stations that Russia would now be treated like any other friendly nation, such as Germany or France. The C.I.A. was no longer in the business of recruiting agents to spy against the Russians. In addition, C.I.A. surveillance apartments were closed and wiretaps turned off throughout the Middle East and Europe. "We'll never know the losses we had in terms of not capitalizing on the Soviet collapse," a retired official said. Former high-level Soviet officials with intelligence information or other data were rebuffed. "Walk-ins were turned away. It was stunning, and, as far as I knew, nobody fought it."

Little changed when Bill Clinton took office, in 1993. Baer, now assigned, at his request, to the tiny C.I.A. outpost in Dushanbe, Tajikistan, near the Afghanistan border, watched helplessly as Saudi-backed Islamic fundamentalists—the precursors of the Taliban—consolidated training bases and began to recruit supporters and run operations inside the frontier nations of the former Soviet Union.

In 1995, the agency was widely criticized after the news came out that a paid informant in Guatemala had been involved in the murders of an American innkeeper and the Guatemalan husband of an American lawyer. The informant had been kept on the C.I.A. payroll even though his activities were known to the Directorate of Operations. John Deutch, the C.I.A.'s third director in three years, responded to the abuses, and to the public outcry, by issuing a directive calling for prior approval from headquarters before any person with criminal or human-rights problems could be recruited. The approval, Deutch later explained, was to be based on a simple balancing test: "Is the potential gain in intelligence worth the cost that might be associated with doing business with a person who may be a murderer?"

The "scrub order," as it came to be known, was promulgated by Deutch and his colleagues with the best of intentions, and included provisions for case-by-case review. But in practice hundreds of "assets" were indiscriminately stricken from the C.I.A.'s payroll, with a devastating effect on antiterrorist operations in the Middle East.

The scrub order led to the creation of a series of screening panels at C.I.A. headquarters. Before a new asset could be recruited, a C.I.A. case officer had to seek approval from a Senior Review Panel. "It was like a cardiologist in California deciding whether a surgeon in New York City could cut a chest open," a former officer recalled. Potential agents were being assessed by officials who had no firsthand experience in covert operations. ("Americans hate intelligence—just hate it," Robert Baer recalls thinking.) In the view of the operations officers, the most important weapons in the war against international terrorism were being evaluated by men and women who, as one of the retired officers put it, "wouldn't drive to a D.C. restaurant at night because they were afraid of the crime problem."

Other bureaucratic panels began "multiplying like rabbits, one after another," a former station chief said. Experienced officers who were adamant about continuing to recruit spies found that obtaining approval before making a pitch had become a matter of going from committee to committee. "In the old days, they'd say, 'Go get them,'" the retired officer said. Yet another review process, known as A.V.S.—the asset-validation system—was put in place. Another retired officer told me, "You'd have to write so much paper that guys would spend more time in the station writing reports than out on the street."

"It was mindless," a third officer said. "Look, we recruited assholes. I handled bad guys. But we don't recruit people from the Little Sisters of the Poor—they don't *know* anything." He went on, "What we've done to *ourselves* is criminal. There are a half-dozen good guys out there trying to keep it together."

"It did make the workday a lot easier," Robert Baer said of the edict. "I just watched CNN. No one cared." The C.I.A.'s vital South Group, made up of eight stations in central Asia—all threatened by fundamentalist organizations, especially in Uzbekistan and Tajikistan, with links to the Taliban and bin Laden—had no agents by the mid-nineteen-nineties, Baer said. "The agency was going away."

Unlike many senior officials at C.I.A headquarters, Baer had lived undercover, in the nineteen-eighties, in Beirut and elsewhere in the Middle East, and he well understood the ability of terrorist organizations to cover their tracks. He told me that when the C.I.A. started to go after the Islamic Jihad, a radical Lebanese group linked to a series of kidnappings in the Reagan years, "its people systematically went through documents all over Beirut, even destroying student records. They had the airport wired and could pick the Americans out. They knew whom they wanted to kidnap before he landed." The terrorists coped with the American ability to intercept conversations worldwide by constantly changing codes—often doing little more than changing the meanings of commonly used phrases. "There's a professional cadre out there," Baer said. Referring to the terrorists who struck on September 11th, he said, "These people are so damned good."

An American Dream, Slightly Apart

Anne Hull

The Washington Post | October 27, 2001

*When Anne Hull was awarded the 2002 Freedom Forum/American Society News-
paper Editors Award for Outstanding Writing on Diversity, the judges noted her
"graceful and elegant narrative style, [which] persuades people to read what they
need to know and understand." Hull's award-winning series of articles included this
touching account of a Muslim-American family's newfound uneasiness in the aftermath of September 11. . . .*

PATERSON, N.J.—Mohammad Al-Qudah fires up his Weber grill and
throws on a few lamb steaks. It's a glorious October evening. He has prayed
three times already and will pray twice more before he goes to sleep.

His wife, Nadia Kahf, third-year law student and mother of two,
mixes hummus in the blender. She's not wearing the hijab she usually
wears in public.

They recently left an apartment for this sprawling split-level in the suburbs, proof that Al-Qudah has come a long way since arriving from Jordan
in 1989 and cramming into a Paterson boarding house with several other
Middle Eastern immigrants.

Yet, on the big-screen TV in the den, he and his wife toggle between
CNN and al-Jazeera, wary of the American news filter.

"It's news when one Jewish person dies," Kahf says. "When they massacre 24 Palestinians, nothing. What really bothers me is when they bring
on Islamic experts who are not Muslim."

Since the Sept. 11 terrorist attacks, and with the United States dropping
bombs on a Muslim country, Kahf and Al-Qudah wrestle with their place
in their adopted nation, a land suddenly rippling with American flags and
a taste for revenge. The crosscurrents are especially strong in this part of
New Jersey, where the FBI believes six hijacking suspects flowed through
this year while plotting their suicide missions.

"Terrible, criminal," says Kahf of the murder of more than 5,000 people.

Yet the seeds of the hijackers' motivations are not mysterious to her.

"People in a lot of places hate America," she says. "It's not hard to understand that."

Born in Syria, Kahf arrived here 17 years ago, when she was 12. America seems to have been good to her. But her embrace is tentative. In a study this year titled "The Mosque in America: A National Portrait," 82 percent of American Muslims strongly agreed that high-tech America offered opportunity; 28 percent said the nation was immoral and corrupt.

For Kahf and her husband—taxpayers, registered voters, law-abiding citizens—assimilation is not a goal. After she graduates from Seton Hall University law school, she hopes to specialize in defending Muslims in civil liberties cases.

"There are so few Muslim lawyers, even fewer female Muslim lawyers, and even fewer female lawyers who cover," she says, referring to the hijab.

"Throughout history," she says, Muslims "will always be separate."

But after Sept. 11, separateness became a liability.

"Do you know who your neighbors are?" a local news segment asked ominously after the Paterson terrorist cell was discovered.

Al-Qudah quickly attached an American flag to his wife's car.

A Mini-Ramallah

When Rep. William J. Pascrell Jr. (D-N.J.) met Yasser Arafat in 1998 in Ramallah, the Palestinian leader asked, "How are my people in Paterson?" The city has one of the largest concentrations of Arab Americans in the country; 20,000 of its 160,000 residents are Muslim. Paterson prints its recycling rules in English, Spanish and Arabic.

The heart of the Arab American community is along Main Avenue in South Paterson, a mini-Ramallah, with halal butchers and men drinking tea and scarved women surveying bins of olives. Turkish techno music pumps from the hot-waxed cars of the Jordanian boys smoking Marlboro Reds.

This is where Mohammad Al-Qudah came when he arrived from Jordan. There was the food he knew, and the language he knew and the faith he knew.

Main Avenue is also where Hani Hanjour came looking for an apartment in February, choosing a $650-a-month one-bedroom unit over a mini-mart. It's where alleged ringleader Mohamed Atta visited a travel office in July and bought a one-way ticket to Madrid.

When Kahf learned that a hijacked plane had crashed into the World Trade Center, 20 miles to the east, her first reaction was horror, followed by something equally desperate:

"Please don't let it be a Muslim."

The collateral damage from the attacks takes shape in a third-floor apartment over Main Avenue, where a woman named Ruby Santos pulls back her lace curtains and watches the sky for low-flying airplanes.

"I have nothing against Arabics," says Santos, a Puerto Rican mother of three who grew up happily in the melting pot of Passaic County. "But I don't trust them after what happened."

When a bearded Middle Eastern man wearing an Army jacket boarded her bus, "all the way to Passaic I had a stomachache," she says.

Her 13-year-old daughter, Melissa, rolls her eyes.

Santos folds her arms. "Melissa, you don't get scared when you see an Arabic with a little scarf?"

"Ma, I see them every day, the lunch ladies in the cafeteria."

Santos's younger daughter, Deidre, pipes in. "Mommy, I thought some Arabics were nice."

"Not all of them are bad, baby." Her eyes go back to the window, the darkness beyond it, the place where she used to feel so comfortable. "Those hijackers, they just messed up everything."

'I Feel Guilty'

With a day off from law school, Kahf joins a group of Muslim "sisters" to visit a friend with a new baby. All are covered from head to toe in hijab and jilbab, the smock worn for modesty. One woman pulls up in a black Lexus SUV, her hand wrapped in a bandage.

"How did you burn your hand?" someone asks.

"Not cooking," says Dalia Fahmy, who is finishing her master's in politics at New York University.

"Her stove is so clean, and she's been married two years!" her sister, Dena, chimes in.

They settle around a table spread with baklava, tea, cashews and dried fruit.

Talk inevitably turns to the tenor of life as a Muslim after Sept. 11. Immediately afterward, the imam at their mosque suggested that women stay inside, particularly if they wore hijab. Fahmy lasted two days in seclusion and then went to Gymboree. "I'm in line and I feel like everyone is feeling weird for me," she says. "At the same time, I feel guilty for the situation."

Sally Amer also stayed home. "Okay, I'll let you lock me down for one day," the pharmacist and mother of two told her husband. On the third day, she went to the mall. A Muslim friend of hers was not so lucky; someone shot an arrow through her child's bedroom window.

Kahf couldn't miss law classes. So her husband taped the flag to her car antenna, and off she drove into the anxieties beyond her driveway.

Not wearing their hijab would have made life easier.

"Would Oprah take off her skin color growing up in the '50s or '60s?" Fahmy asks.

The women oppose Afghanistan's Taliban regime, but they are frustrated, too, by stereotypes of Islam. "Americans confuse culture and religion," Kahf says. "With the Taliban, women are not being educated. That's political, not religious, and it's wrong."

Yet Kahf objects to what she sees as American feminist arrogance toward the practice of covering, even among the Afghan women forced to wear burqas by the Taliban.

"Oh, they must be so hot in those tents," Kahf says, mockingly. "Maybe they want to cover."

Several years ago, Kahf applied for a teaching position in the history department at a community college. With a bachelor's degree in political science and a master's in Middle Eastern studies, she thought she had the job. "The director was very happy until he met me and saw my cover," Kahf says. She was rerouted to the ESOL (English Speakers of Other Languages) department.

From the baby shower, the women disperse into the afternoon to put children down for naps, to pick up children from school. Wearing their hijab, they move like silken ghosts down the sidewalk. The flag on Kahf's Jeep whips in the autumn breeze.

A few days earlier, her son asked her why so many people were flying flags.

"Because everyone is happy to be in America," she told him.

But not necessarily happy with the country's policies. Kahf opposes the war efforts in Afghanistan. "America really does decide whose life is more important," she says. "Think of it from the point of view of an Iraqi child, or a Palestinian child."

Neighbor Avoids Neighbor

Not far from the heart of Paterson's Middle Eastern community, there is a house where retribution is more easily understood. A sign on the front door reads: "Thanks to you for your concerns and prayers. Kenny still missing. I will be waiting for my son now and forever."

Paterson lost one resident in the World Trade Center attack. Kenny Lira was a 28-year-old computer technician who worked on the 110th floor of the North Tower. A Peruvian American, he grew up easily among the Latinos and Arabic kids in this neighborhood.

Now his mother, Marina Lira, sleeps on the couch at night to be near the TV, as if it will deliver the antidote she needs. On CNN, the FBI announces its 22 Most Wanted Terrorists list. The colorful graphic "America Strikes Back" is stripped beneath the 22 photos of dark faces.

"I know that the Muslim religion is not what these people are practicing," Lira says.

Yet she no longer walks to Main Avenue to buy dried cherries and pita bread. "I don't even drive that way," she says. "We drive the other way. A friend said to me, 'I saw them and my anger grew inside.' "

While Lira was in Manhattan putting up fliers for her missing son, a stranger came to her house and spoke with a relative. I'm Muslim, the woman said. My family is Muslim. We apologize for what happened.

"My niece told me this happened, but I did not see it," Lira says. She looks out the front window. The neighbors who used to walk by covered in hijab and burqa no longer pass her house.

"Why?" she asks. "Why?"

'This Makes Me Feel Good'

The next night, while Lira holds a candlelight service at her house in honor of her son, Kahf is starting dinner.

"Finish your math," she tells her daughter.

"Oh, Mom, I hate math," says Mariam, 9, slumping over her backpack on the kitchen counter. "Fifth-grade math is a killer. Can I just get a zero?"

Kahf calls into the living room to her 5-year-old son. "Abdallah, you said you were just going to play one game of Nintendo."

She hears the garage door open. "Daddy's home."

Mohammad Al-Qudah embraces his children. His wife takes the spinach pastries from the oven and kisses him. "How was your day?" she asks. His gas station business is down 15 percent since Sept. 11.

After dinner, a friend calls. President Bush is on TV. Al-Qudah grabs the remote. Bush is saying that Muslim women who cover their heads should not have to be afraid. Al-Qudah leans forward on the couch and points to the president. "This is very important," he says. "You know, he's been very good on this."

More than his wife, he looks for the positive. He keeps several voice-mail messages he received in the days after the hijackings.

Hey, Mo, this is Jimmy. Want to make sure everything is okay. We're thinking about you.

I know that with what happened, certain Americans will look on Muslim groups unfavorably. We're thinking of you. Thanks, Mo.

"This makes me feel good," he says.

They are part of America, but apart. Kahf does not see this as a contradiction. "This is part of living in a democracy," she says. "This saying, 'America, love it or leave it.' I don't buy it. True democracy is being able to question things, even to criticize things, but always wanting to make the situation better."

The next day, Kahf irons her hijab and grabs her keys. A decade ago, local Muslims prayed in a rented room above a restaurant near Main Avenue. Now, the Islamic Center of Passaic County, a former synagogue, welcomes 800 Muslims on Fridays for 1 o'clock prayer. Kahf settles in the back of the mosque with the other women. Kneeling, facing toward Mecca, she bows, her forehead to the carpet.

The imam, Mohammad Qatanani, repeats that Muslims are against terrorists, against what happened at the World Trade Center, but also against "crimes committed against innocent lives in Afghanistan."

From the mosque, Kahf picks up her daughter at the Islamic school. Mariam is standing on the blacktop with three of her friends, all of whom wear hijab. "She looks so grown up in it," Kahf says, beaming.

At home, Mariam goes outside to ride her Razor scooter with a neighbor boy, who by now understands when Mariam is called inside for prayer time. "Come back in five minutes," she will say.

Her father's car pulls into the garage. In a few hours, he will go to the mosque for prayer. He has a business trip to Las Vegas coming up. An airline passenger named Mohammad Al-Qudah! A friend joked that he should show up at airport security wearing a bikini and handcuffs.

"I can't believe you are going," his wife says.

He smiles. "I'm going to do what the president says. I am going to live my life."

Diamonds sparkle in his wife's ears. His son prays beside him on the rug and goes to sleep in zebra pajamas. His daughter began wearing hijab to school this year. His business is expanding.

"I was born in Jordan," Al-Qudah says. "But America makes me feel alive."

The Sentry's Solitude

Fouad Ajami

Foreign Affairs | November/December, 2001

In addition to this eloquent, even poetic, essay in Foreign Affairs, *Fouad Ajami found time last year to pen articles for the* U.S. News and World Report, The New Republic, *and* The New York Times—*and to chat at length on screen with Charlie Rose—all to the same end: to try to communicate to the American public what is going on in the minds of the world's Arab Muslims.*

Not everyone agrees with his take: In responding to Ajami's article in the Times *magazine about the Al-Jazeera television station ("What the Arab World is Watching"), for example, Rime Allaf wrote in the* Lebanon Daily Star, *"the real problem with Al-Jazeera seems to be its reporting on the Arab-Israeli conflict which, for the likes of Ajami, is too pro-Arab . . . "Still, the Lebanese-born Ajami, who is a professor of Middle Eastern studies at Johns Hopkins (after a long stint at Princeton University), has a deep understanding of the psychological and political strains created when traditional, religious-based Arab cultures bump up against modern life—and the dangers these tensions pose for the United States. . . .*

From one end of the Arab world to the other, the drumbeats of anti-Americanism had been steady. But the drummers could hardly have known what was to come. The magnitude of the horror that befell the United States on Tuesday, September 11, 2001, appeared for a moment to embarrass and silence the drummers. The American imperium in the Arab-Muslim world hatched a monster. In a cruel irony, a new administration known for its relative lack of interest in that region was to be pulled into a world that has both beckoned America and bloodied it.

History never repeats itself, but when Secretary of State Colin Powell came forth to assure the nation that an international coalition against terrorism was in the offing, Americans recalled when Powell had risen to fame. "First, we're going to cut it off, then we're going to kill it," he had said of the Iraqi army in 1991. There had been another coalition then, and Pax Americana had set off to the Arab world on a triumphant campaign. But those Islamic domains have since worked their way and their will on the American victory of a decade ago. The political earth has shifted in that world. The decade was about the "blowback" of the war. Primacy begot its nemesis.

America's Arab interlocutors have said that the region's political stability would have held had the United States imposed a settlement of the Israeli-Palestinian conflict—and that the rancid anti-Americanism now evident in the Arab world has been called up by the fury of the second intifada that erupted in September 2000. But these claims misread the political world. Long before the second intifada, when Yasir Arafat was still making his way from political exile to the embrace of Pax Americana, there was a deadly trail of anti-American terror. Its perpetrators paid no heed to the Palestinian question. What they thought of Arafat and the metamorphosis that made him a pillar of President Clinton's Middle East policy is easy to construe.

The terror was steady, and its geography and targets bespoke resourcefulness and audacity. The first attack, the 1993 truck bombing of the World Trade Center, was inspired by the Egyptian cleric Sheikh Omar Abdel Rahman. For the United States, this fiery preacher was a peculiar guest: he had come to bilad al-Kufr (the lands of unbelief) to continue his war against the secular regime of Egyptian President Hosni Mubarak. The sheikh had already been implicated in the 1981 murder of Mubarak's predecessor, Anwar al-Sadat. The young assassins had sought religious guidance from him—a writ for tyrannicide. He had provided it but retained a measure of ambiguity, and Egypt let him leave the country. He had no knowledge of English and did not need it; there were disciples and interpreters aplenty around him. An American imperium had incorporated Egypt into its order of things, which gave the sheikh a connection to the distant power.

The preacher could not overturn the entrenched regime in his land. But there was steady traffic between the United States and Egypt, and the armed Islamist insurgency that bedeviled Cairo inspired him. He would be an Ayatollah Khomeini for his followers, destined to return from the West to establish an Islamic state. In the preacher's mind, the world was simple. The dictatorial regime at home would collapse once he snapped its lifeline to America. American culture was of little interest to him. Rather, the United States was a place from which he could hound his country's rulers. Over time, Abdel Rahman's quest was denied. Egypt rode out the Islamist insurgency after a terrible drawn-out fight that pushed the country to the brink. The sheikh ended up in an American prison. But he had lit the fuse. The 1993 attack on the World Trade Center that he launched was a mere dress rehearsal for the calamity of September 11, 2001. Abdel Rahman had shown the way—and the future.

There were new Muslim communities in America and Europe; there was also money and freedom to move about. The geography of political Islam had been redrawn. When Ayatollah Khomeini took on American power, there had been talk of a pan-Islamic brigade. But the Iranian revolutionaries were ultimately concerned with their own nation-state. And they were lambs compared with the holy warriors to come. Today's warriors have been cut loose from the traditional world. Some of the leaders—the Afghan Arabs—had become restless after the Afghan war. They were insurrectionists caught in no man's land, on the run from their homelands but never at home in the West. In Tunisia, Egypt, and Algeria, tenacious Islamist movements were put down. In Saudi Arabia, a milder Islamist challenge was contained. The counterinsurgencies had been effective, so the extremists turned up in the West. There, liberal norms gave them shelter, and these men would rise to fight another day.

The extremists acquired modern means: frequent flyer miles, aviation and computer skills, and ease in Western cities. They hated the United States, Germany, and France but were nonetheless drawn to them. They exalted tradition and faith, but their traditions could no longer give them a world. Islam's explosive demography had spilled into the West. The militant Islamists were on the move. The security services in their home countries were unsentimental, showing no tolerance for heroics. Men like Abdel Rahman and Osama bin Ladin offered this breed of unsettled men a theology of holy terror and the means to live the plotter's life. Bin Ladin was possessed of wealth and high birth, the heir of a merchant dynasty. This gave him an aura: a Che Guevara of the Islamic world, bucking the mighty and getting away with it. A seam ran between America and the Islamic world. The new men found their niche, their targets, and their sympathizers across that seam. They were sure of America's culpability for the growing misery in their lands. They were sure that the regimes in Saudi Arabia and Egypt would fall if only they could force the United States to cast its allies adrift.

Not in My Backyard

Terror shadowed the American presence in the Middle East throughout the 1990s: two bombings in Saudi Arabia, one in Riyadh in November of 1995, and the other on the Khobar Towers near Dhahran in June of 1996; bombings of the U.S. embassies in Tanzania and Kenya in 1998; the daring attack on the *U.S.S. Cole* in Yemen in October 2000. The U.S. presence in the Persian Gulf was under assault.

In this trail of terror, symbol and opportunity were rolled together—the physical damage alongside a political and cultural message. These attacks were meant for a watchful crowd in a media age. Dhahran had been a creature of the U.S. presence in Saudi Arabia ever since American oil prospectors turned up in the 1930s and built that city in the American image. But the world had changed. It was in Dhahran, in the 1990s, that the crews monitoring the no-fly zone over Iraq were stationed. The attack against Dhahran was an obvious blow against the alliance between the United States and Saudi Arabia. The realm would not disintegrate; Beirut had not come to Arabia. But the assailants—suspected to be an Iranian operation that enlisted the participation of Saudi Shi`a—had delivered the blow and the message. The foreigner's presence in Arabia was contested. A radical Islamist opposition had emerged, putting forth a fierce, redemptive Islam at odds with the state's conservative religion.

The ulama (clergy) had done well under the Saud dynasty. They were the dynasty's partners in upholding an order where obedience to the rulers was given religious sanction. No ambitious modernist utopia had been unleashed on them as it had in Gamal Abdel al-Nasser's Egypt and Iran under the Pahlavis. Still, the state could not appease the new breed of activists who had stepped forth after the Gulf War to hound the rulers over internal governance and their ties to American power. In place of their rulers' conservative edifice, these new salvationists proposed a radical order free from foreign entanglements. These activists were careful to refrain from calling for the outright destruction of the House of Saud. But sedition was in the air in the mid-1990s, and the elements of the new utopia were easy to discern. The Shi`a minority in the eastern province would be decimated and the Saudi liberals molded on the campuses of California and Texas would be swept aside in a zealous, frenzied campaign. Traffic with the infidels would be brought to an end, and those dreaded satellite dishes bringing the West's cultural "pollution" would be taken down. But for this to pass, the roots of the American presence in Arabia would have to be extirpated—and the Americans driven from the country.

The new unrest, avowedly religious, stemmed from the austerity that came to Saudi Arabia after Desert Storm. If the rulers could not subsidize as generously as they had in the past, the foreigner and his schemes and overcharges must be to blame. The dissidents were not cultists but men of their society, half-learned in Western sources and trends, picking foreign sources to illustrate the subjugation that America held in store for Arabia. Pamphleteering had come into the realm, and rebellion proved contagious. A dissident steps out of the shadows, then respectable critics, then others come forth. Xenophobic men were now agitating against the "crusaders" who had come to stay. "This has been a bigger calamity than I had expected, bigger than any threat the Arabian Peninsula had faced since God Almighty created it," wrote the religious scholar Safar al-Hawali, a master practitioner of the paranoid style in politics. The Americans, he warned, had come to dominate Arabia and unleash on it the West's dreaded morals.

Saudi Arabia had been free of the anticolonial complex seen in states such as Algeria, Egypt, Syria, and Iraq. But the simplicity of that Arabian-American encounter now belonged to the past. A fatwa (Islamic decree) of the senior religious jurist in the realm, Sheikh Abdelaziz ibn Baz, gave away the hazards of the U.S. presence in Arabia. Ibn Baz declared the Khobar bombing a "transgression against the teachings of Islam." The damage to lives and property befell many people, "Muslims and others alike," he wrote. These "non-Muslims" had been granted a pledge of safety. The sheikh found enough scripture and tradition to see a cruel end for those who pulled off the "criminal act." There was a saying attributed to the Prophet Muhammad: "He who killed an ally will never know the smell of paradise." And there was God's word in the Koran: "Those that make war against Allah and his apostle and spread disorder in the land shall be put to death or crucified or have their hands and feet cut off on alternate sides; or be banished from the country. They shall be held to shame in this world and sternly punished in the next." The sheikh permitted himself a drapery of decency. There was no need to specify the identity of the victims or acknowledge that the Americans were in the land. There had remained in the jurist some scruples and restraints of the faith.

In ibn Baz's world, faith was about order and a dread of anarchy. But in the shadows, a different version of the faith was being sharpened as a weapon of war. Two years later, bin Ladin issued an incendiary fatwa of his own—a call for murder and holy warfare that was interpreted in these pages by the historian Bernard Lewis. Never mind that by the faith's strictures and practice, bin Ladin had no standing to issue religious decrees. He had grabbed the faith and called on Muslims to kill "Americans and their allies . . . in any country in which it is possible to do so." A sacred realm apart, Arabia had been overrun by Americans, bin Ladin said. "For more than seven years the United States has been occupying the lands of Islam in the holiest of its territories, Arabia, plundering its riches, overwhelming its rulers, humiliating its people, threatening its neighbors, and using its peninsula as a spearhead to fight the neighboring Islamic peoples." Xenophobia of a murderous kind had been dressed up in religious garb.

Into the Shadows

The attack on the *Cole* on October 12, 2000, was a case apart. Two men in a skiff crippled the *Cole* as it docked in Aden to refuel. Witnesses say that the assailants, who perished with their victims, were standing erect at the time of the blast, as if in some kind of salute. The United States controlled the sea lanes of that world, but the nemesis that stalked it on those shores lay beyond America's reach. "The attack on the *U.S.S. Cole* . . . demonstrated a seam in the fabric of efforts to protect our forces, namely transit forces," a military commission said. But the official language could not describe or name the furies at play.

The attack on the Cole illuminated the U.S. security dilemma in the Persian Gulf. For the U.S. Navy, Yemen had not been a particularly easy or friendly setting. It had taken a ride with Saddam Hussein during the Gulf War. In 1994, a brutal war had been fought in Yemen between north and south, along lines of ideology and tribalism. The troubles of Yemen were bottomless. The government was barely in control of its territory and coastline. Aden was a place of drifters and smugglers. Moreover, the suspected paymaster of anti-American terror, bin Ladin, had ancestral roots in Hadramawt, the southeastern part of Yemen, and he had many sympathizers there.

It would have been prudent to look at Yemen and Aden with a jaundiced eye. But by early 1999, American ships had begun calling there. U.S. officials had no brilliant options south of the Suez Canal, they would later concede. The ports of call in Sudan, Somalia, Djibouti, and Eritrea were places where the "threat conditions" were high, perhaps worse than in Yemen. The United States had a privileged position in Saudi Arabia, but there had been trouble there as well for U.S. forces: the terrorist attacks in 1995 and 1996, which took 24 American lives. American commanders and planners knew the hazards of Yemen, but the U.S. Navy had taken a chance on the country. Terrorists moved through Yemen at will, but American military planners could not find ideal refueling conditions in a region of great volatility. This was the imperial predicament put in stark, cruel terms.

John Burns of *The New York Times* sent a dispatch of unusual clarity from Aden about the *Cole* and the response on the ground to the terrible deed. In Yemen, the reporter saw "a halting, half-expressed sense of astonishment, sometimes of satisfaction and even pleasure, that a mighty power, the United States, should have its Navy humbled by two Arab men in a motorized skiff." Such was imperial presence, the Pax Americana in Arab and Muslim lands.

There were men in the shadows pulling off spectacular deeds. But they fed off a free-floating anti-Americanism that blows at will and knows no bounds, among Islamists and secularists alike. For the crowds in Karachi, Cairo, and Amman, the great power could never get it right. A world lacking the tools and the political space for free inquiry fell back on anti-Americanism. "I talk to my daughter-in-law so my neighbor can hear me," goes an Arabic maxim. In the fury with which the intellectual and political class railed against the United States and Israel, the agitated were speaking to and of their own rulers. Sly and cunning men, the rulers knew and understood the game. There would be no open embrace of America, and no public defense of it. They would stay a step ahead of the crowd and give the public the safety valve it needed. The more pro-American the regime, the more anti-American the political class and the political tumult. The United States could grant generous aid to the Egyptian state, but there would be no dampening of the anti-American fury of the Egyptian political class. Its leading state-backed dailies crackled with the wildest theories of U.S.-Israeli conspiracies against their country.

On September 11, 2001, there was an unmistakable sense of glee and little sorrow among upper-class Egyptians for the distant power—only satisfaction that America had gotten its comeuppance. After nearly three decades of American solicitude of Egypt, after the steady traffic between the two lands, there were no genuine friends for America to be found in a curiously hostile, disgruntled land.

Egyptians have long been dissatisfied with their country's economic and military performance, a pain born of the gap between Egypt's exalted idea of itself and the poverty and foreign dependence that have marked its modern history. The rage against Israel and the United States stems from that history of lament and frustration. So much of Egypt's life lies beyond the scrutiny and the reach of its newspapers and pundits—the ruler's ways, the authoritarian state, the matter of succession to Mubarak, the joint military exercises with U.S. and Egyptian forces, and so on. The animus toward

America and Israel gives away the frustration of a polity raging against the hard, disillusioning limits of its political life.

In the same vein, Jordan's enlightened, fragile monarchy was bound to the United States by the strategic ties that a skilled King Hussein had nurtured for decades. But a mood of anger and seething radicalism had settled on Jordan. The country was increasingly poorer, and the fault line between Palestinians and East Bankers was a steady source of mutual suspicion. If the rulers made peace with Israel, "civil society" and the professional syndicates would spurn it. Even though the late king had deep ties with the distant imperial power, the country would remain unreconciled to this pro-American stance. Jordan would be richer, it was loudly proclaimed, if only the sanctions on Iraq had been lifted, if only the place had been left to gravitate into Iraq's economic orbit. Jordan's new king, Abdullah II, could roll out the red carpet for Powell when the general turned up in Jordan recently on a visit that had the distinct sense of a victory lap by a soldier revisiting his early triumph. But the throngs were there with placards, and banners were aloft branding the visitor a "war criminal." This kind of fury a distant power can never overcome. Policy can never speak to wrath. Step into the thicket (as Bill Clinton did in the Israeli-Palestinian conflict) and the foreign power is damned for its reach. Step back, as George W. Bush did in the first months of his presidency, and Pax Americana is charged with abdication and indifference.

The Seige

The power secured during Desert Storm was destined not to last. The United States could not indefinitely quarantine Iraq. It was idle to think that the broad coalition cobbled together during an unusually perilous moment in 1990-91 would stand as a permanent arrangement. The demographic and economic weight of Iraq and Iran meant that those countries were bound to reassert themselves. The United States had done well in the Persian Gulf by Iraq's brazen revisionism and the Iranian Revolution's assault on its neighboring states. It had been able to negotiate the terms of the U.S. presence—the positioning of equipment in the oil states, the establishment of a tripwire in Kuwait, the acceptance of an American troop presence on the Arabian Peninsula—at a time when both Iran and Iraq were on a rampage. Hence the popular concerns that had hindered the American presence in the Persian Gulf were brushed aside in the 1990s. But this lucky run was bound to come to an end. Iraq steadily chipped away at the sanctions, which over time were seen as nothing but an Anglo-American siege of a brutalized Iraqi population.

The campaign against Saddam Hussein had been waged during a unique moment in Arab politics. Some Muslim jurists in Saudi Arabia and Egypt even ruled that Saddam had run afoul of Islam's strictures, and that an alliance with foreign powers to check his aggression and tyranny was permissible under Islamic law. A part of the Arabian Peninsula that had hitherto wanted America "over the horizon" was eager to have American protection against a "brother" who had shredded all the pieties of pan-Arab solidarity. But the Iraqi dictator hunkered down, outlasting the foreign power's terrible campaign. He was from the neighborhood and knew its rules. He worked his way into the local order of things.

The Iraqi ruler knew well the distress that settled on the region after Pax Americana's swift war. All around Iraq, the region was poorer: oil prices had slumped, and the war had been expensive for the oil states that financed it. Oil states suspected they were being overbilled for military services and for weapons that they could not afford. The war's murky outcome fed the belief that the thing had been rigged all along, that Saddam Hussein had been lured into Kuwait by an American green light—and then kept in power and let off the hook—so that Pax Americana would have the pretext for stationing its forces in the region. The Iraqi ruler then set out to show the hollowness of the hegemony of a disinterested American imperium.

A crisis in 1996 laid bare the realities for the new imperium. Saddam Hussein brazenly sent his squads of assassins into the "safe haven" that the United States had marked out for the Kurds in northern Iraq after Desert Storm. He sacked that region and executed hundreds who had cast their fate with American power. America was alone this time around. The two volleys of Tomahawk missiles fired against Iraqi air-defense installations had to be launched from U.S. ships in the Persian Gulf and B-52 bombers that flew in from Guam. No one was fooled by the American response; no one believed that the foreign power would stay. U.S. officials wrote off that episode as an internal Kurdish fight, the doings of a fratricidal people. A subsequent air campaign—"fire and forget," skeptics dubbed it—gave the illusion of resolve and containment. But Clinton did not have his heart in that fight. He had put his finger to the wind and divined the mood in the land: there was no public tolerance for a major campaign against Saddam Hussein.

By the time the Bush administration stepped in, its leaders would find a checkered landscape. There was their old nemesis in Baghdad, wounded but not killed. There was a decade of Clintonianism that had invested its energy in the Israeli-Palestinian conflict but had paid the Persian Gulf scant attention. There was a pattern of half-hearted responses to terrorist attacks, pinpricks that fooled no one.

Having It His Way

It was into this witch's brew that Arafat launched the second intifada last year. In a rare alignment, there had come Arafat's way a U.S. president keen to do his best and an Israeli soldier-statesman eager to grant the Palestinian leader all the Israeli body politic could yield—and then some. Arafat turned away from what was offered and headed straight back into his people's familiar history: the maximalism, the inability to read what can and cannot be had in a world of nations. He would wait for the "Arab street" to rise up in rebellion and force Pax Americana to redeem his claims. He would again let play on his people the old dream that they could have it all, from the river to the sea. He must know better, he must know the scales of power, it is reasonable to presume. But there still lurks in the Palestinian and Arab imagination a view, depicted by the Moroccan historian Abdallah Laroui, that "on a certain day, everything would be obliterated and instantaneously reconstructed and the new inhabitants would leave, as if by magic, the land they had despoiled." Arafat knew the power of this redemptive idea. He must have reasoned that it is safer to ride that idea, and that there will always be another day and another offer.

For all the fury of this second intifada, a supreme irony hangs over Palestinian history. In the early 1990s, the Palestinians had nothing to lose. Pariahs in the Arab councils of power, they made their best historical decision—the peace of Oslo—only when they broke with the maximalism of their political tradition. It was then that they crossed from Arab politics into internal Israeli politics and, courtesy of Israel, into the orbit of Pax Americana. Their recent return into inter-Arab politics was the resumption of an old, failed history.

Better the fire of an insurrection than the risks of reconciling his people to a peace he had not prepared them for: this was Arafat's way. This is why he spurned the offer at Camp David in the summer of 2000. "Yasir Arafat rode home on a white horse" from Camp David, said one of his aides, Nabil Shaath. He had shown that he "still cared about Jerusalem and the refugees." He had stood up, so Shaath said, to the combined pressure of the Americans and the Israelis. A creature of his time and his world, Arafat had come into his own amid the recrimina-tions that followed the Arab defeat in 1948. Palestine had become an Arab shame, and the hunt for demons and sacrificial lambs would shape Arab politics for many years.

A temporizer and a trimmer, Arafat did not have it in him to tell the 1948 refugees in Lebanon, Syria, and Jordan that they were no more likely to find political satisfaction than were the Jews of Alexandria, Fez, Baghdad, and Beirut who were banished from Arab lands following Israel's statehood. He lit the fuse of this second intifada in the hope that others would put out the flame. He had become a player in Israeli politics, and there came to him this peculiar satis-faction that he could topple Israeli prime ministers, wait them out, and force an outside diplomatic intervention that would tip the scales in his favor. He could not give his people a decent public order and employ and train the young, but he could launch a war in the streets that would break Israel's economic momentum and rob it of the normalcy brought by the peace of Oslo.

Arafat had waited for rain, but on September 11, 2001, there had come the floods. "This is a new kind of war, a new kind of battlefield, and the United States will need the help of Arab and Muslim countries," chief Palestinian negotiator Saeb Erekat announced. The Palestinian issue, he added, was "certainly one of the reasons" for the attacks against the United States. An American-led brigade against terrorism was being assembled. America was set to embark on another expedition into Arab-Muslim domains, and Arafat fell back on the old consola-tion that Arab assets would be traded on his people's behalf. A dowry would have to be offered to the Arab participants in this brigade: a U.S.-imposed set-tlement of the Israeli-Palestinian conflict. A cover would be needed for Arab regimes nervous about riding with the foreigner's posse, and it stood to reason that Arafat would claim that he could provide that kind of cover.

The terror that hit America sprang from entirely different sources. The plotters had been in American flight schools long before the "suicide mar-tyrs" and the "children of the stones" had answered Arafat's call for an intifada. But the Palestinian leader and his lieutenants eagerly claimed that the fire raging in their midst had inspired the anti-American terror. A decade earlier, the Palestinians had hailed Saddam Hussein's bid for pri-macy in the Persian Gulf. Nonetheless, they had been given a claim on the peace—a role at the Madrid Conference of October 1991 and a solicitous U.S. policy. American diplomacy had arrived in the nick of time; the first intifada had burned out and degenerated into a hunt for demons and "col-laborators." A similar fate lies in wait for the second intifada. It is reasonable to assume that Arafat expects rescue of a similar kind from the new American drive into Arab and Muslim lands.

No veto over national policies there will be given to Arafat. The states will cut their own deals. In the best of worlds, Pax Americana is doomed to a measure of solitude in the Middle East. This time around, the American predicament is particularly acute. Deep down, the Arab regimes feel that the threat of political Islam to their own turfs has been checked, and that no good can come out of an explicit public alliance with an American campaign in their midst. Foreign powers come and go, and there is very little protection they can provide against the wrath of an angry crowd. It is a peculiarity of the Arab-Islamic political culture that a ruler's authoritarianism is more permissible than his identification with Western powers—think of the fates of Sadat and of the Pahlavis of Iran.

Ride with the foreigners at your own risk, the region's history has taught. Syria's dictator, Hafiz al-Assad, died a natural death at a ripe old age, and his life could be seen as a kind of success. He never set foot on American soil and had stayed within his world. In contrast, the flamboyant Sadat courted foreign countries and came to a solitary, cruel end; his land barely grieved for him. A foreign power that stands sentry in that world cannot spare its local allies the retribution of those who brand them "collaborators" and betrayers of the faith. A coalition is in the offing, America has come calling, urging the region's rulers to "choose sides." What these rulers truly dread has come to pass: they might have to make fateful choices under the gaze of populations in the throes of a malignant anti-Americanism. The ways of that world being what they are, the United States will get more cooperation from the ministers of interior and the secret services than it will from the foreign ministers and the diplomatic interlocutors. There will be allies in the shadows, but in broad daylight the rulers will mostly keep their distance. Pakistan's ruler, Pervez Musharraf, has made a brave choice. The rulers all around must be reading a good deal of their worries into his attempt to stay the course and keep his country intact.

A broad coalition may give America the comfort that it is not alone in the Muslim world. A strike against Afghanistan is the easiest of things—far away from the troubles in the Persian Gulf and Egypt, from the head of the trail in Arab lands. The Taliban are the Khmer Rouge of this era and thus easy to deal with. The frustrations to come lie in the more ambiguous and impenetrable realms of the Arab world. Those were not Afghans who flew into those towers of glass and steel and crashed into the Pentagon. They were from the Arab world, where anti-Americanism is fierce, where terror works with the hidden winks that men and women make at the perpetrators of the grimmest of deeds.

Brave Old World

"When those planes flew into those buildings, the luck of America ran out," Leon Wieseltier recently wrote in *The New Republic*. The 1990s were a lucky decade, a fool's paradise. But we had not arrived at the end of history, not by a long shot. Markets had not annulled historical passions, and a high-tech world's electronic age had not yet dawned. So in thwarted, resentful societies there was satisfaction on September 11 that the American bull run and the triumphalism that had awed the world had been battered, that there was soot and ruin in New York's streets. We know better now. Pax Americana is there to stay in the oil lands and in Israeli-Palestinian matters. No large-scale retreat from those zones of American primacy can be contemplated. American hegemony is sure to hold—and so, too, the resistance to it, the uneasy mix in those lands of the need for the foreigner's order, and the urge to lash out against it, to use it and rail against it all the same.

There is now the distinct thunder of war. The first war of the twenty-first century is to be fought not so far from where the last inconclusive war of the twentieth century was waged against Iraq. The war will not be easy for America in those lands. The setting will test it in ways it has not been tested before. There will be regimes asking for indulgence for their own terrible fights against Islamists and for logistical support. There will be rulers offering the bait of secrets that their security services have accumulated through means at odds with American norms. Conversely, friends and sympathizers of terror will pass themselves off as constitutionalists and men and women of the "civil society." They will find shelter behind pluralist norms while aiding and abetting the forces of terror. There will be chameleons good at posing as America's friends but never turning up when needed. There will be one way of speaking to Americans, and another of letting one's population know that words are merely a pretense. There will step forth informers, hustlers of every shade, offering to guide the foreign power through the minefields and alleyways. America, which once held the world at a distance, will have to be willing to stick around eastern lands. It is both heartbreaking and ironic that so quintessentially American a figure as George W. Bush—a man who grew up in Midland, Texas, far removed from the complications of foreign places—must be the one to take his country on a journey into so alien, so difficult, a world.

The National Conversation:
The War on Terror

Choosing Our Enemy

Tucker Carlson

New York magazine | October 1, 2001

Just because Tucker Carlson is a rising television star doesn't mean he's lost his journalistic chops. In this New York *magazine column, Carlson tries to suss out where the Bush Administration's new War on Terror is headed—and whether Iraq's Saddam Hussein will be served up as the next item on the menu. . . .*

The United States is going to war. That's what we know about American foreign policy at the moment. Now consider all the things we don't know: when we're going to war, where it will be waged, how long it will last, what constitutes victory, and, most striking of all, who the enemy is. We don't know these things partly because they have not yet been fully decided, but also because the administration doesn't want us to know.

Washington is in the middle of a news brownout. The papers arrive every morning filled with fascinating reporting, brilliant writing, and human-interest pieces so moving they've spawned an entire subgenre of stories about how almost no one can read the newspaper these days without crying. But if you're looking for a WHAT NEXT FOR THE U.S.? story, you're out of luck. The press doesn't know.

Neither do most members of Congress. Last week, there was widespread complaining on Capitol Hill after Attorney General John Ashcroft arrived to brief lawmakers on the state of the investigation, and told them . . . virtually nothing. "I learned more on cable," said one frustrated member. This week, there were rumors that administration staff suspected of leaking defense-related information of any kind to the media would have their phone records pulled by the FBI (334, *The Washington Post* exchange, would be a dead giveaway) and would be subjected to polygraph examinations. Are the rumors true? That, too, is hard to verify. But people believe it. That's the mood here.

All of which is to say, we'll know for certain what's going to happen only when it does. In the meantime, here's what appears to be the story line so far:

The administration is divided into two camps. Crudely put, one side wants to go after terrorists; the other, after the states that sponsor them. The president declared last week that all states must choose whether they are with us or against us. He didn't say which ones had to decide. Afghanistan, obviously. But there's still a lot of room beyond that for the two factions to contend over strategy.

The first side, represented by Colin Powell and the State Department, instinctively favors international coalitions and modest, finite goals. It fears protracted military involvement abroad. It would be happy to dispatch bin Laden, uproot his network with the cooperation of Arab coalition members, and declare victory.

The other side doesn't see this as nearly enough. This contingent, represented by Donald Rumsfeld and two of his deputies at Defense, Doug Feith and Paul Wolfowitz, has less confidence in coalitions (and far less in the reliability of foreign intelligence services). It believes the U.S. should mount a broader military campaign in the region. It's likely the September 11 attack was in some way state-sponsored, this group reasons, and in any case, other attacks on Americans have been. Why stop with bin Laden when we can disable the governments that allow him and other terrorists to flourish? Better to kill the roots than to trim the leaves.

Wolfowitz said as much shortly after the attacks, when he explained that the U.S. is committed to "ending" regimes that sponsor terrorism. A few days later, the secretary of state publicly slapped him down. "We're after ending terrorism," Powell said. "And if there are states and regimes, nations that support terrorism, we hope to persuade them that it is in their interest to stop doing that."

"Persuade them that it is in their interest"? It's hard to imagine Rumsfeld saying something like this, except maybe sarcastically. Just as it's hard to imagine anyone at the Defense Department bragging, as Powell did at the same briefing, about the "support" the U.S. has received from Yemen and Syria in the fight against terrorism. Yemen and Syria are part of the reason we have terrorism in the first place.

At this point, with nothing beyond a showdown with Afghanistan declared, it's not clear which side will ultimately win the argument—though Condoleezza Rice will probably be the tiebreaker. Bush is said to listen particularly closely to Rice, not because she is a strategic genius—she's not—but because he considers her loyal and above narrow bureaucratic interests. The president trusts her, and that matters most. It's a theme in the administration.

If the Defense Department position prevails, expect more dramatic reporting from Baghdad. "The elephant in the room is Iraq," says one well-connected foreign-policy player (who, like everyone else I spoke to, refused to be identified even by branch of government). There's some evidence that the elephant is guilty. Earlier this year, Mohamed Atta met with the head of European operations for the Iraqi Intelligence Service. The Israelis are convinced. According to a recent piece in the defense industry monitor, *Jane's,* Israel believes the entire attack was paid for and run by Saddam. Others believe the 1993 Trade Center bombing was also the work of Iraq.

A war on Iraq would likely begin with a bombing campaign against sites thought to house the country's nuclear- and chemical-weapons programs. From there, Bush could send American troops to Baghdad.

If anything like this were to happen, the "coalition" that Powell favors would fray, at best. Is Sudan really going to hang tough when America starts killing Muslims? Once the shooting starts, says one policymaker, "the French will want a cease-fire. The Chinese will want to bring it to the United Nations."

It's not clear which course American foreign policy will take, though there are signs. For one, Condi Rice has turned out to be more hawkish— less of a Powell-ite—than expected. For another, Wolfowitz, despite the embarrassing spanking by Powell, is still espousing the same position and still doing it in public. Most telling of all, Bush himself has not moderated his rhetoric. In his speech to Congress last week—a magnificent perform-ance by any measure, almost unbelievably good considering who gave it— the president again threatened to crush not just terrorists but states that assist them. Powerful nations don't bluff. Bush means it.

This administration, like any, would like to wade in with a detailed plan already in place, and it will try. At the moment, the Wolfowitz position appears to be ascendant. But the Bush people understand that much of the strategy is bound to be ad hoc. The Afghan war is likely to be long. By the end, the Powell doctrine may be back.

As one defense analyst I spoke to put it, wars evolve. Two weeks after Pearl Harbor, no one thought we'd be island-hopping through the Pacific three years later.

The Real War
Thomas Friedman

The New York Times | November 27, 2001

Tom Friedman's reporting on the worldwide impact of terrorism for The New York Times—*including the following column—earned him the 2002 Pulitzer Prize for commentary. "It was the biggest story of my life . . . I just really wanted to get it right," Friedman told the* Times *after learning he'd won his third Pulitzer. "Get it right not only in terms of who they are but in terms of who we are". . . .*

If 9/11 was indeed the onset of World War III, we have to understand what this war is about. We're not fighting to eradicate "terrorism." Terrorism is just a tool. We're fighting to defeat an ideology: religious totalitarianism. World War II and the cold war were fought to defeat secular totalitarianism— Nazism and Communism—and World War III is a battle against religious totalitarianism, a view of the world that my faith must reign supreme and can be affirmed and held passionately only if all others are negated. That's bin Ladenism. But unlike Nazism, religious totalitarianism can't be fought by armies alone. It has to be fought in schools, mosques, churches and synagogues, and can be defeated only with the help of imams, rabbis and priests.

The generals we need to fight this war are people like Rabbi David Hartman, from the Shalom Hartman Institute in Jerusalem. What first attracted me to Rabbi Hartman when I reported from Jerusalem was his contention that unless Jews reinterpreted their faith in a way that embraced modernity, without weakening religious passion, and in a way that affirmed that God speaks multiple languages and is not exhausted by just one faith, they would have no future in the land of Israel. And what also impressed me was that he knew where the battlefield was. He set up his own schools in Israel to compete with fundamentalist Jews, Muslims and Christians, who used their schools to preach exclusivist religious visions.

After recently visiting the Islamic madrasa in Pakistan where many Taliban leaders were educated, and seeing the fundamentalist religious education the young boys there were being given, I telephoned Rabbi Hartman and asked: How do we battle religious totalitarianism?

He answered: "All faiths that come out of the biblical tradition—Judaism, Christianity and Islam—have the tendency to believe that they have the exclusive truth. When the Taliban wiped out the Buddhist statues, that's what they were saying. But others have said it too. The opposite of religious totalitarianism is an ideology of pluralism—an ideology that embraces religious diversity and the idea that my faith can be nurtured without claiming exclusive truth. America is the Mecca of that ideology, and that is what bin Laden hates and that is why America had to be destroyed."

The future of the world may well be decided by how we fight this war. Can Islam, Christianity and Judaism know that God speaks Arabic on Fridays, Hebrew on Saturdays and Latin on Sundays, and that he welcomes different human beings approaching him through their own history, out of their language and cultural heritage? "Is single-minded fanaticism a necessity for passion and religious survival, or can we have a multilingual view of God—a notion that God is not exhausted by just one religious path?" asked Rabbi Hartman.

Many Jews and Christians have already argued that the answer to that question is yes, and some have gone back to their sacred texts to reinterpret their traditions to embrace modernity and pluralism, and to create space for secularism and alternative faiths. Others—Christian and Jewish fundamentalists—have rejected this notion, and that is what the battle is about within their faiths.

What is different about Islam is that while there have been a few attempts at such a reformation, none have flowered or found the support of a Muslim state. We patronize Islam, and mislead ourselves, by repeating the mantra that Islam is a faith with no serious problems accepting the secular West, modernity and pluralism, and the only problem is a few bin Ladens. Although there is a deep moral impulse in Islam for justice, charity and compassion, Islam has not developed a dominant religious philosophy that allows equal recognition of alternative faith communities. Bin Laden reflects the most extreme version of that exclusivity, and he hit us in the face with it on 9/11.

Christianity and Judaism struggled with this issue for centuries, but a similar internal struggle within Islam to re-examine its texts and articulate a path for how one can accept pluralism and modernity—and still be a passionate, devout Muslim—has not surfaced in any serious way. One hopes that now that the world spotlight has been put on this issue, mainstream Muslims too will realize that their future in this integrated, globalized world depends on their ability to reinterpret their past.

An Afghan-American Speaks
Mir Tamim Ansary

salon.com | September 14, 2001

The day after two jet liners crashed into the World Trade Center, Afghan-born writer Mir Tamim Ansary—disturbed by the anti-Afghanistan vitriol he was hearing on his local Bay Area radio station—sent the following e-mail to 20 friends. Within 48 hours, salon.com had posted his essay on its website, and by that Friday night, Ansary told L.A. Weekly, "I was hearing from people in the Netherlands and Australia, even Thailand." Since then, his plea for understanding has become known as "the e-mail read around the world". . . .

I've been hearing a lot of talk about "bombing Afghanistan back to the Stone Age." Ronn Owens, on San Francisco's KGO Talk Radio, conceded today that this would mean killing innocent people, people who had nothing to do with this atrocity, but "we're at war, we have to accept collateral damage. What else can we do?" Minutes later I heard some TV pundit discussing whether we "have the belly to do what must be done."

And I thought about the issues being raised especially hard because I am from Afghanistan, and even though I've lived in the United States for 35 years I've never lost track of what's going on there. So I want to tell anyone who will listen how it all looks from where I'm standing.

I speak as one who hates the Taliban and Osama bin Laden. There is no doubt in my mind that these people were responsible for the atrocity in New York. I agree that something must be done about those monsters.

But the Taliban and bin Laden are not Afghanistan. They're not even the government of Afghanistan. The Taliban are a cult of ignorant psychotics who took over Afghanistan in 1997. Bin Laden is a political criminal with a plan. When you think Taliban, think Nazis. When you think bin Laden, think Hitler. And when you think "the people of Afghanistan" think "the Jews in the concentration camps." It's not only that the Afghan people had nothing to do with this atrocity. They were the first victims of the perpetrators. They would exult if someone would come in there, take out the Taliban and clear out the rats' nest of international thugs holed up in their country.

Some say, why don't the Afghans rise up and overthrow the Taliban? The answer is, they're starved, exhausted, hurt, incapacitated, suffering. A few years ago, the United Nations estimated that there are 500,000 disabled orphans in Afghanistan—a country with no economy, no food. There are millions of widows. And the Taliban has been burying these widows alive in mass graves. The soil is littered with land mines, the farms were all destroyed by the Soviets. These are a few of the reasons why the Afghan people have not overthrown the Taliban.

We come now to the question of bombing Afghanistan back to the Stone Age. Trouble is, that's been done. The Soviets took care of it already. Make the Afghans suffer? They're already suffering. Level their houses? Done. Turn their schools into piles of rubble? Done. Eradicate their hospitals? Done. Destroy their infrastructure? Cut them off from medicine and healthcare? Too late. Someone already did all that. New bombs would only stir the rubble of earlier bombs. Would they at least get the Taliban? Not likely. In today's Afghanistan, only the Taliban eat, only they have the means to move around. They'd slip away and hide. Maybe the bombs would get some of those disabled orphans; they don't move too fast, they don't even have wheelchairs. But flying over Kabul and dropping bombs wouldn't really be a strike against the criminals who did this horrific thing. Actually it would only be making common cause with the Taliban—by raping once again the people they've been raping all this time.

So what else is there? What can be done, then? Let me now speak with true fear and trembling. The only way to get Bin Laden is to go in there with ground troops. When people speak of "having the belly to do what needs to be done" they're thinking in terms of having the belly to kill as many as needed. Having the belly to overcome any moral qualms about killing innocent people. Let's pull our heads out of the sand. What's actually on the table is Americans dying. And not just because some Americans would die fighting their way through Afghanistan to Bin Laden's hideout. It's much bigger than that, folks. Because to get any troops to Afghanistan, we'd have to go through Pakistan. Would they let us? Not likely. The conquest of Pakistan would have to be first. Will other Muslim nations just stand by? You see where I'm going. We're flirting with a world war between Islam and the West.

And guess what: That's bin Laden's program. That's exactly what he wants. That's why he did this. Read his speeches and statements. It's all right there. He really believes Islam would beat the West. It might seem ridiculous, but he figures if he can polarize the world into Islam and the West, he's got a billion soldiers. If the West wreaks a holocaust in those lands, that's a billion people with nothing left to lose; that's even better from Bin Laden's point of view. He's probably wrong—in the end the West would win, whatever that would mean—but the war would last for years and millions would die, not just theirs but ours.

Who has the belly for that? Bin Laden does. Anyone else?

Put Out No Flags
Katha Pollitt

The Nation | October 8, 2001

For those who embrace the theory of the "engaged writer" (the concept that writers should be actively involved in encouraging social and political change), one of the signs of an effective piece of writing is its ability to stir public reaction. By that standard, the following essay by Katha Pollitt scored a direct bulls-eye. Her explanation of why she refused her teenaged daughter's request, in the wake of September 11, to fly an American flag outside the living-room window of their Manhattan apartment evoked cries of outrage from across the political spectrum.

We suggest you read Pollitt's reasoning for yourself, then decide. . . .

My daughter, who goes to Stuyvesant High School only blocks from the World Trade Center, thinks we should fly an American flag out our window. Definitely not, I say: The flag stands for jingoism and vengeance and war. She tells me I'm wrong—the flag means standing together and honoring the dead and saying no to terrorism. In a way we're both right: The Stars and Stripes is the only available symbol right now. In New York City, it decorates taxicabs driven by Indians and Pakistanis, the impromptu memorials of candles and flowers that have sprung up in front of every firehouse, the chi-chi art galleries and boutiques of SoHo. It has to bear a wide range of meanings, from simple, dignified sorrow to the violent anti-Arab and anti-Muslim bigotry that has already resulted in murder, vandalism and arson around the country and harassment on New York City streets and campuses. It seems impossible to explain to a 13-year-old, for whom the war in Vietnam might as well be the War of Jenkins's Ear, the connection between waving the flag and bombing ordinary people half a world away back to the proverbial stone age. I tell her she can buy a flag with her own money and fly it out her bedroom window, because that's hers, but the living room is off-limits.

There are no symbolic representations right now for the things the world really needs—equality and justice and humanity and solidarity and intelligence. The red flag is too bloodied by history; the peace sign is a retro fashion accessory. In much of the world, including parts of this country, the cross and crescent and Star of David are logos for nationalistic and sectarian hatred. Ann Coulter, fulminating in her syndicated column, called for carpet-bombing of any country where people "smiled" at news of the disaster: "We should invade their countries, kill their leaders, and convert them to Christianity." What is this, the Crusades? The Rev. Jerry Falwell issued a belated mealy-mouthed apology for his astonishing remarks immediately after the attacks, but does anyone doubt that he meant them? The disaster was God's judgment on secular America, he observed, as famously secular New Yorkers were rushing to volunteer to dig out survivors, to give blood, food, money, anything—it was all the fault of "the pagans, and the abortionists, and the feminists, and the gays and the lesbians . . . the ACLU, People for the American Way." That's what the Taliban think too.

As I write, the war talk revolves around Afghanistan, home of the vicious Taliban and hideaway of Osama bin Laden. I've never been one to blame the United States for every bad thing that happens in the Third World, but it is a fact that our government supported militant Islamic fundamentalism in Afghanistan after the Soviet invasion in 1979. The mujahedeen were freedom fighters against Communism, backed by more than $3 billion in US aid—more money and expertise than for any other cause in CIA history—and hailed as heroes by tag-along journalists from Dan Rather to William T. Vollmann, who saw these lawless fanatics as manly primitives untainted by the West. (There's a story in here about the attraction Afghan hyper-masculinity holds for desk-bound modern men. How lovely not to pay lip service to women's equality! It's cowboys and Indians, with harems thrown in.) And if, with the Soviets gone, the vying warlords turned against one another, raped and pillaged and murdered the civilian population and destroyed what still remained of normal Afghan life, who could have predicted that? These people! The Taliban, who rose out of this period of devastation, were boys, many of them orphans, from the wretched refugee camps of Pakistan, raised in the unnatural womanless hothouses of fundamentalist boarding schools. Even leaving aside their ignorance and provincialism and lack of modern skills, they could no more be expected to lead Afghanistan back to normalcy than an army made up of kids raised from birth in Romanian orphanages.

Feminists and human-rights groups have been sounding the alarm about the Taliban since they took over Afghanistan in 1996. That's why interested Americans know that Afghan women are forced to wear the total shroud of the burqa and are banned from work and from leaving their homes unless accompanied by a male relative; that girls are barred from school; and that the Taliban—far from being their nation's saviors, enforcing civic peace with their terrible swift Kalashnikovs—are just the latest oppressors of the miserable population. What has been the response of the West to this news? Unless you count the absurd infatuation of European intellectuals with the anti-Taliban Northern Alliance of fundamentalist warlords (here we go again!), not much.

What would happen if the West took seriously the forces in the Muslim world who call for education, social justice, women's rights, democracy, civil liberties and secularism? Why does our foreign policy underwrite the clerical fascist government of Saudi Arabia—and a host of nondemocratic regimes besides? What is the point of the continuing sanctions on Iraq, which have brought untold misery to ordinary people and awakened the most backward tendencies of Iraqi society while doing nothing to undermine Saddam Hussein? And why on earth are fundamentalist Jews from Brooklyn and Philadelphia allowed to turn Palestinians out of their homes on the West Bank? Because God gave them the land? Does any sane person really believe that?

Bombing Afghanistan to "fight terrorism" is to punish not the Taliban but the victims of the Taliban, the people we should be supporting. At the same time, war would reinforce the worst elements in our own society—the flag-wavers and bigots and militarists. It's heartening that there have been peace vigils and rallies in many cities, and antiwar actions are planned in Washington, D.C., for September 29-30, but look what even the threat of war has already done to Congress, where only a single representative, Barbara Lee, Democrat from California, voted against giving the president virtual carte blanche.

A friend has taken to wearing her rusty old women's Pentagon Action buttons—at least they have a picture of the globe on them. The globe, not the flag, is the symbol that's wanted now.

Pulse of Patriotism
Richard Rodriguez

The Los Angeles Times | October 21, 2001

As a Mexican-American son of immigrant parents, Richard Rodriguez has always viewed U.S. culture from a perspective that is somewhat detached from the traditional mainstream, yet at the same time reflective of a deeper truth about our country. As he points out in this post 9/11 column, in the end, its our differences that make us all so American. . . .

SAN FRANCISCO—In peacetime, America is the most original nation in the world. We are the maddest, most inventive; truly a splendid disorder are we. When America goes to war, we become a nation like any other.

Nowadays, I turn on TV and hear Americans gamely stumbling through the national anthem. At an intersection yesterday, I saw a Lexus carrying a socialite alongside a pickup with a kid who was absorbing the thump-thump-thump of rap music—both cars wearing the stars and stripes.

Everywhere I walk in San Francisco, in shop windows, signs of uniform size, identical lettering, proclaim: United We Stand.

Odd. I had always assumed the reverse: That the strength of America derives from our variety and disparate opinions. Which is to say: Disunited We Stand.

In today's nation of wartime unity, television comedians, newspaper columnists, Berkeley politicians and everyday loonies—indeed, anyone who might voice an eccentric opinion about Sept. 11 and our government's response—have been called down by their fellow Americans as unpatriotic. Immediately after Sept. 11, I found it dismaying that opinion turned so uniform. And it was not until I began to hear dissenting voices—opinions I didn't necessarily share—that I knew the America I recognized had survived.

Meanwhile, from his cave emerges Osama bin Laden, a medieval villain, fondling a microphone, to describe the United States as a "Jewish-Christian alliance."

America, of course, is no such thing. America is the Enlightenment's daughter, a nation that someone like Bin Laden cannot comprehend.

America was created as a secular country. Which is why, today, Buddhist, pagan, Methodist and Hindu live side by side.

In my opinion, President Bush was not only shrewd but authentically patriotic in his insistence that Muslims should be regarded by their neighbors as true Americans. Treating Muslims as Americans at this moment of history is not magnanimous, but an act essential to our nation's meaning.

My Mexican immigrant father, I remember, was never less than grateful for the economic freedom of America; never wasted a moment of nostalgia for the country he had left behind. But my father was confused by the variety of America. "There is no unity here; this is not a real country," my father used to remark. Coming from a Mexican village of continuity, my father found metropolitan America a puzzle.

But from the first, I was seduced by America, enchanted by the idea that a nation could be organized, disorganized, around the first-person, singular pronoun. The history of America I read was the history of a young country extending, too slowly and painfully at times, but certainly extending the definition of "the American," decade after decade. It was a marvel to me and the source of my greatest love of this country—the way the country enlarged with every facet, every religion and race and tongue and recipe. America became the jewel of civilization.

Wartime is not the best time to see this America. In wartime, Americans are merely united; the country defines itself by what it must exclude and resist. When I was a boy in the 1950s, I remember hearing adults talk nostalgically about the way the country had been united a decade earlier. Americans in World War II had been galvanized by a sense of a shared enemy, a common purpose. "You wouldn't believe it," a neighbor lady said to me.

But in the peacetime America of the 1950s, America was drawing new worlds to itself—drawing my Mexican family to itself, even while the country was finding its meaning in its disunion. By the late 1950s, rock 'n' roll jackhammered a channel we named the "generation gap." And Americans of every age sped along newly constructed interstates, trying to get as far as possible from in-laws and the inner city. And my neighbor lady was getting a divorce.

I sing the American parade in peacetime: the Chinese teenager with earphones; the Russian woman in a sparkling sweater; the blue-suited Big Deal chattering into her cell phone; the tattoos and the shorts; the big bellies; the prim; the rabbinical; the anarchic.

It is true that the chaos of America can leave us melancholic and lonely. The pace and frenzied desires of our lives often leave us, more than any other people on Earth, addicted to sexual titillation, celebrity (the glamour of the oversized ego) and drugs, "recreational" and not. There are days, I admit, when the fury of America—the determination of each driver to pull ahead—seems a madness and leaves me feeling that America is the thinnest culture in the world, barely a "nation."

But from the American respect for individualism would also come our nation's great originality and creativity. American culture is the mass culture of the world, because the world is hungry for an idea of itself larger than a single creed, nation or color. This is, of course, why the religious fundamentalist, the nationalist and the tribalist must hate America.

It is nothing for me to hate in return. Indeed, I loathe Bin Laden—may his tribe decrease. I resent him most because he has taken away my America at peace, at frenzy, and has replaced it with a nation of uniform opinion and too little sense of its greatness.

I cannot imagine a more patriotic insult America could offer Bin Laden than to become as divided in wartime as we are divided in peace.

Hail and Farewell

Anthony Lewis

The New York Times | December 15, 2001

In his final New York Times *op-ed piece, columnist Anthony Lewis bids adieu, and offers the nation a parting word of caution. . . .*

BOSTON—Everything comes to an end, my friend Sydney Gruson told me long ago. Now the time has come for this column to end. I have been writing it for 32 years. As I look back at those turbulent decades, I see a time of challenge to a basic tenet of modern society: faith in reason.

No one can miss the reality of that challenge after Sept. 11. Islamic fundamentalism, rejecting the rational processes of modernity, menaces the peace and security of many societies.

But the phenomenon of religious fundamentalism is not to be found in

Islam alone. Fundamentalist Christians in America, believing that the Bible's story of creation is the literal truth, question not only Darwin but the scientific method that has made contemporary civilization possible.

Religion and extreme nationalism have formed deadly combinations in these decades, impervious to reason. Serbs in the grip of religion and mystical nationalist history killed thousands and expelled millions in their "ethnic cleansing" of Bosnia. Fundamentalist Judaism and extreme Israeli nationalism have fed the movement to plant settlements in Palestinian territory, fueling Islamic militancy among Palestinians.

Faith in reason was the foundation stone of the United States. The men who met in Philadelphia in 1787 set out to create a nation from struggling states so distant from each other that it took seven days for George Washington to learn that New Hampshire had provided the needed ninth vote to bring their Constitution into being. They wagered that a national government based on written rules could hold the country together.

Intricate checks and balances, they reasoned, would prevent the abuses of power that tempt all politicians. They put their faith not in men but in law: the law of the Constitution.

Without the foundation of law, this vast country could never have survived as one, could never have absorbed streams of immigrants from myriad cultures. With one terrible exception, the Civil War, law and the Constitution have kept America whole and free.

Of course we have not always been faithful to the vision of the Framers. In time of war and stress, we have yielded again and again to fear. Fear of Jacobin terror in France produced the Sedition Act of 1798. In World War I, men and women were sentenced to long prison terms for mildly critical political speech. In World War II, unreasoning fear led to the internment of Japanese-Americans. During the cold war, fear of Communism brought the abuses of McCarthyism.

Today again fear threatens reason. Aliens are imprisoned for months on the flimsiest of grounds. The attorney general of the United States moves to punish people on the basis of secret evidence, the Kafkaesque hallmark of tyranny. Recently F.B.I. agents went to a Houston art museum and, on suspicion that it was promoting terrorism, scrutinized a work that showed a city skyline burning.

I am an optimist about America. But how can I maintain that optimism after Vietnam, after the murder of so many who fought for civil rights, after the Red scare and after the abusive tactics planned by government today? I can because we have regretted our mistakes in the past, relearning every time that no ruler can be trusted with arbitrary power. And I believe we will again.

The hard question is whether our commitment to law will survive the new sense of vulnerability that is with us all after Sept. 11. It is easy to tolerate dissent when we feel safe.

But after all, this has always been a country of unbounded optimism, a country that struggles with itself and conquers corrupting habit. In my lifetime we have carried out two revolutions, unfinished but extraordinary: the ending of racial discrimination and the move toward equality for women. Thirty-two years ago few imagined that the secretary of state could be anything but a white male.

In a speech nearly a century ago, Justice Oliver Wendell Holmes Jr. foresaw racial conflict and destruction of the world's resources. But even that great skeptic concluded: "Beyond the vision of battling races and an impoverished earth I catch a dreaming glimpse of peace."

In the end I believe that faith in reason will prevail. But it will not happen automatically. Freedom under law is hard work. If rulers cannot be trusted with arbitrary power, it is up to citizens to raise their voices at injustice. The most important office in a democracy, Justice Louis Brandeis said, is the office of citizen.

Part Six:
America's Future in an Uncertain World

War in a Time of Peace

David Halberstam

from *War in a Time of Peace*

In this final section, we take a step back to consider the long-range challenges facing the United States in its role as the world's preeminent military and economic power.

In David Halberstam's book War in a Time of Peace—*his first large-scale work on the subject of national security since 1972—he explores the emergence of the new, post-Cold War American foreign policy, as seen through the lens of President Clinton's decision to take military action (albeit reluctantly) against Slobodan Milosevic in Kosovo. While Halberstam's book came out before the 9/11 attacks, his closing words in this excerpt proved all too accurate. . . .*

More than six years after he had first taken office and begun to struggle with the issue of the Balkans, Clinton had finally and quite reluctantly unleashed American airpower in Kosovo and Serbia. He had won that gamble—at least won it for the time being, because winning in the Balkans was always so problematical. But in the end Milosevic had folded his hand. When he had backed down, Clinton had taken a phone call from Senator Joe Biden of Delaware, the ranking Democratic member of the Senate Foreign Relations Committee. Biden had been almost without equal in urging the administration to act militarily in the Balkans. "Congratulations— you've got your sea legs," he told the president. "Joe, you've been pretty rough on me," the president said. Then he paused and added, as if in apology, something revealing: "Remember I came in as a governor and I didn't have any experience in foreign policy?" It was a nice, friendly call, and it took place in the seventh year of Clinton's presidency.

This incomplete and in many ways unsatisfactory war was soon followed by an incomplete and difficult peace. Where in Bosnia some traditional forces were working toward pluralism, the forces at play in Kosovo were much more violent and far less likely to find any common ground. The hatreds there between the Serbs and the Kosovar Albanians went deeper—they were almost organic—and were completely mutual. Any peace that followed the fighting would probably not be a genuine peace. Whichever faction was stronger was sure to try to sabotage any peace-keeping effort and exploit its leverage against the momentarily weaker faction. A few months earlier, the villains, by Western consensus, had been the Serbs, trying to de-ethnicize the land by driving the Albanians off it. Now, based on the Serb defeat, and the use of awesome NATO airpower on behalf of the Albanian cause, it was the KLA and related groups that wanted to drive all Serbs out of Kosovo and parts of southern Serbia, which was triggering violent incidents. To the Western forces trying to bring some degree of stability to one of the most unstable pieces of real estate in the world, that meant their recent semi-allies were now potentially their adversaries. In a region where vengeance was a birthright, the great problem was once again deciding who the good guys and who the bad guys were, because they could so readily switch sides. Those who had so recently worn the white hats could wear the black hats, while the black hats could don the white hats.

The past year had greatly strengthened—and emboldened—the KLA and its allied nationalist groups, turning them into a considerable political and military force. Their goal was complete Albanian independence, yet the Western allies that had just fought to protect these same Albanians were pledged to nothing more than some kind of limited autonomy under what would still be overall Serb rule. Thus, the darkest parts of Balkan history—the raw feelings of the Kosovar Albanians and Serbs toward each other—had not been settled. They had been rekindled and were now likely to tear the region apart, with the Western forces that had defeated Milosevic charged with being the new, unsure referee, and largely resentful of being pulled in.

Bill Clinton, who had long minimized the importance of foreign affairs, was the beneficiary of the NATO victory in Kosovo, though there was little political capital to be gained from it. If the intervention had backfired, if the bombing had not worked and ground troops had been needed, there might well have been a political price to pay. It was a valuable lesson for any leader of America-the-superpower in dealing with these so-called teacup wars. If things worked out, if the most optimistic scenario was reasonably accurate, casualties were low (or almost nonexistent), and there was no damaging media coverage, it would nonetheless be of little domestic advantage. But there was always the potential for a downside, the televised capture of American troops, a repeat of Somalia, and a political disaster.

Peace in Kosovo momentarily and only partially accomplished, Clinton in the fall of 1999 was in an oddly ambiguous political position. He had survived impeachment, he had cleared the long-standing shadow of the Balkans from his presidency, the economy was still vibrant, and his standing in the polls was remarkably high, particularly for someone who had been in office for almost two terms. Yet his accomplishments were not necessarily that significant or at least significant in the ways that historians valued them. Much of his energy had gone into limiting the conservative assault upon a broad liberal agenda rather than creating an agenda of his own. After the victory in Kosovo, he had about a year and a half remaining to try to define his own vision of the proper legacy of what had been a star-crossed presidency. Clinton was *always* campaigning, and in his last year he was campaigning all out for his place in history, his legacy very much in mind. That was true of most presidents, but for Clinton, a passionate reader and a thoughtful amateur historian himself, it was especially true; he wanted to be sure that historians took the full measure of his presidency—as he measured it himself, of course. There had been signs of this early on. In January 1997, after his reelection, he had sat at dinner next to Doris Kearns Goodwin, who was a member of the Society of American Historians, a group that had just rated the various American presidents, himself included, and had placed him somewhere in the middle. Much of the evening had been devoted to his protests over his mediocre rank and his lobbying for a higher one.

Yet a last-minute upgrade in the legacy business was not an easy accomplishment. His years in office were badly tainted by the Lewinsky affair and the failed impeachment process. Stalemated as he was on the domestic front by fierce, highly personal Republican opposition, it was not likely that he could claim any kind of groundbreaking domestic legislation as a part of his political bequest. Only in the world of foreign affairs could Clinton find some daylight. Thus, in his final year, foreign policy ascended to the top of his political agenda. Though as a candidate he had once criticized Bush for globe-trotting, Clinton had traveled more widely than any other American president, the first to set foot in Botswana, Bulgaria, Kuwait, Slovenia, Denmark, and South Africa. "If it's Monday, this must be Turkey," said a *New York Times* headline in November 1999.

To someone like Marlin Fitzwater, the former Bush press secretary, this was ironic for a man who, Fitzwater noted, had once attacked George Bush in New Hampshire for seeming to care more about Liechtenstein than Littletown and Micronesia than Manchester. Other less partisan critics obviously looked at this development somewhat skeptically, as if Clinton was engaged now in first and foremost a legacy hunt. Another headline in the *New York Times* in January 2000 read, "Clinton's Final Chapter: Single-Minded Full Steam Run at a Global Agenda." Suddenly Clinton was always on the move, traveling constantly to foreign capitals, where, as analysts pointed out, people cared nothing about the Lewinsky matter and thought the impeachment process (as Clinton himself did) a political travesty. If foreign policy was his only hope to make a mark on history, then that was where he would place his energies.

The change in priorities was dramatic for a man who had a few days before taking office told Lee Hamilton of the House Foreign Affairs Committee that no one in America cared about foreign policy except for a handful of journalists. The old Clinton might have been cautious in mid-presidency in moving toward official recognition of Hanoi and had had to be pushed forward by Vietnam veterans serving in the Senate in both parties, but now he was eager to visit the country. He did, and the trip was considered a triumph; old wounds could now be healed just a little faster. There was also in the final months of his second term a good chance that he might visit North Korea, which would have been a first. It would not exactly have been the equal in groundbreaking presidential trips to visiting Moscow or Beijing or even Hanoi, but a first was a first, and in a post–Cold War world with fewer and fewer forbidden cities, you had to take your firsts where you could get them.

Most of Clinton's efforts in his last year went into a highly public, all-out attempt to advance the peace process in the Middle East to a new and final settlement. Clearly this one objective was closer to his heart than anything else on his agenda during the late summer and early fall of 2000. Along with the Israeli prime minister, Ehud Barak, he worked relentlessly toward the next level of a peace accord in a series of nonstop meetings with Palestinian leader Yasir Arafat at Camp David, which ran well into the morning hours. It was obviously the kind of foreign policy role Clinton enjoyed the most. Working to bring peace in the Middle East at Camp David was a more natural part for him to play than sitting around the White House weighing whether to bomb targets in downtown Belgrade. Barak, his partner, seemed equally eager to push forward.

For a brief time, the negotiations appeared to be on the verge of a break-through. Arafat was offered a deal that exceeded anything the Israelis had ever before tendered. But because so much of Arafat's position was premised on expected Israeli intransigence, the Palestinian leader seemed totally unprepared by Barak's flexibility. In the end, it was Arafat who blocked the proceedings and the negotiations ended in failure. With the breakup of the Middle East peace process, the last best hope for Clinton to stake his legacy on foreign policy accomplishments collapsed as well.

Clinton liked to tell friends, only partially tongue in cheek, that after the talks failed he received a call from Arafat praising him. "I'm a colossal failure because of you," he answered. Yet what Clinton had done, however reluctantly, in the Balkans was not to be underestimated. The questions facing a president in the post-Cold War years were more difficult to deal with than in the previous, simpler era. This time the enemy was genocide, not Communism. Because there was no direct, immediate threat to the United States during the Balkan crisis, Clinton had received few positive notices for finally using American force in both Bosnia and Kosovo. But quite possibly, with few in the government and even fewer outside realizing it, his administration—and the generation it represented that had come to power after the Cold War—had finally faced a critically important test for the uses of American might, and in answering the question of whether America stood for anything beyond the defense of its own land. Clearly there were no easy answers—or necessarily even right answers—in cases like this, and just as clearly there was little political upside to the intervention. Clinton and his administration had moved slowly at first, perplexed by the equation in front of them and the lack of political support at home. They had frequently stumbled but they had, however awkwardly, and belatedly, met a vital early test of post-Cold War peace keeping.

• • •

In the fall of 2000, Al Gore got his chance to run for the presidency and escape the somewhat neutered role of sitting vice president. He had quietly been the leading hawk in the administration, but because the vice president's duty was *never* to be seen in any disagreement with the president, a great deal of what he believed and had wanted to do in the Balkans had been kept completely private. Some insiders in the Clinton administration spoke of the Kosovo campaign as Gore's War, instead of Madeleine's War. Still, he received no bonus points from that, and there was a danger, given the essential indifference of the American populace to foreign policy issues, that if he campaigned too openly and spoke too candidly about his support for the successful use of force there, it might backfire and he would have to defend himself from accusations of being too much of an interventionist.

Gore was an old-fashioned internationalist, a more committed interventionist than the president he had served. But in the spring and summer of 2000, when he needed to clarify the consistency and independence of his views, neither he nor the people immediately around him did a very good job of it. His chief national security operative, Leon Fuerth, himself a Balkan hawk, was by nature so secretive that, when talking to reporters about the vice president's role during Bosnia and Kosovo, he seemed determined to keep Gore's views as much of a mystery as possible. He treated inquiring reporters as if they were representatives of the KGB, thus, however involuntarily, diminishing Gore's role during the Clinton years. Gore was, in fact, experienced and exceptionally well apprenticed, an uncommonly substantive (sometimes *too* substantive) political figure, but curiously clumsy when it came to making the case for himself with the facility requisite in an age of modern communications.

He seemed to be better at governance than campaigning, and during his presidential run he often came across as not merely awkward and stiff, but also prone to saying things that were self-defeating. It was as if his exceptional résumé, obviously better than anyone else's in Washington, was not quite good enough and he had to juice it up just a bit. To those who had studied both Clinton and Gore, the outgoing president was clearly the more skilled politician, his loyalty always calibrated to the needs of the moment, his allegiances, like his thoughts, always inner-directed. Gore, not by any means as gifted a politician, was by contrast the better human being, a man of greater and more consistent beliefs and personal loyalties.

As a presidential candidate, however, he ran an oddly awkward, almost clunky race, a man never entirely in sync with himself, unsure of which Al Gore he really was. Despite his considerable and active involvement in the critical issues of a largely successful and generally popular two-term presidency, he was never able to exploit his superior background or expertise. He had, for example, cast the deciding vote for the economic policies at the start of the Clinton administration, policies, aimed at limiting the deficit, that had helped lead, in time, to unparalleled prosperity. But it was nearly impossible to tell that from listening to him on the campaign trail. He was judged in his three debates with George W. Bush to have done poorly, too aggressive and condescending in the first, then too amenable and almost lobotomized in the second. Rarely had greater knowledge of the issues and a superior curriculum vitae been of less value in a series of presidential debates. Gore, in the end, was generally judged by network pundits to be less likable than George W. Bush, as if they were assessing a college fraternity election, which it often seemed they were.

Despite the economic prosperity the country enjoyed, no small part of Gore's problem was the dilemma of coming to the campaign from the political house of Bill Clinton, and his quite personal (rather than political) need to separate himself from Clinton over the Lewinsky-impeachment scandal. Perhaps a more deft and nimble politician could have done it readily, managing at once to take some credit for the successes of the Clinton years, while avoiding the taint of the administration's lesser aspects. One can easily imagine, if the roles had been reversed and there had been a Gore scandal, that the new candidate, Bill Clinton, finally released from his long years of servitude as vice president, would have embraced the positive in the Gore record while neatly dodging the shadow of the scandal. But Gore was never able to find the proper degree of separation, and his animus toward Clinton appeared very personal for the world of high-level politicians, more like a son who felt betrayed by a parent than a vice president who had learned to be extremely cautious about a talented but careless president.

Foreign policy, an area where Gore held a significant edge in knowledge, experience, and interest over Bush, remained a marginal part of the campaign, and Gore was never able to exploit his vastly greater expertise. To the degree that the Clinton administration was considered a success, it was because of the improvement in the economy; to the degree that it was considered a failure, it was over the scandals that his personal behavior had precipitated. Clinton's foreign policy decisions—most particularly in the Balkans—were barely an issue. The nation's interest still remained inner-directed. To much of the rest of the world, America was immensely powerful, but for a nation that powerful, it was shockingly self-absorbed. George W. Bush, the son of the former president, for whom foreign policy had been his primary political passion, appeared to have little interest in the rest of the world. He had apparently never traveled to Europe, though he had visited Mexico and had stayed with his father when he was the American diplomatic representative to China. George W. Bush's campaign autobiography, as the *New York Times* columnist Maureen Dowd noted, devoted all of one paragraph to his six-week visit to China. The trip, she wrote, "made him applaud free markets and long for Midland [Texas]." In his campaign rhetoric, his foreign policy was limited to the belief that we should spend more money on the military, which he claimed was in bad shape because of Clinton's budget cuts.

In general, when the subject of foreign policy came up, Bush was uneasy and tentative, as if he had walked into the wrong classroom and was being asked to take an exam for a course he had never signed up for. In an obvious difference with Gore in their respective views of the world around them, Bush did say he wanted to pull back from any use of the military in peacekeeping or humanitarian missions. He referred to the Clinton policy in the Balkans as nation-building, which it was not, and Condoleezza Rice, one of his top foreign policy advisers, implied during the campaign that if Bush were elected, he would quickly bring American troops back from the Balkans. That statement enraged people like retired general John Shalikashvili, who had been one of the principal architects of the small American force that was actually helping to keep the peace at a relatively low cost. In all, the debate over the use of the military, such as it was, fit the shrewd assessment of Bruce Herschensohn, the conservative commentator, filmmaker, and political activist who had once run for the Senate in California. The Democrats, he said, always want a small army, but want to send it everywhere, while the Republicans want a very big army and don't want to use it at all.

George W. Bush was considered a more authentic Texan than his father, and the key to his campaign was said to be his likability, as if he were the successor to the much-revered Ronald Reagan rather than to Reagan's more awkward vice president. From the start of the primaries, he had been the candidate of the smart (and big) Republican money, the agreeable young man bearing a famous name who had done so well in Texas that he had been reelected virtually without opposition. The Republicans, believing they were a majority party (they were most certainly a majority *white* American party), and still smarting from two Clinton election victories (they seemed to think that the victories were illegal, that Clinton had somehow stolen the presidency from them), were determined not to stumble on the issue of abortion again. For that purpose, a great deal of money—some $60 million—had been raised for Bush early in the game, the idea being that he would be able to get by the early ambushes the question of abortion might trigger and thus easily outdistance otherwise minor candidates who might have superior connections to the fundamentalists on the one issue they cared so passionately about. That strategy almost worked, but Senator John McCain, the former POW, ran what was by far the most zestful campaign of all the candidates in both parties, choosing to speak out on what were for many centrist, independent Americans two hot-button issues: the sleaziness of contemporary campaign financing and the power of the fundamentalists in the Republican Party. The McCain campaign eventually forced Bush into a more passionate embrace of the fundamentalists than he wanted during the South Carolina primary. To the degree that any candidate fired the imagination of ordinary centrist Americans in what was generally a grim political year, it was McCain, and his campaign was a reminder that on occasion presidential candidates should have in their curriculum vitae something besides running for office. It was McCain's larger life experience, his ability to survive six years in a North Vietnamese prison camp and come out a richer, more tolerant, more complex human being who appealed to millions of ordinary people. He had created a serious challenge to Bush until he simply ran out of money in midcampaign.

Those who questioned Bush's preparation and readiness for the presidency, his right to lead the world's only superpower, and who were also bothered by what appeared to be glaring deficits in his attention span and curiosity, were reassured by their friends that if he was not exactly a big boy himself, he was surrounded by all the big boys from his father's administration. Just to encourage those people who thought the ticket might be a little short on gravitas, Dick Cheney, good at governance but short on natural charm, and the victim of several heart attacks at a very young age, was made the vice-presidential nominee. Other former top figures from Bush One, such as Colin Powell, often appeared with Bush during the campaign. Even James Baker, in partial exile from the inner Bush circle since the disastrous 1992 campaign, which he had helped manage, was resurrected to be the signature figure in charge of spin during the prolonged struggle over the Florida votes.

The election was extremely close. Gore won the popular vote and might have won the electoral vote as well if the governor of Florida had been a Democrat and not the brother of the Republican candidate. The divisions that had first appeared on the American political landscape starting in the late sixties after the Voting Rights Act of 1965 were still apparent, and the map that the television anchors put up on election night reflected two Americas, a red one and a blue one, which existed uneasily side by side.

One America, the smaller, less populated states, with a decided white majority, where what were considered traditional cultural values still dominated, and where the women's movement was not especially powerful, went Republican, often by margins close to 60–40 and sometimes even larger. That particular political-cultural breakdown also placed the senior military on the Republican side of the ledger, for more and more it tended to align itself with the Republicans over issues of values.

In the other America, much stronger in the more populous states, those with larger cities and dramatically different demographics and changed values, the Democrats did well because there were far larger black and Hispanic populations, the women's movement was more powerful, and gays represented a more defined and well-organized political force. In the end some 105 million Americans had voted, 539,897 more for Gore than Bush on the certified results. But on the most important vote of all, that of the Supreme Court of the United States, Bush won a cliff-hanger, 5–4.

Bill Clinton, whose political sense had always been so sure, departed the White House as ingloriously as any president in recent years, save only Richard Nixon. Buoyed in his last months by surprisingly high approval ratings that reached into the mid-sixties, he had been the omnipresent American figure, flying everywhere and appearing on every television news show to thank people. He clearly enjoyed the final few weeks of his presidency, letting the people of the country know—especially after the grimness of the Bush-Gore campaign—how much they were going to miss him. It was as if he was not merely an outgoing president, but the popular culture's reigning master of ceremonies. Some critics (and friends) might have been left wondering if it was an entirely good thing for a president to exit office so popular. Did that mean he had squirreled away too much of his own political power for too long and not taken enough risks?

Not to worry. Bill Clinton never wore too much success too well for too long, and disaster, as it always did with him, lurked just around the corner. Almost as soon as he left the White House, a firestorm arose over a number of inexplicable pardons he had granted in the last minutes of his presidency, most particularly the one to a fugitive financier named Marc Rich, whose financial and political dealings were one giant mountain of sleaze and corruption. Rich was one of those remarkable refugees who rewards a country that takes him in by seeking to circumvent all its financial laws, and believes as well that his earnings should not go to anything as mundane as paying taxes. Rich had shown not the slightest element of remorse about his thievery, but had devoted himself in his years as a fugitive in Europe to buying access to powerful people through allegedly good works that were the very embodiment of me-first charity. In the Rich case, as in a number of other pardons, Clinton had clearly not checked with the prosecutors, and what he had done was brazen, ugly, and careless, the handiwork of a man who thought he could always get away with whatever he did and would always be forgiven because he was so talented. The pardon to Rich, and a number of other equally improbable and undeserving pardons, stunned even the most loyal of Clinton's inner circle and were devastating to the Democratic Party's leadership.

Oddly enough, another incident was just as revealing about the contradictions within this immensely gifted and equally flawed man. Quietly, in the final hours of his presidency, Clinton worked out a deal with Robert Ray, Ken Starr's successor as independent counsel. Ray would drop the grand jury investigation against Clinton, and as part of the quid pro quo, Clinton agreed to forfeit his Arkansas law license for five years, pay a $25,000 fine to cover legal fees, and not to seek reimbursement for his own attorneys' fees. His had been a long, unpleasant struggle with the independent counsel's office, and though much of it was Clinton's own fault, the righteousness of Starr's pursuit was unbecoming, and one could hardly blame Clinton for seeking on his last day in office what was, in effect, his own pardon. But, in the opinion of some people watching, the deal was distasteful because of Clinton's failure, once it had been agreed upon, to come forward and explain it to the country. Up until then, he who had been everywhere at once, holding impromptu news conferences wherever he went, suddenly disappeared from public view. Instead he sent the White House lawyer and John Podesta, one of his top staff people, to face the country in his place. This, the unwillingness to deal with something so messy, had echoes of the young Clinton who had not merely managed to avoid service in Vietnam, but had played so skillfully with Colonel Holmes, the Arkansas ROTC officer.

Clinton's disastrous farewell allowed George W. Bush a lengthy honeymoon in his early weeks in the White House because so much of the nation's attention was focused—malevolently—on the bizarre final acts of his predecessor. When Bush emerged from the transition period, he was surrounded by those who had been the leading figures in Desert Storm, arguably his father's most dramatic accomplishment. There was Dick Cheney, then secretary of defense, now the vice president, who quickly became the driving force within the White House, and Colin Powell, then chairman of the Joint Chiefs, was now secretary of state. Donald Rumsfeld had been a political opponent of the senior Bush and had often spoken caustically in private of what he considered Bush senior's intellectual limitations. But Rumsfeld was the original sponsor of some of the key Bush people—he had discovered Cheney and had promoted Frank Carlucci, who had, in turn, reached down for Colin Powell. Rumsfeld was named secretary of defense. Condoleezza Rice, the national security adviser, was a Brent Scowcroft protégé. Thus, in terms of foreign policy Bush Two was like something of a reunion of Bush One. Most of the senior people appeared to be cautious about any use of the military for the kind of humanitarian missions that the Clinton people, tentatively and on occasion erratically, had been moving toward. Bush Two was composed of men— and now women—who had dealt well with the final months and weeks of the Cold War, but had not been particularly deft in adapting to the very different circumstances in a changed post–Cold War world.

If anything symbolized that, it was Rumsfeld's passion for a missile shield, something he had been involved with in the past and that loomed as an exceptionally expensive piece of hardware, which might not ever work, and which, if we went after it, would surely siphon immense amounts of money from other very demanding military projects. To many nonpartisan analysts in the world of national security and intelligence, the shield was a kind of high-tech Maginot Line, the wrong idea at the wrong time. America's lead in traditional weaponry was vast and growing greater because of the staggering expense of the technology involved. Thus, rogue states would probably see the gap in aerospace power widen rather than narrow in the years to come. That was one reason not to invest in a missile shield. The other was more basic—a belief among many senior intelligence analysts that the greatest threat to an open society like America came from terrorists, rather than the military power of rogue states, which offered exceptional targets themselves. The real danger to an open society like America was the ability of a terrorist, not connected to any sitting government, to walk into an American city with a crude atomic weapon, delivered, as it were, by hand in a cardboard suitcase.

Early in the new Bush administration, during the inevitable struggle for territory and power, something of a fault line appeared within the national security world, with Rumsfeld and a few people in the White House taking in general a harder line, and Powell at State taking a more moderate one. Of the two factions, the hard-liners appeared to be more influential with this young, neophyte president. On humanitarian issues, the attitude of the new Bush team, said one Washington analyst who had watched them deal with these questions, was more and more like that reflected in the old Jim Baker line, "We don't have a dog in that fight." A dozen years after the end of the Cold War, tensions between the United States and Russia were on the rise, though in no way resembling the continual bipolar crisis that had dominated so much of the second half of the twentieth century. Most Americans did not care very much about Russia as long as it was not a threat, and the ongoing struggle within Russia to keep some form of democracy alive, a great and important story of the new century, did not interest many Americans, especially the executive producers and the anchors of the evening news shows. The role of America in the post–Cold War world, which had not been clearly articulated or defined during the Clinton years, was still murky in January 2001 when the presidential guard changed. Foreign policy was not high on the political agenda, primarily because whatever the forces that might threaten the future of this country were, they were not yet visible.

The World According To Powell
Bill Keller

from *The New York Times Magazine* | November 25, 2001

Of all the internal conflicts in the Bush administration (and every executive branch is rife with them), none has garnered more press than the tensions between Colin Powell's State Department and the more hawkish elements of the administration, personified by Vice President Dick Cheney and Defense Secretary Donald Rumsfeld. It seems difficult to believe that a four-star general who successfully led the prosecution of the Gulf War could be considered soft on national security—but the feeling among many right-wing foreign-policy types was that Powell had a little too much of the diplomat in him to be fully trusted.

As 2001 wore on, however, bringing with it both the war on terror and escalating violence in the Middle East, Powell's emphasis on diplomacy increasingly began to look like it might not be such a bad thing, after all. The New York Times' Bill Keller caught up with Powell in the midst of this transformation. . . .

The night of Oct. 15 found Colin Powell inside the heavily fortified residence of the American ambassador in Islamabad, dining with his improbable new best friend, the president of Pakistan. Just a few months earlier, when the Bush administration was beginning to compose its tableau of friends and foes, a Powell deputy was sent to court India, a democracy and possible counterweight to China, as America's darling in South Asia. Pakistan was passed over as a terrorist-cradling rogue nation. But war changes everything, and Gen. Pervez Musharraf was now our partner against the terrorists in neighboring Afghanistan. This was Powell's first face-to-face meeting with the Pakistani strongman, and he was impressed with what he found. Like Powell himself, Musharraf was a pragmatic military man, brimming with self-assurance, equally at ease talking tactical soldiery or political strategy, a man given to thinking three or four steps ahead.

Powell was in Islamabad to reassure the Pakistanis that the United States would not, as it had in the past, abandon Pakistan once the war was over and to proffer some tangible rewards, including an end to sanctions imposed to punish Pakistan's nuclear testing and help in rescheduling a staggering national debt. This was a gamble for Musharraf, enlisting with America against a viral Islamic hatred incubated, among other places, in Pakistan. The streets were simmering with angry protests. As a precaution against a stray shoulder-fired missile, Powell had ended his 17-hour flight with a lights-out, banking dive into the Islamabad airport. And for security reasons, the dinner was not listed on the schedule handed out to his traveling press entourage.

The Secret Service bodyguards were not the only ones feeling twitchy about the visit. Twice, as the two business-suited generals huddled over their meal, cellphones trilled—first in the pocket of the Pakistani head of intelligence, then in that of the C.I.A. station chief—with news that India was firing artillery in the disputed border province of Kashmir. Now India was feeling jilted. "It's a way of saying, 'What about us?' " said one member of the Islamabad dinner party.

Such is the volatile, expedient new world of American foreign policy in which Colin Powell presides. And for now at least, he does preside, his comforting charisma, his ally-charming skills and his experience of war all placed at a premium by the terror attacks of Sept. 11.

• • •

The campaign against terror has created the kind of crisis-management world in which Powell thrives. Before Sept. 11, Powell was the lonely hope of European allies, Congressional centrists, global business and most of the media commentariat to the left of *The Weekly Standard*, who viewed him as the adult in a mosh pit of moralists and America-firsters. "In the land of the blind, he's the one-eyed king," said a prominent Democrat shortly before the terror attacks. Since the dawn of a common international cause, though, the Bush administration has been sounding more like Colin Powell than like anyone else. The terrorists have, for now, disarmed the lone-super-power ideologues within the Republican Party and created a sense of global common purpose in which trust among competitive nations seems a little more plausible. The way Powell puts it is that the attack on America "hit the reset button" on foreign policy. Tense American relationships with Russia and China and even in the intractable Middle East, he says, now seem more amenable to breakthroughs. He contends that America has not only moved, at long last, beyond the Cold War but has also vaulted past the "post-Cold-War period," that confusing interim search for purpose in a world without a center of gravity.

With the rout of the Taliban from Kabul and other cities and, in the same week, halting steps toward a new strategic bargain with Russia, the new Powell doctrine of diplomatic opportunity seems all the more plausible. Whether it survives the frustrations of imposing stability in Afghanistan— which could mean, among other things, winning a guerrilla war—or the ultimate test of our allies' competing self-interests remains to be seen. You can find many within the administration and outside it who believe that the Powell view is naive or amoral in a dangerous world. But one man who appears to share Powell's fresh sense of opportunity, who talks about the world with the same tone of bright promise, is President Bush.

On Sept. 11, Powell was sitting down to breakfast in Lima with Alejandro Toledo, the president of Peru, when an aide handed him a note saying that a plane had hit the World Trade Center. "Oh, my God," he said to his host. "Something terrible has happened." It would be 10 hours before he could get through to President Bush, who was being ferried around the country by a nervous Secret Service.

Until that point, the conventional wisdom about Powell was reflected in an end-of-summer *Time* magazine cover that asked, "Where Have You Gone, Colin Powell?" The new secretary of state had endured a series of minor humiliations—over North Korea, over the Kyoto Protocol on global warming, over the American peacekeeping commitment in the Balkans. Moreover, he seemed invisible, which in Washington is taken to mean impotent. "We've had our little hiccups," he said a couple of days after that issue of *Time* appeared.

Even by then, however, Powell's influence had been steadily growing. He had negotiated a relatively unacrimonious end to the administration's first international crisis, the collision of an EP-3 spy plane with a Chinese fighter, opening the way for a less prickly relationship with China, which President Bush has now embraced. He had reassured the Europeans that despite the Bush camp's belittling talk of nation-building in Bosnia and Kosovo, the Americans who went in with the allies would not leave without them. Bush had, almost impetuously, abandoned his campaign suspicion of Russia. And despite the administration's scorn for Bill Clinton's personal diplomacy in the Middle East, the president had agreed in a National Security Council meeting, the conclusions of which were later artfully leaked, to reaffirm American support for Palestinian statehood and authorize a more active American role in the region. In all of this, the president was following the instincts of his secretary of state.

By Friday, Sept. 14, when Powell helicoptered to Camp David for dinner with Vice President Cheney, Defense Secretary Rumsfeld and Condoleezza Rice, the national security adviser, crucial preparations for war were already under way. Powell's most trusted deputy, Richard Armitage, had already called in the Pakistani intelligence chief to lay the foundations of a military squeeze on Afghanistan. Armitage, a Vietnam vet with a body-builder's imposing bulk, was once decorated by the government of Pakistan for helping arm Afghan rebels in their insurgency against Soviet control. Now he delivered a seven-point, with-us-or-against-us ultimatum calling on the Pakistanis to close their border with Afghanistan, open their intelligence files and provide access for American forces. The Pakistani diplomat left and returned the next day with Musharraf's unqualified concurrence, and Powell cinched it in a phone call to the Pakistani leader. The bombing was still three weeks away, but the group that gathered at Camp David quickly came to the conclusion that the American response would be military and that it would be careful and methodical.

"There is always the pressure to go back and smack somebody right away," Powell, who likes to quote Thucydides on the military virtue of restraint, told me the following week. But, Powell went on to say, the question was "who that somebody was, one, and how to do it so that you were hitting that someone or some group and not just hitting for the sake of hitting."

Over dinner, the foursome kept the conversation light, but the next morning they were joined by the president, George Tenet, the C.I.A. director, and an array of deputies in a Camp David conference room. For four hours they turned over the options, the risks, how to make the declared war more than a figure of speech. They ran through the Soviet experience in Afghanistan, the genesis of the Taliban, the question of how far to trust Pakistan. They talked about whether the initial phase of the war should extend beyond Al Qaeda to target terrorist groups with popular backing in the Middle East, like Hamas and Hezbollah, and whether it should encompass sponsoring states—Syria, Iran and especially Iraq.

"What was kicked around at Camp David was, You have a lot of other countries in the world that support terrorism," said one participant. "What are we going to do about them? Obviously there's Al Qaeda and there's Afghanistan, but we don't want to send a message that there's good terrorism and bad terrorism. You know, you can't be against Al Qaeda and then support Hezbollah."

Powell pointed out that there was no evidence connecting Iraq to the Sept. 11 attacks. Others said that that was irrelevant, that the administration came to power promising to do more to bring about an end to Saddam Hussein. Powell said the coalition would not hold if the United States targeted Iraq, and without the coalition there could be no shutting off of terrorist finances, no intelligence sharing, no international arrests.

After a lunch break, when Bush asked the cabinet principals to sum up their views of the discussion, there was general agreement that Afghanistan and Al Qaeda would be plenty for the first stage. The next day, back at the White House, the president called in Rice and said that he had made up his mind. Iraq was left for the future.

"Iraq will be sitting there after this campaign is well along," Powell told me a few days later. "Iraq isn't going anywhere. It's in a fairly weakened state. It's doing some things we don't like. We'll continue to contain it. But there really was no need at this point, unless there was really quite a smoking gun, to put Iraq at the top of the list.

"With respect to what is sometimes characterized as taking out Saddam," he added, "I never saw a plan that was going to take him out. It was just

some ideas coming from various quarters about, Let's go bomb." He said
raining bombs on Iraq would be no more effective now than it was when
President Clinton did it in December 1998. "What was the result of the
bombing? He's still there, except you put him back on Page 1. 'Here I am!'
And you've spent a billion dollars. So, we'll take that in stride, in sequence.
He'll be there, unfortunately, a week, a month, two months from now."

For Powell's Republican critics inside and outside the administration,
Iraq remains the nagging test of whether this war should or will be fought
on his terms, and it is a battle postponed rather than resolved. When and
if President Bush becomes convinced that he should attack Iraq, Powell
will hew loyally to the policy, but so far he doesn't see the point.

On the plane back from Asia last month, I asked if he had seen anything
to change his mind about targeting Iraq. He said he had not. I asked about
the mission that James Woolsey, the former director of central intelligence,
had recently undertaken to gather evidence of an Iraqi role in the twin
towers attack. Powell was clearly irritated. Woolsey "wasn't working for
me," he said. "All I know is what I read in the newspapers. And I assume
he's doing something for the Pentagon."

Powell's most vociferous critics trace his reluctance to go after Iraq now
to his role in the Gulf War, when he was chairman of the Joint Chiefs of
Staff. It is, they contend, a continuation of an earlier mistake that Powell
refuses to admit.

It is true that the advice Powell gave the first President Bush after Iraq
invaded Kuwait was consistently cautious. As documented by Michael R.
Gordon and Gen. Bernard E. Trainor in their meticulous account of the war,
"The Generals' War: The Inside Story of the Conflict in the Gulf," Powell
opposed using ship movements to send Saddam a signal of American
resolve, a reluctance some say emboldened the Iraqi leader to move against
Kuwait. (The man who advocated moving ships toward the Persian Gulf to
deter an invasion was Paul Wolfowitz, then under secretary of defense.)
Powell advocated a longer period of economic and political sanctions before
sending troops. He at first wanted the focus to be on defending Saudi Arabia
rather than on liberating Kuwait. Based on what proved to be overgenerous
Pentagon estimates of Iraqi strength, he insisted that the war could be undertaken only with half a million troops. And in the end, after the Iraqi Army
had fled home, he recommended ending the war after five days, although (as
intelligence would later show) half of Saddam's lethal Republican Guard had
escaped with its tanks back into Iraq, where they would help crush Shiite

and Kurdish uprisings and assure Saddam's hold on power. Powell feared that bombarding the retreating Iraqis along the so-called Highway of Death would make America seem brutal, and President Bush agreed.

This record persuades conservatives that Powell was too fainthearted. William Kristol, editor of the conservative *Weekly Standard*, wrote in late September in *The Washington Post* that the first President Bush went to war against Iraq over the resistance of Powell, and he challenged the current president to do likewise.

I put this complaint to former President Bush, who sent back a furious written reply.

"Kristol said Powell opposed the use of force," he wrote. "That is a vicious slander, totally untrue. I valued Colin's opinion that when force was needed we'd use sufficient force to keep our casualties to a bare minimum. . . . That Colin did not want to use force is a grossly unfair, insupportable lie."

As for the contention that Powell persuaded the president to stop short of neutering Saddam Hussein, the former president wrote: "Our mission was to end the aggression and kick Saddam out of Kuwait. My commanders told me, 'Mission accomplished.' I ended the fighting. For the reasons I have often stated, I have no regrets that we avoided changing the mission. I admit that based upon the opinion of all our coalition partners I did feel Saddam would flee Iraq or be killed given the magnitude of his defeat. All of us underestimated Saddam's cruelty and brutality to his own people, which keeps him in office."

Powell himself concedes a little bit of ground. "You can reasonably argue that we should have gone for another day or two," he told me. "We would have destroyed more tanks, we would have killed more people, we would have lost more lives, there would have been more destruction along the Highway of Death. But we weren't going to Baghdad. And so when you read things, as I read in an article not too long ago, that Powell insisted on keeping Saddam Hussein in place in Baghdad, that gets my dander up. It's like I'm some Rasputin figure that was all alone causing all this to happen or not to happen."

Administration officials will tell you that the philosophical differences between Powell and his colleagues are exaggerated. One White House official scoffed at what he called the MTV "Celebrity Death Match" version of policy-making that comes across in news accounts. Rice, whose job is to protect against internecine conflict, insists, "It's actually a very collegial national security team, and it's rare that we even go to the president with some split decisions." It is true that since Sept. 11, differences have been muted, and with the National Security Council meeting often and the cabinet principals gathering every evening, Bush's advisers seem to have grown quite comfortable with one another.

But while the division has been bridged for now, relegated to the sniping of deputies and surrogates in the press, it is a real fault line that runs through the administration, and it could open again.

On one side is a neoconservative school that flowered in President Reagan's first term, before he fell in love with arms control. Those in this group tend to see the world in darker tones. They are suspicious of treaties and alliances that constrain American power and generally unsentimental about humanitarian interventions where explicit American interests are not at stake. But they harbor a pronounced sense of America's moral obligations, reflected most powerfully in a devotion to beleaguered democracies like Israel and Taiwan (and for some of them during previous administrations, Bosnia). This group includes Defense Secretary Rumsfeld and his deputy, Paul Wolfowitz—who half-joked around the time he accepted the job that the reason he enlisted in the new administration was to keep an eye on Powell—and a number of outside advisers they have assembled at the Pentagon. The group includes Vice President Cheney, who has been an important sponsor of Powell but who as defense secretary during the gulf war sometimes jousted with Powell over what he saw as the general's foot-dragging. Rice, while she has settled rather successfully into the national security adviser role of honest policy broker, is at heart more impatient with make-nice diplomacy than Powell.

The second group reflects a more traditional Republican foreign policy of the kind that prevailed under the first President Bush—comfortable with alliances, treaties and international institutions, less assertive in the promotion of American values abroad, more Realpolitik in its judgments, more "sandpapered" in its language, as one aide put it. Powell is the standard-bearer for this camp, which includes most of the upper ranks of the State Department and some sympathizers in the White House, along with an outside chorus that notably includes the president's father.

Since Sept. 11, any frictions have tended to occur at the margins of policy, and they have been played out through deputies putting their spin into briefing papers and whispering to sympathizers in the press. Powell says that the cabinet is "in full accord" on the conduct of the antiterror campaign. He is particularly sensitive about any suggestion that he imposes himself in the

Pentagon's business; aides say that he confines his advice to occasions when the president or vice president ask for it. Powell slapped down as "absolute nonsense" reports by Rumsfeld sympathizers in the press that he had dictated a go-slow approach to the early bombing in Afghanistan. "I know enough not to do something I used to do for a living when there's somebody else better qualified than me to now do it," he told me last week.

Powell himself has not spent all those years in the executive branch without becoming adept at close bureaucratic combat. His in-fighting style is patient and discreet. He gives his interviews on the record, so he cannot be accused of badmouthing rivals, except implicitly. (Asked about reports of some jostling with Rice for influence, Powell firmly denied it, then added that he regarded the national security adviser "like a daughter," which was probably not meant to sound condescending but left no doubt about who was the alpha dog.) Powell has plenty of loyalists in the government and Congress who are willing to get more personal. A recent flurry of press reports that characterized Wolfowitz, the Pentagon deputy, as a right-wing zealot—shrewdly not aiming at Rumsfeld himself—was helped along by Powell supporters in the administration and on Capitol Hill.

Powell is careful not to undercut a presidential decision, but he is willing to put forward spin on a policy before the president has formally staked a position. When the first Bush administration was wrestling with the question of whether to intervene in Bosnia, Powell gave an impassioned interview to this newspaper on the folly of intervention, which those who favored air strikes viewed as bordering on insubordination. Last month in Shanghai, he gave a speech to business leaders that was, by several degrees, more optimistic about the benign direction of China's leadership than President Bush has been.

Those who have worked with him say that Powell is usually the best-prepared person in any meeting and has anticipated the arguments several steps out. He can draw on experience of every war since Vietnam. There are seven seats on the National Security Council, including the president and vice president; Powell has held three of them.

"He's a smart linear thinker, with iron self-control, tremendous pride and self-confidence, great leadership skills, great presentational skills, limited analytical skills and a commanding presence," said a diplomat who has sparred with Powell. "It's an amazing package."

Plus, there is the aura. The decorated warrior. The intimate of, now, four presidents. The man many felt could become the first African-American president. His story of accomplishment is the subject of more than 20 books, including his own best-selling memoir. None of this is likely to awe men of comparable experience, like Cheney and Rumsfeld, but it cannot fail to impress a president with none of those credentials.

• • •

"Still got your voice, Andrea?"

A dozen reporters dragged themselves onto the State Department plane home from Shanghai to find Powell presiding over the press seats, tending his entourage. Andrea Koppel, the ailing CNN correspondent, nodded that she was still fit to file.

"That's too bad," Powell said, smiling, and ducked forward into his cabin. He would be back after a few hours' sleep, changed into his traveling uniform of crisp white T-shirt and blue-and-green windbreaker, for a stand-up briefing that would range from the details of China's nuclear deterrent to developments in Israel, managing the seasoned briefer's trick of breaking no news while not sounding canned.

For a man who decided, after a long and public introspection in 1995, that he did not have the stomach for campaign politics, Powell is nimble at the parts of his job that resemble campaign politics—the flattering wisecrack, the command of detail, the much-repeated answer that sounds fresh and the ability to be alert when everyone else is fall-down tired.

All of this has served him during the accelerated diplomacy of assembling a war coalition, which is a little like playing chess on 20 boards at once against challengers with wildly differing opening gambits. There are the Europeans, who came to the antiterror campaign as volunteers and require consulting but no persuading. One thing the Europeans want from Powell, though, is assurance that the United States is doing what it can to defuse the Israeli-Palestinian conflict, and Powell calls regularly with reports on his conversations with Prime Minister Sharon, Foreign Minister Peres and Yasir Arafat. He does the same with Saudi Arabia, one of the few countries where Powell's contacts from the Gulf War are still in power. Japan is another story. The Japanese are being courted to help in the reconstruction of Afghanistan after the war, but they also want to be talked to about the military aspects because they see themselves emerging as more than just a one-dimensional economic power. Powell obliges.

He has met the Russian foreign minister, Igor Ivanov, 13 times and speaks with him routinely to discuss counterterrorism and the full menu of issues. More delicately, using his policy-planning deputy, Richard N. Haass, and working through multilateral committees, Powell has tried to draw Iran into the antiterrorism effort. The Iranians have been helpful in the distribution of food to refugees and have agreed to provide search-and-rescue help if American warplanes run into serious trouble in Afghanistan. The United States wants them to use their influence to help assemble a broad alternative government in Afghanistan.

To support him in all of this, Powell has brought back to life a neglected and demoralized instrument: the State Department. Under previous administrations, the State Department has watched its power be siphoned off to political operatives in the White House and places like the Treasury Department, its network of trained diplomats eroded, its facilities starved and mismanaged. From Powell's first day at the State Department, his reliance on the career Foreign Service has been a rejuvenating tonic to an institution that had felt marginalized. Powell has filled many of his key assistant-secretary jobs, the people who oversee the six regions of the globe, with career Foreign Service officers, to whom he has delegated the kind of authority a general gives to his division commanders. Whether by design or not (Powell's people insist not), this has had the additional effect of assuring that those jobs would not go to White House political appointees whose views were to the right of his own.

The business of management rarely engages secretaries of state, but it is an obsession in the modern American military—developing and motivating talent, delegating authority while holding subordinates to account, dispensing praise and trust in exchange for loyalty and hard work, tending to morale. One retired general who worked closely with Powell recalled his arrival as chairman of the Joint Chiefs of Staff. He inherited a "Joint Staff" of two-star and three-star generals assigned by—and loyal to—the individual services. They reported to him through a tightknit outfit called the Chairman's Staff Group, which filtered and homogenized the conflicting advice of Air Force and Army. His first day on the job, Powell called in the Staff Group and said: "Here's the drill: You're out of it." Thereafter, he took his information directly from the bright officers assigned by the services, bolstering their loyalty to him and assuring a flow of unvarnished information.

State Department insiders say that Powell operates much the same way with dissenters inside his department. A notable example is John Bolton, the under secretary of state for arms control and international security, who is an ardent hawk whose appointment Cheney lobbied for. Rather than isolate Bolton, whose views on Russia and arms treaties are considerably to the right of his own, Powell uses the under secretary to test and sharpen his own thinking.

"Washington players can be divided into those who know how to work the institution and those who don't," said the retired general. "Madeleine Albright didn't. Rumsfeld, in his first months, didn't. Powell plays the institution like a damn orchestra."

The restoration of the State Department has, of course, only elevated the alarm of hawks, who see the career Foreign Service as a bastion of over-polite cookie-pushers and status-quo pragmatists. For all his towering reputation and managerial gifts, Powell started in his job with two serious operational handicaps. He was not an intimate of the new president, and he was viewed with mistrust by the unilateralists who seemed to have custody of the unschooled president's worldview.

New presidencies often start out as extensions of the campaign war room, driven by the glib convictions of the debate briefing book and powered by the loyalties tested in the heat of political combat. Compared, for example, with Condoleezza Rice, who had been the candidate's foreign-policy tutor and spent her weekends grafted to the president's side, or to Dick Cheney, Powell had not really been there. Powell spent the campaign year giving speeches at $75,000 apiece, promoting his program for poor kids, America's Promise, and savoring a life beyond his official duties—a wife he reveres, a hobbyist's devotion to tinkering with old Volvos, a reading list that extends beyond the daily intelligence digest. His most conspicuous role in the Bush campaign had been a speech at the Republican convention in Philadelphia, in which he scolded the party for being insensitive to the condition of minorities. The speech played well at a gathering designed as a showcase of inclusiveness, but it compounded the doubts of party zealots that Powell was a Republican in his soul.

• • •

Powell's temperance in affairs of state matches an instinctive caution honed in a meteoric military career that depended heavily on the patronage of admiring, mostly Republican, civilians. He has never been a boat-rocker, although along the way he has occupied some boats that wanted rocking. As military assistant to Reagan's defense secretary, Caspar Weinberger, for example, he acquiesced in a White House scheme to sell missiles to Iran in the hope of liberating American hostages; his conduct brought him a mild rebuke from the independent counsel—and a promotion.

His old mentor Weinberger sums up Powell this way: "Colin is quintessentially a good soldier. He does his duty and carries out orders."

Like many soldiers of his generation, Powell took from Vietnam, along with two wounds and a chestful of decorations, a disillusioning lesson in the politics of war, a determination not to agree to what he called "half-hearted warfare for half-baked reasons." In 1984, when he was Weinberger's military aide, he was impressed by a speech the defense secretary gave articulating a series of tests a commander in chief should apply before using military force. During the Balkan conflict, when Powell was chairman of the Joint Chiefs of Staff, a reporter for this newspaper compiled these guidelines and labeled them the "Powell Doctrine." In brief, it calls for the use of force to be clearly synchronized with political ends and for force to be applied decisively. (Powell has used the word "overwhelming," though he now disavows it.) The doctrine does not specify that wars should be quick, low-casualty and popular, but it certainly smiles on such wars. Powell says that he has always regarded his rules as guidelines, not dogma—a safeguard against wars, like Vietnam, that demoralize the country and damage American prestige. He argues that the people he calls "Kmart parents"—working-class Americans who tend to be the parents of soldiers—should understand why their children are being put at risk and should never doubt that the country will back them to the hilt.

His rules for the application of force have been maligned by more interventionist critics, liberal and conservative, as an excuse for inaction.

"He is exceedingly cautious," said an official who, like everyone with aspirations of influence, refused to criticize Powell for the record. "Cautious to the point where he will reject audacious options, even well-considered ones." When asked about this, Powell retorted: "Caution is not a vice. I think it's a virtue. I know when to act. And if caution is such a terrible vice, then I'm sure the various people I've worked for over the years probably would not have hired me."

The most controversial application of the Powell Doctrine was in Bosnia, where Powell's aversion to committing American force was outspoken and adamant, verging on coldhearted. Powell worried at each step that ostensibly limited American involvement—airdrops of food and medicine for Bosnian Muslims, air strikes against Serbs—would lead inexorably to a deep and bloody American involvement. He seemed to sense something ordained by history in the war of Muslims and Serbs. He approvingly quoted Bismarck's remark that all the Balkans were not worth the life of one of his soldiers.

Powell's reluctance matched the sentiment in the first Bush White House, where President Bush was running a difficult re-election campaign against a public sense that he was too preoccupied with foreign policy. Powell still had eight months to serve as chairman when President Clinton came to office, fresh from a campaign in which he excoriated Bush for sitting by while Serbs slaughtered Muslims in Bosnia. But the new president's attention was on health care and the economy, and his national security team was haunted by ghosts of the Vietnam entanglement. Madeleine Albright, then the ambassador to the United Nations, and James Woolsey, the C.I.A. director, argued for intervention, but they were outnumbered, and overshadowed by the impressive figure of Powell.

There is a famous encounter between Powell and the Clintonites that gets recounted with different emphasis depending on who is doing the telling. The president's foreign policy advisers were agonizing over Bosnia, Powell arguing as usual that only a large ground force could change the behavior of the Serbs and that it was hard to envision a political goal for which the public would support the risk of American lives.

Those who favored intervention recount with relish Albright's outburst: "What's the point of having this superb military that you're always talking about if we can't use it?"

Supporters of Powell are more likely to recall his reaction, unvoiced but noted in his autobiography: "I thought I would have an aneurysm. American G.I.'s were not toy soldiers to be moved around on some sort of global game board."

But the revealing contribution came from Anthony Lake, the national security adviser, reflecting the disposition of an administration cowed by history: "You know, Madeleine, the kinds of questions Colin is asking about goals are exactly the ones the military never asked during Vietnam."

• • •

As Powell is well aware, the war on terrorism strains his ideal of clear objectives and decisive commitments. The war is unconventional and likely to become more so as the Taliban retreat into the mountains. The broader declared purpose of making the world inhospitable for terrorists is murky and open-ended. But as one administration official put it: "If you deconstruct the so-called doctrine into a set of questions, they are still important questions, and they're the questions Powell will keep asking: What, exactly, is the objective? Have we brought the right resources to bear? What happens next?"

That Powell now seems to be in tune with the president should not be so surprising. Apart from his more ideologically ardent handlers, Bush has always seemed to have an essentially optimistic temperament and an instinctive trust in personal relationships and in the ability of reasonable people to work things out. The issue on which Powell has worked hardest to close a gulf between himself and the president is Bush's apparently devout belief in missile defense. Before the antiterror campaign, the issue of missile defense was the single most important test of how the Bush administration would balance the new primacy of unfettered American self-interest against a pragmatic respect for the rest of the civilized world. The intramural debate on that issue continues, and it is as good a window as you can find into how Powell thinks and how he operates.

In the months of deliberations leading up to Vladimir Putin's inconclusive visit to the president's ranch in Crawford, Tex., Powell was the most forceful voice for a compromise on missile defense that would allow American testing to proceed without demolishing the scaffolding of arms-control agreements. Like many career soldiers, Powell has always been a skeptic about wizard weapons that promise to make warfare antiseptic, simple and safe. He likes his advances in military technology incremental and tested. In his view, civilian leaders who put their faith in smart bombs and high-altitude air power usually end up sending divisions of soldiers to die finishing the job.

Powell's suspicion of missile defense was nourished at its genesis, President Reagan's Strategic Defense Initiative, which the young Pentagon aide watched with a kind of amused horror.

"Reagan, God bless him, was forever talking about this shield and, you know, We're just going to make all offensive weapons useless," Powell recalled, rolling his eyes. Powell saw antimissile technology at the time not as a utopian dream but as a useful way of throwing a scare into the war planners of the Soviet Union. Once U.S. negotiators had placed missile defense on a back burner as part of a deal cutting nuclear arsenals on both sides, Powell was happy to let it revert to a low-priority research project.

Fifteen years later, Powell says that the technology is more plausible and well worth advanced testing. What he has in mind is not a missile-tight umbrella of defenses in space, but sea-based rockets that might intercept a nuclear missile soon after launch and installations on American territory that might stop a missile as it descends. Powell invariably refers to "limited" missile defense, a phrase the president has now adopted. Powell is wary, though, of making missile defense the tail that wags the dog of foreign policy.

"One can argue whether you should give it this amount of attention, this amount of passion, and give it the foremost position on your agenda," Powell told me in September. If the United States can calculate a way around the A.B.M. treaty, which prohibits advanced testing, then "it's just another defense program that will go into a more routine level of development without the kind of attention it's now getting."

The argument within the administration has focused on exactly how to get around the A.B.M. treaty constraints. Rice and others at the Pentagon and in the White House wanted to drop the A.B.M. treaty altogether as a demonstration that America accepts no artificial limits on its national interest. They have argued that amending the treaty would entail a time-consuming ratification battle in the Senate and that even something less than a formal amendment—a Russian side letter promising not to challenge certain tests—would give the Russians too much leverage.

Powell's first preference is for an amendment to the treaty, which would assure the full blessing of Congress and avoid controversy he said the president didn't need. Failing that, he said he would be content with a less-formal understanding that certain specific tests were O.K.—an agreement the Russians have so far balked at providing. The important thing, he said, was to avoid abandoning the treaty altogether, with the probable high price in Russian, European and Congressional good will. He argued that a concession to the Russians on the formalities of the A.B.M. treaty would be more than repaid in other ways—their acquiescence in the expansion of NATO, the continued reform of their economy and, of course, their cooperation in the war against terror.

Powell is sympathetic to their anxieties.

"The one thing that scares them—and I'd be scared if I were them, and we've got to figure out a way to deal with this: 'Powell, we love you like a brother. We don't care what the magazines in Washington say, we think you're great. But you'll be gone one day. Putin will be gone. Bush will be gone. Igor will be gone. And we will have made some kind of a deal now, and, great, it's a limited defense. Well, one day another president comes in, and he decides: "I'll replicate it. I'll clone it. I'll geneticize it." And it goes from being a limited defense to: POW! Reagan's back. How do you persuade us that's not going to happen? We can't do this on the basis of personal relations. It has to be on the basis of our national interest over time.' " Which means, Powell said, "You codify it somehow.

"A good argument you get on the other side, probably from Condi, is:

'Let's just do what we think is right. We really don't have to be bound up in the legal documents like we used to be with the Soviet Union.' We will see."

Powell paused and pursed his lips in a grim smile. Referring to the Russians, he said: "You could just say, 'The heck with you.' I would rather not."

Won't the Russians get over it if we decide to go it alone?

"They may get over it," he replied. "But they also will be under no constraints as to what they might do in the future."

Given Powell's stature—Senator John McCain calls him "the most popular person in America"—and the uncertain state of the vice president's health, there's considerable curiosity about whether Powell would ever revisit the question of higher office. What if, for example, Cheney's heart troubles were to recur and President Bush invited Powell to become vice president—meaning a campaign role in 2004 and considerable pressure to run for president in 2008, when he would be 71?

I asked this question of everyone I interviewed who was close to Powell, and the reaction was almost universally dismissive. The attacks of Sept. 11 have certainly not diminished the powerful fears of his wife, Alma, that as a candidate Powell would be a target for every kind of madman. And Powell seems to have come to terms with his own visceral reluctance.

"Absolutely not," said Richard Armitage, probably Powell's closest friend in government. "He's slept soundly from the time he made the decision on it. He said at the time: 'On mornings when I woke up and thought, I'm going to run, I felt terrible, it was a terrible day. On mornings I got up and said, I'm not going to, I had a wonderful day. And I finally came to realize, with all these people telling me, You have to run, they were looking for a shortcut, they wanted someone on a white horse. That's not the way our system works.' "

Powell's son, Michael, said it was "very, very doubtful" that his father would revisit the question, having "resolved it in a pretty fundamental way."

"But, and I guess this is an important but, he does have a sort of consummate commitment and love of service and serving the country," he continued. "In the extreme, if the country was at war, if there were the kind of challenges with which he could come to grips, if there was some reason he was the right person for the right time—I do think it would have to be some element that rose to that level in his mind to entice him to do it." That was the week before we declared ourselves at war.

If Powell wants a larger job, though, he need only stay put. Because now, with the rapid advances of anti-Taliban forces in Afghanistan, it gets really complicated.

In a phone conversation last week, with the Taliban collapsing, Powell cited his own scripture: "By Powell Doctrine standards, you keep your eye on the political objective, which is Osama bin Laden and the Al Qaeda network."

But among the things Powell has committed America's diplomats to do, even before the military work is fully accomplished: help assemble a Muslim-led peacekeeping force in Afghanistan and then a reasonably stable, polyglot government without precedent; repay and reassure the government of Pakistan; try to defuse the explosive border dispute in Kashmir; and calculate a new relationship with the highly problematic government of Iran. He also appears set to inject himself, and possibly President Bush, in the cynics' nest of what America now freely calls Palestine. Powell will probably be spending a lot more time with yet another longtime coddler of terrorists, Yasir Arafat, and with yet another problematic general, Ariel Sharon.

And the minute the Afghan phase of the war on terror seems near an end, he may again have his hands full maintaining that other troublesome coalition, the Bush administration.

New Weapon for a New World Order
Richard Perle

American Enterprise Magazine | April/May 2001

Did the 9/11 attacks strengthen or weaken the rationale for missile defense? Opponents of the proposed scheme point out that missile defense will never stop a terrorist bomb on the ground, while its advocates point out that September 11 was yet another reminder of our own vulnerability, and that we need missile defense now more than ever.

While such debates can make for entertaining cocktail party conversation, there are people who get paid to think about this sort of thing. One of them is Richard Perle, former Assistant Secretary of Defense for International Security Policy under

Ronald Reagan. In this essay, Perle lays out the case for missile defense. As of this writing, by the way, his proposed scenario for India and Pakistan suddenly looks a lot less hypothetical. . . .

The question is not *whether* a ballistic missile with a nuclear or chemical or biological warhead capable of killing hundreds of thousands of Americans will wind up in the hands of a hostile power. The question is *when*.

Pinpointing the exact date is a game played by intelligence agencies, rather like an office pool on the outcome of the Super Bowl. In the Super Bowl, though, you at least know who the players are. When it comes to the acquisition of a ballistic missile or a nuclear warhead, there is no sure way of telling.

That is why it is so urgent we begin now to build a system capable of intercepting the missile that we know is coming. The argument for getting on with it is overwhelming. The arguments against are unconvincing—and drawn mostly from ideas that developed during the Cold War but have been rendered irrelevant by its end.

The best argument in favor of building a missile defense system is a moral one: It will save lives, in large numbers, in other countries as well as our own. It will discourage the proliferation of missiles and warheads of mass destruction. It will make the world stabler and safer.

Consider the following scenario, for example. Imagine a sharp rise in tension between traditional adversaries India and Pakistan, both of which have nuclear weapons and ballistic missiles. Suppose the United States Navy could dispatch an Aegis cruiser to the region with instructions to intercept any ballistic missile fired by either side. Such a capability in American hands would be highly stabilizing, discouraging hair-trigger missile attacks, reducing the likelihood of conflict breaking out in the first place, reassuring both sides.

Nations like Iran, Iraq, and North Korea are trying to acquire long-range missiles. They believe that possessing even a single missile will catapult them into a select class of powers, gaining great leverage because they will be capable of inflicting massive damage on the United States or its friends and allies. And given time and money, these countries can reasonably hope to possess a single missile, or even several.

But suppose we constructed a defense that could intercept all the warheads and decoys carried by 100 or 200 enemy missiles. A Saddam Hussein in Iraq or a Kim Jong Il in North Korea would lose any confidence he could land a missile on New York or Chicago or an allied capital. The relatively easy task of acquiring a missile or two would become the impossible burden of acquiring hundreds.

In that case, even a determined adversary is likely to throw up his hands and conclude that enhancing his power with nuclear long-range missiles is simply too hard. Imagine a meeting of Saddam Hussein with his military advisors. The general in charge of Iraq's armored force pleads for money to buy new tanks and spare parts for old ones, while the general in charge of missile development requests billions of dollars for construction and testing of a new missile. If the United States has the ability to defend itself and its allies against 100 such missiles, how does the general in charge of the missile program answer Saddam's question, "What good is a $10 billion missile if the Americans can knock it down?"

In short, the best way to protect against missile dangers is to discourage our adversaries from investing in the missiles in the first place. There can be no more powerful disincentive than to have a shield that guarantees their hugely expensive programs will fail. It is that shield, based on our most advanced technology, that will protect America best—not the flotsam of the 1972 Anti-Ballistic Missile Treaty to which the opponents of missile defense cling like shipwrecked sailors.

Some Americans still treat the ABM Treaty with reverence. It remains a primary obstacle to our going forward with missile defense, so a short history lesson is needed to explain why the treaty is hopelessly obsolete.

Cold War nuclear theology held that if one side were to deploy a defense against ballistic missiles, the other side would simply build more missiles in numbers sufficient to overwhelm the defense. Thus the specter of an arms race, often described as an "ever upward spiral," became a central theme in foreign offices and ministries of defense around the world.

So, in 1972 the United States and the Soviet Union signed a treaty banning the deployment of national missile defenses. Reflecting the logic of the Cold War, the ABM Treaty sought to assure each side that the other was vulnerable to a retaliatory missile attack. Given the deep political, ideological, and military divisions between the superpowers at that time, the notion gained currency that vulnerability to a missile attack with many nuclear weapons was a good thing. This "Mutual Assured Destruction" would keep anyone from attacking and thus make us safe.

Though it prohibits the deployment of a national missile defense, the ABM Treaty does allow certain research short of deployment, as well as the actual deployment of no more than 100 interceptor missiles at a single location in each country. The Russians long ago built such a system around Moscow, which they maintain today. The United States, which abandoned its own fledgling system after the 1972 treaty, has none.

In April 1983, President Reagan announced a new program of research and development to determine whether the United States could build an effective defense against ballistic missiles. The initiative was vehemently opposed by the Soviet Union, by many American intellectuals, and by anxious Europeans. Following the 1983 announcement, a succession of Soviet leaders tried to negotiate further restrictions on the deployment of defensive systems. The most important such negotiation took place in Iceland in 1986 at a summit meeting between President Reagan and Communist Party Secretary Mikhail Gorbachev. The Reykjavik summit ended when President Reagan refused to accept Soviet proposals to confine further development of missile defenses to the laboratory, a technological straitjacket which would have throttled any serious defense in its infancy.

Because we cling to an obsolete treaty with a nation that no longer exists, the United States stands naked today before its enemies, unable to intercept even a single ballistic missile aimed, by accident or design, at our territory. Many Americans are shocked to learn that this condition of abject vulnerability is the freely chosen policy of the government of the United States and widely insisted upon by America's allies.

Frozen in the Cold War like a fly in amber, the Clinton administration's policies were based on the outdated idea that our exposure to attack by ballistic missiles actually made us safer. Clintonites argued the vulnerability that developed during the Cold War should become a permanent feature of American policy, enshrined in a trivially modified—and thereby reinvigorated—ABM Treaty.

Under political pressure in the last election year not to cede the issue of missile defense to the Republicans, President Clinton toyed with deployment of a manifestly inadequate system in Alaska that could not protect all of the U.S. or any of our allies. It was a system designed more to remain within the confines of the ABM Treaty than to actually defend the country. Clinton chose to develop a system so modest and ineffective as to be useless for all but political purposes.

Mired in Cold War thinking, the Clinton administration argued that a technologically serious defense, even if limited, would precipitate an arms race. The administration actually assured the Russians in meetings that even if the U.S. built an effective defense in Alaska, Russia would still be able to incinerate the United States at any time. It is hard to imagine a mind-set more reflective of the Cold War than that.

The idea that the ABM Treaty is a cornerstone of stability is especially popular among America's European allies. But it seems fair to ask: How can a treaty that was the cornerstone of stability in 1972 remain our foundation in the year 2001? After all, there is almost nothing in common between the geopolitical situation in the middle of the Cold War and the situation today. Former Secretary of State Henry Kissinger, who negotiated the ABM Treaty, has argued convincingly that it no longer serves American interests. I think that argument can be broadened to include Western interests generally.

Some Europeans have claimed that Europe could become a target of convenience if an American missile defense left potential adversaries unable to attack the U.S. directly. In this scenario, a Saddam Hussein or a Kim Jong Il might think, "If I can't destroy New York, I'll just have to destroy Berlin or Paris instead." I suppose one can't rule out such a development, though it surely is not high on the list of things French President Jacques Chirac or German Chancellor Gerhard Schroeder ought to be worrying about.

The idea, though, gives rise to several thoughts. First, this bizarre concern shows that the Europeans recognize there may indeed be a threat from ballistic missiles in the hands of unpredictable, vindictive, malicious leaders. After hearing any number of learned Europeans tell us that there is no threat, or that we are overstating it, this is a welcome acknowledgment. Second, any missile defense we plan can and should cover our European allies. I believe the Bush administration will think in those terms, even if the Clinton administration did not.

In any case, what are the Europeans expecting of us? Do they think their concerns will have America responding, "Oh, how silly of us to think we should defend ourselves. If you're worried that could put you in harm's way, we'll just drop the whole idea and remain vulnerable. We certainly would not want our defense to cause you any concern."

Consider: with no missile defense, even one incoming warhead could do catastrophic harm to Los Angeles or Washington or New York. A handful would mean destruction beyond imagination. Now, suppose we were to deploy a defense capable of countering not one or a handful, but a few hundred incoming warheads. With such a defense, we might no longer be vulnerable to such nuclear powers as, say, Great Britain or France, which have their own deterrent forces. Would the British then feel compelled to build more nuclear weapons to overpower our defense?

Of course not. Why not? *Because they don't regard the United States as an enemy.* They don't fear an American attack. (Actually the French do fear an attack but (a) it comes from Hollywood and not the U.S. military, (b) it is truly devastating, and (c) while Chirac may think our anti-missile system won't work, I know his defense against American culture will fail.) In other words, it is the political context, not the weapons themselves, that determines whether, and to what extent, any particular military capability is threatening.

Now that the Cold War is over, should Russia regard us as an enemy? We are more likely to send Mr. Putin a check than a barrage of missiles with nuclear warheads. We have sought in countless ways to work with, not against, the Russians. We have muted our criticism—wrongly in my view—of Russia's outrageous assault on civilians in Chechnya. It is unimaginable that we would launch thousands of nuclear weapons against Russia and hope to benefit thereby. And that would be true even if we had a defense that could knock down every missile that might be launched in retaliation.

Would it make sense for Mr. Putin to respond to an American defense against North Korea or Saddam Hussein by building more missiles? Is the Russian economy in a condition where such a vast investment in new weapons would benefit his country? And what about China? We recently sent them an invitation into the world trading system. Should they fear an American missile attack? Or regard an American defense as a threat to China? And even if they did think in these terms, should we remain vulnerable to all the world just to reassure them?

Sometimes we hear that perceptions, not reality, are what counts: If the Russians or the Chinese perceive the United States as a threat and therefore regard any anti-missile system we may build as a danger, shouldn't the U.S. stand down?

This seems a particularly unwise line of argument. In psychiatry it would lead to humoring paranoids by accepting their paranoia and acting to accommodate baseless fears. In science it would mean the abandonment of rigor and discipline, pretending instead of proving. And in international politics it would mean nurturing rather than finding ways to correct false, dangerous, and even self-fulfilling ideas.

The final argument in favor of ballistic missile defense is an ethical one, and the most compelling: During the great clash of the Cold War, it may have been defensible to threaten to kill millions of innocents with nuclear weapons in order to deter massive Soviet attacks on the West. But it is not morally defensible now to say we will kill, say, tens of thousands of innocent men and women in Afghanistan if Osama bin Laden launches a single rather crude missile at Naples. It is now terrorists and tyrants who threaten us, not empires, and we must therefore have more selective and sophisticated ways of defending ourselves.

The Cold War is over, but we will not realize the full benefit of its passing until everyone involved behaves accordingly—abandoning the fears and apprehensions of half a century of conflict, and the outdated ideas about security that flowed from that long, dark struggle.

Clinging to the notion that the security of others is diminished if the United States is protected against missile attack only perpetuates the anxiety of the Cold War. And that is a climate we must transcend now—so that we may protect ourselves and our allies against the real threats we face today.

Dump the ABM Treaty
Jeane Kirkpatrick

American Enterprise Magazine | April/May 2001

One of the big knocks against missile defense is that it would require abandoning the 1972 Anti-Ballistic Missile (ABM Treaty). In the ABM treaty, the Soviet Union and the U.S. each officially bought into the concept "mutually assured destruction": Neither country would dare launch a first-strike nuclear attack, because they would inevitably suffer an equally devasting response.

Here another old Reagan hand, former U.N. ambassador Jeane Kirkpatrick, explains why giving the ABM Treaty the boot is actually a terrific idea. . . .

What George Washington called our "blessed location" between two vast oceans can no longer protect America from weapons of mass destruction. Contemporary missile technology is evaporating those oceans. And our failure to develop a defense in response leaves Americans vulnerable to a degree that we have never been vulnerable in the entire life of our nation.

Too many in Congress and among allies abroad are wedded to an "arms control" approach to this threat. They are more concerned with preserving paper barriers like the Anti-Ballistic Missile Treaty than with reliably protecting millions of American men, women, and children. Their strategy does not work.

For example, we hear the Nuclear Non-Proliferation Treaty (NPT) praised, even though it has actually helped spread the technology needed to produce nuclear weapons. Under the treaty's terms, countries like Iran gained the right to assistance in developing their (supposedly peaceful) nuclear capacities from other signatories like Russia. Iraq was actually on the governing board of the International Atomic Energy Agency—charged with ensuring compliance with the NPT—at the same time it violated promises not to develop nuclear weapons. In short, a treaty intended to halt nuclear proliferation has been the principal source of that proliferation.

If treaties and diplomatic control regimes actually worked, Iraq, North Korea, India, and Pakistan would not have bombs today. But they do. Nor have countries like Iraq been prevented by various treaties and conventions from developing and using chemical weapons. What happens when a nation violates a weapons treaty? Little or nothing. A country attacked by the resulting weapons, however, will experience devastation.

The Anti-Ballistic Missile Treaty has not, despite its defenders' claims, stabilized international relations. The country with which we signed the ABM Treaty no longer exists, and when it did exist it violated the treaty—as Soviet Foreign Minister Edouard Schevardnadze admitted soon after the Cold War ended. Today, Russia retains a huge arsenal of weapons of mass destruction and is much less stable than we would prefer.

Meanwhile, China is dramatically increasing the reach and accuracy of her missiles. Her leaders are pushing for preservation of the ABM Treaty—paying lip service to "strategic stability"—while simultaneously using their new power to threaten Japan, Taiwan, the Philippines, and the U.S. The Chinese are also aiding the spread of nuclear and missile technology to Pakistan, Iran, and North Korea.

Meanwhile, the number of other countries with nuclear weapons and the missiles to deliver them is increasing alarmingly. In 1998 the bipartisan Rumsfeld Commission concluded that any of several small anti-American nations may, if they choose, "be able to inflict major damage on the U.S. within about five years of a decision to acquire such a capability." Worse, "during several of those years the U.S. might not be aware that such a decision had been made."

The archaic ABM Treaty was ratified during a time when only the United States and the Soviet Union had the capacity to reach the other's territory with ballistic missiles. Whether the treaty contributed to America's security during the Cold War is a question for historians. The question today is whether it contributes to our security now. The answer is a resounding no.

By allowing the ABM Treaty to constrain our ability to defend ourselves, we allow dangerous governments to acquire power they would not otherwise have. The United States should give notice of our intention to withdraw from the treaty and immediately focus on building a missile defense system to protect our most vital interest: our national survival.

Yes, there will be complaints from abroad. Russia clearly has an interest in keeping America vulnerable to its missiles. The Russian military, lacking its former size and power, has chosen to place ICBMs at the center of its national strategy.

The ABM Treaty also serves China's long-term ambition to become the dominant power in East Asia, because a missile defense system developed by the U.S and shared with its Asian allies would neutralize China's ability to blackmail its neighbors. If we do not provide an adequate missile defense for our Asian allies, a regional nuclear arms race may indeed result. Japan, for instance, may feel compelled to develop nuclear weapons to counterbalance those coming in China and North Korea.

The ABM Treaty is without legal standing. Under international and U.S. law, it expired with the Soviet Union's demise in 1991. Yet its restrictions prohibit our scientists from developing the effective, economical system they know how to create. The right of self-defense is undisputed in courts of law and the U.N. Charter. It is time to unleash the creativity of American scientists and allow them to solve the problems of defending the United States, its allies, and world peace generally from potentially grievous harm.

Editor's note: On June 13, 2002, after the required six-month waiting period, the United States formally withdrew from the 1972 ABM Treaty.

American Policy in the Persian Gulf
Henry Kissinger

from *Does America Need a Foreign Policy?*

It's been almost three decades since Henry Kissinger stepped down as U.S. Sec-retary of State, but he remains one of the most formidable foreign-policy minds in the business. When his most recent book, Does America Need a Foreign Policy? *was published last spring, the scuttle-butt surrounding it was that it was aimed prima-rily at an audience of one: Newly elected President George W. Bush, who was notice-ably wet behind the ears where international affairs were concerned.*

The following excerpt concentrates on one of the most volatile corners of the world, the Persian Gulf, including Iraq and Iran. In this region, as elsewhere, Kissinger sees United States policy constrained by a central paradox: The U.S. has never been more powerful—yet out-dated Cold War maxims and the influence of domestic politics raise the prospect of America's "becoming irrelevant to many of the currents affecting and ultimately transforming the global order". . . .

No area of the world confronts American precepts with greater complexi-ties than the Gulf. Wilsonian principles cannot guide America's actions in this region. The rationale for preventing its domination by a hostile power is, from the Wilsonian point of view, a choice among evils; there are no democracies to defend. But the United States—and the other industrial democracies—have a compelling national interest in preventing the region from being dominated by countries whose purposes are inimical to ours. The advanced industrial economies depend on supplies of energy from the Gulf, and a radicalization of the area would have consequences extending from North Africa through Central Asia to India.

But this geopolitical imperative has to be implemented against a back-ground in which the two strongest nations in the Gulf, Iran and Iraq, are hos-tile to the United States and in their conduct toward their neighbors. How does one achieve stability in the Gulf against its two strongest powers simul-taneously without permanent bases and supported only by brittle allies?

Traditional diplomacy would counsel improving relations with either Iraq or Iran so that at least one of them can form part of the balance of power in the region. As these lines are being written, neither option appears very promising. So long as Saddam Hussein remains in power in Iraq, a rapprochement with Baghdad will be perceived throughout the region, probably in the rest of the world, and surely by Saddam as a major American defeat and humiliation. And improved relations with Iran, while desirable in principle, face major internal obstacles in Tehran as the ayatollahs work out their domestic deadlocks.

For the time being, no dramatic initiatives are available to reverse this state of affairs. Watchful waiting, not a favorite American pastime, is required. Challenges to the stability of the Gulf must be firmly rebuffed; any encroachment by Iraq on the existing United Nations framework must be resisted in a manner leaving no doubt that the gradualism of the past decade is over and that challenges will be met decisively.

In that period, it is important to strengthen the relationship with allies whose support in possible confrontations would be crucial. Principal among them is Turkey. Adjoining Iraq, Iran, and the tumultuous Caucasus, its cooperation in any crisis becomes indispensable. There has been too much of a tendency in the United States, and even more so in Europe, to take Turkey for granted, to act as if it could be subordinated to domestic politics without cost and as if Turkish national pride or its special circumstances could be ignored. The industrial democracies—especially Europe and the United States—must remember that crucial elements of their basic national security are at stake. Their preferences regarding Turkey's domestic structure must be balanced against these imperatives.

The same sensibilities should govern our attitudes toward Saudi Arabia and the Gulf states. Their comparative weakness in relation to the two regional giants imposes on them a certain caution which creates a gap between what they recommend publicly and what they hope the United States will carry out. The United States must take care not to compound their insecurity by leaving its commitment uncertain or by excessive intrusion into fragile domestic structures.

With the passage of time, India's role in the region will become more important. There is a certain commonality of interests between India and the United States with respect to stability in the Gulf, especially regarding the spread of fundamentalism in the region. But, as has been pointed out in the previous chapter, India is at least as worried about Saudi and Taliban support for its own dissidents as it is about the security balance in the Gulf. And it is occasionally tempted to play the role of mediator between the United States and the Gulf radicals—a role America will find helpful only if it is coordinated with U.S. long-range strategy. Still, as time passes, the Gulf should play a major role in an increasingly intensive strategic dialogue with India.

Iraq

Iraq became a British mandate after the First World War when the Ottoman Empire in the Middle East was divided up between France and Britain. Created to serve strategic and economic interests, the new multi-ethnic state was governed after independence by a Hashemite dynasty and served as a pillar of British strategy in the Gulf. In 1958, the dynasty was overthrown in the wake of Britain's humiliation in the Suez operation of 1956. The radical nationalist Baath party took over, led by a group of military officers out of which Saddam Hussein emerged as the dominant figure in the 1970s.

Since then, Iraq has been the scourge of its neighbors. In 1980, it invaded Iran, plunging itself into a debilitating ten-year war in the course of which it was gradually thrown on the defensive. The United States had no interest in the outcome other than to prevent the domination of the region by one of the combatants. Iran, because of its greater resources, larger population, and radical fundamentalism, was considered the greater threat. The Reagan administration restored diplomatic and economic relations with Iraq and encouraged America's European allies to supply military equipment to Saddam Hussein. After the conclusion of the war with Iran in 1988, Saddam chose a new target and annexed Kuwait in 1990, triggering a massive American military deployment to the Gulf, followed by a victorious military campaign in 1991.

The end of the 1991 Gulf War brought about yet another demonstration of America's congenital difficulty with translating military success into political coin. Because the United States has traditionally viewed force and power as discrete, separate, and successive phases, it has fought its wars either to unconditional surrender, which obviates the need of establishing a relationship between force and diplomacy, or it has acted as if, after victory, the military element is no longer relevant and diplomats are obliged to take over in a kind of strategic vacuum. This is why the United States stopped military operations in Korea in 1951 as soon as negotiations began and why it halted the bombing in Vietnam in 1968 as an entrance price to negotiations. In each case, the easing of military pressures reduced the incentives that had produced the enemy's willingness to negotiate. Prolonged stalemates and continued casualties were the consequence.

The end game of the Gulf War revealed that the United States had not learned from this history. For it allowed an utterly defeated adversary to escape the full consequences of its debacle. The war aims had been defined too narrowly and too legalistically. The war having started over the Iraqi occupation of Kuwait, American policymakers concluded that, with the liberation of that country, they had achieved both their objective and the limits of the U.N. authorization. They justified this decision by stressing the risk of casualties in going on to Baghdad and the public impact of inflicting casualties after the battle seemed to be won. They remembered the stalemates in Korea and Vietnam but not the causes of them.

The George H. W. Bush administration, as its predecessors, had made a case for its course of action. The highest officials of the U.S. government had testified before Congress and assured the international community that America's sole objective was the liberation of Kuwait. With that objective accomplished or exceeded, domestic or international support for continuing the war was believed to be in danger of eroding.

Fear of the disintegration of Iraq was another justification for ending the war quickly. A Shiite rebellion had broken out in Basra and might have produced an Iran-leaning republic. In the long term, Iran was considered the ultimate danger in the Gulf. Also it was feared that an independent Kurd republic in the north of Iraq might disquiet Turkey and undermine its commitment to support American policy in the Gulf. Finally, it was expected that the impact of defeat and the return home of tens of thousands of Iraqi prisoners of war would lead to the overthrow of Saddam.

These arguments, plausible as they seemed, underestimated Saddam's staying power and its effect on America's position in the Gulf. So long as Saddam remained in office, Iraq could not be part of any effort to achieve an equilibrium in the region. Too weak to balance Iran, too strong for the safety of its Gulf neighbors, too hostile to the United States, Iraq would turn into a permanent wild card. Nor were the military options adequately defined. The choice was not marching on to Baghdad or ending the war; the best course would have been to continue the destruction of the elite Iraqi units—the Republican Guards—which were, and remain, the foundation of Saddam's rule. Had this strategy been followed, it is probable that the Iraqi army would have removed Saddam. While his successor would have been no great advertisement for democracy, the symbolic effect of Saddam's removal would have been considerable, and the victorious allies could have begun restoring Iraq to a regional system.

The argument that continuing the war another week would have outrun public and international support must be weighed against the scale of respect President Bush had garnered with the victory his leadership had made possible. The Arab leaders most immediately affected, especially in Saudi Arabia, subsequently claimed that they would have preferred to go on until Saddam was removed from power.

The attempt to calibrate the extent of Iraq's defeat created a long-term political dilemma. United Nations Security Council Resolution 687 established a cease-fire; its disarmament provisions could be enforced only by intrusive international supervision, while the rapid withdrawal of American forces progressively eliminated the credibility of a threat to reintervene. Saddam seized the opportunity and has since tenaciously restored his position and that of a radical Iraq.

The Clinton administration accelerated this deterioration. When Saddam remained in office after the Gulf War, the United States was left with three policy options: (1) to reconcile with a hopefully chastened Saddam; (2) to keep Saddam "in his box" by obliging him to fulfill the terms of Resolution 687; (3) to make it a national policy to overthrow him.

The Clinton administration pursued all three options simultaneously and achieved none of them. Once Saddam survived the Gulf War, his conduct reinforced the fears of his neighbors. He systematically undermined the provisions of the cease-fire that had ended the Gulf War. In 1996, he overthrew the autonomous institutions established under American aegis for the Kurdish areas. Hundreds were killed, and at least three thousand individuals associated with the United States were exiled. Starting in November 1997, Saddam methodically sabotaged the U.N. inspection system meant to monitor Iraq's programs for building weapons of mass destruction. The Clinton administration repeatedly threatened to use force and recoiled each time, enabling Saddam to dismantle the U.N. inspection system. When the United States finally used force for four nights in December 1998, it was a threadbare camouflage for giving up on inspections altogether.

With the inspection system dismantled, Saddam turned to undermining the economic sanctions set up to reinforce the inspection system that were supposed to remain in place until the certification of the demolition of all weapons of mass destruction and the means to produce them. Three months after Iraq over threw the cease-fire arrangements in the Kurdish area, the United States, in December 1996, went along with a United Nations-sponsored program which allowed Iraq to sell $2 billion worth of oil annually for the purchase of food and medicines. The rationale was to "isolate" Saddam by separating enforcement of the military provisions from the well-being of the population. The idea that strengthening Saddam's domestic position would ultimately weaken him showed little grasp of Gulf realities. Since then, the so-called oil-for-food program was increased to $6 billion annually and now has no limit. Thus, in the year 2000, Saddam exported $16 billion in crude—roughly the same as Iraq's annual earnings before the Gulf War. Of course, money being fungible, the resources thus freed can be used for the purchase of far more dangerous materials.

The hesitant American response to all these challenges was motivated by two psychological legacies of the Vietnam protest: the enormous reluctance to use power, and the insistence on justifying any threat of force by enlisting the widest multilateral backing. Thus, in response to an alleged Iraqi plot against former President Bush's life on a visit to Kuwait in 1993, Clinton ordered a few cruise missiles fired into a single building that the Pentagon reassuringly announced had been unoccupied. In 1996, when Saddam crushed the American-sponsored Kurdish forces, the Clinton administration responded with cruise missiles against radar stations situated hundreds of miles to the south. And, as noted, a gesture of four nights of inconsequential bombing signaled American acquiescence in the collapse of the U.N. inspection regime in December 1998. Throughout this period, the Clinton administration also had a tendency to take at face value statements by Gulf leaders urging restraint. These were more likely intended to serve as an alibi which the various rulers—only too well aware of the threat posed by Saddam—were secretly hoping the United States would ignore.

Saddam's political survival has forced the United States into a policy of "dual containment" against both Iran and Iraq. Saudi Arabia, Kuwait, and the Gulf states are not strong enough to resist either of these countries alone, much less the two together. And there seemed to be ambiguity about America's purpose with respect to Saddam's longtime role. Thus, President Clinton, after aborting a retaliatory attack already, in fact, launched, stated in November 1998:

> If we can keep UNSCOM [the U.N. inspection group] in there working and one more time give him [Saddam] a chance to become honorably reconciled by simply observing U.N. resolutions, we see that results can be obtained.

None of our allies in the Gulf or in the area remotely believed in the prospect of "honorable reconciliation" based on observing U.N. resolutions for a few months. All were convinced that Iraq would bend every effort to rearm as soon as sanctions were lifted and that the major powers were already straining to find pretexts for lifting U.N. sanctions entirely. The countries in the region that rely on the United States will, in the end, judge America's relevance to their security by its ability either to depose Saddam or to weaken him to a point where he can no longer represent a threat—no matter what their public declaration.

With the United States as de facto guarantor of all the frontiers in one of the most volatile regions of the world, the security of the Gulf has come to depend on the widespread perception of America's ability to deal with the consequences of Saddam's continued rule and growing strength. The Gulf states are at once very conscious of their dependence on America and very nervous about too visible a collaboration, especially when America vacillates.

Saddam's strategy is geared to three objectives: (1) to focus the world's attention on Iraq's grievances; (2) to force into the open the latent split between the permanent members of the United Nations Security Council regarding Iraqi sanctions; and (3) to shift the focus of the debate from inspection to lifting the sanctions. He is well on the way to achieving each of these objectives. There is no serious effort to restore the U.N. inspection system; most of the international debate concentrates on easing or lifting the sanctions—indeed, several nations, led by Russia, China, and France, are in open noncompliance with them. Notably, Iraq seems to have become a test case for another French effort to define a European identity distinct from and in opposition to the United States.

At the end of a near-decade of shilly-shallying, the United States has maneuvered itself into a position where, in major parts of the world—especially in Europe—America, not Saddam, appears as the obstacle to easing tensions in the Gulf. Iraq's sponsors in the United Nations have a good chance of obtaining the necessary Security Council majority to suspend sanctions altogether. Though the United States would not doubt exercise its veto, such an outcome would advertise America's growing isolation and probably cause other countries to relax their compliance with the sanctions.

America's yielding to the chorus would gain no advantage. The countries undermining sanctions would learn that there is no penalty for flouting U.S. policy backed by U.N. resolutions. The Gulf states would be relieved about the temporary surcease from Iraqi pressures but worried about American steadfastness during the next crisis.

The issue posed by the "smart sanctions" suggested as an alternative is whether they wind up as a method of abdication or a form of pressure that will, in fact, be sustained. If smart sanctions are interpreted as a way of abandoning sanctions altogether, the question is whether, in a retreat amounting to a rout, the United States is better off leading the parade or should let others assume the responsibility. If the smart sanctions are serious, it depends on their nature and America's willingness to insist on their enforcement.

Comparable considerations apply to the often heard proposal that covert operations backed by the United States can enable it to sidestep the complexities of the sanctions policy. In principle, I favor encouraging internal Iraqi resistance but, having witnessed such covert enterprises from the inside, I would advance three cautionary notes: such covert operations must be run by professionals, not adventurers; they must take into account the interests of neighboring countries, especially Turkey, Saudi Arabia, Iran, and Jordan, to prevent their being drawn into consequences they are unable or unwilling to tolerate and that the United States is not prepared to sustain; and the United States must be prepared to back the resistance movement militarily when it gets into trouble, or else it will repeat the debacle of the Bay of Pigs and of northern Iraqi in 1975 and 1996, when most of those it supported were wiped out or exiled. If these conditions cannot be met, the call for massive covert operations turns into a dangerous trap.

Even America's European allies undermining the sanctions regime cannot wish to bring about an Iraqi capacity to turn OPEC into a weapon against the industrial democracies, in the process gradually undermining moderate governments in the region. Only after Saddam is gone—even if by actuarial causes—is a more flexible American policy toward Iraq possible and indicated.

• • •

An ominous development in the fall of 2000 occurred with Saddam's increasing effort to manipulate the light oil market by periodically reducing the flow of oil permitted under the sanctions regime. This effort should be treated for what it is: not a problem of supply and demand in the energy market but a national security challenge. A coherent cooperative energy policy on the part of the industrial democracies is essential, but it cannot be equated with kowtowing to Iraq.

It is not too soon to focus on the kind of Iraq to be hoped for after Saddam's removal from office. Iraq should be neither too strong for the balance of power in the region nor too weak to preserve its independence against covetous neighbors, including especially Iran. One of the causes of the Gulf crisis in 1991 was the laxity of the Western nations in the wake of the Iran-Iraq war by ignoring that Iraq might become the next aggressor. It would be ironic if another bout of tunnel vision produced the opposite outcome: an Iraq so weak that its neighbors, especially Iran, rush to refill the vacuum. But a balanced approach to Iraq cannot be achieved with Saddam in office; it is for the future, after he is removed.

To preserve America's assets in the Gulf, determined purposefulness is preferable to the thrashing about characteristic of the 1990s. It is also—paradoxically—important for America's relationship with Iran, the most powerful and largest country in the region. The United States will not be able to moderate fundamentalist Iran if it cannot handle a defeated Iraq, or if Tehran's leaders, looking across their border, see how easy and effective it is to defy the United States. What incentive would the ayatollahs then have for a moderate course?

Iran

There are few nations in the world with which the United States has less reason to quarrel or more compatible interests than Iran. Though, in the 1970s, the shah had come to symbolize the friendship between the two countries, those interests did not depend on one personality. They reflected political and strategic realities that continue to this day. The United States has no conceivable interest in dominating Iran as the ayatollahs now governing it insist. During the Cold War, America's interest had been to preserve Iran's independence from the threat of the Soviet Union, the historical source of pressures and invasions of the country. In the nineteenth century, British intervention, motivated by the defense of India and of the sea lanes to it, prevented large parts of Iran from being incorporated into Imperial Russia in much the same way as the neighboring Central Asian states had been conquered by the tsars. In 1946, but for American intervention, Iran's northwestern province of Azerbaijan would have been seized by the Soviet Union as a first step toward dismembering the country. Throughout the Cold War, Iran helped resist Soviet pressure on Afghanistan and penetration of the Middle East.

America's interest in Iran paralleled Iran's own quest for independence. Many American policymakers of that era, myself included, felt deep gratitude for the shah's support of the United States in various Cold War crises. But our basic motivation was less sentiment than an appreciation of the importance of the sum total of Iran's geography, resources, and the talents of its people.

There is no American geopolitical motivation for hostility between Iran and the United States. Iran, however, continues to provide reasons for America to keep its distance. In several administrations, the United States has made it clear that it is prepared to normalize relations. Iran is destined to play a vital—in some circumstances, decisive—role in the Gulf and in the Islamic world. A prudent American government needs no instruction on the desirability of improving relations with Iran.

The chief obstacle has been the government in Tehran. Since the overthrow of the shah in 1979, the ayatollah-based regime has engaged in a series of actions in violation of accepted principles of international conduct, many of them aimed explicitly at the United States. From 1979 to 1981, it held fifty American diplomats hostage for fourteen months. Throughout the 1980s, organizations financed and supported from Tehran were responsible for the kidnappings of Americans and other Westerners in Beirut. The Tehran regime provided the main support to groups which killed several hundred American soldiers in Beirut. It is closely linked with and also finances camps in Sudan for the training of terrorists. Evidence exists linking Iran-sponsored groups to the bombing of the American military barracks at Khobar Towers in Saudi Arabia, which killed nineteen Americans in 1996. In France, a senior Iranian living in exile was assassinated by Iranian agents who were then released from prison in exchange for a French hostage being held in Beirut. The Iranian ayatollahs have pronounced a death sentence on the author Salman Rushdie that has not yet been revoked, though the Tehran government has "distanced" itself from it, whatever that means.

Beyond these individual acts, Iran does its utmost to undermine Middle East peace diplomacy. Tehran is the patron of Hezbollah, which continues armed opposition to peace with Israel. Iran provides substantial financial support to Hamas and the Palestine Islamic Jihad, both of which regularly claim responsibility for terrorist attacks on Israeli civilians.

The Iranian regime is now building long-range missiles capable of striking the Middle East and most of Central Europe. It is developing a clandestine nuclear capability assisted by dual technology from the West and with some support from Russia, despite its signing of the Non-Proliferation Treaty (China seems to have ended its previous assistance).

The key question for American policymakers is whether these acts are integral to the nature of the Tehran regime, or whether a relationship based on reciprocal nonhostility is possible. That issue has become part of an agenda of disagreements with America's European allies that is testing the Atlantic relationship.

On one level, the dispute is over whether European companies and American companies domiciled in Europe are subject to the penalties legislated by the United States Congress against violators of sanctions. I have elsewhere in these pages indicated my concern about the extent to which sanctions have been overused. Extraterritorial application, especially against allies, is difficult to justify and requires a new look. The fundamental issue, however, is not the legal basis of American strategy but whether improvement of relations with Iran is helped by unilateral concessions undertaken without any demand for reciprocity. Or is the rush to Tehran an *obstacle* to a rapprochement which is in itself not in dispute? Will continuing unilateral concessions in the face of rigid Iranian policies help or hinder the agreed goal of a better relationship?

At the heart of the disagreement is the insistence of the European allies on what they call a "critical dialogue" with Iran. The allies argue that their dialogue is designed to explore the prospects of moderating Iran's policy and would always include criticism of Iran's human rights violations and other misdeeds; in short, it would by its very existence contribute to easing tensions (not to speak of the signing of lucrative oil and gas deals).

So far there has been little productive dialogue, critical or otherwise, with Europe although the hint of Iranian President Mohammad Khatami suggesting a "dialogue of civilizations" might in time provide an opening wedge. Nor was there any response to the Clinton administration's offer of an official dialogue. It was rebuffed by an Iranian regime that seems incapable of deciding on rapprochement with the United States and was unimpressed by formal and abject apologies for past American conduct.

In essence, the proposition that unilateral gestures will somehow ease Iranian hostility represents the application of "politically correct" psychiatric theory to politics: the perpetrator of a crime is perceived as victim, allegedly deformed by pressures outside his control. But when applied to Iran's transgressions, there is not a shred of evidence to support it. Unilateral concessions of any magnitude are much more likely to reinforce intransigence than to moderate it. After all, why change when the targets of the ideology-based policy are so abjectly eager to accommodate?

• • •

While there is little doubt that Khatami is seeking to implement more moderate domestic policies in the face of considerable resistance, there is little evidence so far that this moderation extends to the international scene or that Khatami will be permitted to execute a change of course if he were to attempt it. It is as likely that he will purchase maneuvering room in domestic reconstruction by demonstrations of ideological vigilance on the international scene. In fact, Khatami has publicly identified himself with support for Islamic and Palestinian terrorist groups in Damascus and Beirut.

The debate should move beyond theoretical speculation. If there is to be an improvement of relations with the Iranian Islamic regime, it seems elementary to link it with abandonment of the export of revolution by force and subversion, a curb on terror, and an end to interference in the Middle East peace diplomacy. Simultaneously, progress must be made with respect to Iran's acquisition of missiles and nuclear weapons.

If there were a serious willingness by Iran to move toward an improvement of relations, a series of reciprocal parallel steps could surely be devised to achieve a significant improvement, provided the rulers in Iran are prepared to embrace a normal relationship. The mechanism of such an approach would not be difficult to construct. The new American administration could designate a trustee representative—or an "unofficial" trusted spokesman—to explore, at first secretly, whether it is possible to agree on a series of reciprocal measures leading to a step-by-step improvement of relations. The United States might even agree after the initial dialogue to take a few symbolic steps first, provided they are followed by Iranian moves in a time frame clearly relevant to the initial action.

If America's allies believe that it has not adequately explored the diplomatic options, the United States should be prepared to undertake a serious effort of joint diplomacy. And, at least theoretically, there should be a community of interests. The European nations will be the first victims of the spread of Islamic fundamentalism and of Iranian medium-range missiles. As a nuclear power, Iran will in the long run prove far more threatening to Europe (and Russia) than to the United States. And, if the Gulf blows up, the European nations will be the first to ask for access to American energy supplies to avoid an economic catastrophe.

Foreign policy always comes down to making choices. An effective counterterrorist and counterproliferation policy for the West requires the willingness to accept sacrifices for the sake of a greater long-term goal. There are times when commercial interests must be prepared to give way to broader security interests. American leadership is essential to reach this trade-off with respect to Iran. At the same time, if an alliance turns into a free ride for one side, it will not be sustained by public opinion.

A major effort should be made to achieve a transatlantic consensus that relates diplomacy to reasonable pressures and agreed diplomatic overtures vis-à-vis Iran. Only by a firm, consistent, and conciliatory policy can the day be hastened when Iran will be prepared to take the concrete policy actions which represent the only reliable basis for a long-term cooperative relationship.

Contributors

Fouad Ajami is a professor of Middle Eastern studies at the School of Advanced International Studies at Johns Hopkins University. He is a contributing editor for *U.S. News & World Report*, a member of the editorial board of *Foreign Affairs*, and the author of four books including, most recently, *The Dream Palace of the Arabs: A Generation's Odyssey*.

Mir Tamim Ansary is a writer who specializes in nonfiction books for children. His latest book, written for adult readers, is *West of Kabul, East of New York*, a memoir of his childhood in Aghanistan.

Dan Balz is the national political correspondent for *The Washington Post*.

Fred Barnes is executive editor of *The Weekly Standard*. He is also co-host of the FOX television program *The Beltway Boys*, and the host of a weekly radio show on the media, *What's the Story?*

David Brooks is a senior editor of *The Weekly Standard*, a correspondent for *The Atlantic Monthly*, and a columnist for *The New York Times Magazine*. He is also a regular panelist on *PBS's The NewsHour with Jim Lehrer*, and the author of *Bobos in Paradise: The New Upper Class and How They Got There*.

Vincent Bugliosi is a former Los Angeles deputy district attorney. He is the author of several books, including *Helter Skelter*, the story of his prosecution of Charles Manson, and *Betrayal of America*, a critique of the U.S. Supreme Court's role in the 2000 presidential election.

George W. Bush was inaugurated in January 2001 as the 43rd president of the United States.

Daniel Callahan is director of international programs and co-founder of The Hastings Center, a nonprofit research group devoted to the exploration of ethical questions in health care, biotechnology and the environment. He is the author of *False Hopes: Why America's Quest for Perfect Health Is a Recipe for Failure*.

Margaret Carlson is a columnist for *Time* magazine, and a regular panelist on CNN's *Inside Politics* and *The Capital Gang*.

Tucker Carlson writes the "National Affairs" column for *New York* magazine, where he is a contributing editor. He is also a contributing editor for *The Weekly Standard*, a political analyst for CNN, and a co-host of CNN's *Crossfire*.

Barbara Ehrenreich is a journalist and political essayist whose work has appeared in a wide variety of publications, including *Time*, *Harper's*, *The Nation*, *The New Republic*, *The Atlantic Monthly*, and many others. She is the author of numerous books including, most recently, *Nickel and Dimed: On (Not) Getting by in America*.

Howard Fineman is chief political correspondent, senior editor, and deputy Washington bureau chief for *Newsweek* magazine, and a political analyst for NBC News.

Thomas Friedman is the foreign affairs op-ed columnist for *The New York Times*. He won the Pulitzer Prize for international reporting in 1983 and again in 1988, and was recently awarded the 2002 Pulitzer Prize for distinguished commentary. He is the author of several books, including *From Beirut to Jerusalem*, which won the 1989 National Book Award for nonfiction.

Jeff Greenfield is a senior political analyst and anchor for CNN. He has written nine nonfiction books on politics and is also the author of *The People's Choice*, a novel about the electoral college.

Meg Greenfield was the editorial page editor of *The Washington Post*, where she won the 1978 Pulitzer Prize for editorial writing, a columnist for *Newsweek* magazine, and the author of the posthumously published *Washington*, a book about Washington D.C.'s political class. She passed away in 1999.

Lani Guinier is a professor of law at Harvard Law School, specializing in the area of voting rights law. She is the author of several books including, most recently, *The Miner's Canary: Enlisting Race, Resisting Power, Transforming Democracy* (co-authored with Gerald Torres).

David Halberstam is the author of numerous books, including *The Best and the Brightest,* his classic study of the origins of the Vietnam War. His most recent book is *Firehouse,* about a New York City engine and ladder company which lost 12 of its 13 men in the World Trade Center attacks. He shared the 1964 Pulitzer Prize for national reporting for his coverage of the Vietnam war as a reporter for *The New York Times.*

Ted Halstead is the president and chief executive officer of the New America Foundation. He is the co-author (with Michael Lind) of *The Radical Center: The Future of American Politics.*

Bob Herbert is an op-ed columnist for *The New York Times,* where he writes on politics, urban affairs and social trends.

Seymour Hersh is a staff writer for *The New Yorker* magazine and a contributing editor for the *Atlantic Monthly.* He won the 1970 Pulitzer Prize for international reporting for his exposé of the My Lai massacre during the Vietnam War. He has is the author of numerous books including, most recently, *Against All Enemies: Gulf War Syndrome: The War Between America's Ailing Veterans and Their Government.*

Hendrik Hertzberg is editorial director for *The New Yorker* magazine, where he reports on national politics.

Anne Hull is a staff writer for *The Washingon Post.* She received a 2002 American Society of Newspaper Editors Award for diversity writing, and was a finalist for the 2000 Pulitzer Prize in both national reporting and feature writing.

Molly Ivins is a nationally syndicated columnist for the *Dallas-Fort Worth Star-Telegram.* She is author of two collections of essays on politics and journalism, *Molly Ivins Can't Say That, Can She?* and *Nothin' But Good Times Ahead.*

David Kaplan is a senior writer for *Newsweek,* and has twice shared the American Bar Association's Silver Gavel Award for his coverage of the Supreme Court nomination process. He is the author of several books including, most recently, *The Accidental President: How 413 Lawyers, 9 Supreme Court Justices, and 5,963,110 Floridians (Give or Take a Few) Landed George W. Bush in the White House.*

Leon Kass, M.D., is a professor in the College and Committee on Social Thought at the University of Chicago. He is the author of several books, including *The Ethics of Human Cloning* (co-authored with James Wilson).

Dan Keating is database editor at *The Washington Post.* He was part of the Miami Herald team that won the Pulitzer Price for investigative reporting in 1999 for its exposure of vote fraud in Miami.

Bill Keller is an op-ed columnist for *The New York Times* and senior writer for *The New York Times Magazine.* He has held numerous other posts at the *Times,* including managing editor, foreign editor, Johannesburg bureau chief, and Moscow correspondent. He won a Pulitzer Prize in 1989 for his coverage of the Soviet Union.

Randall Kennedy is a professor at Harvard Law School. He is the author of several books, including *Race, Crime, and the Law* and, most recently, *Nigger: The Strange Career of a Troublesome Word.*

Jeane Kirkpatrick is Leavy Professor at Georgetown University and a senior fellow at the American Enterprise Institute. She served as the U.S. Ambassador to the United Nations from 1981 to 1985, and was awarded the Presidential Medal of Freedom in 1985. She is the author of numerous books including, most recently, *The Withering Away of the Totalitarian State.*

Henry Kissinger is the chairman of Kissinger Associates, an international consulting firm. He was the U.S. secretary of state from 1973 to 1977, and also served as national security adviser to the president from 1969 to 1975. He shared the Nobel Peace Prize in 1973, and was awarded the Presidential Medal of Freedom in 1977. He is the author of numerous books incuding *Diplomacy* and, most recently, *Does America Need a Foreign Policy?*

Elizabeth Kolbert is a staff writer for *The New Yorker* magazine.

Charles Krauthammer is a nationally syndicated columnist for *The Washington Post*. He was awarded the 1987 Pulitzer Prize for distinguished commentary.

Paul Krugman is a professor of economics and international affairs at Princeton University, and an op-ed columnist for *The New York Times*. He written numerous books, including *Fuzzy Math: The Essential Guide to the Bush Tax Plan*.

Nicholas Lemann is a staff writer for *The New Yorker*. He has written several books including, most recently, *The Big Test: The Secret History of the American Meritocracy*.

Anthony Lewis was an op-ed columnist for *The New York Times* from 1969 to 2001. He won the Pulitzer Prize for national reporting in 1955, and again in 1963. He is the author of several books, including *Gideon's Trumpet* and *Make No Law: The Sullivan Case and the First Amendment*.

Michael Lind is a senior fellow with the New America Foundation. He is the author of several books including, most recently, *The Radical Center: The Future of American Politics* (co-authored with Ted Halstead).

Glenn Loury is a professor of economics and the director of the Institute on Race and Social Division at Boston University. He is the author of several books, including *One by One from the Inside Out: Essays and Reviews on Race and Responsibility in America*, winner of a 1996 American Book Award.

Warwick McKibbin is a nonresident senior fellow in economic studies with the Brookings Institution.

Dana Milbank is a White House correspondent for *The Washington Post*. He is the author of *Smashmouth: Two Years in the Gutter with Al Gore and George W. Bush*.

Arthur Miller is one of America's foremost playwrights. He won the 1949 Pulitzer Prize for drama for his play *Death of a Salesman*.

Richard Perle is a resident fellow at the American Enterprise Institute. He served as U.S. assistant secretary of defense for international security policy from 1981 to 1987.

Katha Pollitt writes the "Subject to Debate" column for *The Nation* magazine. The winner of a National Magazine Award in 1992, she has published several books including, most recently, *Subject to Debate: Sense and Dissents on Women, Politics, and Culture.*

William Raspberry is a nationally syndicated columnist for *The Washington Post.* He won the Pulitzer Prize for distinguished commentary in 1994.

Frank Rich is an op-ed columnist for *The New York Times* and a senior writer for *The New York Times Magazine.* He has written several books including, most recently, *Ghost Light: A Memoir.*

Richard Rodriguez is an editor at the *Pacific News Service,* an op-ed columnist for the *Los Angeles Times,* a regular essayist for the *PBS NewsHour with Jim Lehrer,* and a contributing editor for *Harper's* and *U.S. News & World Report.* He is the author of three books including, most recently, *Brown: The Last Discovery of America.*

Jennifer Senior is a contributing editor for *New York* magazine.

Jake Tapper is the Washington correspondent for *salon.com.* He is the author of *Down and Dirty: The Plot to Steal the Presidency.*

Michael Tomasky writes "The City Politic" column for *New York* magazine, where he is a contributing editor. He has written two books including, most recently, *Hillary's Turn: Inside Her Improbable, Victorious Senate Campaign.*

Douglas Waller is the congressional correspondent for *Time* magazine. He has written six books including, most recently, *Big Red: Three Months On Board A Trident Nuclear Submarine.*

Peter Wilcoxen is a nonresident senior fellow in economic studies with the Brookings Institution.

Marjorie Williams is a contributing editor for *Vanity Fair* magazine.

James Wolcott is a contributing editor for *Vanity Fair* magazine, and the author of a novel, *The Catsitters*.

Michael Wolff writes the column "This Media Life" for *New York* magazine, which won the 2002 National Magazine Award for columns and commentary. He is a contributing editor for *New York* and the author of numerous books including, most recently, *Burn Rate: How I Survived the Gold Rush Years on the Internet.*

Permissions